Command	Key Combination	
Compare Versions of Document	Alt-U, *then* V	Utilit...
Copy Selection to Clipboard	Alt-E, *then* C Ctrl-Ins	Edit/Copy
Customize Word Features	Alt-U, *then* U	Utilities/Customize
Cut Selection to Clipboard	Alt-E, *then* T Shift-Del	Edit/Cut
Display Options, Select	Alt-V, *then* E	View/Preferences
Document, Format	Alt-T, *then* D	Format/Document
Draft Document View	Alt-V, *then* D	View/Draft
Exit from Program	Alt-spacebar, *then* C Alt-F, *then* X Alt-F4	Word Control/Close *or* File/Exit
Field, Insert	Alt-I, *then* D	Insert/Field
Fields, Show Codes/Results	Alt-V, *then* C	View/Field Codes
Find Document	Alt-F, *then* F	File/Find
Footnote, Insert Reference	Alt-I, *then* N	Insert/Footnote
Footnote Window, Open/Close	Alt-V, *then* F	View/Footnotes
Format Character	Alt-T, *then* C	Format/Character
Format Document	Alt-T, *then* D	Format/Document
Format Paragraph	Alt-T, *then* P	Format/Paragraph
Format Section	Alt-T, *then* S	Format/Section
Glossary Entry, Define or Insert	Alt-E, *then* O	Edit/Glossary
Go To Position in Document	Alt-E, *then* G F5	Edit/Go To
Header or Footer, Edit	Alt-E, *then* H	Edit/Header/Footer
Help, Show Index	Alt-H, *then* I	Help/Index
Help, on Keyboard Commands	Alt-H, *then* K	Help/Keyboard
Help, on Active Window	Alt-H, *then* W	Help/Active Window
Help on Help Command	Alt-H, *then* H	Help/Using Help
Hyphenate Selection	Alt-U, *then* H	Utilities/Hyphenate
Index, Compile and Insert	Alt-I, *then* I	Insert/Index
Index Entry, Define	Alt-I, *then* E	Insert/Index Entry
Insert Document Contents	Alt-I, *then* F	Insert/File
Insert Page, Column, or Section Break	Alt-I, *then* B	Insert/Break
Keyboard Commands, Customizing	Alt-M, *then* K	Macro/Assign to Key
Macro, Record	Alt-M, *then* C	Macro/Record
Macro, Run	Alt-M, *then* R	Macro/Run

MASTERING MICROSOFT WORD FOR WINDOWS

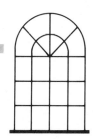

MASTERING MICROSOFT® WORD FOR WINDOWS™

Michael J. Young

SYBEX® San Francisco • Paris • Düsseldorf • Soest

Acquisitions Editor: Dianne King
Editors: Tanya Kucak, Cheryl Holzaepfel
Technical Editors: Nick Dargahi, Michael Gross
Word Processors: Winnie Kelly, Deborah Maizels, Lisa Mitchell
Chapter Art & Layout: Suzanne Albertson
Screen Graphics: Cuong Le
Typesetter: Elizabeth Newman
Proofreader: Patsy Owens
Indexer: T.G. McFadden
Cover Designer: Thomas Ingalls + Associates
Cover Photographer: Mark Johann

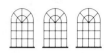

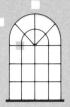

CONTENTS AT A GLANCE

Introduction   xxi

PART I AN INTRODUCTION TO WORD FOR WINDOWS

1 Creating a Word Document   3
2 Editing, Previewing, and Printing the Document   19

PART II EDITING

3 Basic Editing Skills   31
4 Navigating through a Document   63
5 Using Block Editing Commands   83
6 Searching and Replacing   105
7 Checking Your Spelling and Finding Synonyms   125
8 Using Word Tables   143
9 Including Graphics in Your Document   185
10 Adding Headers, Footers, and Footnotes   207
11 Creating Indexes and Tables of Contents   237

PART III FORMATTING AND PRINTING

12 An Overview of Formatting and Printing   263
13 Formatting Documents   273

14 Formatting Sections   287
15 Formatting Paragraphs   307
16 Formatting Characters   347
17 Previewing and Printing Your Document   365
18 Printing Form Letters   385

PART IV DOCUMENT TEMPLATES AND OTHER SPECIAL FEATURES

19 An Overview of Document Templates   401
20 Defining Styles to Simplify Formatting   415
21 Using the Glossary to Save Typing   437
22 Writing Macros to Save Work   445
23 Customizing Menus, Keyboard Commands, and Other Features 455

PART V LARGE PROJECTS

24 Outlining Your Documents   471
25 Adding Annotations and Marking Revisions   489
26 Managing Collections of Documents   503
A Understanding the DOS File System   523
B Entering Measurements in Word   529
Index   531

TABLE OF CONTENTS

INTRODUCTION   xxi

PART I
AN INTRODUCTION TO WORD
FOR WINDOWS

1 CREATING A WORD DOCUMENT   3

Installing Word for Windows   4
Starting Word for Windows   5
The Opening Screen   6
Entering Text into the Document   8
Saving the Document   9
Help!   13
Exiting from Word for Windows   13
Summary   15

**2 EDITING, PREVIEWING, AND PRINTING THE
DOCUMENT**   19

Starting Word and Opening the Document   20
Making the Revisions   20
  Moving the Insertion Point   21
  Making the Changes   22
  Revising the Example Document   22
Saving the Document and Quitting Word   24
Previewing the Document   24

Printing the Document   26
Exiting from Word   27
Summary   28

PART II
EDITING

3   BASIC EDITING SKILLS   **31**

Creating a New Document   32
   Starting Word and Creating a New Document   32
   Creating a New Document within Word   33
Opening an Existing Document   35
   Starting Word and Opening a Document   35
   Opening a Document within Word   36
Entering and Revising Text   39
   Creating Text Breaks   41
   Entering Special Characters and Symbols   45
   Correcting Mistakes   47
   Repeating Editing Actions   51
Saving a Document   52
   The Save Command   53
   The Save As Command   53
   The Save All Command   58
   The Autosave Option   58
Summary   59

4   NAVIGATING THROUGH A DOCUMENT   **63**

Using the Keyboard   64
Using the Mouse   65
Using the Go To Command   69
   Specifying the Target Location   70
   The Go Back Key (Shift-F5)   76

Using Other Methods	76
Edit/Search	76
Using Draft View	77
Display Options for Efficient Scrolling	77
The Status Bar	78
Summary	80

5 USING BLOCK EDITING COMMANDS — **83**

Selecting Text and Graphics	84
Selecting with the Keyboard	85
Selecting with the Mouse	87
Removing the Selection	90
Deleting, Moving, and Copying	90
Deleting the Selection	91
Moving and Copying Using the Clipboard	93
Moving and Copying without Using the Clipboard	97
Other Copying Techniques	100
Summary	100

6 SEARCHING AND REPLACING — **105**

Searching	105
Searching for Text	106
Searching for Formatting	110
Searching for Combinations of Text and Formatting	113
Using Other Search Methods	114
Replacing	115
Replacing Text	115
Replacing Formatting or a Style	120
Replacing Combinations of Text and Formatting	121
Summary	122

7   CHECKING YOUR SPELLING AND FINDING SYNONYMS   **125**

Checking Spelling   125
 Working with a Single Word   127
 Checking Spelling within Your Document   129
 Using the Spell Key (F7)   135
Finding Synonyms with the Thesaurus   136
Summary   139

8   USING WORD TABLES   **143**

Creating a Table   143
 Entering Text into a Table   147
 Navigating through a Table   148
 Paragraphs within a Table   148
 Converting Text to a Table   149
 Converting a Table to Text   151
Editing a Table   152
 Inserting or Deleting Cells   152
 Merging Cells   157
 Dividing Tables   158
 Deleting, Moving, and Copying Text within a
  Table   159
Using the Table Formatting Options   161
Calculating and Sorting in a Table   168
 Calculating   168
 Sorting   173
Summary   180

9   INCLUDING GRAPHICS IN YOUR DOCUMENT   **185**

Inserting Pictures   186
 Pasting a Picture from the Clipboard   186
 Pasting from the Clipboard and Linking   189
 Inserting a Picture from a Disk File   191

Inserting a Blank Picture Frame 192

Formatting a Picture 193

Selecting a Picture 194

Cropping or Scaling a Picture 195

Placing a Border around a Picture 200

Deleting, Moving, or Copying a Picture 201

Positioning a Picture 201

Summary 204

10 ADDING HEADERS, FOOTERS, AND FOOTNOTES 207

Working with Headers and Footers 207

Creating a Simple Page Number Header or Footer 208

Creating and Formatting Complete Headers or Footers 209

Using Header and Footer Options 216

Using Footnotes in Your Document 221

Inserting a Footnote 222

Editing a Footnote 224

Deleting, Moving, or Copying a Footnote 225

Specifying Footnote Separators 226

Specifying the Footnote Position and Numbering Scheme 227

Summary 231

11 CREATING INDEXES AND TABLES OF CONTENTS 237

Creating Indexes 238

Inserting Index Entries 238

Inserting the Index 246

Creating Tables of Contents 253

Inserting Table of Contents Entries 253

Inserting the Table of Contents 256

Summary 259

PART III
FORMATTING AND PRINTING

12 AN OVERVIEW OF FORMATTING AND PRINTING 263

Formatting and Printing Your Document:
The Basic Steps 264

Finding the Correct Formatting Command 265

Features Formatted at Several Levels 269

Summary 269

13 FORMATTING DOCUMENTS 273

Setting the Page Size 274

Setting the Document Margins 275

Setting Margins *without* the Mirror Margins
Option 275

Setting Margins *with* the Mirror Margins Option 278

Setting the Default Tab Stops 281

Assigning Footnote Placement 281

Enabling Widow Control 281

Changing the Document Template 282

Altering the Default Settings 283

Overriding Document Formatting 283

Summary 284

14 FORMATTING SECTIONS 287

Dividing a Document into Sections 287

Going to a Section 290

Formatting a Section 291

Specifying Where the Section Starts 292
Specifying the Vertical Alignment 294
Setting the Number of Columns 297
Numbering Lines 302
Including Footnotes 304
Summary 304

15 FORMATTING PARAGRAPHS 307

Creating and Selecting Paragraphs 307
Using the Format/Paragraph Command 309
Setting the Indents 311
Setting the Alignment 314
Setting the Spacing 316
Assigning the Style 317
Adding Borders 317
Controlling Page Breaks 318
Enabling Line Numbering 319
Setting Tab Stops 320
Using the Ruler 324
Using the Ruler with the Mouse to Format
Paragraphs 325
Using the Ruler with the Keyboard to Format
Paragraphs 331
Using the Ruler to Set Document Margins and
Inner Column Boundaries 333
Using the Ruler to Set Cell Widths in Tables 335
Using the Keyboard 336
Positioning a Paragraph 338
Summary 343

16 FORMATTING CHARACTERS 347

Selecting Characters 348
Viewing Character Formatting 348

Using the Format/Character Command 349
    Choosing the Font 350
    Setting the Character Size 352
    Specifying the Character Color 353
    Assigning Character Enhancements 354
    Adjusting the Vertical Position of Characters 356
    Altering the Character Spacing 357
Using the Ribbon 357
Using the Keyboard 360
Summary 362

17 PREVIEWING AND PRINTING YOUR DOCUMENT 365

Performing Automatic Hyphenation 365
Previewing Your Document 370
    Page View 372
    Print Preview 373
Setting Up Your Printer 376
Printing Your Document 379
Summary 381

18 PRINTING FORM LETTERS 385

Creating the Main Document 386
Creating the Data Document 388
Merging the Main Document and Data Document 390
Using Other Print Merge Instructions 393
    The IF Field 393
    The NEXT Field 394
    The NEXTIF Field 395
    The SKIPIF Field 397
Summary 397

PART IV
DOCUMENT TEMPLATES AND OTHER SPECIAL FEATURES

19 AN OVERVIEW OF DOCUMENT TEMPLATES   401

Features That Can Be Assigned to Templates   402
   Text and Formatting   402
   Styles   403
   Glossary Entries   403
   Macros   403
   Menu and Keyboard Assignments   403
NORMAL and Other Templates   404
The Relationship between a Document and Its
Template   405
   Text, Graphics, Formatting, and Styles   405
   Glossary Entries, Macros, and Menu and
   Keyboard Assignments   406
Changing the Template Assigned to a Document   406
Creating or Modifying a Template   407
   Creating a New Template   407
   Modifying a Template   409
Summary   411

20 DEFINING STYLES TO SIMPLIFY FORMATTING   415

The Predefined Styles   416
Applying a Style   420
   Using the Format/Styles Command   421
   Using the Ruler   423
   Using the Keyboard   423
Defining Styles   424
   Using the Format/Define Styles Command   424

Defining or Modifying Styles by Example   431
Using the Ruler or Keyboard   432
Using the Format/Styles Menu Command   433
Summary   433

21 USING THE GLOSSARY TO SAVE TYPING   437

Storing a Selection in a Glossary   438
Inserting a Glossary Entry into a Document   439
Using the Spike   440
Summary   441

22 WRITING MACROS TO SAVE WORK   445

Recording a Macro   445
Automatic Macros   447
Editing a Macro   449
Running a Macro   450
Summary   452

23 CUSTOMIZING MENUS, KEYBOARD COMMANDS, AND OTHER FEATURES   455

Customizing Menus   456
Assigning Keystrokes   459
Assigning a Keystroke to a Command or Macro   460
Removing a Keystroke Assignment   462
Restoring the Original Keyboard Assignments   462
Customizing Other Word Features   463
The Utilities/Customize Command   463
The View/Preferences Command   464
Summary   466

PART V
LARGE PROJECTS

24 OUTLINING YOUR DOCUMENTS 471

Working with Outline View 472
    Selecting in Outline View 474
    Promoting and Demoting Outline Text 474
    Collapsing and Expanding Headings 476
    Moving a Heading and Its Subtext 478
    Using Outline View to Find Topics 479
Numbering Outline Headings 480
Creating a Table of Contents from Outline Headings 483
Summary 484

25 ADDING ANNOTATIONS AND MARKING REVISIONS 489

Adding Annotations 489
    Changing Annotation Formatting 492
    Finding Annotation Marks and Reading Annotations 492
    Printing Annotations 493
    Locking a Document 493
Marking Revisions 494
    Marking Changes As You Make Them 495
    Comparing with a Previous Version of the Document 497
    Searching for Revisions 498
    Accepting or Undoing Revisions 499
Summary 500

26 MANAGING COLLECTIONS OF DOCUMENTS 503

Retrieving Documents 503
    Obtaining a List of Documents 504
    Sorting the List 510
    Opening Documents 511
    Printing Documents 511

Deleting Documents 512

Reading and Editing Document Summary
Information 512

Working with Windows in Word 514

Working with the Word Window 515

Working with a Document Window 516

Opening Several Document Windows 518

Splitting a Window 518

Summary 519

APPENDIXES

A UNDERSTANDING THE DOS FILE SYSTEM 523

How Files Are Organized 523

Specifying Full Path Names 524

Specifying Partial Path Names 525

Using Wildcards in File Names 526

B ENTERING MEASUREMENTS IN WORD 529

INDEX 531

INTRODUCTION

WORD FOR WINDOWS IS A WORD PROCESSING program designed specifically for the Microsoft Windows operating environment. It provides all of the sophisticated features offered by traditional text-mode word processors, such as Microsoft Word for DOS. In addition, it takes full advantage of the graphics interface provided by Windows, allowing you to view and control the precise printed appearance of your document. Also, as a Windows application, it permits close interaction with other Windows programs, such as spreadsheets and graphics applications. This book covers Microsoft Word for Windows through version 1.1.

Word for Windows is ideal for writing simple documents or for creating complex camera-ready art. It is easy to use for standard word processing tasks, but also provides many of the features of dedicated desktop publishing applications.

The large number of features, however, can make learning Word for Windows a challenging task. This book is designed to help you quickly learn the basic word processing tasks, so that you can rapidly become a productive user of Word for Windows. It also provides thorough explanations of Word's more advanced features to help you take full advantage of the program.

The book provides tutorial exercises, step-by-step procedures, and many examples. It also contains discussions to help you *understand* Word's features, many of which are complex, subtle, and confusing even to users experienced with word processing.

AN OVERVIEW OF THE BOOK

The book is divided into five parts. Part I provides a tutorial introduction. Parts II and III present the most essential information on creating, altering, formatting, and printing a document. Parts IV and V discuss more advanced methods, which can save you time and extend your word processing abilities.

The tutorial introduction in **Part I** covers the basic tasks of creating, formatting, and printing a document. By working through the exercises given in the two chapters in this part, you will gain a clear overview of Word's features and you will begin to use the program productively.

Part II, on editing, focuses on the techniques for creating the document *content*. In this part, you will learn how to enter and revise the text and graphics that constitute the document. You will learn how to use program features that help you enter, correct, and organize document text, and you will learn how to add special elements to your document, such as headers, footnotes, and indexes.

Part III, on formatting, explains how to control the printed *appearance* of your document, and how to produce the final printed copy. You will learn how to assign formatting features to each level of your document, ranging from the entire document to individual characters. You will also learn how to preview and print the document, and how to generate form letters.

Part IV discusses document templates (a template is the basic framework upon which a document is built), and the timesaving features that can be assigned to them. You will learn how to speed up your work by defining styles, storing text within glossaries, and automating tasks using macros. You will also learn how to customize menus, keyboard commands, and other program features.

Part V focuses on techniques for working with large documents, and for creating documents in conjunction with other writers or editors. You will learn how to edit or view the document as an outline, how to add annotations and mark revisions, and how to manage collections of documents.

REQUIREMENTS FOR USING WORD FOR WINDOWS

To use Word for Windows, you will need the following hardware and software:

- The Word for Windows software package from Microsoft

- Microsoft Windows, version 2.11 or higher, is required for performing certain tasks described in this book, and for running other Windows programs together with Word for Windows; using Windows version 3.0 is strongly recommended

Releases of Word for Windows later than version 1.0 may not include a runtime version of Windows, since Microsoft is phasing it out.

(if you do not have Windows, you can use the *runtime* version of Windows supplied with Word for Windows version 1.0, described in Chapter 1)

- An IBM-compatible microcomputer, with an 80286 or later-model processor

- At least 640K of memory, or 1Mb if you are using Windows with other applications; 1–3 Mb of expanded or extended memory is strongly recommended

- One hard disk drive, and one floppy disk drive

- An EGA or higher-resolution monitor

- A Microsoft or compatible mouse is almost essential

Before using Word for Windows, you should be familiar with basic Windows techniques, such as:

- Maximizing, minimizing, and restoring a window

- Moving a window on the screen

- Adjusting the size of a window

If you need more information on any of these methods, read the user's guide accompanying your copy of Windows, or the booklet *Basic Skills for Windows Applications,* supplied with Word for Windows. Another way to learn some of these basic skills is to run the tutorial program that comes with Word for Windows.

Also, this book frequently refers to the Word *User's Reference* and the Word *Technical Reference.* The *User's Reference* is supplied with the Word for Windows package; its full title is *Microsoft Word for Windows User's Reference.* The Word *Technical Reference* must be obtained separately from Microsoft or through a bookstore; its full title is *Microsoft Word for Windows Technical Reference.*

I

AN INTRODUCTION TO WORD FOR WINDOWS

This part of the book is designed to give you a quick overview of Word for Windows before you begin exploring the detailed features of the program in the remaining chapters. By following the step-by-step instructions given here, you will learn the most essential word processing tasks: creating, saving, and printing a document. You will learn each task by actually performing it.

You will discover that because of its intuitive graphics interface, the basic features of Word are easy to learn and simple to perform. Although many techniques, shortcuts, subtleties, and advanced features will be discussed in this book, what you learn in these two chapters will give you a good start toward becoming a productive user of Word for Windows.

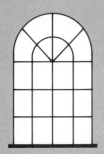

1

CREATING A
WORD DOCUMENT

IN THIS CHAPTER, YOU WILL CREATE A NEW WORD
for Windows document. A *document* is a body of text—and possibly
graphics—that you create using the Word for Windows program.
Once you have created a document in Word, you can revise it, print
it, and store it permanently in a disk file. Once the document has
been stored in a disk file, you can later *open* it in Word (that is, read it
from the disk back into the program) to make further revisions or
print additional copies.

In this chapter, you will first learn how to install and start Word for
Windows. You will then enter a short block of text into a new document, and discover how to designate separate paragraphs and how to
correct minor typing errors. Finally, you will save the document and
exit from the program. In Chapter 2, you will open this same document, make several revisions to it, preview the printed appearance of
the document, and generate a copy of the document on your printer.

INSTALLING WORD FOR WINDOWS

Word for Windows is designed to run within Microsoft Windows (version 2.11 or later, or Windows/386). Microsoft Windows is a graphics environment that allows you to load several programs at the same time, running each program within a separate window on the screen. It also allows you to manage disk files and perform program tasks by directly manipulating menus and graphic symbols (known as *icons*) with a mouse.

The run-time version of Windows may not be included in Word releases later than 1.0.

If you do not have Windows, you can still install and use Word, since the Word package includes a special *run-time version* of Windows that is installed when you install Word for Windows. The run-time version allows you to run Word for Windows, but it does not permit you to run other Windows applications. If you want to take complete advantage of the Windows environment, you should obtain a copy of the full Windows version. You will need the full Windows version to perform certain tasks described in this book, such as exchanging data with other applications.

The basic hardware and software requirements for installing Windows and Word for Windows are outlined in the Introduction under the heading "Requirements for Using Word for Windows."

You should install Windows on your hard disk before installing Word for Windows. To install Windows, place the Windows Setup disk in drive A. If drive A is not the current active disk drive, first type

A:

at the DOS prompt and then press ←┘. Once A is the active disk drive, type

setup

and then press ←┘. These steps will run the Windows setup program. To complete the installation, simply follow the instructions that appear on the screen.

If you have completed installing Windows, or if you are using the run-time Windows version, you should install Word for Windows on your hard disk by performing the following steps:

1. Place the Word for Windows *Setup* disk in drive A.

2. If drive A is not the current active drive, type

   A:

   at the DOS prompt and press ←┘.

3. Type

   setup

   at the DOS prompt and press ◄┘.

4. The setup program will ask you several questions regarding your computer equipment, and will prompt you to insert the appropriate disks. Simply follow these instructions to complete the installation.

If you are using Windows version 3.0 or later, once you have installed Word for Windows you might want to add the Word for Windows icon to the Windows Program Manager, so that it will be easier to start the program. To add the icon, use the File/New command of the Program Manager, as described in the *User's Guide* that accompanies your version of Windows.

STARTING WORD FOR WINDOWS

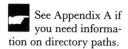

See Appendix A if you need information on directory paths.

Start the Word for Windows program using the following steps. To perform these steps, the disk directory containing the Windows files and the disk directory containing the Word for Windows files must both be included in the current DOS directory path, as specified by the PATH command. This requirement is normally taken care of by the Windows and Word setup programs.

If you are using the run-time version of Windows, start Word by simply typing **winword** and pressing ◄┘ at the DOS command prompt rather than within Windows.

The first part of Chapter 3 describes alternative methods for starting Word for Windows.

1. If Windows is not currently running, start it by typing

   win

   at the DOS prompt and pressing ◄┘.

2. Run the program file WINWORD.EXE. If you have Windows version 3.0 or later, choose the File/Run command from the main menu of the Program Manager. The expression "File/Run" is typical of the notation used to refer to Word commands throughout the book. The first word, File, refers to the

main menu name, and the second word, Run, refers to the specific item on this menu. The Program Manager is the first application that comes up when you start Windows; it allows you to organize and run other programs.

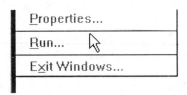

If you have a version of Windows prior to 3.0, choose the File/Run command from the MS-DOS Executive menu. The MS-DOS Executive is the first application that appears when you run a pre-3.0 version of Windows; it permits you to run programs, manage disk files, and perform other tasks. With either Windows version, the File/Run command will prompt you for the name of the program to run.

3. Type the name of the program

Run
Command Line: winword
☐ Run Minimized
OK   Cancel

and press ⏎.

THE OPENING SCREEN

For convenience, an illustration of the Word screen is also printed on the inside front cover of the book.

When Word for Windows begins running, you will see the screen illustrated in Figure 1.1. As you work through the chapters of this book, you will learn about each of the parts of this screen; you can refer back to the illustration for reference.

For now, the most important part of this screen is the large rectangular area labeled the *document window*. This is the window in which

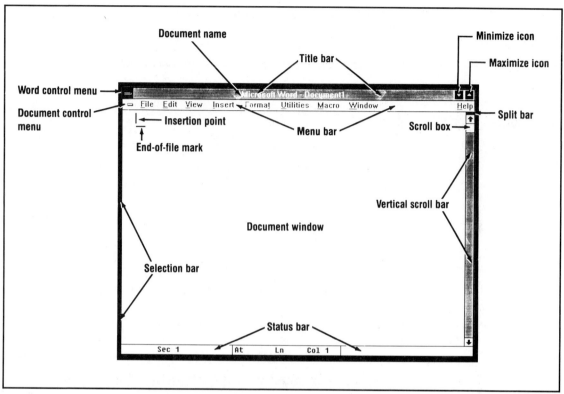

Figure 1.1: The Word for Windows opening screen

The first time you run Word for Windows, the program asks you for your name. The name you enter will be used to identify the author of the documents created using the program. You can change this name later through the Utilities/Customize menu command.

Word displays the contents of the document you are creating or modifying. The window is initially blank, since Word begins by opening a new empty document. As you can see in the *title bar* above the document window, the new document is temporarily named Document1; when you save the document as described later in the chapter, you will assign it a permanent name.

Although the document window does not yet display text, it does contain two important objects: the *end-of-file mark* and the *insertion point*. The end-of-file mark is a short horizontal line placed after the last character in the file. The insertion point is a blinking vertical line that marks the point where the characters you type will be inserted into the document. The insertion point is where most of the action takes place within the Word program. As you will see later, in addition to inserting characters you can also delete characters, change the appearance of characters, mark blocks, and perform many other tasks at the insertion point. You can move the insertion point throughout the document. You cannot, however, move it beyond the end-of-file mark, since this mark indicates the end of the document.

ENTERING TEXT INTO THE DOCUMENT

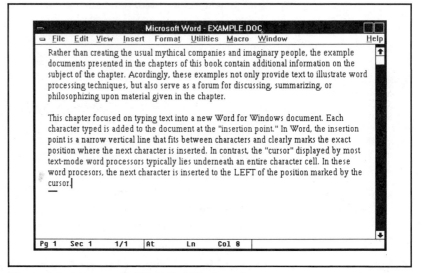

PC keyboard models are illustrated in Figure 3.3.

This chapter assumes that you are in the insert mode rather than in the overtype mode. If the letters **OVR** appear on the status bar, indicating that the overtype mode is active, press the Ins key once to restore the insert mode. See Chapter 4 for an explanation of the overtype mode.

Begin by typing in the text shown in Figure 1.2. Simply type each character using the computer keyboard as if it were a typewriter. For example, you insert an uppercase letter—as well as the upper character on a key with two characters—by holding down the Shift key while pressing the key.

Before typing the first line, be aware of an important difference between using a typewriter and entering text into a Word document: When using Word, you *should not press the* ← *key at the end of each line* (as you will see, if you pressed ←, you would create a new paragraph rather than simply insert a new line). As you approach the end of the

Figure 1.2: An example Word for Windows document

first line of text, simply continue typing as if the line extended forever to the right. Notice that when you finally type a word that is too long to fit at the end of the current line, Word automatically moves the word—together with the insertion point—down to the beginning of the next line. This feature is known as *automatic word wrap*.

When you are typing your document, each line may break at a different point than illustrated in Figure 1.2. The exact position at which Word breaks a line (through automatic word wrap) depends upon the number of characters that can be printed on a line with your printer.

Continue typing in the first paragraph, remembering not to press the ◄— key at the end of the lines. When you have completed typing the entire paragraph (that is, when you have typed through the words **in the chapter.**), you should press ◄— to generate a new paragraph. Before typing the second paragraph, press ◄— again so that there will be a blank line between the two paragraphs; this blank line is actually a separate paragraph that contains no characters.

Notice that as you type each character, it is inserted into the document at the current position of the insertion point, and that the insertion point instantly moves to the right, marking the position where the *next* character will be inserted. Type the text exactly as shown; in Chapter 2 you will correct the misspellings and make several other revisions to this document.

If you make a mistake of your own while typing the text, you can correct it by using the Backspace key. Each time you press Backspace, Word erases the character immediately preceding the insertion point, and then moves the insertion point one character position back. If you continue to hold down the Backspace key, this action is automatically repeated so that you can erase an entire series of previously typed characters. (In the following chapters, you will learn much more efficient ways to correct your errors.)

In the same manner, type in the second paragraph to complete the document. Notice that quote characters are used around the words **"insertion point"** and **"cursor,"** and that the word **LEFT** is emphasized by using all capital letters. With Word, however, you can do much better than this; in Chapter 16, you will learn how to emphasize characters by using italics or boldface.

Press the ◄— key only when you want to create a new paragraph; do not use it to generate a new line within a paragraph.

CII. 1

To save the document, you will choose the File/Save menu command. If you have a mouse, follow these steps (if you do not have a mouse, see the next set of instructions):

1. Place the pointer on the word **File** on the menu bar (see Figure 1.1) and press the left mouse button.

Word allows you to display either short menus, which list only a portion of the menu commands, or long menus, which list all of the commands. While you are working through this book, you should display full menus; if the item Full Menus is included on the View menu (indicating that short menus are currently displayed), choose this item to display full Word menus.

2. The menu of file commands immediately appears below the menu bar. While holding down the mouse button, drag the highlight down to the Save item and release the mouse button to choose this command (see Figure 1.3).

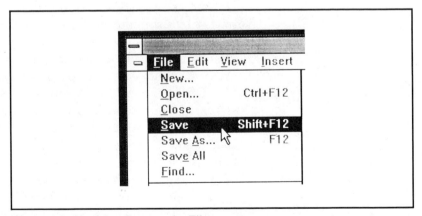

Figure 1.3: Choosing Save on the File menu

If you do not have a mouse, you can choose the File/Save menu item by performing these two steps:

1. Press the Alt key and F key simultaneously. This will open the File menu.

2. Press the S key to choose the Save menu item.

Word will request a file name only the *first time* you choose the File/Save menu command. If you later want to change the name under which the document is stored, use the File/Save As menu command instead.

Once you have chosen the File/Save menu command, Word will display a *dialog box* requesting the name of the file in which the document is to be stored (Figure 1.4). A dialog box is a window that Word displays to obtain additional information. You must supply a file name the first time you save the document because the name appearing on the title bar, **Document1**, is only temporary.

The file name you type into the dialog box should include the full directory path, so that Word knows exactly where to place the file on your disk. For example, if you wanted to name the example document EXAMPLE.DOC and place it in the directory PRACTICE, you would type this into the dialog box:

```
Save File Name:
┌────────────────────────────┐
│\PRACTICE\EXAMPLE│          │
└────────────────────────────┘
```

The directory PRACTICE must already exist. For information on creating directories, see Appendix A.

You do not need to include an *extension* in the name you specify when saving a file. The extension is the optional one to three final letters that follow a period. If you do not provide an extension, Word automatically adds the extension .DOC. For example, if you type **TABBY**, Word will name the document TABBY.DOC.

3. Create a directory named PRACTICE and name the document EXAMPLE—type **\PRACTICE\EXAMPLE**.

To abort saving the file, click the Cancel button or press Esc. In general, pressing the Esc key will remove a dialog box or menu without performing any action, or will interrupt a lengthy process such as printing a file.

As you will see in Chapter 3 (in the section "Saving a Document") you can also use the list of directory and disk names within the dialog

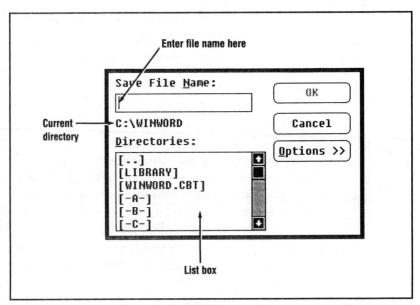

Figure 1.4: The dialog box displayed when you first save a new file

box to search through the entire file system and to select an existing directory (using this method, you do not have to remember the names of your directories or type in the directory name).

4. When you have finished typing the file name, click the OK button or press ←.

Once you click OK or press ←, Word will display another dialog box requesting *summary information*. The summary information associated with a document is used primarily to make it easier to find and identify documents (through the File/Find command, discussed in Chapter 26). Filling in these fields is completely optional.

5. For now, simply click the OK button or press ← to quickly save the document.

Word will request summary information only the *first time* you choose the File/Save command. If you later want to change this information, choose the Edit/Summary Info menu command (see Chapter 26). Maintaining and using document summary information is discussed in Chapter 3.

Word will now save the document in a disk file named EXAMPLE.DOC, within the requested directory, and will remove the dialog box. Notice that after you perform the save operation, the file name you assigned, EXAMPLE.DOC, now appears on the window title bar.

HELP!

Before proceeding further in your exploration of Word for Windows, you might want to learn about the program's help facility. By using the help feature, you can discover how to use many of Word's functions without referring to the printed documentation.

The easiest way to access help is to simply press the F1 key. When you press this key, a window will appear that contains information pertaining to the current task you are performing; Word for Windows help is therefore described as *context sensitive*. For example, if the Save menu item is highlighted on the File menu when you press F1, the help window will display information on the File/Save command. Likewise, if the File/Open dialog box (that is, the one displayed when you select the File/Open command) is open when you press F1, the help window will display information on the fields within this dialog box. If no particular command is in progress when you press F1, a general index of help topics will appear in the help window (Figure 1.5).

If you press F1 when the help window is already active, the window will display information on how to use the help facility. In summary, all you have to remember to obtain help is to press F1.

EXITING FROM WORD FOR WINDOWS

Once you have saved your document, you can exit from the Word for Windows program. To quit Word, choose the Exit item from the File menu.

CII. 1

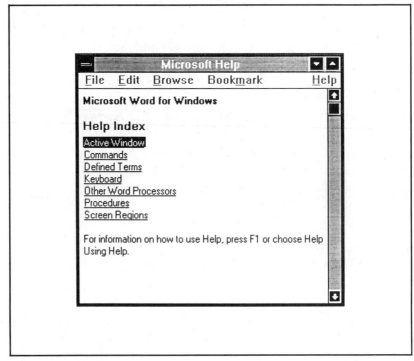

Figure 1.5: The Word help utility

See the *User's Guide*
that accompanies
your version of Windows
or the *Basic Skills for
Windows Applications*
booklet that comes with
Word for more informa-
tion on using the mouse.

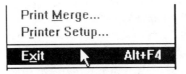

Alternatively, you can terminate the program by choosing the
Close item from the Word *control menu,* as shown in Figure 1.6.

You can also quit the program by rapidly clicking the left mouse
button twice while the pointer is on the Word control menu box (a
process known as *double-clicking*).

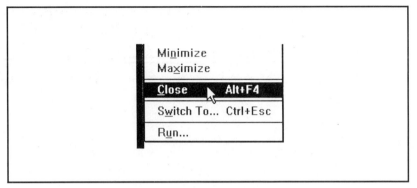

Figure 1.6: Choosing Close from the Word control menu

SUMMARY

- Start the Word program by choosing the File/Run menu command from the Program Manager (with Windows version 3.0 or later) or from the MS-DOS Executive (with a pre-3.0 version of Windows), typing **winword** at the prompt, and pressing ←┘.

- Enter the text for the new document by typing the letters on the keyboard as if you were using a typewriter; the characters will be added to the document at the current position of the insertion point. Do not, however, press the ←┘ key at the end of each line.

- Correct typing mistakes by pressing the Backspace key.

- Press ←┘ each time you want to create a new paragraph.

- Save the document in a disk file by choosing the File/Save menu command. The first time you activate this command, you will have to type the name of the file in which you want to save the document. Word will also prompt you for document summary information; entering this information is optional.

- Anytime you want to access Word's online help facility, press the F1 key.

- Exit from Word for Windows by double-clicking the Word control menu box (shown in Figure 1.1).

2

EDITING, PREVIEWING, AND PRINTING THE DOCUMENT

IN CHAPTER 1, YOU CREATED A NEW DOCUMENT BY entering text in much the same manner as you would type a paper using a typewriter. In this chapter, you will learn one of the great advantages of using a word processor such as Word for Windows: the ability to revise an existing document, freely inserting, deleting, or changing characters.

You will begin by running Word and opening the document you created in Chapter 1. You will then make several revisions to this document by moving the insertion point to the appropriate locations, and then deleting or inserting characters. Next, you will save the revised version. Finally, you will preview the printed appearance of the document and produce a printed copy.

STARTING WORD AND OPENING THE DOCUMENT

If you are using the run-time version of Microsoft Windows described in Chapter 1, you should start Word by typing **winword** followed by the document name *at the DOS prompt* rather than from within Windows.

If Windows is not currently running, start it by typing **win** at the DOS prompt. To run Word for Windows, choose the File/Run command from the Windows Program Manager (or from the MS-DOS Executive for versions of Windows prior to 3.0), as described in Chapter 1. This time, however, when you are prompted for the program name, type **winword** followed by the *full path name* of the document you created in the previous chapter. For example, if you stored the document in the file EXAMPLE.DOC, within the PRACTICE directory on drive C, you should start Word by typing

---

Run

Command Line: winword C:\PRACTICE\EXAMPLE

☐ Run **M**inimized

OK   **Cancel**

---

and pressing ←⊥.

Because you included a file name when starting Word, the program will initially open and display the specified document rather than creating a new empty document. The screen should appear as shown in Figure 1.2. (Remember that the exact location of the line breaks in your document depends upon the printer that is installed.)

In Chapter 3, you will learn how to open an existing document once the Word program has already started.

MAKING THE REVISIONS

As you saw in Chapter 1, the insertion point marks the position in the document where characters are inserted or deleted. Accordingly, making a revision normally requires the following two steps:

1. Move the insertion point to the place in the document you want to change.

2. Delete and/or insert characters as required to make the change.

This section discusses these two procedures individually, and then gives step-by-step instructions for revising the example document.

MOVING THE INSERTION POINT

This section describes two methods for moving the insertion point: using the arrow keys and using the mouse.

See Figure 3.3 for the location of the arrow keys (←, →, ↑, and ↓) on various keyboard models.

If you are using the arrow keys on the numeric keypad (the set of keys at the right side of the keyboard), make sure that the Num Lock state is not on. When this state is on, **NUM** appears on the right side of the Word status bar; you can turn it off by pressing the Num Lock key once.

Pressing an arrow key (↑, ↓, ←, →) moves the insertion point one character position in the corresponding direction. Holding down an arrow key causes the insertion point to continue moving, character by character. Using the arrow keys is a convenient method for moving the insertion point a short distance; it can be quite slow, however, for moving horizontally across an entire line or vertically through an entire paragraph.

Using the mouse is a faster method for moving the insertion point a distance greater than a few characters. While the mouse pointer is within the document window, it has an I-beam shape:

Rather than creating the usual

Simply move the mouse pointer to the location in the document where you would like to place the insertion point, and press the left mouse button. The insertion point will instantly appear at the designated position. You can't position the insertion point beyond the last character in the file.

In Chapter 3, you will learn several other methods for efficiently moving the insertion point, as well as techniques for scrolling the document if the text does not fit entirely within the window.

MAKING THE CHANGES

Once you have moved the insertion point to the desired location, you are ready to make the change to the document. You can delete existing characters using either the Backspace key or the Del key. As you saw in Chapter 1, pressing the Backspace key deletes the character immediately *preceding* the insertion point and moves the insertion point one character space back. Pressing the Del key erases the character immediately *following* the insertion point. Remember that holding down either Backspace or Del causes the erasing action to repeat automatically.

Chapter 5 will discuss more efficient methods for deleting large amounts of text, and methods for deleting or copying a block of text and then inserting the block into another location in the document (or another document).

After you have erased any characters you want to eliminate, the next step is to insert, if necessary, one or more new characters at the insertion point.

REVISING THE EXAMPLE DOCUMENT

In this section, you will practice the techniques just discussed by making several changes to the example document you created in Chapter 1. The original version of this document is shown in Figure 1.2, and the revised version is presented in Figure 2.1.

To make the first revision, move the insertion point immediately in front of the words **the example documents** in the first sentence. Type the words

most of

followed by a space character.

Next, move the insertion point in front of the words **the chapters of this book contain...**, also in the first paragraph. Now press the Del key repeatedly to erase the words **the chapters of**.

Notice that as you erase or insert characters, Word maintains the paragraph margins, automatically adjusting line breaks as necessary.

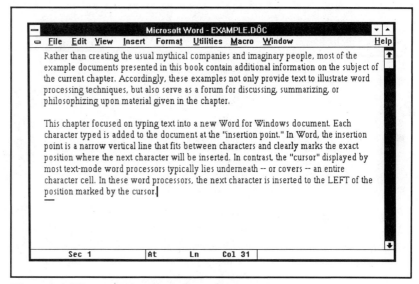

Figure 2.1: The revised example document

Now place the insertion point in front of the words **chapter. Acordingly, these examples**, and add the word

current

followed by a space character. Also, move the insertion point a few characters forward and add a second **c** to the word incorrectly spelled **Acordingly**.

Moving to the second paragraph, place the insertion point immediately after the word **is** in the expression **is inserted,** near the middle of the paragraph. Press the Backspace key twice to erase the **is**, and then type the words

will be

(not followed by a space).

Finally, move the insertion point in front of the expression **an entire character cell** near the end of the second paragraph, and insert

-- or covers --

followed by a space.

You have now finished revising the document. Compare your result with the completed document shown in Figure 2.1.

SAVING THE DOCUMENT AND QUITTING WORD

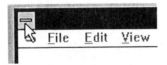

If you want to save the document under a new name, choose the File/Save As command, which will be explained in Chapter 3.

Before continuing, save the document using the File/Save menu command as described in Chapter 1. Since you have already assigned the document a permanent name (EXAMPLE.DOC), Word will immediately save the document without prompting you for a file name or document summary information.

If you want to take a break before previewing and printing the document, you can quit Word by double-clicking the Word control menu box.

PREVIEWING THE DOCUMENT

See Table 17.2 in Chapter 17 for a summary of all the document views provided by Word.

Now you will see some tangible results from the efforts you have expended so far. Word for Windows provides several alternative document views. A *document view* is a particular way of looking at and working with a document. When you start Word and open a document, you begin in galley view. *Galley view* is the normal editing view you have seen in the previous two chapters. In galley view, characters and paragraphs are normally displayed as they will be printed. However, in this view you cannot see the page margins, multiple columns, or elements such as headers and footers (all of these items are discussed later in the book).

In this section, you will see another document view, known as *Print Preview*, which allows you to view the overall printed appearance of each page of the document.

If you are not already running Word, first start the program, opening the example document you created in the previous chapter. Follow the instructions given in the first section of this chapter. You should see the example document in galley view. To switch into Print

Remember that you should enable full Word menus, if necessary, by choosing the File/Full Menus menu command.

To view one page, click the One Page button; to view two pages, click the Two Pages button. See Chapter 17 for complete details on Print Preview.

Preview, choose the Print Preview command from the File menu. This new view of the document is illustrated in Figure 2.2.

In Print Preview, you will see a representation of one or two entire document pages as they will be printed. Although the individual characters are too small to be read, this view shows you the overall composition of the page. As you will see in Part III, Print Preview is especially valuable when you have added headers or footers, or when you have placed paragraphs of text or graphics at specific positions on the page. You cannot perform normal editing tasks such as inserting or deleting characters while in Print Preview; however, as you will also see in Part III, you can adjust the positions of various objects on the page so that you can refine the final page layout.

To exit from Print Preview and return to galley view, click the Cancel button

or press the Esc key.

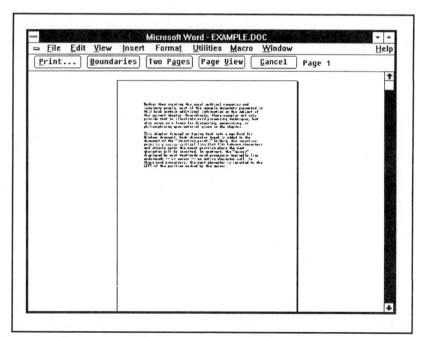

Figure 2.2: The Print Preview view of the example document

When you are creating a more complex document, you will normally go into Print Preview just before printing the document to verify that the page layout is correct and to make any necessary layout adjustments.

PRINTING THE DOCUMENT

You can print the document while you are still in Print Preview, or after you have returned to normal galley view. To print from Print Preview mode, choose the File/Print Preview menu command, click the Print button, or simply press P. In order to print from galley view, choose the File/Print menu command. Make sure the printer is connected to the computer, is turned on, and is "selected" before issuing the print command.

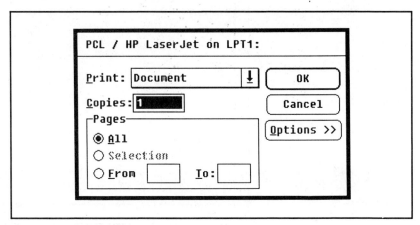

Remember that you can generally remove a dialog box or menu, or cancel a long process, by pressing Esc.

Once you have chosen the print command, Word will display the dialog box shown in Figure 2.3. At the top of this dialog box, you will see the name of the *default* printer, which is the printer that currently receives all printed output. You supply the name of the default printer when you install Windows. You can change the name of the printer to receive output by issuing the Word menu command File/Printer Setup. The dialog box also allows you to set printing options, such as the number of copies of the document that are to be printed. For now, simply click the OK button, or press ←, to accept the default options and to begin printing. Word will remove the dialog box and will print your document. You can

PCL / HP LaserJet on LPT1:

Print: Document

Copies: 1

Pages
- ● All
- ○ Selection
- ○ From ____ To: ____

OK

Cancel

Options >>

Figure 2.3: The Print dialog box

cancel printing the document and remove the dialog box by clicking the Cancel button or by pressing Esc. You can also abort the printing process after the dialog box is removed by pressing Esc.

The printed document is illustrated in Figure 2.4. In addition to the printing options you can set through the print dialog box, you can also change the default printer (if you change printers or have more than one printer installed), and you can set certain options associated with this printer, such as the paper size, by issuing the File/Printer Setup menu command. See Chapter 17 for more information on this command; also, refer to Chapter 17 if you have any difficulties printing your document.

Rather than creating the usual mythical companies and imaginary people, most of the example documents presented in this book contain additional information on the subject of the current chapter. Accordingly, these examples not only provide text to illustrate word processing techniques, but also serve as a forum for discussing, summarizing, or philosophizing upon material given in the chapter.

This chapter focused on typing text into a new Word for Windows document. Each character typed is added to the document at the "insertion point." In Word, the insertion point is a narrow vertical line that fits between characters and clearly marks the exact position where the next character will be inserted. In contrast, the "cursor" displayed by most text-mode word processors typically lies underneath -- or covers -- an entire character cell. In these word processors, the next character is inserted to the LEFT of the position marked by the cursor.

Figure 2.4: The top part of the printed example document

EXITING FROM WORD

If you made any changes to the document after you opened it, you should save it before exiting from Word by choosing the File/Save menu command.

When you have finished working with the document, you can exit from Word by double-clicking on the Word control menu box.

SUMMARY

- You can start Word and open an existing document by choosing the File/Run menu command from the Windows Program Manager, and typing **winword** followed by the document name.

- To make revisions to a document, first move the insertion point to the desired location, and then delete or insert characters as necessary.

- To move the insertion point a short distance, it is convenient to use the arrow keys.

- To move the insertion point a greater distance, place the mouse I-beam pointer at the desired location and press the left mouse button.

- Use the Backspace key to delete characters *preceding* the insertion point, and use the Del key to delete characters *following* the insertion point.

- Choose the File/Save command to quickly save the document under its current name.

- Word provides several document views, each of which offers a different way of looking at and working with your document. The normal editing view is termed *galley view*.

- You can examine and adjust the overall layout of the pages of your document by switching into the Print Preview document view.

- Activate Print Preview by choosing the File/Print Preview menu command. Return to galley view by clicking the Cancel button or by pressing Esc.

- To print your document on the default printer, choose the File/Print menu command (in Print Preview, you can also print the document by clicking the **Print** button or by pressing P).

- You can change the default printer or adjust the printer options through the File/Printer Setup menu command, which is described in Chapter 17.

EDITING

This part of the book focuses on techniques for creating the *content* of your documents. It shows you how to enter and revise text, graphics, tables of information, headers, and footers. It also explains how to check your spelling and find synonyms, and how to automatically generate indexes, tables of contents, and footnotes.

The next part of the book then focuses on methods for adjusting the printed *appearance* of your documents, and explains how to generate the final printed copies.

3

BASIC EDITING SKILLS

IN THIS CHAPTER, YOU WILL LEARN FUNDAMENTAL
Word for Windows editing skills: how to create a new document or
open an existing one, how to enter text and perform minor revisions,
and how to save a document in a disk file. If you worked through the
tutorial in Part I of this book, you will already be familiar with some
of these techniques; this chapter, however, treats these topics in much
greater detail. To get some practice with editing techniques, you'll
create two new short documents.

This chapter assumes that you have installed both Windows and
Word for Windows on your hard disk as described at the beginning of
Chapter 1. It also assumes that you are familiar with basic Windows
skills, such as choosing a command from a menu; if you need more
information on Windows techniques, please see the *User's Guide* that
comes with your version of Windows or the *Basic Skills* booklet that comes
with Word.

To use the techniques described in this chapter, the disk directory containing the Windows files and the disk directory containing the Word for Windows files must both be included in the current DOS directory path, as specified by the PATH command. This requirement is normally taken care of by the Windows and Word for Windows setup programs. See Appendix A for information on directory paths and the PATH command.

CREATING A NEW DOCUMENT

This section explains how to start the Word for Windows program so that it automatically opens a new document when it begins running. It also shows you how to create a new document after you have started Word.

STARTING WORD AND CREATING A NEW DOCUMENT

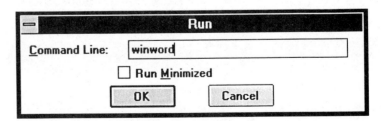

If you are using the run-time version of Windows described in Chapter 1, you start Word by typing **winword** *at the DOS prompt* rather than running Word from within Windows.

If Windows is not already running, you can start it by typing **win** at the DOS command prompt and pressing ◄┘. The first program that normally appears when you start Windows is the Program Manager (or the MS-DOS Executive for versions of Windows prior to 3.0). You can use the Program Manager (or the MS-DOS Executive) to start Word for Windows—creating a new document—in one of three ways.

First, you can start Word by choosing the File/Run menu command. When prompted for the name of the program to run, type **winword** and then press ◄┘.

See the *User's Guide* that accompanies your version of Windows for information on using the File Manager and other basic Windows skills.

Second, you can start the Windows File Manager from the Program Manager, and use the File Manager to open the directory containing the Word for Windows files (which is usually named WINWORD). Once you have opened this directory, double-click the file name WINWORD.EXE (which includes an icon under Windows version 3.0 and later), or highlight this name and press ←↵.

Third, if you have installed Word for Windows within a program group of the Program Manager (see Appendix B), you can simply open this group and either double-click the Word icon, or highlight the icon and press ←↵.

When Word begins, it automatically opens and displays a new document, which is temporarily named Document1. The opening screen is illustrated in Figure 1.1 and on the inside front cover of the book.

CREATING A NEW DOCUMENT WITHIN WORD

You can also open a new document at any time you are running Word (provided that you have not exceeded the limit of nine open windows). You might, for example, be working on an existing document and decide that you want to open a new document. To create the new document from within Word, choose the File/New menu command.

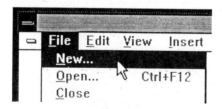

When you create a new document through the File/New command, Word prompts you for the name of the *document template* to be associated with the new document (see Figure 3.1). A template is a file that serves as the framework upon which a document is built. Various document elements can be assigned to a given template, such as text, formatting styles, custom menu designs, and other features. When a new document is created based upon a particular template, it automatically acquires all of the features assigned to that template.

When prompting you for the document template, Word displays a list of existing templates, all of which have the .DOT file extension. Several templates are supplied with the Word program, and you can

---

If you are using a version of Windows prior to 3.0, use the MS-DOS Executive to open the WINWORD directory and start the program.

If you already have a document open when you create a new document through the File/New command, *both* documents will be open simultaneously in Word. See Chapter 26 for information on techniques for managing multiple windows.

Document templates, and all of the features that can be assigned to them, are described in Part IV.

CH. 3

If you start Word so that it automatically creates a new document, this document is based upon the template NOR-MAL.DOT.

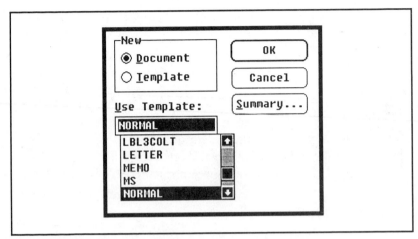

Figure 3.1: The File/New dialog box

create additional ones. Notice that Word initially selects the template NORMAL.DOT, which contains the standard (default) program values. For the exercises in this chapter, simply click the OK button or press ◄—┘ to create a new document based upon NORMAL.DOT. The document you create will then have the standard formatting styles, menu designs, and other features.

In Part IV of the book you will learn how to create and use templates and how to alter NORMAL.DOT. While you are working through the exercises in this book, however, you should use and not change the NORMAL.DOT template, since the descriptions of program features in the book are based upon the default values initially assigned to NORMAL.DOT.

Notice that while Word is displaying the dialog box for choosing the document template, you can also assign summary information to the document by clicking the Summary button. You need not assign this information now, since, as mentioned in Chapter 1, you will automatically be prompted for summary information the first time you save the document. You can also supply this data at any time by choosing the Edit/Summary Info menu command. See the section "Saving a Document," later in this chapter, for information on maintaining and using document summary information.

When Word opens the new document, it will be assigned a temporary name (Document2 if it is the second document you have opened, Document3 if it is the third, and so on). The opening screen you will see is illustrated in Figure 1.1, and on the inside front cover of the book.

OPENING AN EXISTING DOCUMENT

You can open an existing document either when you run Word for Windows, or at any time after the program has already started. This section describes these two methods.

STARTING WORD AND OPENING A DOCUMENT

See Chapter 26 for information on opening files in formats other than the standard format used for Word documents.

If you are using the run-time version of Windows described in Chapter 1, you should start Word by typing **winword**, followed by the document name, *at the DOS prompt* rather than running Word from within Windows.

If Windows is not already running, start it by typing **win** at the DOS command prompt and pressing ◄─┘. Once Windows is running, you can start Word—and have it open an existing document— in one of two ways.

When starting Word and opening a document, you must type the *full path name* of the document so that the system can locate the file. See Appendix A for more information on specifying file paths.

First, you can choose the File/Run command from the menu of the Program Manager (or the MS-DOS Executive in versions of Windows prior to 3.0). When you are prompted for the name of the file to run, type **winword** followed by the *full path name* of the document you would like to open. For example,

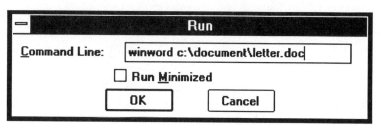

As a shortcut, if you type the expression **/mfile1** following the file name, Word will automatically open the file that was last opened when you previously ran the program, as in

winword   /mfile1

Be sure to leave a space between **winword** and the /.

Note that to start Word by double-clicking the file name, the line

doc = winword.exe   ^.doc

must be in the EXTENSIONS section of your WIN.INI file. The Word setup program should have added this line for you. For more information on WIN.INI settings, see your Windows manual.

Second, you can also start Word and automatically open an existing document by directly selecting the document name from the File Manager (or from the MS-DOS Executive with pre-3.0 versions of Windows). The procedure is as follows:

1. Run the Windows File Manager (if you are using a version of Windows prior to 3.0, run the MS-DOS Executive).

2. Use the File Manager (or the MS-DOS Executive) to open the directory containing the desired Word document.

3. Double-click the name of the document you would like to open. The file must have the .DOC extension. (If you don't have a mouse, highlight the name and press ←┘.)

Word will begin running and will automatically open the selected document.

OPENING A DOCUMENT WITHIN WORD

If you do not close the current document before opening a new document through the File/Open command, *both* documents will be open simultaneously in Word. See Chapter 26 for information on techniques for managing multiple windows.

There are three methods of opening an existing document within Word: you can use the File/Open command, choose a file from the File menu, or use the File/Find command.

When you execute the File/Open menu command, Word will display the dialog box shown in Figure 3.2. To open any document file, you can simply type its full path name into the text box at the top of the dialog box, as in

\LETTERS\MOM01

When you are ready to open the document, click the OK button or press ←┘. In this example, Word would open the file MOM01.DOC, located in the LETTERS directory on drive C.

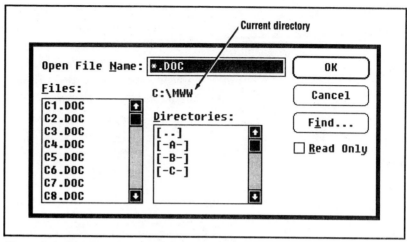

Current directory

Figure 3.2: The File/Open dialog box

See Appendix A for an explanation of the DOS directory structure and a definition of the current directory.

You can save typing, however, if you understand the concept of the *current directory*. The current directory is the disk directory displayed above the Directories list box within the File/Open dialog box (see Figure 3.2). You can *omit* the current directory path from the file name that you type into the dialog box. For example, if the current directory is C:\LETTERS, you could simply enter

MOM01

rather than the full path, C:\LETTERS\MOM01, which was shown in the previous example.

You can change the current directory to any directory within your file system by using the Directories list box (see Figure 3.2). This list box displays the following items, which can be used to choose the current directory (you can scroll through the list box by means of either the vertical scroll bar or the arrow keys):

- The names of all disk drives in your system. If you want the current directory to be located on another drive, double-click the letter for this drive (or highlight it and press ◄—⏎). The drive letters are surrounded by the [- and -] characters (for example, drive A is listed as [-A-]).

- The names of all directories contained within the current directory. The name of each directory is surrounded by the [and] characters; for example, the WINDOWS directory is displayed as **[windows]**. To make one of these directories the current directory, double-click the name, or highlight the name and press ⏎.

- The symbol **[..]**, which indicates the directory that contains the current directory (that is, the *parent* directory). To change the current directory to the parent, double-click this symbol, or highlight it and press ⏎.

When you set the current directory in the File/Open list box, it also becomes the current directory used by other commands, such as File/Save As.

Using the three elements found in the Directories list box, you can navigate through the entire file system to reach the desired directory.

You can also save typing and obtain the names of all document files in the system by using the Files list box. This box normally lists the names of all files with the .DOC extension (that is, all Word document files) that are within the current directory. To open one of these files, double-click the file name, or highlight the name and press ⏎. You can view the document files within any other directory by changing the current directory as just described.

You can also view—and possibly open—files with extensions other than .DOC by entering an asterisk character (∗) into the text box, immediately followed by the desired extension. For example, to view all files with the .TXT extension in the current directory, type

    ∗.TXT

and click the OK button or press ⏎. Rather than attempting to open a file, Word will recognize the asterisk character and will display all files with the desired extension in the Files list box. In the next section, you will see how to open files that are not in standard Word document format.

If you select the Read Only option in the File/Open dialog box,

Read Only

Word will open the file and allow you to freely make editing changes. However, you will not be able to save such a document under its original name. If you have changed the document and want to save the modified version, use the File/Save As command to save a copy of the document under a new name, while leaving the original version intact. The Read Only option is thus a safeguard that prevents you from modifying an original copy of a document.

If you want to remove the dialog box without opening a document, click the Cancel button or press Esc.

In addition to the File/Open command, Word provides two other methods for opening an existing document. First, Word displays the names of the four most recently opened or saved files in a numbered list at the bottom of the File menu. To open one of these files, simply choose the corresponding menu item.

```
┌─────────────────────────────┐
│ E_xit              Alt+F4    │
├─────────────────────────────┤
│ 1 C3.DOC                     │
│ 2 C2.DOC                     │
│ 3 EXAMP02.DOC  ▷             │
│ 4 C1.DOC                     │
└─────────────────────────────┘
```

You must enable full menus to choose the File/Find command. If full menus are not currently enabled, execute the View/Full Menus menu command.

> You can also access the Word Find feature by clicking the Find button within the File/Open dialog box.

Second, you can open a document by means of the File/Find menu command. This command allows you to search for a file or group of files based upon a wide variety of criteria. Once you have located the desired file or files, you can then open or print one or more of them. The File/Find command is described in Chapter 26.

ENTERING AND REVISING TEXT

> Because Word runs in the Windows environment, the keyboard lights indicating the Caps Lock, Num Lock, and Scroll Lock states may be disabled.

As you saw in Chapter 1, when creating a new document or adding to an existing one, you insert characters by simply typing on the keyboard as if you were using a typewriter. An uppercase letter—as well as the upper character on a key with two characters—is inserted by holding down the Shift key while typing the character. If you press the Caps

Lock key, the letters **CAPS** will appear on the Word status bar at the bottom of the screen, and all alphabetical characters will be entered in uppercase. (If the status bar is not visible on your screen, you must enable it by choosing the View/Status Bar menu option.) If you press Caps Lock again, the letters **CAPS** will be removed and alphabetical keys will again generate lowercase characters. Figure 3.3 illustrates several common keyboard models.

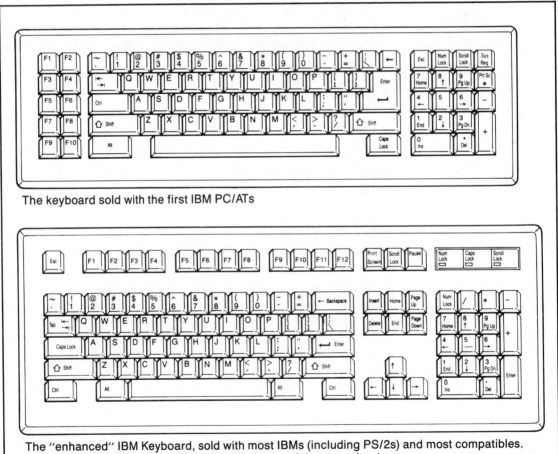

The keyboard sold with the first IBM PC/ATs

The "enhanced" IBM Keyboard, sold with most IBMs (including PS/2s) and most compatibles. In some cases, the three indicator lights at the top right are omitted.

Figure 3.3: PC keyboards used with Word for Windows

Remember that when you enter text you should *not* press the ← key at the end of each line. Rather, Word will automatically wrap each word that does not fit on the current line down to the next line—a feature known as *automatic word wrap*.

The Tab key moves the insertion point to the next tab stop, and causes the subsequent character that is typed to be aligned at this stop. (See Chapter 15 for information on setting and using tab stops.) Note, however, that using tabs to create tables of side-by-side information is an obsolete method under Word; employing Word's table feature, described in Chapter 8, is a much easier technique.

> Remember, hyphenated keystrokes, such as Shift-←, indicate that the specified keys are to be pressed *simultaneously*.

As Word performs automatic word wrap, it may insert a line break between any two words (Word places on each line the maximum number of words that can fit between the text margins). If you want to prevent Word from breaking a line between two particular words, you can insert a *nonbreaking* space between these words. You enter a nonbreaking space by typing the Ctrl-Shift-spacebar key combination.

Normally, a tab character appears on the screen as one or more spaces, and a nonbreaking space appears as a single space. You can, however, make these two characters visible through the View/Preferences menu command. To make tabs visible, select the Tabs item within the Preferences dialog box. To make nonbreaking spaces visible, choose the Spaces option (this option will make both space characters *and* nonbreaking spaces visible). Figure 3.4 shows the symbols that are used to indicate these special characters.

If you hyphenate a word (for example, Rimsky-Korsakov), Word may insert a line break following the hyphen character. See Chapter 17 for a discussion on the special hyphen characters you can enter (specifically, *nonbreaking* and *optional* hyphens).

CREATING TEXT BREAKS

As explained in Chapter 1, while you are typing text, you can press the ← key to create a new paragraph. Word will begin inserting characters on a new line, within a new paragraph.

Alternatively, you can press the Shift-← key combination to generate a line break *within* a paragraph (that is, the next character will be inserted on a new line, but will be contained within the same paragraph). When you press Shift-←, Word enters a character into the

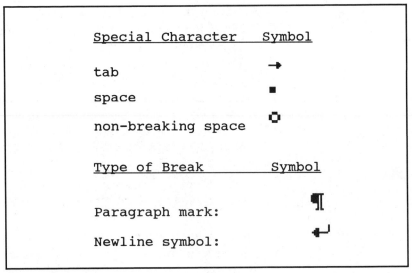

Figure 3.4: Special characters and text breaks and their corresponding symbols

document known as a *newline*. Although this keystroke may seem to have the same effect as pressing ↵, all characters you subsequently type will be in the *same* paragraph and will therefore share all paragraph formatting with the preceding characters (paragraph formatting is explained in Chapter 15).

When you create a new paragraph or a line break within a paragraph, Word actually inserts a special character into the document (see Figure 3.4). Normally, this character is invisible. However, if you choose the View/Preferences menu command, and select the Paragraph Marks item in the dialog box, Word will make the character visible.

☐ **S**paces
☒ **P**aragraph Marks
☐ **O**ptional Hyphens

You can create a *hard page break* by pressing the Ctrl-↵ keystroke. A hard page break forces Word to begin printing on a new page at the exact position in the document where you insert it. A hard page break is indicated by a tight dotted line extending across the document.

This line comes immediately before a hard page break inserted by pressing **Ctrl-Enter**.

This line comes immediately after a hard page break.

You can also insert a hard page break by choosing the Insert/Break menu command, and then selecting the Page Break item within the dialog box that Word displays.

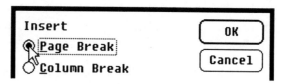

Finally, you can insert a hard page break by formatting the paragraph with the Page Break Before option, as explained in Chapter 15.

When Word prepares a document for previewing or printing, it automatically divides it into separate pages (a process known as *re-pagination*). The division between each of these pages is known as a *soft page break*. A soft page break is indicated by a loose dotted line extending across the document.

This line comes immediately before a soft page break inserted by Word.
This line comes immediately after a soft page break.

If you change the formatting or content of the document, the next time Word repaginates, it will automatically adjust the position of soft page breaks as necessary to maintain the document page length. In contrast, Word will not change the position of a hard page break, though you can always delete or move a hard page break. (In Chapter 17, you will see how to quickly adjust the position of hard or soft page breaks within the Print Preview document view.) Two other types of document breaks, *column breaks* and *section breaks*, are discussed in Chapter 14.

To practice entering the different types of characters discussed so far in this section, you can create the short document shown in Figure 3.5.

1. Open a new document by choosing the File/New menu item and pressing ↵ as soon as the dialog box is displayed.

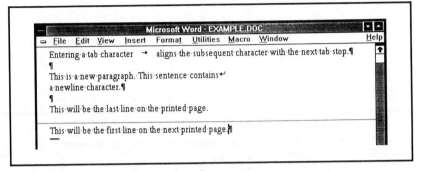

Figure 3.5: An exercise in entering characters

2. Choose the View/Preferences menu command and check the Show All * item (if it is not already checked). This will make *all* characters visible on the screen.

3. Begin typing the text below; when you have completed entering the words **tab character**, press the Tab key.

      Entering a tab character →

    Notice that a right arrow appears on the screen (the symbol for a tab character), and that the insertion point jumps several spaces forward. (It moves to the next tab stop; in Chapter 15 you will learn how to have Word display the positions of the tab stops and how to adjust these positions.) Notice that Word displays a small dot indicating each space character.

4. Finish typing the first sentence; press ◄┘ at the end of the sentence:

      aligns the subsequent character with the next tab stop.

    Notice that Word inserts the symbol for a new paragraph and moves the insertion point down to the first line of the next paragraph. Press ◄┘ again to insert a blank line between the paragraphs.

5. Begin typing the next paragraph, which begins with **This is**. When you have finished typing the word **contains**, press the Shift-◄┘ keystroke to enter a newline character, and then finish typing the sentence. Notice that the newline character

is represented by an arrow symbol, and forces Word to begin a new line (normally, the first line would be much longer). Notice also that both lines of the sentence are contained in the same paragraph.

6. Again, press ◄─┘ twice when you finish typing the sentence, to insert a blank line and start a new paragraph.

7. Now type the next sentence (beginning with **This will be the last line**). When you get to the end of the sentence, press the Ctrl-◄─┘ keystroke—rather than just ◄─┘—to enter a hard page break. Notice that Word inserts a dotted line indicating the page break. When you print the document, the page break will force Word to begin printing on the next page.

8. Finally, enter the last line, beginning with **This will be the first**. This line will be printed at the top of the second page of the document.

When you have completed these steps, you might want to print the document to see the final results. You might also want to save it for future use.

ENTERING SPECIAL CHARACTERS AND SYMBOLS

In addition to the characters pictured on the keyboard, you can enter various special characters and symbols into your document. Most of the fonts used in the Windows environment consist of the collection of characters known as the ANSI (American National Standards Institute) character set. The ANSI character set includes all of the characters on the keyboard, plus many foreign letters, mathematical operators, and other symbols. The ANSI character set used by Windows is different from the IBM character set, which is used for text mode programs on IBM-compatible microcomputers. The complete ANSI character set, showing the code for each character, is given in Appendix C of the Word *User's Reference*. Table 3.1 lists some of the more useful special characters in the ANSI set, and provides their codes.

Table 3.1: Several Useful ANSI Characters

SYMBOL:	KEYSTROKE:	DESCRIPTION:
'	Alt-0145	Single opening quotation mark
'	Alt-0146	Single closing quotation mark
"	Alt-0147	Double opening quotation mark
"	Alt-0148	Double closing quotation mark
•	Alt-0149	Bullet
—	Alt-0150	Em dash
–	Alt-0151	En dash
¢	Alt-0162	Cent sign
©	Alt-0169	Copyright symbol
¼	Alt-0188	One-quarter
½	Alt-0189	One-half
¾	Alt-0190	Three-quarters

Each of the ANSI characters has a unique code, which is a value between 0 and 255. You can insert any character by using its ANSI code, as follows:

1. Make sure that the Num Lock state is on (if the letters **NUM** do not appear on the status bar, press the Num Lock key).

2. While holding down the Alt key, type the number 0 followed by the ANSI code for the character. You must use the numeric keypad to type the numbers. For example, you can insert a bullet character by typing 0149 on the numeric keypad while holding down Alt, since 149 is the ANSI code for this symbol.

To practice entering special characters into a document, you can create the short table shown in Figure 3.6, as follows:

See Chapter 21 for a discussion on using the Word *glossary* to quickly insert frequently used special characters.

1. Open a new document by choosing the File/New menu command and pressing ↵.

2. Type the word **Symbol**, press the Tab key to move the insertion point to the next tab stop, and then type **Description**.

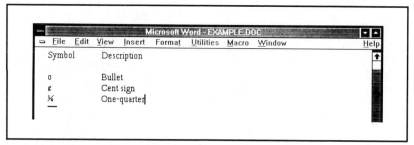

Figure 3.6: An exercise in entering special characters

3. Press ◄─┘ twice: first to insert a blank line and then to start a new paragraph.

4. If the letters **NUM** do not appear within the status bar, press the Num Lock key to turn on the number lock state.

5. Press the Alt key, and while holding the key down, type the numbers **0149** *on the numeric keypad*. Word will insert the bullet character.

6. Press the Tab key twice and type the word **Bullet** to complete the first line of the table. Then press ◄─┘ to begin the next line.

7. Finish typing the table using the same techniques. The code for the cent sign is **0162** and the code for the one-quarter symbol is **0188**.

Word will not display or print Symbol characters unless your printer supports this font. If you have an HP LaserJet, the Word setup program provides you the option of installing a downloadable version of the Symbol font.

In addition to fonts that consist of the ANSI character set, Windows provides a font called Symbol, which consists entirely of special symbols such as Greek letters.

To determine the keystroke required to insert each symbol in the Symbol font, you can open the document KEYCAPS.DOC, which is provided with the Word for Windows package and is normally located in the \WINWORD\LIBRARY subdirectory. This document displays the symbol associated with each key on the keyboard.

CORRECTING MISTAKES

As you saw in Part I of the book, the easiest way to correct typing errors that you notice as you are entering text is to simply press the

Paragraph format-
ting is described in
Chapter 15.

Backspace key one or more times. This key erases the character immediately preceding the insertion point, and if you hold it down, it automatically repeats this action.

If two paragraphs have the same formatting, you can combine them into a single paragraph by backspacing over the paragraph mark that separates them (whether it is visible or invisible). If, however, the paragraphs have different formats, Word will not allow you to delete the paragraph mark with the Backspace key (you can, however, use the Del key or another deleting method).

As you saw in Chapter 2, you can delete the character immediately *following* the insertion point by pressing the Del key. To save time, you can press the Ctrl-Del keystroke to delete the entire *word* following the insertion point (if the insertion point is within a word, this keystroke will delete all characters from the insertion point to the end of the word). You can also press Ctrl-Backspace to delete the entire word preceding the insertion point (if the insertion point is within a word, this keystroke will delete all characters from the beginning of the word to the insertion point).

In the next chapter, you will learn methods for quickly moving the insertion point to the document location where you want to make the revisions. Also, Chapter 5 discusses efficient ways for deleting and copying entire blocks of text.

Using the Overtype Mode

Word has two editing modes: the *insert* mode and the *overtype* mode. When Word begins running, it is automatically in the *insert* editing mode. Pressing the Ins key switches into the overtype mode; when the overtype mode is active, the letters **OVR** appear in the status bar. Pressing the Ins key again restores the insert mode. (Thus, the Ins key toggles between the two modes.)

The descriptions given so far in this book have assumed that you are in the insert editing mode. As you have seen, if you are in the insert mode and place the insertion point within existing text, all characters you type are inserted into the text, causing the existing text to be *moved forward* in the document.

In contrast, if you are in the overtype mode and place the insertion point within existing text, all characters you type *replace* the existing text. Each character is written over the existing character to the immediate

If you are simply
adding text to the
end of a document, there
is little apparent dif-
ference between the in-
sert and overtype modes.

right of the insertion point. Thus, when you are making corrections to a document, you can switch into the overtype mode to avoid the need to erase existing characters before inserting the new text.

Now practice using the different techniques that have been presented so far for correcting mistakes by typing the following sentence into a new document:

The quick brown fox jumped over the lazy dog.

Make sure that you are not in the overtype mode when performing the first four steps. If the letters **OVR** appear in the status bar, press the Ins key once to restore the insert mode.

You might try issuing the Edit/Undo command if you make any mistakes while performing this exercise. This command reverses your most recent editing action.

1. Place the insertion point immediately after the first **The** and press the backspace key three times to erase this word. Now type the letter **A**.

2. Place the insertion point immediately before the word **quick** and press the Del key five times to delete this word. Now type the word **swift**.

3. Place the insertion point immediately before the word **brown** and press the Ctrl-Del keystroke. This will delete the entire word **brown** together with the following space. Now type **red** followed by a space character.

4. Place the insertion point immediately after the word **fox** and press the Ctrl-Backspace keystroke. This will delete the entire word **fox** together with the preceding space. Now type a space character followed by the word **rabbit**.

5. Press the Ins key to turn on the overtype mode; the letters **OVR** will appear in the status bar. Place the insertion point immediately in front of the word **jumped**. Now simply type the letters **lea**. When you are done with this step, press Ins once again to restore the insert mode.

If you have followed each of these steps, the sentence should now be:

A swift red rabbit leaped over the lazy dog.

Undoing and Redoing

The *Undo* command provides another way to correct not only typing errors but also many other types of mistakes made while working with Word. When you issue the Undo command, Word reverses the effect of your most recent action, provided that the action is reversible. To issue the Undo command, either press the Alt-Backspace key combination, or choose the Edit/Undo menu command.

The Alt-Backspace keystroke immediately undoes the last action, unless the action is not reversible. If the action is not reversible, Word simply beeps.

When you choose the Undo command from the Edit menu, you will notice that the menu item (which is at the top of the menu) is labeled with the name of the action that will be reversed. For example, if you have just typed several characters, the label will read Undo Typing, or if you have just deleted some characters with the Del key, the label will be Undo Edit Clear. If the action cannot be reversed, the label will be displayed in light gray letters and cannot be chosen. For your reference, the reversible Word commands are listed in this section; however, if you are uncertain whether your last action is reversible (or if you are uncertain what your last action was!), you can simply pull down the Edit menu and check the Undo command label at the top of the menu.

The following Word actions can be reversed through the Undo command:

- Entering text. Undo erases all text typed since the insertion point was last moved. Pressing the Backspace key to delete characters is considered part of the typing to be reversed.

- Deleting characters. Undo restores the last character or block of characters deleted with the Del key, as well as characters cut or copied to the Clipboard (see Chapter 5).

- Pasting. Undo removes a block of text pasted from the Clipboard (see Chapter 5).

- Formatting (see Part III).

- Field operations (these operations are performed through the F9 key; they are explained in the Word *User's Reference* or *Technical Reference*, under the topic "Fields").

- All Edit menu commands, except Search and Go To. The Undo command itself is included. Undo will reverse *all* changes made through the Replace command if the Confirm Changes option was not selected; if Confirm Changes was selected, only the last change made is reversed. (See Chapter 6 for an explanation of the Replace command.)

- All Insert menu commands except Page Numbers.

- All Format menu commands except Define Styles.

- All Utilities menu commands except Repaginate Now and Customize.

It is important to remember that the Undo command reverses only the immediately preceding action. (In contrast, some text editors continue to reverse prior editing actions as you repeat the Undo command.) Accordingly, you must issue the Undo command *immediately after making the error you want to correct*.

Notice that the Undo command itself is among the reversible Word actions. Therefore, if you choose the Undo command to reverse some action, and then immediately choose Undo again, you will reverse the "undoing," thereby restoring the effect of the original action ("redoing" it). When you have just issued the Undo command, the menu label reads Undo Undo. For example, if you move the insertion point, type a sentence, and then issue the Undo command, the sentence will be erased. If you immediately issue the Undo command again, the sentence will be restored. If you choose the Undo command yet again, the sentence will once more be removed. If you continue to choose Undo, the sentence will alternately be erased and restored.

REPEATING EDITING ACTIONS

This section completes the discussion on entering and revising text by discussing the *Repeat* command, which allows you to automatically repeat your last editing or formatting action. Note, however, that just as not every action is reversible through the Undo command, not every action is repeatable through the Repeat command. You issue this command by pressing F4 or by choosing the Edit/Repeat menu item.

When you press F4, the last action is immediately repeated, if possible. If the action is not repeatable, Word simply beeps.

The title for the Repeat command displayed on the Edit menu indicates the previous action that will be repeated. For example, if you had just typed some characters, the title would read Repeat Typing, and if you had just deleted a character by pressing Del, the title would be Repeat Edit Clear. If the previous action cannot be repeated, the title Can't Repeat is displayed in gray letters, and the command cannot be chosen. You should therefore consult the Edit menu if you are uncertain whether the last action can be repeated, or if you are not sure exactly what action will be repeated when you issue the Repeat command.

You can repeat these actions through the Repeat command:

- The File menu commands New, Open, and Print.

- The Edit menu commands Undo, Repeat, Cut, Copy, Paste, and Table. You can repeat the Search or Go To command by pressing the Shift-F4 key combination.

- The Insert menu commands Break, Footnote, File, Table, Annotation, Picture, and Field.

- All of the Format menu commands, *except* Position and Define Styles.

- All of the Utilities menu commands, *except* Revision Marks, Repaginate Now, and Customize.

- The Macro menu commands Run, Assign to Key, and Assign to Menu.

- The Window menu commands New Window and Arrange All.

When you repeat certain commands, Word may display the dialog box associated with the command.

SAVING A DOCUMENT

It is important to remember that while you are creating or modifying a document in Word, your work is saved only in the computer's temporary memory (that is, in random access memory, or RAM) until you explicitly save the document in a disk file. Each time you save the document, the current document contents are written to a permanent file on the disk. If the power is interrupted, or if the computer stops operating due to a software or hardware error, data stored in temporary memory is lost; data written to a disk file, however, is preserved.

In Chapters 1 and 2, you learned the basic method for saving a Word document. In this section, you will learn about the three commands Word provides for saving documents—Save, Save As, and Save All—and the options available with these commands; and about the Autosave feature.

THE SAVE COMMAND

Normally, when you want to save the document you are working on, you simply choose the File/Save menu command, or press the Shift-F12 or Alt-Shift-F2 key combination. If the document has already been saved one or more times, the Save command immediately saves it under its current name (which is the name that appears on the title bar). In this case, Word displays a message in the status bar, but does not prompt you for further information.

If, however, you are saving a new document for the first time, the Save command performs two special actions. First, it activates the Save As command (described in the next section). As you will see, the Save As command prompts you to specify a document name. You must provide a name because the name assigned to the new file (a name such as Document1 or Document2) is only temporary.

Second, before the Save As command saves the new document, it displays a dialog box prompting you for document *summary information*. As you will see in Chapter 26, the summary information is used primarily for helping you retrieve the document later. You do not need to supply any of this information to save the file; when Word displays the summary information dialog box, you can simply click the OK button or press ← to complete the saving process.

You can add or revise the document summary information at any time the document is open by choosing the Edit/Summary Info menu command. See Chapter 26 for a discussion on maintaining and using document summary information.

THE SAVE AS COMMAND

As you saw, the Save As command is automatically invoked when you first save a new document. You might also want to choose this com-

See Chapter 26 for a discussion on converting Word documents to other formats when saving them.

mand, rather than the Save command, in the following situations:

- If you want to save a copy of the document under a new name.

- If you want to save a copy of the document in a different format (such as pure text, or the format used by another word processor).

- If you want to select one or more of the options that control the way Word saves documents.

Each of these uses for the Save As command will be discussed shortly.

You can issue the Save As command by choosing it from the File menu, or by pressing the F12 or Alt-F2 keystroke. Word will display the dialog box shown in Figure 3.7.

If the document is being saved for the first time, the text box will be empty and you *must* enter a file name.

If you have previously saved the document at least once, the document name you assigned will appear in the text box at the top of the dialog box. If you simply click the OK button or press ⏎, the Save As command will have the same effect as the Save command; that is, it will immediately save the document under its existing name.

If you enter a new name, Word will create a *copy* of the document under the new name, leaving the original document file unchanged.

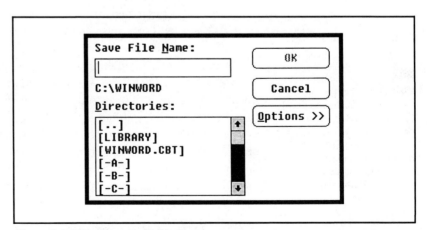

Figure 3.7: The Save As dialog box

Word will also display the new name within the title bar, and will use this name whenever you subsequently save the document.

The Save As command is thus useful for creating an exact copy of a document under a new name, or a copy under the same name within a new directory. You can also use it to preserve copies of various versions of a document. Each time you create a new document version, you can use the Save As command to save it under a new name.

If you type a simple file name, such as CATS, into the Save As dialog box, the document will be saved in the current directory under the name CATS.DOC. The name of the current directory is displayed in the File/Save dialog box, directly above the Directories list box (see Figure 3.7). If you want to save the document in *another* directory, you can type the full directory path. For example, you could save the document CATS.DOC in the PETS directory on drive C, even if this is not the current directory, by typing the following path name:

> C:\PETS\CATS

Alternatively, you can use the Directories list box to view the names of all directories in your file system, and to change the current directory to any one of them. The procedure is the same as that described previously for the Open dialog box (in the section "Opening a Document within Word" in this chapter).

Once you have set the current directory to the directory where you want to store your document, you can type the simple file name and click the OK button or press ◄─┘.

If you type a *new* file name when using the Save As command, and this name is the same as that of an existing file, Word will ask you if you want to replace the original document. Don't click OK unless you are sure you want to erase the original file.

Also, the first time you save a document under a new name, Word will prompt you for document summary information, as described in the previous section.

Finally, before you click the OK button or press ◄─┘, thereby dismissing the Save As dialog box, you might want to choose one or more of the options discussed in the sections below.

If you do not include an extension in the name you specify for the Save As command, Word will automatically append the .DOC extension.

See Appendix A for more information on the MS-DOS directory structure, and for instructions on specifying full directory paths.

Setting the current directory in the Save As dialog box affects the current directory used by other commands, such as Open. Also, the directory you set will be remembered the next time you use the Save As command, even if you remove the dialog box by clicking the Cancel button or pressing Esc.

The Save As command also allows you to choose one or more of the following three options:

- Fast Save

- Create Backup

- Lock for Annotations

To access these options, you must click the Options >> button—or press Alt-O—when the Save As dialog box appears. Your choice of options will go into effect when you click the OK button or press ⏎ to save the document.

Fast Save

When Word performs a *full save* on a document, it writes the *entire body* of text to the disk file, in the order in which this text appears in the document. For a large document, this can be a lengthy process.

If you select the Fast Save option, however, rather than performing a full save, Word merely appends to the disk file a description of any *changes* you have made to the document since the last time you saved it. Although these changes are merely appended to the disk file, Word will incorporate them into the document when it displays the document on the screen or prints the document.

If you continue to save a document using the Fast Save option, the appended list of changes will eventually become too long, and Word will have to perform a full save to permanently incorporate the changes into the body of the document. In this case, Word displays the message **Fast Save Failed** in the status bar and automatically proceeds with the full save.

Word also will automatically disable the Fast Save option if you select the Create Backup option, since Word must write the entire file when creating a backup.

When you start Word, the Fast Save option is initially selected. *Each time* you want to perform a full save, you must use the Save As command and unselect this item before saving the file. After Word performs the full save, it automatically turns the Fast Save option back on.

If you frequently use the File/Find command to search for documents that contain a specific block of text, you should disable Fast Save when you save the document. See Chapter 26 for a description of the File/Find command.

Create Backup

If you select the Create Backup option, Word will *keep* the file that was created the last time you saved the document, and will write a new file containing the current document version. The previous version will be given the same file name, but with the .BAK extension. For example, if your document is named FELIX, when you issue a save command the existing disk file FELIX.DOC will be renamed FELIX.BAK, and then the current version of the document will be written to a new file named FELIX.DOC.

When you install Word, the Create Backup option is initially *not* selected. Once you select it, however, it will remain in effect until you explicitly disable it (even if you quit and restart Word). Also, the option will cause Word to create backups not only when you save through the Save As command, but also when you save through the Save or Save All command.

Lock for Annotations

Annotations are notes that you append to specific locations in a document. Annotations are discussed in Chapter 25.

If you select the Lock for Annotations option, your document will be saved as a *locked* document file. If you are the author of a document, *you* can freely open, modify, and save it even if it has been locked; you can also unlock the document by unselecting the Lock for Annotations option before saving it again with the Save As command. However, any *other* user who opens the document can add annotations, but *cannot* make other modifications. Locking a file thus preserves the original document content, while allowing one or more reviewers to read and comment on the manuscript.

Any user can modify a locked document by entering the name of the document author into the area labeled Your Name within the Utilities/Customize dialog box.

The document author is the person whose name is stored by Word when the document is first saved. Word obtains this name when the program is first run (it displays a dialog box asking you for your name). You can change this name at any time by entering another name into the Your Name area within the dialog box displayed by the Utilities/Customize menu command.

THE SAVE ALL COMMAND

Document templates and the items that may be assigned to them are discussed in Part IV.

When you choose the File/Save All menu command, Word saves not only the document itself, but also any document template that you have modified while working with the document. A document template is modified whenever you add, delete, or change a macro, a glossary entry, a keyboard assignment, a menu assignment, or a style (when you have chosen the Add to Template option).

When you issue the Save All command, Word prompts you before saving each unsaved item. The same sequence of prompts occurs as when you quit the program without saving a modified document or template.

THE AUTOSAVE OPTION

If you enable the *Autosave* feature, Word will periodically remind you to save your document. To turn on this feature, choose the Utilities/Customize menu command and select the High, Medium, or Low option within the box labeled Autosave Frequency.

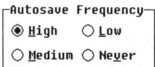

```
Customize
┌Autosave Frequency┐
  ⦿ High     ○ Low
  ○ Medium  ○ Never
└                  ┘
```

When Word is first installed, the Never option is selected, which disables Autosave.

These options cause Word to prompt you to save your document at the following frequencies:

OPTION	FREQUENCY OF PROMPT
Low	Every 30–60 minutes
Medium	Every 20–45 minutes
High	Every 10–30 minutes

The actual time between prompts depends upon the amount of editing you are doing. If you have made many editing changes since

If you have more than one open document, as described in Chapter 26, Word will prompt you to save *each* document that has been modified since the last time it was saved.

the last save, the time will be near the low value of the range; otherwise, the time will be near the upper value. You will not be prompted if you have not modified the document.

Word prompts you to save your document by displaying the following dialog box:

You then have three choices:

1. You can click the OK button to save the document.

2. You can select the Postpone option to have Word prompt you again after a specified period. You can enter the desired number of minutes or accept the default value of 5 minutes, and then click OK or press ⏎.

3. You can click the Cancel button or press Esc to remove the dialog box without saving the document. Word will prompt you again after the usual period.

SUMMARY

*   You can create a new document by starting Word without specifying a file name, or by choosing the File/New menu command once Word is already running.

*   You can open an existing document by specifying the file name when starting Word, or by choosing the File/Open command while Word is running.

*   The File/Open command allows you to convert a document created by one of several other word processors into a Word document.

*   You can also use Word to open, modify, or generate text files, which are suitable for computer programs, data communications, and other purposes.

- You enter text into a Word document by using the computer keyboard like a typewriter. You should press the ← key, however, only to create a new paragraph.

- Press Shift-← to create a line break within a paragraph, or Ctrl-← to generate a new page. You can also generate a new page through the Insert/Break menu command.

- You can enter a variety of characters that do not appear on the keyboard, such as the copyright symbol, by pressing the Alt key while typing 0 (zero) followed by the ANSI code for the character (the Num Lock state must be on, and you must use the numeric keypad). You can also generate a wide variety of symbols by choosing the Symbol font.

- You can correct errors by pressing the Del or Backspace key to remove the character following or preceding the insertion point.

- You can undo your entire previous editing or formatting action by choosing the Edit/Undo menu command or by pressing Alt-Backspace.

- You can repeat your previous editing or formatting action by choosing the Edit/Repeat menu command or by pressing F4.

- Choose the Save menu command, or press Shift-F12 or Alt-Shift-F2, to save the document under its current name.

- Choose the Save As menu command, or press F12 or Alt-F2, to save a copy of the document under a different name or in a different format. You can also use the Save As command to choose options that affect the way Word saves documents.

- The Fast Save option provided by the Save As command allows Word to save documents much more rapidly.

- The Create Backup option causes Word to save the previous version of the document in a backup file (with the .BAK extension) each time you save.

- The Lock for Annotations option locks the file so that other users can enter annotations but cannot change the content of the document you save.

- Choose the Save All command to save the document *and* any modified templates associated with the document.

- The Autosave feature periodically reminds you to save your document. It is enabled through the Utilities/Customize menu command.

4

NAVIGATING
THROUGH A DOCUMENT

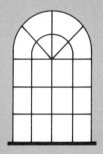

AS YOU HAVE SEEN, THE INSERTION POINT MARKS
the location in the document where the insertion or deletion of characters takes place. Once you have entered text into a new document, or once you have opened an existing document, you need to be able to move the insertion point efficiently to any position in the text.

This chapter explains each of the following methods that Word provides for moving the insertion point or scrolling the document within the window:

- Using the keyboard
- Using the mouse
- Using the Go To command
- Other methods

The chapter concludes with an explanation of the status bar at the bottom of the window, which shows you the current location of the insertion point within the document.

USING THE KEYBOARD

In Chapter 2, you saw how to use the arrow keys to move the insertion point one character position in the desired direction. Word provides several other simple keystrokes for quickly moving the insertion point to various positions in the document. These keystrokes are summarized in Table 4.1.

Table 4.1: Keystrokes for Moving the Insertion Point

PRESS THIS KEY:	TO MOVE TO:
←	Previous character
→	Following character
↑	Previous line
↓	Following line
Ctrl-←	Previous word
Ctrl-→	Next word
Home	Beginning of line
End	End of line
Ctrl-↑	Previous paragraph
Ctrl-↓	Following paragraph
Ctrl-PgUp	First character in window
Ctrl-PgDn	Last character in window
PgUp	Previous windowful
PgDn	Following windowful
Ctrl-Home	Beginning of document
Ctrl-End	End of document

As you can see in the table, pressing the PgUp key moves you toward the beginning of the document by one *windowful*, which is the amount of document content that can be viewed through the current window. Similarly, the PgDn key moves you toward the end of the document by one windowful.

The Word Go To command, described later in the chapter, also allows you to move to various document positions using keyboard commands.

To practice using the keyboard methods for moving the insertion point, perform the following steps:

1. Open one of the example documents provided with the Word program. When you install Word, the setup program normally copies a collection of example documents to the \WINWORD\LIBRARY directory on your hard disk. To open one of these documents, MEMO.DOC for example, follow the instructions given in Chapter 3 (in the section "Opening an Existing Document").

2. Once the document has been opened, try each of the keystrokes given in Table 4.1, namely ←, →, ↑, ↓, Ctrl-←, and so on. To help locate these keys, see the illustrations of keyboards in Figure 3.3.

USING THE MOUSE

You can use the mouse to scroll vertically through the document by means of the vertical scroll bar, and horizontally through the document by means of the horizontal scroll bar. When you first install Word, only the vertical scroll bar is displayed (see Figure 1.1 or the illustration on the inside front cover of the book). You can display or hide either the vertical or the horizontal scroll bar by checking or unchecking the Vertical Scroll Bar or Horizontal Scroll Bar item in the dialog box shown by the View/Preferences menu command. Figure 4.1 illustrates the basic components of a scroll bar.

Table 4.2 summarizes the actions you can perform using the mouse with the vertical scroll bar, and Table 4.3 summarizes the actions you can perform with the horizontal scroll bar.

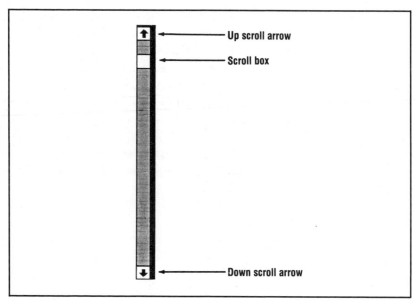

Figure 4.1: The components of a scroll bar

Table 4.2: Actions You Can Perform Using the Vertical Scroll Bar

PERFORM THIS ACTION WITH THE MOUSE & VERTICAL SCROLL BAR:	TO SCROLL WITHIN THE DOCUMENT:
Click up arrow	One line up
Click down arrow	One line down
Click scroll bar above scroll box	One windowful up
Click scroll bar below scroll box	One windowful down
Drag scroll box	To any relative position

If you *scroll up*, as shown in Table 4.2, the view through the window moves toward the beginning of the document, and if you *scroll down*, the view moves toward the end of the document. A *windowful* is the amount of the document content that can be viewed through the current window. To *drag* the scroll box, you click the mouse while the

Table 4.3: Actions You Can Perform Using the Horizontal Scroll Bar

PERFORM THIS ACTION WITH THE MOUSE & HORIZONTAL SCROLL BAR:	TO SCROLL WITHIN THE DOCUMENT:
Click left arrow	Several columns to the left
Click left arrow while holding down the Shift key	Left into the margin area
Click right arrow	Several columns to the right
Click scroll bar to left of scroll box	One windowful toward the left margin
Click scroll bar to right of scroll box	One windowful toward the right margin
Drag scroll box	To any relative horizontal position

pointer is on the scroll box, and, while holding down the button, move the arrow to the desired location and then release the button. The relative position of the scroll box within the scroll bar indicates the relative position of the text displayed in the window with respect to the whole document. If, for instance, the scroll box is at the top of the vertical scroll bar, you are viewing the beginning of the file; if it is in the center of the scroll bar, you are viewing the middle of the document; and so on.

Similarly, as described in Table 4.3, if you *scroll left*, the document view moves toward the left margin, and if you *scroll right*, it moves toward the right margin. Normally, you can scroll left only until you reach the left margin; however, if you press the Shift key while clicking the left scroll bar arrow, you can continue scrolling into the left-margin area. You might need to scroll into the left-margin area to view a paragraph that has been assigned a negative left indent (that is, a paragraph that extends into the left-margin area; setting indents is described in Chapter 15.)

Scrolling with a scroll bar causes Word to display a different portion of the document within the window. Scroll bar actions, however, *do not move the position of the insertion point*. Also, if you have scrolled away from the insertion point and then type a character, the view in the window will instantly scroll back to the portion of the document containing the insertion point. You can use these features to your advantage; the following typical scenario shows how you could quickly view another document position without losing the current position of the insertion point:

1. You are entering text into a document, and want to temporarily view a previous section of the document.

2. You click the vertical scroll bar above the scroll box to move up through the document, one windowful at a time. After clicking three times, you find the portion of the document you want to see. The insertion point will no longer be visible within the window.

3. To return to your original position, you type a character (the next character you were going to type, or any other character). Word instantly scrolls back to the portion of the document containing the insertion point.

4. You resume entering text.

Thus, the insertion point is not always located within the portion of the document displayed in the window. The insertion point, however, will instantly move to the first character position currently within the window if you press an arrow key or issue any command that moves the insertion point, such as Edit/Go To, Edit/Search, or Edit/Replace. For example, if you scroll the document vertically so that the insertion point is no longer visible, and then press the → key, the insertion point will initially move to the first character position in the window (in the upper left corner) and will then move one character position to the right.

To practice using the mouse methods for scrolling through a document, you can open one of the example documents provided with the Word program, as described in the previous section. Once you have opened the document, try each of the scrolling methods described in Tables 4.2 and 4.3.

USING THE GO TO COMMAND

You can use the Go To command to move the insertion point to a precise location in the document. When using the Go To command, you can specify the desired location employing a wide variety of methods. There are two ways to issue the Go To command. First, you can choose the Edit/Go To menu command; Word will display the dialog box shown in Figure 4.2. Type the desired target location into the text box—using one of the methods described in this section—and click the OK button or press ◄┘. You can also choose one of the *bookmarks* (explained later in this section) displayed in the list box as the target location.

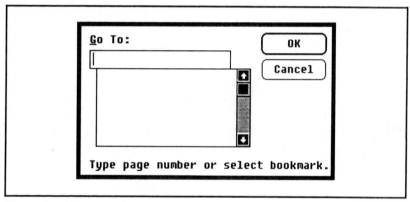

Figure 4.2: The Edit/Go To dialog box

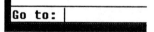
If you have issued the Search command (explained in Chapter 6) since the last time you issued the Go To command, the Shift-F4 keystroke will repeat the Search command rather than the Go To command.

Second, you can press F5 (Go To) and type the desired location at the prompt that Word displays within the status bar.

If you press F5 twice, Word will display the same dialog box activated by the Edit/Go To menu command.

Once you have issued the Go To command, you can quickly go to the same location specified in the command by pressing Shift-F4.

SPECIFYING THE TARGET LOCATION

Whether you have chosen the Edit/Go To menu command or have pressed the F5 key, you can express the desired target location by specifying one or more of the following document features:

- Page
- Section
- Line
- Percentage of the document
- Footnote
- Annotation
- Bookmark
- A combination of features

Go to a Page

When specifying a location, you must *not* type a space between the **p**, **s**, l, %, **f**, or **a** character and the associated number.

To go to a specific page in the document, type **p** followed immediately by the page number, or simply type the page number by itself. For example, to go to page 5, type

> p5

or

> 5

When you press ← (or click the OK button in the Go To dialog box), Word will immediately place the insertion point at the first character position within the specified page.

Note that before you can go to a specified page in a document, the document must be *paginated*, or divided into pages. The document is automatically paginated when you print it, or when you issue one of the following menu commands, which are discussed in Chapter 17:

- Utilities/Repaginate Now
- Utilities/Customize and enable the Background Pagination option

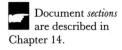
Document *sections* are described in Chapter 14.

The document will also be paginated up to the page you are currently viewing when you activate the Print Preview or Page View mode, also discussed in Chapter 17.

When you specify a page number, the Go To command simply counts pages from the beginning of the document (*not* from the beginning of the current *section*). It ignores any page numbers that are displayed when you print the document. For example, although you may have specified that printed page numbers begin with 100 on the first page of the document, the Go To command still regards the first page as number 1.

To go to a location a specified number of pages *after* the current page, type a + in front of the page number. To go to a page a specified number of pages *before* the current page, type a − in front of the page number. For example, to move five pages forward in the document, type

    p + 5

or

    + 5

To go to the next page, you can also simply type **p** or leave the specification field blank.

Go to a Section

To go to a specified document section (see Chapter 14), type **s** followed by the section number. To go to a section a given number of sections *after* the current section, type a + in front of the section number. To go to a section a given number of sections *before* the current section, type a − in front of the number.

To go to the next section, you can also simply type **s**. When you specify a section with the Go To command, Word will place the insertion point at the *first character position* within that section (you will see later how to go to a given line within a specific section).

Go to a Line

To go to a specific line within the document, type **l** (the letter el) followed by the line number. To move a given number of lines toward the end of the document, type a + in front of the line number, and to move a given number of lines toward the beginning of the document, type a − in front of the line number.

When going to a specific line, the Go To command simply counts lines from the beginning of the document (the first line in the document is number 1). It ignores any line numbering you may have enabled for one or more document sections (as described in Chapter 14), which does not necessarily start with 1. Word places the insertion point at the first character position within the specified line.

Go to a Location a Given Percentage through the Document

You can also move to a point that is a given percentage of the way through the document by typing % followed by the percentage. For example, to go to a point midway through the document, type

```
%50
```

The % sign can also *follow* the number; for example, 50%.

Go to a Footnote or Annotation

Footnotes are discussed in Chapter 10, and annotations in Chapter 25.

You can use the Go To command to go to a specific footnote or annotation within the document. To go to a footnote, type **f** followed by the number of the footnote, and to go to an annotation, type **a** followed by the number of the annotation. The Go To command numbers footnotes and annotations from the beginning of the document, including *all* footnotes or annotations. It ignores the numbers assigned to specific footnotes or annotations.

You can also move to a footnote or annotation a given number of footnotes or annotations *after* the current one by typing a + in front of the number, and you can move a specific number of footnotes or annotations toward the *beginning* of the document by typing a − in front of the number.

Go to a Bookmark

You can use the Go To command to move to a position in a document that is labeled as a *bookmark*. A bookmark is a name that you assign to a specific document position. To assign a bookmark, place the insertion point at the desired location, choose the Insert/ Bookmark menu command, type the name of the bookmark, and click the OK button or press ←. Figure 4.3 shows the bookmark dialog box.

A bookmark name must begin with a letter; it can contain only letters, numbers, or underline characters (_); and it must be from 1 to 20 characters in length.

The dialog box also displays a list of bookmarks that have already been assigned. You can select one of these names to either reassign the name to the current position of the insertion point, or to delete the bookmark (by clicking the Delete button).

Alternatively, you can assign a bookmark to the current position of the insertion point by pressing the Ctrl-Shift-F5 key combination, and typing the bookmark name at the prompt that appears within the status bar (following the same rules just stated for typing a bookmark name into the Insert/Bookmark dialog box).

Once you have defined a bookmark, you can quickly move the insertion point to the corresponding document position by issuing the Go To command and typing the bookmark name when prompted for the target location. Alternatively, if the Go To dialog box is displayed, you can select a bookmark from the list box and then click the OK button or press ← (or just double-click the bookmark name).

Using bookmarks, you can tag an entire set of document locations, and then go instantly to any one of these locations by means of the Go To command.

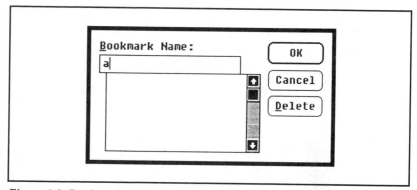

Figure 4.3: Bookmark dialog box

Note that you can also assign a bookmark to an entire block of characters, rather than to a single insertion-point position. To make such an assignment, you must first *select* the block, and then assign the bookmark as just explained. Techniques for selecting text are discussed in Chapter 5. If you specify a bookmark that refers to a block of text, the Go To command will select that block rather than simply moving the insertion point to a position within the block.

Go to a Location Specified as a Combination of Elements

When specifying a target location for the Go To command, you can *combine* any of the elements discussed previously in this section, subject to the following two rules:

1. If you specify a bookmark or document percentage (%), you cannot also specify a page, line, or other element.

2. The specification may contain only *one* of the following elements: line (l), footnote (f), or annotation (a). (Specifying more than one of these elements would make no sense.)

To understand how multiple elements combine, it is useful to divide the elements into the following three levels:

Level 1   Section

Level 2   Page

Level 3   Line, Footnote, or Annotation

This division is based upon the fact that a section can contain pages, and a page can contain lines, footnotes, or annotations.

Here are some examples of how you can combine elements:

s2p5   Go to the fifth page from the beginning of section 2 of the document.

p5l8   Go to the eighth line on page 5 of the document (the pages are counted from the beginning of the document).

s3f5   Go to the fifth footnote from the beginning of section 3 of the document.

s2p5l3   Go to the third line on the fifth page of section 2 of the document.

> When you specify a number, the Go To command always counts from the beginning of the document, section, or page (depending on the specification) and *ignores* any numbering you may have assigned to an element (such as the page numbers or footnote numbers that will appear on the printed document copy).

As you saw in the previous sections of this chapter, when you specify a single element, the Go To command always counts from the beginning of the document. For example, p5 means the fifth page from the beginning of the document. If, however, you include a higher-level element in the specification, the Go To command counts from the beginning of the higher-level element. For example, s2p5 means the fifth page from the beginning of section 2 (regardless of the page number that might appear on the printed page).

A final guideline is that you can include the + or − symbol (to specify a relative move) only for the highest-level element in a combined specification. Thus, the expression **s − 2p3** is allowed (meaning the third page in the section that comes two sections before the current section). However, the expression **s2p − 3** is not allowed.

An Exercise in Using the Go To Command

To practice using the Go To command, complete the following exercise:

1. Open one of the example documents provided with the Word program. The setup program normally copies these documents to the \WINWORD\LIBRARY directory on your hard disk. The document should be longer than one page.

2. Once you have opened the document, issue the Utilities/Repaginate menu command to have Word divide the document into pages.

3. Move the insertion point to the beginning of page 2 by pressing F5, typing **p2** or simply **2**, then pressing ←⏎.

4. Move the insertion point to the tenth line *from the beginning of the document* by pressing F5, typing **l10**, then pressing ←⏎.

5. Move the insertion point to the tenth line *on the second page* by pressing F5 and then typing **p2l10**.

6. Move to a point halfway through the document by pressing F5 and then typing **50%**.

THE GO BACK KEY (SHIFT-F5)

Pressing the Shift-F5 key moves the insertion point back to its *previous location*. The previous location refers to the most recent position of the insertion point where an action, such as one of the following, occurred:

- You inserted or deleted characters.
- You issued a Go To command.
- The insertion point was positioned via a Go To command.
- You saved the document.

If you press Shift-F5 again, the insertion point will move to the next most recent position. Each subsequent press will continue to move the insertion point to prior positions. Word, however, remembers only three locations before the present location; therefore, on the fourth consecutive press of Shift-F5, the insertion point is returned to the location where Shift-F5 was first pressed.

When you first open an existing document, you can press the Shift-F5 key to bring you to the point in the document where you last issued a Save command before closing the document or exiting from Word.

USING OTHER METHODS

This section summarizes the following additional ways to move the insertion point to specific document positions, or to enhance the efficiency of scrolling through a document:

- Using the Edit/Search command
- Employing other document views
- Choosing efficient display options

Most of these methods are discussed in detail in other chapters of the book.

EDIT/SEARCH

The Edit/Search menu command allows you to search for a particular sequence of characters, or for a particular format, within the document. The command moves you to the first occurrence of the characters or format (which it highlights). Chapter 6 discusses the Edit/ Search command in detail.

You can also use the Edit/Search command or the Utilities/ Revision Marks command to search for *revision marks* in your document. Revision marks are discussed in Chapter 25.

USING DRAFT VIEW

See Chapter 17 for a summary of all the document views provided by Word.

You saw in Chapter 2 that Word provides several alternative document views, which are different ways of looking at and working with your document. The default document view is called galley view, also known as normal editing view. In Chapter 2, you also saw the Print Preview document view. Two other document views are mentioned here because they can help you navigate through your document: *draft view* and *outline view*.

Normally, Word displays characters and paragraph formatting so that the document's appearance on the screen is quite similar to its printed appearance (in general, Word for Windows abides by the WYSIWYG—what you see is what you get—rule). However, displaying various fonts and other features required to simulate the printed document is time-consuming.

You will learn about character formatting in Chapter 16.

As you will see in Chapter 17, you can also save time when printing your document by selecting the Draft option in the File/Print dialog box.

You can increase the speed of scrolling through the document by switching into *draft view*. In draft view, all characters are displayed using a single typeface and character size (employing a font known as the System font). Also, all character enhancements, such as boldface and italic, are displayed as simple underlined characters. Furthermore, draft view eliminates the time-consuming display of graphics (see Chapter 9). Draft view is especially valuable for slower computer models.

To activate draft view, choose the View/Draft menu item. To deactivate draft view, choose this menu item again.

DISPLAY OPTIONS FOR EFFICIENT SCROLLING

The View/Preferences menu item displays a dialog box that allows you to enable or disable a variety of display options. This dialog box is illustrated in Figure 4.4.

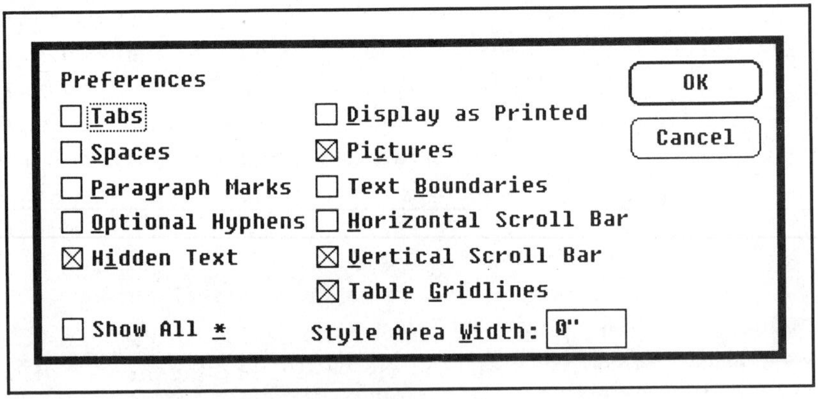

Figure 4.4: The View/Preferences dialog box

Making the following choices in the View/Preferences dialog box can increase the speed of scrolling through a document:

1. Do *not* select the Display as Printed option. Word will then not have to calculate the printed length of each line and insert line breaks at the exact positions where they will occur on the printed page.

2. Do *not* select the Pictures option. Word will then display any graphic image you have inserted into your document as an empty box the same size as the graphic, rather than engaging in the time-consuming process of fully drawing the graphic each time it appears within the document window. Using graphics is discussed in Chapter 9.

3. Do *not* select the Table Gridlines option. Word will then be relieved of the task of drawing lines around each cell of any table that appears within the document window. Tables are discussed in Chapter 8.

THE STATUS BAR

The status bar displayed at the bottom of the window can help you navigate through a document by showing you the current position of the insertion point. The relevant status bar fields are labeled in Figure 4.5.

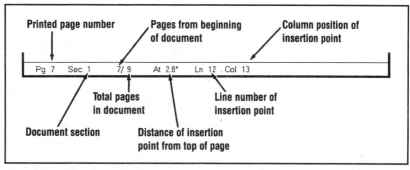

Figure 4.5: Status bar fields showing your current document position

The following is an explanation of each of these fields, going from left to right along the status bar:

The methods for including a page number in a header or footer are explained in Chapter 10.

Pg — The number of the page containing the insertion point. If you have included a page number in a header or footer, the page number in the Pg field is the number that would be printed for the current page. By default, page numbering begins with 1 at the beginning of the current section.

Sec — The number of the document section that contains the insertion point. Sections are always numbered beginning with 1 at the start of the document. See Chapter 14 for an explanation of sections.

c/t — The first number, c, is the number of the current page, and the second number, t, is the total number of pages in the document. Word derives both of these numbers by simply counting pages *from the beginning of the document*. These numbers are not necessarily the same as page numbers printed in headers and footers (which may not start from 1). Thus, the number c may not equal the Pg field.

At — The distance of the insertion point from the top edge of the page.

Ln — The number of the line containing the insertion point. Lines are numbered starting at the beginning of the current page.

Col   The column containing the insertion point. Columns are numbered beginning with 1 at the leftmost position within the paragraph, and increase by 1 with each character position to the right.

Note that the page numbers displayed in the status bar are not necessarily accurate unless the document has recently been repaginated. The repagination process was explained in Chapter 3, in the section "Creating Text Breaks." Word repaginates the entire document at the following times:

- When you print the document.

- When you issue the Utilities/Repaginate Now command.

- If the Background Pagination option within the Utilities/ Customize dialog box is enabled, Word will *maintain* correct pagination while you work on the document. Word can update the pagination, however, only when it is not busy performing some other task. Therefore, you should issue the Utilities/Repaginate Now command if you want to make sure that pagination is up to date.

SUMMARY

- You can move the insertion point to any position in the document using the keyboard. Pressing an arrow key moves the insertion point one column or row position in the corresponding direction. Word also provides keystrokes for efficiently moving greater distances.

- You can scroll through a document by using the mouse in conjunction with the vertical or horizontal scroll bar. Scrolling with a scroll bar does not automatically move the insertion point.

- The Go To command allows you to move the insertion point instantly to a specific position in the document. It is activated by choosing the Edit/Go To menu command, or by pressing the F5 key. You can specify the position using a wide variety of methods.

- You can label a position in a document using a *bookmark*. You can later move instantly to this position by means of the Go To command.

- The *Go Back* key, Shift-F5, moves the insertion point to its previous location.

- The Edit/Search menu command moves you to the first occurrence of a given sequence of characters within the document.

- You can switch to the *draft* document view to increase the speed of scrolling through a document (choose the View/Draft menu item).

- Choosing appropriate options in the dialog box displayed by the View/Preferences menu command can increase the speed of scrolling through a document.

- The Word status bar shows you the current position of the insertion point within the document.

5

USING BLOCK
EDITING COMMANDS

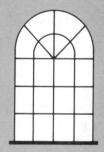

SO FAR, YOU HAVE SEEN HOW TO INSERT OR DELETE
text one character at a time. In this chapter, you will learn how to
work with entire blocks of text or graphics, ranging in size from a
single character to an entire document.

The first step in performing a block editing command is to *select* (or
highlight) the block of data. Once you have selected the block, you
can quickly delete it, copy it, or move it to another location. Each of
these procedures is described in this chapter. Selecting a block of text
is also the first step in applying many of the Word formatting commands, which are explained in Part III.

The techniques discussed in this chapter apply to the normal editing views of the document (that is, *galley*, *draft*, and *page* views). The
outline document view provides many special, highly efficient ways for
working with blocks of text or graphics (see Chapter 24).

SELECTING TEXT AND GRAPHICS

Many Word editing and formatting commands are performed in two distinct steps: you first select the text or graphics, and then apply the command to the selection. For example, to delete a line of text, you first select all of the characters on the line, and then press the Del key.

When you select a block of data, Word highlights the selection on the screen. If, for example, your system displays black characters on a white background, the selected block will appear as white characters on a black background.

It is important to distinguish the *insertion point* from the *selection*. As you have seen, the insertion point is the position where characters are inserted into the document, and it is marked by a blinking vertical line that fits *between* two characters. In contrast, a selection is a highlighted area that encompasses at least one entire character. At any given time, the document in the active window contains *either* an insertion point *or* a selection; these two elements cannot be present at the same time. The insertion point or selection, however, may not be currently visible in the window (you may have positioned the insertion point or selection and then scrolled to another place in the document using a scroll bar).

Word provides many techniques for selecting text or graphics. You should choose the method that is most efficient for the size of block you want to select. The techniques conform to basic Windows conventions, and can be divided into those that use the keyboard and those that use the mouse.

Once you have selected a block, you are ready to perform one of the block editing commands described later in the chapter, or to apply a formatting command as explained in Part III.

See Chapter 8 for an explanation of the techniques for selecting within a Word *table*. Also, Chapter 24 covers the copying methods available in outline view.

You can also label a selection using a Word bookmark. First, select the desired text or graphics as described later in this chapter, and then assign the bookmark as explained in Chapter 4, in the section "Go to a Bookmark." Such a bookmark refers to an entire block of data rather than to a single insertion point. When you issue the *Go To* command (also described in Chapter 4) and specify the bookmark as the target location, Word will select the entire block.

Although this chapter frequently refers to blocks of *text*, the techniques given here can be used to manipulate text *or* graphics, or a combination of both. When performing a block editing command, a graphic image, which is known as a *picture*, is treated as a single text character. A picture can be included in a larger selection or can be selected separately. See Chapter 9 for a description of using graphics.

SELECTING WITH THE KEYBOARD

The easiest way to select a small block of text is to press an arrow key while holding down the Shift key. First, position the insertion point at one end of the block of text you want to select. Then, while holding down the Shift key (you can use either one), press the appropriate arrow key—repeatedly if necessary—to select the desired area. If you press the → key, the insertion point will be transformed into a selection that encompasses the following character. The ← key will select the preceding character.

If you press the ↓ key while holding down Shift, Word moves the insertion point down one line and selects *all* of the characters that fall between the beginning and ending positions.

Try this selection method by following the steps in the exercise below.

1. Open a new document and type in the text shown in Figure 5.1.

2. Create the selection shown in Figure 5.1 by placing the insertion point immediately in front of the word **you** on the third line. While holding down the Shift key, press the ↓ key once

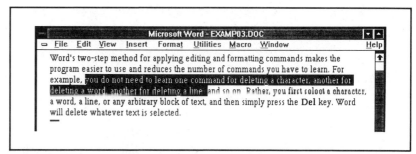

Figure 5.1: A sample paragraph showing selected text

and then hold down the → key until the highlight encompasses the comma following the word **line**. Your screen should now look like Figure 5.1.

3. Remove the selection by pressing any arrow key.

Keep this document on your screen; in a moment you'll use it to practice some other editing techniques.

Pressing the ↑ key in conjunction with Shift moves the insertion point up one line, and, like the ↓ key, selects all characters in the document that fall between the starting and ending positions. If you want to select a *rectangular* block of text, you should use one of the column selection techniques discussed later in the chapter.

In a similar manner, you can also hold down Shift and press the Home, End, PgUp, or PgDn key to select text or graphics from the insertion point to the beginning of the line, to the end of the line, to a point one page up, or to a point one page down (the term *page* is used here to mean the number of document lines that fit within the current window).

As an alternative method for selecting text or graphics, you can first press F8 to turn on the *extend selection* mode. When you activate this mode, the letters **EXT** appear in the status bar, and pressing an arrow key (or the Home, End, PgUp, or PgDn key) will extend the selection as if Shift were held down. Pressing F8 twice will select the word containing the insertion point. Continuing to press F8 will select, in order, the entire sentence, paragraph, section, and finally, the whole document. To turn off the extend selection mode, press Esc. It will also be turned off automatically if you execute an editing or formatting command on the selection.

Use the practice document you just created to try the extend selection mode.

1. Create the same selection as in the previous exercise. First, place the insertion point immediately in front of the word **you**, and then press and release the F8 key once.

2. Press the ↓ key once, and then hold down the → key until the selection covers the comma following the word **line**.

You can also use the Shift key in combination with the ←, →, Home, or End key to select text that you have typed into a dialog box.

Simply press and release F8; do not hold this key down.

3. Remove the selection by pressing Esc and then any arrow key.

Keep the document on your screen.

While the extend selection mode is active, you can also type a letter key to expand the selection through the next occurrence of that letter in the document. For example, if you press F8 to activate the extend selection mode and then type the character **a**, Word will select all text or graphics from the current insertion point through the first occurrence of the letter **a** in the document. You can then type **a** again, or some other character, to further extend the selection through the next occurrence of the specified character. Once you are finished, press Esc to exit from the extend selection mode.

Finally, you can use any of the following keystrokes to select the entire document:

- Ctrl-5 (5 on the numeric keypad)

- Ctrl-Home, then Ctrl-Shift-End

- Ctrl-End, then Ctrl-Shift-Home

See "Deleting a Column of Text" for a practice exercise illustrating column selection.

To select a rectangular block of text that includes more than one line, you must first activate the *column selection mode* by pressing the Ctrl-Shift-F8 key combination. When this mode is active, the words **COL** appear in the status bar, and pressing an arrow key extends a rectangular selection in the corresponding direction. Unlike the selection methods described previously, column selection does *not* automatically include all text between the starting and ending positions, but only the text that falls within a rectangular block.

Like the extend selection mode, the column selection mode is terminated when you issue an editing or formatting command on the selection, or press Esc.

Table 5.1 summarizes selection methods using the keyboard.

SELECTING WITH THE MOUSE

You can also use the mouse to select text that you have entered into a dialog box.

To select a block of text or graphics with the mouse, place the mouse pointer at either end of the desired block, press the left mouse button, and while holding down the button, drag the highlight over

Table 5.1: Keyboard Methods for Selecting Text or Graphics

TO SELECT:	PRESS:
Following character	Shift-→, or F8 then →
Preceding character	Shift-←, or F8 then ←
Following line	Shift-↓, or F8 then ↓
Preceding line	Shift-↑, or F8 then ↑
Through end of line	Shift-End, or F8 then End
Through beginning of line	Shift-Home, or F8 then Home
Through following page	Shift-PgDn, or F8 then PgDn
Through preceding page	Shift-PgUp, or F8 then PgUp
Current word	F8 twice
Current sentence	F8 again
Current paragraph	F8 again
Current section	F8 again
Entire document	F8 again, or Ctrl-5 (on numeric keypad), or Ctrl-Home then Ctrl-Shift-End
Through a given character	F8 then character key
Rectangular block	Ctrl-Shift-F8 then: arrow key, Home, End, PgUp, or PgDn

the area you want to select. Notice that when you drag the highlight up or down in the document, Word includes all text on each line that falls between the starting and ending points. To select a rectangular block spanning more than one line, use one of the column selection techniques described later in the chapter.

Alternatively, you can select by clicking one end of the desired block, and then holding down the Shift key while clicking the other end. If you need to scroll the document to reach the other end of the block, be sure to use a scroll bar rather than a keyboard command so that you do not inadvertently move the insertion point before marking the opposite end of the block. You can also click the start of the block, press the F8 key, and then click the end of the block.

To quickly select an entire word, double-click the word. To quickly select an entire sentence, click the sentence while pressing the Ctrl key.

Using the Selection Bar

If the style name area is displayed, as explained in Chapter 20, the selection bar is between the style name area and the document text.

You can also use the mouse in conjunction with the *selection bar* to quickly select various blocks of text or graphics. The selection bar is the area within the window to the immediate left of the text; it is labeled in Figure 1.1 and in the illustration on the inside front cover of the book. When the mouse pointer is within this area, it becomes an arrow pointing up and to the right.

> program easier to use and
> example, you do not need .
> deleting a word, another f

Thus, although the selection bar is not explicitly marked on the screen, you can tell when the pointer is within this area by observing its shape.

To select a single line, click the selection bar to the immediate left of the line. To select a series of lines, place the pointer next to the first or last line, and hold down the left mouse button while dragging the highlight over the desired lines. To select a single paragraph, double-click the selection bar anywhere next to the paragraph. To select a series of paragraphs, double-click the selection bar and, while holding down the left button after the second click, drag the highlight over the desired paragraphs.

Finally, to select the entire document, click anywhere in the selection bar while pressing the Ctrl key.

Unless otherwise stated, click with the *left* mouse button.

Using the practice document you created earlier in this chapter, follow these steps to try selecting with the mouse:

1. Create the selection shown in Figure 5.1 using the mouse. Place the pointer immediately in front of the word **you** on the

third line. Press the left mouse button and, while holding down this button, drag the highlight to the comma following the word **line**. Remove the selection by clicking at any position in the document.

2. Create the same selection using the following alternative mouse method: Click immediately in front of the word **you** on the third line, and, while holding down the Shift key, click to the right of the comma following the word **line**. Remove the selection by clicking at any position in the document.

You can also use the mouse to select a rectangular-shaped block of text. As you have seen previously in the chapter, this procedure is known as *column selection*. First, place the mouse pointer on one corner of the area you want to select. Then, while holding down the *right* mouse button, drag the highlight to the opposite corner.

Table 5.2 summarizes the methods for selecting text or graphics using the mouse.

REMOVING THE SELECTION

Once you have used one of the techniques just described to select a block of text or graphics, Word will display a selection rather than an insertion point. You can now perform one or more actions on the selection, such as copying the data or converting text characters to italic. After you have performed an action, the selection remains marked on the screen (unless, of course, you have deleted it).

You can remove the selection marking and restore the insertion point at any time simply by performing an action that moves or positions the insertion point. For example, you can press an arrow key, press the PgUp key, or click on a character position.

Also, if you type a character while a selection is marked, Word removes the selection marking, restores the insertion point, and inserts the character immediately in front of the former selection.

If you have chosen the Typing Replaces Selection option from the Utilities/Customize dialog box, described in the next section, Word will *delete* all selected text or graphics if you type a character key.

DELETING, MOVING, AND COPYING

In this section, you will learn how to delete, move, or copy a selected block of text or graphics.

Table 5.2: Methods for Selecting Text or Graphics with the Mouse

TO SELECT:	USE THE MOUSE TO:
A series of characters in the document	Click one end of desired block and, while holding down the button, drag the highlight to the other end of block, *or* click one end of block and then click the other end while holding down the Shift key
A word	Double-click the word
A sentence	Click the sentence while holding down the Ctrl key
A line	Click selection bar to the immediate left of line
A series of lines	Press left button in selection bar and hold down button while dragging highlight
A paragraph	Double-click the selection bar anywhere next to the paragraph
A series of paragraphs	Double-click selection bar and drag while holding down button after second click
Entire document	Click anywhere in selection bar while pressing Ctrl
A rectangular block (a column selection)	Hold down the right mouse button while dragging highlight from one corner of the desired rectangle to the opposite corner

The Undo command is discussed in Chapter 3, in the section "Undoing and Redoing."

Since performing an editing operation on a selection can effect a radical change in your document (you could easily delete the entire document with a short series of commands!), you should remember that you can reverse the effect of your last editing command through the Edit/Undo menu command or the Alt-Backspace keystroke. You must, however, issue the Undo command *immediately after* performing the action you want to reverse.

DELETING THE SELECTION

You can delete any size block of text or graphics by selecting the block and then pressing the Del key.

While text is selected, you cannot use the Backspace key for deleting; rather, this key behaves like the ← key.

Once you have deleted a portion of your document in this manner, the only way you can restore it is by issuing the Undo command immediately after the deletion. As a precaution, therefore, if you are deleting a large block you might want to *cut* it to the Clipboard, as described in the next section, rather than using the Del key. As you will see, data stored in the Clipboard can easily be inserted back into the document until another selection replaces it.

The Typing Replaces Selection Option

Choosing the Typing Replaces Selection option from the Utilities/ Customize dialog box provides another way to delete a selection. As you have seen, if you type a character while a selection is marked, Word normally removes the selection marking, restores the insertion point, and inserts the character in front of the text that was formerly selected.

If, however, the Typing Replaces Selection option is enabled, when you press a character key, Word immediately deletes the selection, inserts the character in its place, and positions the insertion point to the right of this character. Thus, if you select a block of text and then type one or more characters, these characters effectively *replace* the selected text.

When Word is first installed, this feature is not in effect. To enable it, choose the Utilities/Customize menu command, and select the Typing Replaces Selection option.

☐ Typing Replaces Selection

Deleting a Column of Text

By deleting a column selection, you can quickly eliminate a portion of several lines. The exercise below illustrates using this technique to remove the numbers from a list of items within a document. Use the practice document you created earlier.

1. Press ← twice and type in the text shown in Figure 5.2.

2. Place the insertion point in front of the **1**.

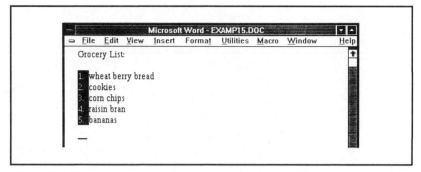

Figure 5.2: The sample document with a column selected

3. Enable column selection by pressing Ctrl-Shift-F8.

4. Use the arrow keys to move the highlight over the numbers and space characters in front of the lines of text. Your screen will look like Figure 5.2.

5. Press the Del key. The numbers and leading spaces will be deleted, and the remaining portions of the lines will move to the left margin. Your screen will look like Figure 5.3.

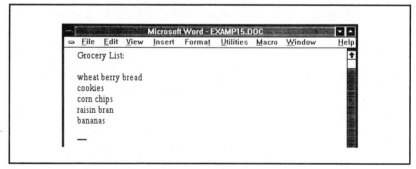

Figure 5.3: Deleting a column of text

You could also select the column of text using the mouse, as described previously in the chapter.

MOVING AND COPYING USING THE CLIPBOARD

Once you have selected a portion of your document, you can move or copy it to another location by using the Windows *Clipboard*. The

Clipboard is a facility that Windows maintains for temporarily storing and transferring selections of text or graphics.

In Word, you access the Clipboard through the following three commands:

- Cut
- Copy
- Paste

The Cut command stores the current selection in the Clipboard and deletes it from your document. You issue this command by choosing the Edit/Cut menu item or by pressing the Shift-Del key combination. The selection remains in the Clipboard until you store a new selection through the Cut or Copy command. You can use this command to delete a selection, or as described later in this section, to move a selection to another location. If there is currently no selection, the Cut command is displayed in gray letters on the menu and cannot be chosen.

The Copy command stores the current selection in the Clipboard, but leaves the selection intact in your document. You issue this command by choosing the Edit/Copy menu item or by pressing the Ctrl-Ins key combination. If there is currently no selection, the Copy command is displayed in gray letters on the menu and cannot be chosen.

The Paste command inserts the current contents of the Clipboard into your document at the insertion point. You issue this command by choosing the Edit/Paste menu item, or by pressing the Shift-Ins key combination. After pasting, the selection *remains* in the Clipboard and can therefore be pasted into one or more additional locations. If the Clipboard is currently empty, the Paste command is displayed in gray letters and cannot be chosen.

Table 5.3 summarizes these three Clipboard commands.

You can use the Cut or Copy command together with the Paste command to move or copy a selection to another document location.

To *move* the selection, issue the Cut command, position the insertion point at the desired new location for the selection, and issue the Paste command.

> The Clipboard can hold only a single data selection. When you add a selection through the Cut or Copy command, it *replaces* the selection (if any) currently held in the Clipboard.

Table 5.3: The Cut, Copy, and Paste Commands

ISSUE THIS MENU COMMAND:	OR PRESS THIS KEY COMBINATION:	TO PERFORM THIS ACTION:
Edit/Cut	Shift-Del	Store selection in Clipboard and delete it from document
Edit/Copy	Ctrl-Ins	Store selection in Clipboard and leave it in document
Edit/Paste	Shift-Ins	Insert selection from Clipboard into document at insertion point

To *copy* the selection, issue the Copy command, place the insertion point where you would like to insert the copy, and issue the Paste command.

Since the selection remains in the Clipboard after you have pasted it, you can insert the selection into one or more additional locations after you have performed the initial move or copy operation.

Not only can you use the Clipboard to move and copy data within a single Word document, but you can also use it to exchange data among separate Word documents, or even among separate Windows applications (see Chapters 9 and 26). For example, you can use the Copy command to copy a block of data from one document into the Clipboard, switch to another document, and then paste the data into the second document. The second document need not be open at the time you copy the data into the Clipboard, since the data remains in the Clipboard as long as you are running Windows and you have not replaced it with another selection.

Because the Clipboard is available to all applications running under Windows, you can also use it to exchange data between a Word document and a file in another application, such as an Excel spreadsheet or a Windows graphics application.

If you have stored a large selection in the Clipboard, Word will ask you if you want to save the data when quitting Word. Unless you answer yes, the Clipboard contents will be lost. Also, if you quit Windows, the Clipboard contents are lost unless you have explicitly saved the data in a file, as explained in the next section.

See Chapter 26 for a discussion on managing multiple documents within Word.

Accessing the Clipboard

You can directly access the Clipboard at any time you are running Windows. To access it from within the Word program, choose the Run command from the Word control menu (see Figure 5.4), or type Alt-spacebar and then **u**. Word will display a dialog box. Select the Clipboard item, and then click the OK button or press ◄─┘. The Windows Clipboard window will now appear, as shown in Figure 5.5.

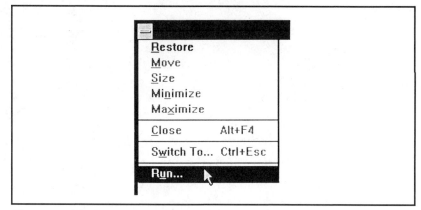

Figure 5.4: The Word control menu

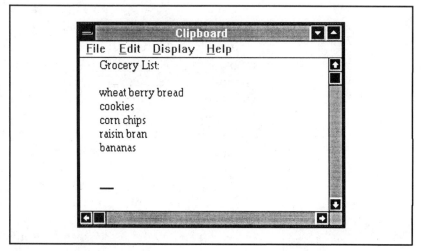

Figure 5.5: The Windows Clipboard window

See your Windows manual or refer to the online help for an explanation of the Clipboard commands.

The Clipboard window displays the current contents of the Clipboard. You can thus use it to determine exactly what is contained in the Clipboard before you paste the data into a document. If necessary, you can scroll the window using the scroll bars or keyboard in the same manner as scrolling through a Word document.

You can also save the Clipboard contents in a file by choosing the File/Save As Clipboard command. Doing so will allow you to quit Windows without losing the Clipboard data. You can later read this data back into the Clipboard by issuing the File/Open command from the Clipboard menu.

To remove the Clipboard window and resume working in Word, double-click the control menu icon in the upper left corner, or type Alt-spacebar and then **c**.

MOVING AND COPYING WITHOUT USING THE CLIPBOARD

Word also provides several methods for moving or copying data that do not use the Windows Clipboard. An advantage of using these techniques is that you can avoid deleting the current contents of the Clipboard. A disadvantage is that once you have completed the move or copy operation, you cannot continue to insert additional copies of the selection.

You can also use the Word glossary to move or copy a selection from one position to another position within the same document or within a different document. (The glossary is a Word feature that allows you to store blocks of text; using the glossary is fully explained in Chapter 21.) The advantage of using the glossary to move or copy text or graphics is that you can permanently save more than one selection, and then insert the desired selection at any time by specifying its name. Also, you are less likely to overwrite a glossary entry than a Clipboard selection; therefore, the glossary provides a safer method for moving large blocks of text.

The techniques explained in this chapter are categorized by those that use the keyboard and those that use the mouse.

Using the Keyboard

You can *move* a selection by pressing the F2 key. When using this key, you can either select the text you want to move and *then* indicate the target location, or you can indicate the target location and *then* select the text that you want to move. The first method for moving a selection is as follows:

1. Select the block of text or graphics you want to move.

2. Press the F2 key. The insertion point will become a *dotted* vertical line.

3. Move the dotted insertion point to the location where you want to move the text, using the keyboard or mouse.

4. Press ◄┘, and Word will move the selection.

The following is the second method for moving a selection:

1. Place the insertion point at the position where you want to move the block.

2. Press the F2 key.

3. Select the block of text or graphics you want to move to the location indicated in step 1. Word will underline the selection rather than highlighting it.

4. Press ◄┘, and Word will move the selection.

Whichever method you are using, you can cancel the move operation before completing step 4 by pressing Esc.

You can *copy* a selection by pressing the Shift-F2 key combination. You can either select the text you want to copy and *then* indicate the target location, or you can indicate the target location and *then* select the text you want to copy. Both of these techniques are the same as those just described for moving a selection, except that you press Shift-F2 rather than F2.

You can use these methods to move or copy a selection from one Word document to another, provided that *both* the source and the target documents are open in Word at the time you issue the command. For example, you could use the following steps to copy a block of text from document A to document B.

Chapter 26 des-
cribes techniques for
working with multiple
documents in Word.

1. Make sure that both document A and document B are open in Word.

2. Select the source text in document A.

3. Press the Shift-F2 key combination.

4. Switch to document B (for example, by choosing the name of document B from the Window menu).

5. Place the insertion point at the desired target location in document B.

6. Press ⏎; Word will copy the data from document A to document B.

Using the Mouse

You can also use the mouse to move or copy a selection to another location, without involving the Clipboard. To move a selection, use the following procedure:

1. Select the block of text or graphics you want to move.

2. Place the mouse pointer at the position to which you want to move the selection.

3. Click the *right* mouse button while pressing the Ctrl key.

To copy a selection, perform the following steps:

1. Select the block of text or graphics you want to copy.

2. Place the mouse pointer at the position where you want to insert the selection.

3. Click the *right* mouse button while pressing the Ctrl-Shift key combination.

Unlike the keyboard methods presented in the previous section, to move or copy a selection from one Word document to another with the mouse, *both* documents must be visible simultaneously on the screen.

OTHER COPYING TECHNIQUES

This section summarizes two other methods for copying a block of text or graphics, or the formatting that is assigned to a selection of text.

You can copy data from another Windows application to a Word document in such a way that the data within Word will be updated when the source of the data is changed in the other application. This feature is known as *dynamic data exchange* (or *DDE*).

You can also copy the current character or paragraph *formatting* belonging to a selection without copying the text. However, you must have a mouse to use this method. Character formatting is discussed in Chapter 16 and paragraph formatting in Chapter 15. Use the following procedure to copy either character or paragraph formatting:

1. Select the text you want to format.

2. If you want to copy character formatting, place the mouse pointer on the character that has the format you want to apply to the selection.

3. If you want to copy paragraph formatting, place the mouse pointer in the selection bar adjacent to the paragraph that has the format you want to apply to the selection.

4. Click the left mouse button while pressing the Ctrl-Shift key combination. Word will copy the formatting to the selected text.

> You may not be able to copy the character formatting in certain fonts, depending on the printer you use.

SUMMARY

- Many Word editing and formatting commands are performed by *first* selecting a block of text or graphics, and *then* applying the command to the selection.

- You can select a block of text or graphics using either the keyboard or the mouse.

- To select any size block with the keyboard, hold down the Shift key while using the arrow keys to move the highlight over the desired area. You can also select larger areas by holding down Shift while pressing the Home, End, PgUp, or PgDn key.

- You can select the entire document by pressing the Ctrl-5 keystroke (5 on the numeric keypad).

- To select a rectangular block of data with the keyboard, press Ctrl-Shift-F8 to activate the column selection mode, and then use the arrow keys to expand the highlight over the appropriate area.

- To select a block with the mouse, place the pointer at one end of the block, and, while holding down the left mouse button, drag the highlight over the text or graphics you want to select.

- You can rapidly select larger document areas by clicking in various ways within the selection bar (which is to the left of the text; see Table 5.2).

- You can select a rectangular block with the mouse by holding down the *right* mouse button and dragging the highlight over the desired area.

- To *delete* the current selection, press the Del key.

- You can move or copy the current selection with or without the use of the Windows Clipboard.

- To *move* the current selection using the Clipboard, choose the Edit/Cut menu command (or press Shift-Del), place the insertion point where you want to move the block, and then issue the Edit/Paste menu command (or press Shift-Ins).

- To *copy* the current selection using the Clipboard, choose the Edit/Copy menu command (or press Ctrl-Ins), place the insertion point where you want to insert the copy, and then issue the Edit/Paste menu command (or press Shift-Ins).

- You can *move* the current selection without disturbing the Clipboard by pressing the F2 key, moving the insertion point to the target location, and then pressing ←┘.

- Alternatively, you can also move the current selection by placing the mouse pointer at the target location and clicking the *right* button while pressing Ctrl.

- You can *copy* the current selection without disturbing the Clipboard by pressing the Shift-F2 key combination, moving the insertion point to the target location, and then pressing ⬅.

- Alternatively, you can also copy the current selection by placing the mouse pointer at the target location and clicking the *right* button while pressing Ctrl-Shift.

- You can also copy a selection using the Word glossary, which is explained in Chapter 21.

6

SEARCHING AND REPLACING

THIS CHAPTER DESCRIBES THE SEARCH COMMAND and the Replace command. These two commands are great time-savers, especially when you are working with a document longer than a few pages. The Search command allows you to find all occurrences of a specified sequence of characters or text formatting within your document. The Replace command allows you to search for either of these items, and to automatically replace one or more instances with the alternative text or formatting you specify.

SEARCHING

With the Search command, you can look for occurrences of specified text, formatting, or a combination of text and formatting within your document.

Selecting a block of text prior to issuing the Search command has no effect; it will *not* confine the search to the selection.

To use the Search command, first place the insertion point at the appropriate position within your document. Word will search from the insertion point to the end of the document, or from the insertion point to the *beginning* of the document if you chose the Up option, which is described shortly.

Next, choose the Edit/Search menu command. Word will display the Search For dialog box. In this box, you enter the information you want to search for—a sequence of characters, a special character, a large block of text, a formatting feature, or a format style.

You can also pick a direction for the search. The Down option causes Word to search from the current insertion point (or from the beginning of the current selection) to the end of the document. The Up option causes Word to search from the current insertion point (or from the end of the current selection) to the beginning of the document.

If desired, you can limit the search by choosing the Whole Word, the Match Upper/Lowercase option, or both options. When you are ready to begin the search, click the OK button, or press ⏎.

SEARCHING FOR TEXT

Methods for copying text into the Clipboard are discussed in Chapter 5.

When searching for text, you normally issue the Edit/Search command and type the sequence of characters directly into the Search For dialog box (Figure 6.1). You can also paste the contents of the Clipboard into this box by typing Shift-Ins. If you have previously issued the Search or Replace command, the Search For box will contain the information you formerly entered. You can accept this information or type in a new search specification. The maximum number of characters you can type or paste into the Search For text box is 256

Figure 6.1: The Search For dialog box

(although it is difficult to imagine why you would need to search for anywhere near this number of characters).

When entering text into the Search For box, you can specify one of several special characters by entering the appropriate code. The available codes are listed in Table 6.1. For example, the sequence ^n represents a newline character. Accordingly, the expression

Casper^n

would match the word **Casper** only when this word comes immediately before a new line.

As mentioned in Chapter 3, you enter a newline character into your document by pressing Shift-↵. It causes a line break within a paragraph, and is normally invisible.

Table 6.1: Codes for Specifying Special Characters

To specify:	Type:
Caret character (^)	^^
Newline character (entered by typing Shift-↵; see Chapter 3)	^n
Nonbreaking hyphen (see Chapter 17)	^~
Nonbreaking space (see Chapter 3)	^s
Optional hyphen (see Chapter 17)	^-
Paragraph mark (see Chapter 3)	^p
Section mark (see Chapter 14)	^d
Tab character (see Chapter 3)	^t
White space (one or more space or tab characters) (*Search For only*)	^w
Character whose ANSI code is *nnn* (see Chapter 3)	^*nnn*
Any single character (*Search For only*)	?
Question mark	^?
Exact text (*Replace With only*)	^m
Clipboard contents (*Replace With only*)	^c

The sequence ^w matches any amount of *white space*. White space consists of one or more space or tab characters. This option is useful if a variable amount of space may fall between two words you want to find. For example, the expression

Friendly^wGhost

would match

Friendly Ghost

or

Friendly   Ghost

A question mark (?) embedded in a search expression represents *any single character*. For example, the expression

a?e

would match **Abe**, **ace**, **age**, **ale**, **axe**, and so on. If you want to include an actual question mark as part of the expression, you must precede it with a caret character (^), as in the expression

say what^?

If, however, your search expression consists of a question mark *only*, then Word will also search for an actual question mark in the document. Thus, if no other characters are included in the search expression, ? is equivalent to ^?.

Once you have entered the desired text into the Search For dialog box, you have the option of limiting the search by choosing the Whole Word or Match Upper/Lowercase option.

The Whole Word option causes Word to ignore matches with any text that is *part* of a word. For example, if you typed **cat** into the Search For box, Word would find **cat** but not **caterpillar** or **concatenation**. This option applies also to formatting; that is, Word will search for the specified format only where it is assigned to one or more entire words.

The Match Upper/Lowercase option causes Word to ignore matches with any text that varies from the specified text in the case of one or more letters. For example, if you typed **cat** into the Search For box, Word would find **cat** but not **Cat** or **CAT**.

To begin the search, choose the Up or Down option as described previously, then click the OK button or press ◄─┘. Word will proceed to search from the insertion point toward the end of the document (if you chose the Down option) or toward the beginning of the document (if you chose the Up option).

If the specified text or formatting is not found, if you chose the Down option, and if you did not start the search at the beginning of the document, Word will display the message

> **Reached end of document. Continue search at beginning?**

If the specified text or formatting is not found, if you chose the Up option, and if you did not start the search at the end of the document, Word will display the message

> **Reached beginning of document. Continue search at end?**

In either case, you now have the opportunity to search the entire document, or to terminate the search at the end (or beginning) of the document.

If Word searches the entire document but does not find a match, it displays the message

> **Search text not found**

If you have issued the Go To command (described in Chapter 4) since the last time you issued the Search command, the Shift-F4 keystroke will repeat the Go To command rather than the Search command.

If you have not issued the Search command since starting Word, the Repeat Search command (Shift-F4) will display the Search dialog box.

If Word finds a match, it highlights the matching text. If you want to search for *another* occurrence of the same object, you can issue the Repeat Search command by pressing the Shift-F4 keystroke. This command immediately initiates a search from the current document position. It does not display the Edit/Search dialog box; rather, it uses all of the information you entered when you last issued the Edit/Search menu command. You can continue to use the Repeat Search command to find *all* occurrences of the specified text or formatting throughout the document.

CH. 6

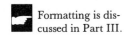

Formatting is discussed in Part III.

SEARCHING FOR FORMATTING

You can also use the Search command to find occurrences of specific formatting within your document. *Formatting* refers to the set of features assigned to the text in a document that determine the printed appearance of the document. You can specify formatting for characters, paragraphs, document sections, or an entire document. When you assign formatting to individual characters, you specify the character font (such as Courier or Tms Rmn), the character size, character enhancements such as italics, and other features. When you assign formatting to entire paragraphs, you specify the alignment style (such as left-justified or centered), paragraph indents, and other features.

If you specify one or more formatting features, the Search command will look for text that has been assigned the specified features, ignoring any other formatting that may also have been assigned to the text. If it finds a match, it highlights all adjoining characters that have the designated formatting.

You can specify the following types of formatting:

You will see later in the chapter how to *combine* text and the various types of formatting in your Search specification.

- Character formatting

- Paragraph formatting

- A format style

Once you have specified the desired formatting, proceed with the search as described previously in the chapter.

You must specify character or paragraph formatting features while the insertion point or highlight is within the Search For box. If the box does not contain the insertion point or highlight, you can place it there by clicking within the box or by pressing Alt-S.

Specifying Character Formatting

You can specify a character formatting feature by pressing the appropriate keystroke (see Table 6.2). You can designate one or more of these formatting features. Each time you specify one, Word adds the description of the feature to the line below the Search For box.

For example, if you typed Ctrl-B and then Ctrl-I to specify bold italic characters

```
Search For:
┌─────────────────────────────────────────┐
│|                                         │
└─────────────────────────────────────────┘
Bold Italic
```

Table 6.2: Codes for Specifying Character Formatting Features

Character formatting is discussed in Chapter 16.

TO SPECIFY THIS CHARACTER FORMAT:	TYPE:
Bold	Ctrl-B
Capitals, small	Ctrl-K
Color, next	Ctrl-V (each press specifies next available color)
Color, previous	Ctrl-Shift-V (each press specifies previous available color)
Deleted text in mark revisions mode (see Chapter 25)	Ctrl-Z (*Search For only*)
Double underline	Ctrl-D
Font, next	Ctrl-F (each press specifies next available font)
Font, previous	Ctrl-Shift-F (each press specifies previous available font)
Hidden	Ctrl-H
Italic	Ctrl-I
New text in mark revisions mode (see Chapter 25)	Ctrl-N (*Search For only*)
Point size, next	Ctrl-P (each press specifies next available point size)
Point size, previous	Ctrl-Shift-P (each press specifies previous available point size)
Remove all character formatting specifications	Ctrl-spacebar
Subscript (3 points)	Ctrl-= (equal character)
Superscript (3 points)	Ctrl-+ (plus character)
Underline	Ctrl-U
Underline, word	Ctrl-W

Word would search for text that is *both* bold *and* italic. It would ignore any other formatting features assigned to the text.

To remove a given character formatting feature from your search specification, press the corresponding keystroke again. For example, pressing Ctrl-U specifies underlined characters; pressing this keystroke again removes underlining. To remove *all* character formatting features from the specification, press Ctrl-spacebar.

Specifying Paragraph Formatting

Paragraph formatting is discussed in Chapter 15.

You can also specify a paragraph formatting feature by pressing the appropriate keystroke (see Table 6.3). You can specify one or more of these features; Word displays a description of each one underneath the Search For box.

For example, if you typed Ctrl-C and Ctrl-2,

<u>S</u>earch For:

```
|
```

Centered, Line Spacing: 24pt

Table 6.3: Codes for Specifying Paragraph Formatting

TO SPECIFY THIS PARAGRAPH FORMATTING FEATURE:	TYPE:
Centered lines	Ctrl-C
Close space before paragraph	Ctrl-E
Double-spaced lines	Ctrl-2
Justified lines	Ctrl-J
Left-aligned lines	Ctrl-L
One-and-one-half-spaced lines	Ctrl-5
Open space before paragraph	Ctrl-O
Remove all paragraph formatting specifications	Ctrl-X
Right-aligned lines	Ctrl-R
Single-spaced lines	Ctrl-1

Word would search for text that has been assigned the centered *and* double-spaced paragraph format features, ignoring any other formatting assigned to the text.

If you specify *only* paragraph formatting, Word will highlight all characters in the first paragraph that has been assigned the specified formatting. Even if several adjoining paragraphs have the specified formatting, Word will select only the first one (if, however, you then issue the Repeat Search command, Shift-F4, Word will highlight the next paragraph).

To remove a given paragraph formatting feature from your search specification, press the corresponding keystroke again. To remove *all* paragraph formatting features, press the Ctrl-X key combination.

Specifying a Style

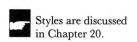
Styles are discussed in Chapter 20.

To search for a specific style, enter the following expression into the Search For box:

> ^ystyle-name

where *style-name* is the name of the style. For example, to search for the style named **heading 1** (the top-level heading style), type

> ^yheading 1

Notice that there is no space between the **y** and the style name. Also, you can specify only a single style, and you cannot combine a style specification with text.

When you search for a style, Word will highlight all characters in the first paragraph that has been assigned the specified style. If several adjoining paragraphs have the style, Word will select only the first one (if you then issue the Repeat Search command, Shift-F4, Word will highlight the next paragraph).

SEARCHING FOR COMBINATIONS OF TEXT AND FORMATTING

When specifying the object you want to find with the Search command, you can freely combine text, character formatting, and paragraph formatting. If you combine character and paragraph formatting in your specification, Word will search for text that has been assigned *all* of the specified features. The text may or may not have been assigned other formatting features; Word ignores all other features and searches only for the specified ones.

If you specify text *and* one or more formatting features, Word will search for the first occurrence of this text that has all of the specified formatting features. For example, if you combine text with a paragraph formatting feature, Word will highlight the first occurrence of the specified text that is contained within a paragraph that has the specified formatting.

Although you cannot specify both text and a style, you *can* specify both a style name and character or paragraph formatting. If you do so, Word will highlight the first block of text that has the specified formatting and is within a paragraph that has been assigned the specified style.

> Contrary to the Word *User's Reference*, you *can* specify both a style and one or more formatting features.

USING OTHER SEARCH METHODS

This section briefly summarizes several other search methods provided by Word that are not accessed through the Search command. These techniques are fully explained elsewhere in the book.

Finding File Locations

You can use the Go To command to find document sections, pages, lines, footnotes, or annotations. You specify each of these target locations by giving its relative number within the document. For example, you can find the fifth page from the beginning of the document, or the third line on the second page, and so on. The Go To command is explained in Chapter 4.

Finding Fields

> For a full explanation of fields, see the topic "Fields" in the Word *User's Reference* or *Technical Reference*.

You can find the *next* field within the document by pressing F11 or Alt-F1, and you can find the *previous* field by pressing Shift-F11 or Alt-Shift-F1.

Finding Revision Markings

As shown in Table 6.2, you can use the Search command to search for new text or deleted text that has been marked in the *mark revisions mode.* You can also use the Utilities/Revision Marks command to search for either of these types of revision markings. Revision marking is discussed in Chapter 25.

Finding Documents

Finally, you can use the File/Find command to help find specific Word documents. You can search for documents that contain specific text, or documents that have been assigned specified summary information. As mentioned in Chapter 1, Word requests summary information when you save a document for the first time. The File/Find command is discussed in Chapter 26.

REPLACING

By using the Word Replace command, you can automatically replace one or more occurrences of the specified text or formatting within your document. You can replace text, character formatting, paragraph formatting, styles, or combinations of these elements.

First, as with searching, you place the insertion point at the appropriate position within your document. Word will search from the current position of the insertion point to the end of the document (when Word reaches the end, however, you will have the opportunity to search the remainder of the document). Alternatively, if you *select* a block of text, Word will replace only within the selection. You then choose the Edit/Replace command, and at the Replace dialog box enter the text, formatting, or style you want to find and replace. Just as with the search operation, you can specify the direction of the search and indicate any limits you want to place on the operation. You also can have Word stop at each found item and confirm that you want to replace that item. When you've made all your specifications, just click OK or press ← to begin the search and replace.

REPLACING TEXT

To begin replacing text, first place the insertion point where you want to begin. Next, choose the Edit/Replace menu command. Word will display the dialog box shown in Figure 6.2.

If you have previ-
ously issued the
Search or Replace com-
mand, the Search For box
will contain the informa-
tion you formerly en-
tered. You can accept this
information or type in a
new search specification.

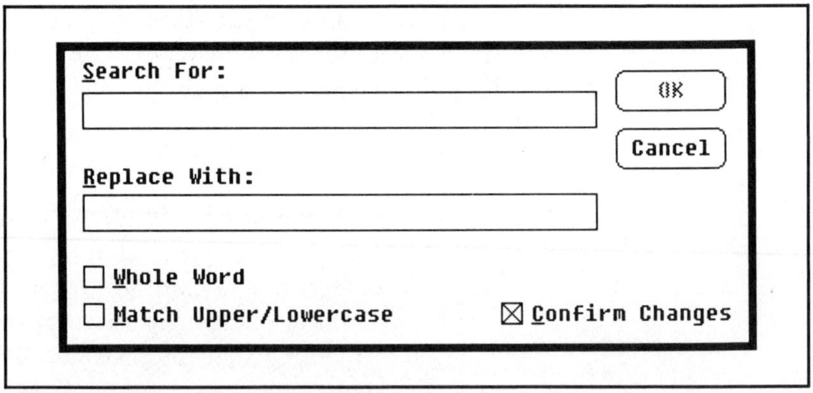

```
┌─────────────────────────────────────────────────────────┐
│                                                          │
│    Search For:                              ┌────────┐   │
│    ┌──────────────────────────────────┐     │   OK   │   │
│    │                                  │     └────────┘   │
│    └──────────────────────────────────┘     ┌────────┐   │
│    Replace With:                            │ Cancel │   │
│    ┌──────────────────────────────────┐     └────────┘   │
│    │                                  │                  │
│    └──────────────────────────────────┘                  │
│                                                          │
│    ☐ Whole Word                                          │
│    ☐ Match Upper/Lowercase       ☒ Confirm Changes      │
│                                                          │
└─────────────────────────────────────────────────────────┘
```

Figure 6.2: The Replace With dialog box

You can enter text into the Search For and Replace With boxes in the same way that you enter text when using the Search command, which was explained previously in the chapter. You can type, or paste from the Clipboard (using the Shift-Ins keys), up to 256 characters into either of these boxes.

To specify special characters, you can use the codes listed in Table 6.1. However, you cannot use the codes ? (any single character) and ^w (white space) in the Replace With box.

You can enter two additional codes into the Replace With box only. First, the code ^m represents the exact text that was matched. For example, if you typed

Chapter ?

into the Search For box, and

"^m"

into the Replace With box, Word would replace

Chapter 1

with

"Chapter 1"

and

Chapter 2

with

"Chapter 2"

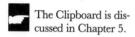
The Clipboard is discussed in Chapter 5.

effectively placing quote characters around all chapter titles.

The second special code you can enter into the Replace With box is ^c, which represents the current contents of the Clipboard. You can enter this code by itself, or in conjunction with other text. Consider, for example, entering the following word into the Search For box:

pets

and the following expression into the Replace With box:

^c, etc.

If the Clipboard currently contains the list

dogs, cats, birds, alligators

then Word would substitute every occurrence of the word **pets** with

dogs, cats, birds, alligators, etc.

Although you can usually paste the contents of the Clipboard directly into the Replace With box (by means of the Shift-Ins keystroke), using the ^c code has two important advantages:

- The number of characters you can paste or type into the Replace With box is limited to 256. If you want to replace using a greater number of characters, you can copy the replacement text into the Clipboard and include the ^c code in the expression you type into the Replace With box.

- You cannot enter a graphic directly into the Replace With box. However, you can replace text with a graphic by copying the graphic into the Clipboard and entering the ^c code into the Replace With box.

If desired, you can limit the search and replacement by choosing the Whole Word option, the Match Upper/Lowercase option, or both options from the Replace With dialog box.

The Whole Word option affects the way the Replace command searches for text; it causes Word to ignore matches with any text that is *part* of a word. For example, if you typed **cat** into the Search For box, Word would find **cat** but not **caterpillar** or **concatenation**. This option also applies to formatting; that is, Word will search for the specified format only where it is assigned to one or more entire words.

The Match Upper/Lowercase option affects both the way Word searches for text and the way it replaces text. If you do *not* choose this option, Word ignores the case of all letters when searching for text. Also, when replacing text, it matches the capitalization style of the existing text. For example, if you entered **tabby** into the Search For box and **Manx** into the Replace With box, Word would replace **tabby** with **manx**, **Tabby** with **Manx**, and **TABBY** with **MANX**.

If, however, you choose the Match Upper/Lowercase option, Word searches only for text that matches the case of all letters typed into the Search For box. Also, it replaces text *exactly* as you typed it into the Replace With box. For example, if you entered **tabby** into the Search For box and **Manx** into the Replace With box, Word would replace **tabby** with **Manx**, and would ignore **Tabby** and **TABBY**.

Select the Confirm Changes option in the Replace With dialog box if you want Word to stop and ask you whether to make each replacement.

When you are ready to begin making replacements, click the OK button or press ↵. Word will begin searching from the insertion point toward the end of the document, or from the beginning of the current selection toward the end of the selection.

If you do *not* choose the Confirm Changes option, Word automatically replaces all occurrences it encounters through the end of the document. If, however, you choose the Confirm Changes option, each time Word finds a match, it pauses and displays the dialog box shown in Figure 6.3.

You can now perform one of the following actions:

- Click the Yes button or press ↵ to make the replacement and then search for the next match.

- Click the No button to search for the next match without replacing the current one.

The dialog box for confirming replacements is movable. You can therefore change its position on the screen if it is covering a portion of the document you want to see.

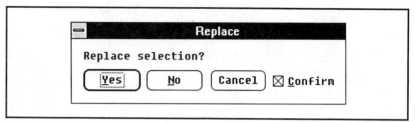

Figure 6.3: The Confirm Changes dialog box

- Click the Cancel button to stop the Replace operation without replacing the current match (replacements already made will remain).

- Click the Confirm box (removing the check mark), and then click the Yes button to replace the current match and to replace the remaining occurrences without pausing for confirmation.

- Click the Confirm box (removing the check mark), and then click the No button to leave the current match unchanged and to replace the remaining occurrences without pausing for confirmation.

If you did not start the Replace operation from the beginning of the document, Word will display the following message when it reaches the end of the document:

> Reached end of document. Continue search at
> beginning?

Click the No button to stop replacing at the end of the document, or Yes to continue replacing from the beginning of the document so that you can make replacements throughout the entire document.

If Word does not find a match after searching the entire document or selection, it displays the following message:

> Search text not found

When the Replace command is finished, Word displays within the status bar the total number of replacements made.

Later in the chapter, you will learn how to specify a combination of text and formatting when using the Replace command.

If you chose the Confirm Replacements option, you can reverse the *last replacement that was made* by issuing the Edit/Undo command. If you did not choose this option, you can reverse *all* replacements by issuing the Edit/Undo command. The Undo command is discussed in Chapter 3, in the section "Undoing and Redoing."

REPLACING FORMATTING OR A STYLE

To search for a specific formatting feature, type the appropriate code while the insertion point is within the Search For box. To replace with a specific formatting feature, type the code while the insertion point is within the Replace With box. Word will display a description of each formatting feature you specify underneath the appropriate box.

To specify formatting features, follow the instructions given previously in the "Searching for Formatting" subsections. You can use any of the character formatting codes listed in Table 6.2 except Ctrl-N and Ctrl-Z. You can use any of the paragraph formatting codes listed in Table 6.3. As with the Search command, you can combine character and formatting codes.

You can specify a style in the Search For or Replace With box in the same manner described for the Search command. As you saw, you can indicate a style by typing the following expression into the box:

^y*style-name*

where *style-name* is the name of the style. Remember that if you specify a style, you cannot enter other text into the same box.

You can also use **^m** to remove one or more character formatting features. Suppose, for example, that you wanted to convert all boldface characters to normal characters. Simply leaving the Replace With box empty would *erase* the characters rather than converting them to a normal typeface. You could, however, use the following procedure:

1. While the insertion point is within the Search For box, press Ctrl-B to have Word find all boldface characters. Do not type text into this box.

2. Type the expression **^m** into the Replace With box. Do not type additional characters into this box, and do not indicate any formatting features.

3. Click OK to begin the replacement.

In the next section, you will learn how to specify a combination of formatting, styles, and text when using the Replace command.

REPLACING COMBINATIONS OF TEXT AND FORMATTING

The exact effect of combining text, formatting, and styles in the Search For and Replace With boxes may not be obvious. Table 6.4 summarizes the result of various combinations.

For example, the first item in the table shows how to replace a block of text while leaving the existing formatting intact: specify text, formatting, or a combination of text and formatting in the Search For box, and specify text only in the Replace With box.

In Table 6.4, the term *formatting* means character formatting, paragraph formatting, a combination of character and paragraph formatting, or a style. Note, however, that you can combine a style with other formatting but you cannot combine it with text.

Table 6.4: Specifying Text and Formatting for the Replace Command

TO OBTAIN THIS RESULT:	SPECIFY IN THE SEARCH FOR BOX:	SPECIFY IN THE REPLACE WITH BOX:
Replace existing text but leave existing formatting intact	Text, formatting, or combination of text and formatting	Text
Add formatting to existing text and formatting	Text	Formatting
Replace existing formatting	Formatting, or combination of text and formatting	Formatting
Replace existing text and add formatting to existing formatting	Text	Text and formatting
Replace existing text and formatting	Formatting, or combination of text and formatting	Text and formatting
Erase existing text and formatting	Text, formatting, or combination of text and formatting	Nothing (leave blank)

Finally, leaving the Replace With box empty causes Word to erase instances of text that match what you specified in the Search For box.

SUMMARY

- You can use the Search command to look for specified text or formatting, or a combination of text and formatting within your document.

- To issue the Search command, choose the Edit/Search menu item. Word will display a dialog box.

- Enter the text you want to find into the Search For box. While the insertion point is within this box, you can also specify any formatting you would like to locate.

- Choose a search direction by selecting the Down or Up option.

- You can limit the search by specifying the Whole Word option, Match Upper/Lowercase, or both options.

- When you are ready to perform the search, click the OK button or press ←┘. Word will highlight the first match, if any, within your document.

- You can search for another occurrence of the same text or formatting you previously specified by pressing the Shift-F4 key combination.

- When entering text into the Search For box, you can specify a special character—such as a paragraph mark—by typing one of the codes given in Table 6.1.

- While the insertion point is in the Search For box, you can specify one or more character or paragraph formatting features by entering the appropriate code or codes from Tables 6.2 and 6.3.

- You can search for a style by entering ^y*style-name* into the Search For box, where *style-name* is the name of the style you want to find.

- You can use the Replace command to automatically replace one or more occurrences of specified text or formatting within your document.

- Issue the Replace command by choosing the Edit/Replace menu item. Word will display a dialog box.

- Enter the text you want to find into the Search For box, and the text you want to replace each occurrence with into the Replace With box.

- As with the Search command, you can limit the search by choosing the Whole Word option, the Match Upper/Lowercase option, or both options.

- If you choose the Confirm Changes option, Word will pause and ask you whether to replace each occurrence. Otherwise, it will make all replacements automatically.

- When you are ready to begin replacing text, click the OK button or press ←.

- When entering the search specification into the Search For box, or the replacement into the Replace With box, you can specify special characters, formatting, and styles in the same manner as using the Search command.

7

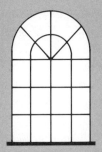

CHECKING YOUR SPELLING AND FINDING SYNONYMS

THIS CHAPTER DESCRIBES TWO IMPORTANT TOOLS Word for Windows provides to help you compose your documents: the spelling checker and the thesaurus. You use the spelling checker to verify your spelling. You can check the spelling of one or more words as you create a document, or you can check the spelling of an entire completed document.

The thesaurus is used to find synonyms for the words in your document, and it can help you add variety to your writing. It provides both a definition and a list of synonyms for the word you choose, and allows you to replace the chosen word with an appropriate synonym.

CHECKING SPELLING

You can use the Word Spelling command to confirm the spelling of a single word, a group of words, or all the words in a document. The

You cannot use the spelling checker when you are in outline view.

spelling checker looks up each word in one or more internal dictionaries of correctly spelled words. If it finds the word in a dictionary, it assumes that it is correctly spelled; if it does not find the word, it flags it as a possible misspelling and allows you to make a correction.

The spelling checker, however, is not infallible. The following are two important limitations:

- All words that are not contained in an internal dictionary are flagged, even if they are actually correctly spelled. Word's dictionaries may not contain some of the proper names, unusual words, or technical terms that you use. As you will see, you can gradually minimize this problem by adding these words to a supplemental dictionary.

- More importantly, the spelling checker will not flag correctly spelled words that are used inappropriately. For example, it will not flag the word **their** used instead of **there**.

Although the spelling checker is not unerring, it can catch many mistakes and is a valuable adjunct to other forms of proofreading. In addition to flagging misspellings, the spelling checker will signal repeated words, words with unusual capitalizations (such as **bAt**), and words in which the first letter should be capitalized (for example, **american**).

There are two basic ways to check spelling with Word. You can use the Spell key (F7) for a quick check of a single word or a block of text, or you can use a more detailed method that uses options within dialog boxes.

When you use the dialog boxes, you must place the insertion point at the appropriate position in your document. Word checks the spelling of all words from the position of the insertion point to the end of the document. (Alternatively, if you *select* one or more words prior to issuing the Spelling command, Word will check the spelling of only the selected words.)

As you will see, if you don't start the check at the beginning of the document, when the spelling checker reaches the end, you will have the opportunity to continue from the beginning so that the entire document can be checked.

The Spelling command uses two dialog boxes: the Check Spelling dialog box, which is displayed when you first issue the command, and the Spelling dialog box, which is displayed when an unrecognized word is encountered.

Let's look at the dialog box method first. Once you have positioned the insertion point, the next step is to choose the Utilities/ Spelling menu command. Word will display the Check Spelling dialog box, which is illustrated in Figure 7.1. Once this dialog box is displayed, you have four basic choices:

- You can check the spelling of any single word by entering it into the box labeled **Word**.

- You can click the Options button to select one or more options before beginning the spelling check.

- You can click the Start button to begin checking the spelling within your document.

- You can click the Cancel button to remove the Check Spelling dialog box and return to the editing window.

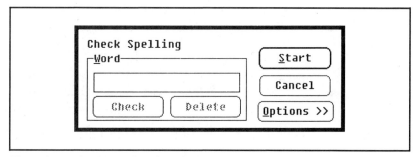

Figure 7.1: The Check Spelling dialog box

The first three choices are discussed in the following sections.

WORKING WITH A SINGLE WORD

The Word box contains the insertion point when the Check Spelling command is first displayed, so that you can modify any word it contains or type in a new word.

The rectangular area within the Check Spelling dialog box that is labeled **Word** can be used either to check the spelling of a single word, or to delete a word from a supplemental dictionary.

If you selected a single word prior to issuing the Spelling command, this word will automatically appear within the Word box. If you selected more than a single word, or if there was no selection when you activated the spelling checker, the Word box will be empty;

in this case, you can type any single word into the box. Try it:

1. Open a new document and choose the Utilities/Spelling command.

2. At the Check Spelling dialog box, enter **acessory** into the Word box.

Once the Word box contains a word, you have two options. If you click the Check button or press ←, the spelling checker will verify the spelling of the word. If it finds the word in one of its dictionaries, it displays a message box indicating which dictionary contains the word. If it does not find the word, it displays the Spelling dialog box, which allows you to view alternative spellings for the word, to add the word to a supplemental dictionary, and to perform other tasks.

> Supplemental dictionaries are discussed in the next section. You can insert a new word into a supplemental dictionary by typing the word into the Word box, clicking the Check button, and then clicking the Add button in the Spelling dialog box.

3. Click the Check button or press ←. You see the Spelling dialog box illustrated in Figure 7.2. (This box is described in more detail later in the chapter.)

Second, if you click the Delete button, and if the word can be found in a supplemental dictionary, it will be removed from this dictionary. You *cannot* use the Delete button to delete a word from the main dictionary, which is described in the next section.

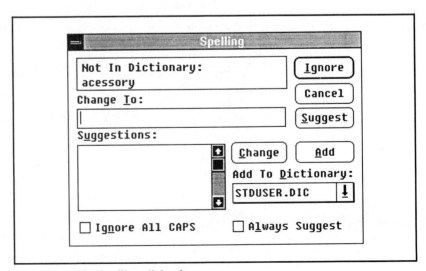

Figure 7.2: The Spelling dialog box

CHECKING SPELLING WITHIN YOUR DOCUMENT

To check your entire document for spelling errors, you begin with the Utilities/Spelling command. Word then displays the Check Spelling dialog box (see Figure 7.1), just as it does when you check a single word. You can begin checking by choosing the Start button, but most likely you'll want to choose one of the spelling options to get optimum use of the spelling check feature.

To choose one or more spelling options, click the Options >> button in the Check Spelling dialog box. The dialog box will expand to reveal several additional options. The expanded dialog box is illustrated in Figure 7.3.

If you select the Ignore All CAPS option, the spelling checker will not check words that are in all capital letters (such as DNA and ASCII). It will also ignore words that have uncommon capitalizations (such as SoftWrite).

Selecting the Always Suggest option causes the spelling checker to automatically display a list of alternative spellings whenever it encounters a word it cannot find in its dictionaries. As you will see in the next section, if this option is *not* selected, you must click the Suggest button in the Spelling dialog box to obtain a list of alternative spellings.

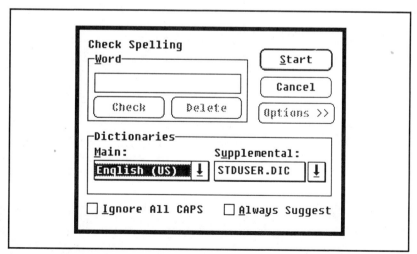

Figure 7.3: The Check Spelling dialog box with additional options

When you choose a main or supplemental dictionary, your choice remains effective only during the current Word session. The next time you start Word, it reverts to its default dictionaries.

You cannot add or delete words from a main dictionary.

When a main dictionary is installed, the appropriate files are copied to the Word for Windows directory (\WINWORD).

The Dictionaries area of the Check Spelling dialog box allows you to choose the *main* dictionary that Word uses, and also to specify an additional *supplemental* dictionary. When the spelling checker searches for a word, it first looks in the main dictionary. If it can't find the word here, it then checks either one or two supplemental dictionaries. If the spelling checker can't find the word in any of its dictionaries, it highlights the word in your document and displays the Spelling dialog box, which you saw in the previous section.

The main dictionary is included with the Microsoft Word package. It contains a large number of words, and it is designed for a specific language. When you install Word, normally only one main dictionary, appropriate for your language, is copied to the hard disk. If, however, you have installed one or more additional main dictionaries for alternative languages, you can have the speller use the desired one by selecting it from the Main list box.

To view the choices in the list, click the ↓

Main:

English (US) ↓

or type Alt-M followed by Alt-↓.

Select the desired dictionary by clicking the name, or by moving the highlight to the name using the arrow keys. Note that you cannot type a main dictionary name into the Main box; rather, you must select one from the list.

In contrast, a supplemental dictionary is one that you create. It consists of the words you add individually when you use the spelling checker, less any words that you delete. You will see later in the chapter how to add words during a spelling check through the Spelling dialog box. You have already seen how to delete words from a supplemental dictionary using the Check Spelling dialog box.

Word will use either one or two supplemental dictionaries. When you start Word, it initially uses a single supplemental dictionary called STDUSER.DIC, which is located in the Word for Windows directory (\WINWORD). Like any supplemental dictionary, it is originally empty, but will retain any words you add to it.

Word always uses the supplemental dictionary STDUSER-.DIC. You can, however, have the program use another supplemental dictionary *in addition* to STDUSER.DIC, by specifying this dictionary in the Supplemental box.

See Appendix A for information on designating directory paths.

You must click the Start button, as described in the next section, before the selected supplemental dictionary is activated. If you simply click Cancel, Word will ignore your dictionary choice.

Notice that the dictionary name initially displayed in the Supplemental box is STDUSER.DIC. You can have the spelling checker use an additional supplemental dictionary during the current Word session by entering the name of this dictionary into the Supplemental box.

If the additional supplemental dictionary does not already exist, type the desired file name into the Supplemental box. If you do not want to store it in the \WINWORD directory, you must specify the full path name for the file. When you click the Start button to begin checking spelling in your document, Word will ask you if you want to create a new supplemental dictionary. If you click the Yes button, Word will create and begin using the new dictionary.

If the desired supplemental dictionary already exists, and if it is located in the \WINWORD directory, its name will appear in the Supplemental pull-down list. In this case, you can simply select it from the list, using the method described for the Main box. If, however, an existing dictionary is located in another directory, you will have to type the full directory path into the box at the top of the list.

Once you have specified a new or existing supplemental dictionary, Word will begin consulting this dictionary in addition to the main dictionary and STDUSER.DIC. You can also begin adding or deleting words from this dictionary, as described in the next section.

Supplemental dictionaries are valuable for storing words not found in the main dictionary, which you commonly use in your documents. For example, you might frequently use proper names, such as Jeremiah or Biff, or technical terms, such as acetabulum or onomastic.

By using a variety of supplemental dictionaries, you can increase the efficiency and accuracy of your spelling checks. For example, if you write books on computers *and* articles on psychiatry, you could use one additional supplemental dictionary while writing on computers (called COMPUTER.DIC) and another while writing on psychiatry (called PSYCH.DIC). You could store the general terms you employ in all types of documents in STDUSER.DIC (which is always used). While writing on computers, you could store computer terms in COMPUTER.DIC, and while writing on psychiatry, you could store psychological terms in PSYCH.DIC. In this manner, the spelling checker will need to search only the supplemental words that are relevant to your current writing topic.

Once you have chosen the desired options, you can begin checking the spelling of words within your document by clicking the Start button. Word will start checking words from the current position of the insertion point or at the beginning of the current selection. When it encounters a word not found in one of the dictionaries it is currently using, it displays the Spelling dialog box (see Figure 7.3). The unknown word is copied to the box at the top of the dialog box, and is labeled **Not in Dictionary:**.

Word also displays the Spelling dialog box in the following two cases:

- If a word is repeated. In this case, the word is labeled **Repeated Word:**.

```
Repeated Word:
the
```

- If the word uses nonstandard capitalization, such as **bAt**. In this case, the word is labeled **Uncommon Capitalization:**.

Once the Spelling dialog box is displayed, you have the following five options in dealing with the word that has been flagged:

- Ignore the word
- Change the word
- View alternative spellings for the word
- Add the word to a supplemental dictionary
- Cancel the Spelling command

These options correspond to the five buttons displayed on the Spelling dialog box (Figure 7.2), and are now discussed individually.

Ignore the Word

Click the Ignore button or press ◄┘ to leave the unknown word unchanged in the document, and to continue the spelling check. If the spelling checker encounters this word again in the same spelling session, it automatically ignores it. However, when the spelling checker is run at a later time, the word will again be flagged the first time it is encountered. To have the spelling checker permanently ignore the word, you should add the word to a supplemental dictionary, as explained later.

Change the Word

To change the flagged word, you can type an alternative spelling into the Change To box and click the Change button (the insertion point is initially placed in this box).

```
Not In Dictionary:
funy
Change To:
funny|
```

Unfortunately, Word does not provide a method for checking the spelling of the word you type into the Change To box. If you misspell the correction, it will be inserted into your document without warning. It might be safer, therefore, to select one of the spellings suggested by Word, as described in the next section.

If you want to erase the word from your document, leave the Change To box empty when you click the Change button. Using this method, you can easily eliminate a repeated word.

Word will display the Spelling dialog box for each subsequent word that it cannot find in its current dictionaries. If the insertion point was not at the beginning of the document when you issued the Spelling command, Word will display a box with the following message when it reaches the end of the document:

Continue checking from beginning of document?

If you click the Yes button, Word will check from the beginning of the document to the point where you started the spelling check, thus covering the entire document. When Word has finished checking the complete document or selection, it briefly displays the **Spell check completed** message in the status bar.

View Alternative Spellings

If you choose the **Always Suggest** option, Word will automatically display a list of suggested spellings. In this case, you need not click the Suggest button.

Click the Suggest button to have Word display a list of alternative spellings. The words will appear in the Suggestions list box. Scroll, if necessary, to view all the suggested words. You may be surprised how often Word comes up with the word you were attempting to spell. If you want to accept one of the suggested spellings, simply highlight it and click the Change button. Notice that as each word is highlighted, it is automatically copied to the Change To box, as shown in Figure 7.4.

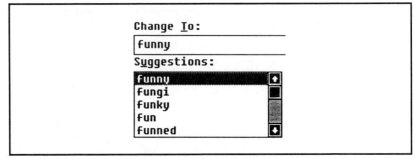

Figure 7.4: Selecting suggested words

Add the Word to a Supplemental Dictionary

You cannot add the word to the main dictionary; you can add it only to a supplemental dictionary.

If you click the Add button, the flagged word will be left unchanged in your document, and will be added to the supplemental dictionary indicated in the Add to Dictionary box (see Figure 7.2).

If Word is using *two* supplemental dictionaries (that is, you specified an additional supplemental dictionary as described previously in the chapter), make sure that the Add to Dictionary box displays the name of the desired dictionary before clicking the Add button. If you would like to choose the other supplemental dictionary, open the pull-down list and select the other name. You can open the list box by clicking the down arrow, or by typing Alt-D and then Alt-↓. Select the desired dictionary by clicking its name, or by using the arrow keys to move the highlight to the name, as shown in Figure 7.5.

The dictionary that appears in the Add to Dictionary box is also the one from which names are deleted when you click the Delete button in the Check Spelling dialog box, as described previously.

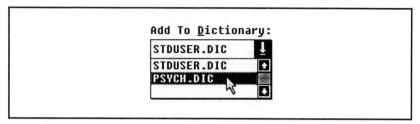

Figure 7.5: Selecting a dictionary to add

Once you have added a word to a supplemental dictionary, the spelling checker will no longer flag the word whenever that dictionary is in use (Word always uses the STDUSER.DIC dictionary).

Cancel the Spelling Command

Finally, you can click the Cancel button to immediately terminate the spelling session and return to the editing window. Any corrections you have already made will remain.

Setting Other Options

While the Spelling dialog box is displayed, you can also set the following options:

- Ignore All CAPS
- Always Suggest

These options are described earlier in this section. Once you set one or both of these options, they will remain in effect throughout the remainder of the spelling session.

USING THE SPELL KEY (F7)

You can press the F7 key to quickly check the spelling of a selection of text, or of a single word. If you have selected a block of text within your document, pressing the F7 key will cause Word to immediately begin checking the spelling of all words within the selection, *without displaying the Check Spelling dialog box*. As usual, if the spelling checker finds an unknown word or another suspected error, it displays the Spelling dialog box and permits you to make a correction. Since the F7 command does not display the Check Spelling dialog box, the spelling checker uses the previous setting for all spelling options.

If no text is selected when you press F7, Word will immediately check the word containing the insertion point, without displaying the Check Spelling dialog box. Unless the insertion point is within the word—or to the *immediate* left of the word—the *previous* word will be checked. If the line containing the insertion point does not have a word, Word will beep in response to the F7 key.

FINDING SYNONYMS WITH THE THESAURUS

You cannot activate the thesaurus while you are in the outline document view.

When Word displays the Thesaurus dialog box, it attempts to place it on the screen as far away as possible from the word in your document. If the dialog box covers some portion of the window you want to see, you can move it on the screen.

You can use the Word for Windows thesaurus to look up synonyms for words in your documents, thereby lending variety and precision to your writing style. To find a list of synonyms for a word, first place the insertion point on, immediately before, or immediately following the desired word, and then choose the Utilities/Thesaurus menu command or press the Shift-F7 keystroke. If the insertion point falls *between* two words, the thesaurus uses the preceding word. You can also *select* the desired word prior to activating the thesaurus. Word will display the Thesaurus dialog box, which is shown in Figure 7.6. The dialog box in this figure was displayed while the insertion point was on the word **pretty**.

The thesaurus looks up synonyms for the word that contained the insertion point, or the word that was selected, when you issued the Thesaurus command. This word is displayed in the Look Up box at the top of the Thesaurus dialog box; in this discussion, it will be referred to as the *current word*.

If the line with the insertion point does not contain a word, or if you have selected more than one word, the Look Up box will initially be empty. In this case, you can type a word into the box and click the Synonyms button to obtain a list of synonyms.

The Definitions box contains a list of different meanings for the current word. At a given time, *one* of these meanings is selected (as indicated by the highlight). As you can see in Figure 7.6, the text for one or more of the meanings listed in the Definitions box may be

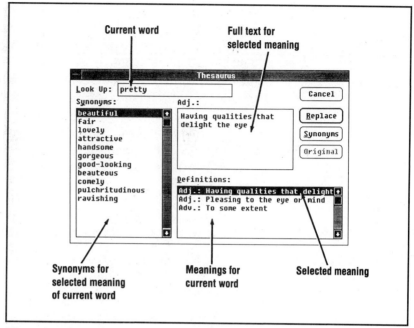

Figure 7.6: The Thesaurus dialog box

truncated. However, the full text of the selected meaning is displayed
in the area above the Definitions box.

The Synonyms box contains a list of synonyms *for the selected meaning*
of the current word. If the thesaurus cannot find the word, it displays
the message **No Synonyms** in the Synonyms box.

Once the Thesaurus dialog box has been displayed, you should first
make sure that the most appropriate meaning is selected within the
Definitions box. Selecting the best meaning will give you a list of synonyms that are as close as possible to your intent. You can select a meaning by clicking it within the Definitions box, or by pressing Alt-D and
then moving the highlight to the word using the arrow keys.

As you select each meaning, a list of corresponding synonyms
immediately appears in the Synonyms box (you don't have to click a
button to obtain this list). You can scroll, if necessary, to view the
entire synonym list.

If you would like to replace the word in your document with one
of the listed synonyms, first select the word by clicking it, or by moving the highlight to the word with the arrow keys. Then click the

To see a list of synonyms for a word in the Synonyms box, you can also simply double-click the word. The word you double-click becomes the new current word (displayed in the Look Up box), and a new list of synonyms appears.

Replace button. The dialog box will be removed, and the selected synonym will replace the word in your document

To see a list of synonyms for an entirely different word, first highlight a word in the Synonyms box, or, if the desired word is not listed there, type it into the Look Up box. Next, click the Synonyms button. The word you highlighted or typed will become the new current word; you will see its meaning or meanings in the Definitions box, and a list of synonyms for it in the Synonyms box.

Using this technique for finding synonyms of synonyms can help you find the most appropriate word for your document. The following scenario illustrates how you might apply this method:

1. You type the word **devious** into your document, but would like to find a more apt term.

2. You therefore activate the thesaurus by pressing Shift-F7 while the insertion point is to the immediate right of the word.

3. You choose the second meaning for **devious** in the Definitions box: **Marked by treachery or deceit**.

4. Among the synonyms that are now listed, you see the word **sneaky**. This word is much closer to your intended meaning, but is not the precise word you want. Therefore, you highlight **sneaky** in the Synonyms box and click the Synonyms button.

5. Once **sneaky** becomes the current word in the thesaurus, you select the second meaning in the Definitions box, **So slow, deliberate, and secret as to escape observation**.

6. Among the synonyms now displayed, you see the word **feline**. You decide that this is the word you want in your document. You therefore select it and click the Replace button.

While the Thesaurus dialog box is still displayed, you can go back to the original word that was in the Look Up box (that is, the word that contained the insertion point when you activated the thesaurus). Simply click the Original button; the original word will again become the current word.

You can also click the Cancel button to remove the thesaurus and return to the editing window without performing a replacement.

SUMMARY

- You can use the Word spelling checker to verify the spelling of the words in your document.

- If the document contains an *insertion point*, the Spelling command will check the spelling of all words from the position of the insertion point to the end of the document. If the document contains a *selection* of one or more words, the Spelling command will check all words within the selection.

- To activate the Spelling command, choose the Utilities/ Spelling menu command. Word will display the Check Spelling dialog box.

- When the Check Spelling dialog box is displayed, you can check the spelling of a single word by entering it into the Word dialog box.

- Before checking the spelling of words in your document, you can click the Options >> button to choose one or more options for the spelling command.

- To begin checking the spelling of words in your document, click the Start button.

- Each time the spelling checker encounters an unrecognized word, it displays the Spelling dialog box.

- Click the Ignore button in the Spelling dialog box to leave the word unchanged in your document and to continue the spelling check.

- To correct the word, type an alternative spelling into the Change To box in the Spelling dialog box, and then click the Change button.

- To view alternative spellings, click the Suggest button in the Spelling dialog box. If you want to replace the word in your document with one of the suggested spellings, highlight the desired spelling and click the Change button.

- Click the Add button in the Spelling dialog box to leave the word unchanged in your document, and to add it to a supplemental dictionary so that it will not be flagged in the future.

- Rather than choosing the Utilities/Spelling menu command, you can simply press the F7 key to immediately check the spelling of the word containing the insertion point, or to check the spelling of the current selection. When you press F7, Word does not display the Check Spelling dialog box; however, it exhibits the Spelling dialog box whenever it encounters an unfamiliar word.

- You can use the Word thesaurus to obtain a definition and list of synonyms for a specified word.

- To activate the thesaurus, first place the insertion point within, immediately before, or immediately following the desired word. Then choose the Utilities/Thesaurus menu command or press the Shift-F7 keystroke. Word will display the Thesaurus dialog box.

- Once the Thesaurus dialog box has been displayed, you should first select the most appropriate meaning for the word from the Definitions list box. When you select a meaning, a corresponding list of synonyms immediately appears in the Synonyms box.

- To replace the word in your document, select the desired replacement in the Synonym box and then click the Replace button.

- While the Thesaurus dialog box is still open, you can obtain a list of synonyms for a different word by typing the word into the Look Up box, or by selecting the word in the Synonym box, and then clicking the Synonym button.

8

USING WORD TABLES

A WORD *TABLE* IS A PROGRAM FEATURE THAT ALLOWS
you to arrange text in an array of rows and columns. The Table feature is quite flexible, and makes it easy to organize tabular data. In
this chapter, you will learn how to create tables, how to edit tables,
and how to format tables. You will also learn how to perform calculations on numeric data contained in tables or elsewhere in a document. Finally, you will learn how to sort document text, either inside
or outside of a table.

CREATING A TABLE

If the Table feature were not available, you would have to arrange
tabular data using the Tab key, together with appropriate paragraph
formatting. Figure 8.1 illustrates two simple tabulations of text

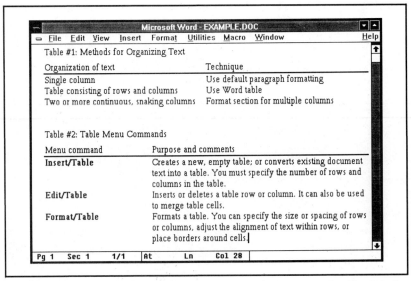

Figure 8.1: Simple tables created by using tab characters and adjusting the paragraph indents

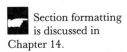
The Tab key is discussed in Chapters 3 and 15. Chapter 15 explains how to set indents and other paragraph formatting features.

Section formatting is discussed in Chapter 14.

within a Word document. The first was created simply by using tab characters; the second was generated by using tab characters and setting the paragraph indents. The table in Figure 8.2 would be quite difficult to create with these methods. As you will see, however, it can easily be produced using the Table feature.

When you create a table in Word, you begin with a framework, which is a collection of separate *cells*, or boxes, arranged in rows and columns. You then insert text or graphics into each cell.

Alternatively, you can arrange text in two or more continuous snaking columns, like those appearing in a newspaper. Snaking columns are created using section formatting commands rather than the Table feature.

To create a new empty table, first place the insertion point at the position in your document where you would like the table, and then choose the Insert/Table menu command. Word will display the dialog box illustrated in Figure 8.3.

Enter the number of columns (which run horizontally) you want into the Number of Columns field, and the number of rows (which run vertically) into the Number of Rows field.

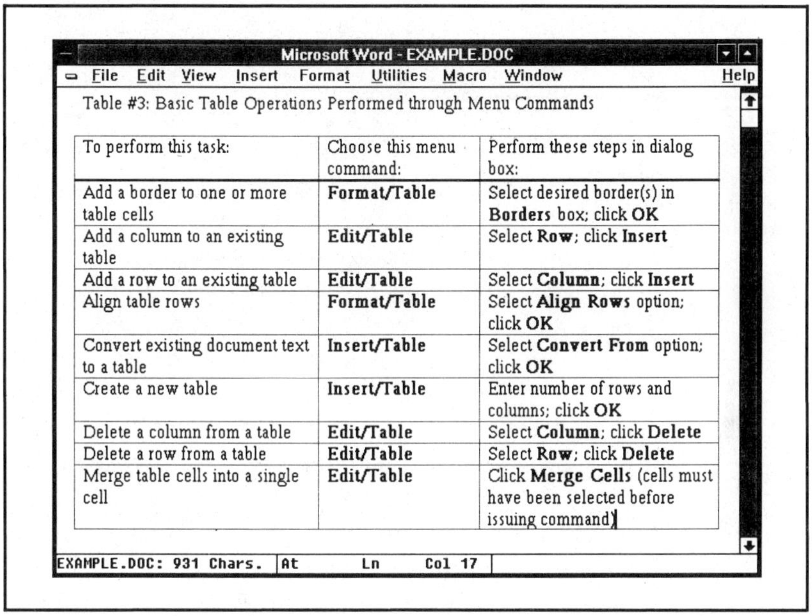

Table #3: Basic Table Operations Performed through Menu Commands

To perform this task:	Choose this menu command:	Perform these steps in dialog box:
Add a border to one or more table cells	**Format/Table**	Select desired border(s) in **Borders** box; click **OK**
Add a column to an existing table	**Edit/Table**	Select **Row**; click **Insert**
Add a row to an existing table	**Edit/Table**	Select **Column**; click **Insert**
Align table rows	**Format/Table**	Select **Align Rows** option; click **OK**
Convert existing document text to a table	**Insert/Table**	Select **Convert From** option; click **OK**
Create a new table	**Insert/Table**	Enter number of rows and columns; click **OK**
Delete a column from a table	**Edit/Table**	Select **Column**; click **Delete**
Delete a row from a table	**Edit/Table**	Select **Row**; click **Delete**
Merge table cells into a single cell	**Edit/Table**	Click **Merge Cells** (cells must have been selected before issuing command)

Figure 8.2: A complex table created with the Word Table feature

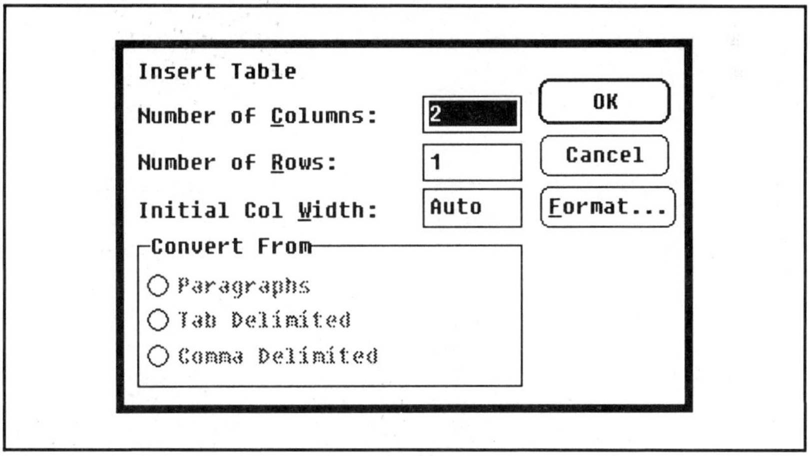

Figure 8.3: The Insert Table dialog box

Word initially suggests 2 columns and 1 row. It is important to enter the actual number of columns you want. However, if you are not sure how many rows you will need, you can simply accept the suggested value of 1. As you will see, it is easy to add new rows as you enter text into the table. Also, you can later adjust the number of rows or columns in a table you have already created, using the Edit/ Table menu command. This command is discussed in the section "Editing a Table."

When creating a table, you can also specify the width of each column by typing a measurement into the Initial Col Width field. The default value that Word suggests is Auto. The Auto value causes Word to automatically calculate the column width by evenly dividing the total distance between the left and right page margins. For example, if the total width of the text between the margins is 6 inches, and if you insert a table with three columns, the width of each column will be 2 inches. (The actual usable width is slightly less, since Word normally leaves space between table columns. You will see how to adjust the amount of space between columns in the section "Formatting a Table.")

Alternatively, you can enter a numeric column width value. For example, if you enter 1 inch into the Initial Col Width field, and if you specify 2 columns, the table will have a total width of 2 inches, and each of the columns will be 1 inch wide. Thus, when you first create a new table, the columns in the table are always equally wide. In the section "Using the Table Formatting Options," you will see how to adjust the width of each column individually, so that you can give the columns different widths.

To insert the table and return to the editing window, click the OK button. Alternatively, you can click the Format button; this button causes Word to close the Insert Table dialog box and open the Format Table dialog box before displaying the table and returning you to the editing window. Clicking this button allows you to format the table immediately. You will see how to use the Format Table dialog box in the section "Using the Table Formatting Options."

When you return to the editing window, the insertion point will be within the first cell of the new table; in the next exercise, you will begin entering text. So that you can see the boundaries of the table cells, Word displays *grid lines* around each cell. To see these lines, however, you must have selected the Table Grid Lines option within the Preferences dialog box. The Preferences dialog box is displayed through the View/Preferences menu command.

See Appendix B for a discussion on entering measurements into Word dialog boxes.

Page margins are discussed in Chapters 13 and 15.

Displaying grid lines makes it easier to work with a table. These lines are shown on the screen, but do *not* appear on printed copies of the document.

ENTERING TEXT INTO A TABLE

As you saw, when you insert a new table into your document, the insertion point is initially placed at the beginning of the *first* cell (that is, the cell in the upper left corner of the table). You can place the insertion point within any cell in the table by clicking anywhere within the boundaries of the cell. You can also quickly move the insertion point from cell to cell in an empty table by using the arrow keys. In the next section, you will see several other keystrokes for efficiently moving through a table that contains text.

Once the insertion point is within the desired cell, you can enter text as if you were creating a normal paragraph. As usual, simply continue typing without pressing the ◄┘ key at the end of each line; Word will automatically insert line breaks as needed.

Notice that as you type, all text is kept within the boundaries of the cell. If additional space is needed to accommodate the text, Word automatically increases the *height* of the cells in the current row; it does *not* expand the *width* of the cell. The cells in a given row always have the same height. As illustrated in Figure 8.2, Word normally makes a row just high enough to accommodate the tallest cell in the row. However, as you will see in the "Using the Table Formatting Options" section, you can specify a minimum row height.

NAVIGATING THROUGH A TABLE

You can place the insertion point at any character position within a table simply by clicking the desired position.

You can move through a table in any direction—character-by-character—by using the arrow keys. When the insertion point reaches the last character in a cell, it moves to the next cell; when it reaches the boundary of the table, it moves outside of the table.

You can also move from cell to cell by pressing the Tab or Shift-Tab keystroke. Wherever the insertion point is within a cell, pressing the Tab key moves it to the *next* cell. Specifically, it moves the insertion point to the cell to the immediate right until reaching the end of the row; it then moves it to the leftmost cell in the row below. If the next cell contains text, pressing the Tab key will select this text. In a similar manner, the Shift-Tab key moves the insertion point to the *previous* cell, selecting any text it contains.

You can also insert a graphic into a table cell. Methods for inserting graphics are discussed in Chapter 9. You cannot, however, insert another table into a table (that is, tables cannot be nested).

Although the cells in a given row always have the same height, they can be assigned varying widths. See the "Using the Table Formatting Options" section.

The maximum height for a single cell is one document page.

If you press the Tab key when the insertion point (or selection) is in the *last* cell of the table (that is, the rightmost cell in the bottom row), Word *automatically inserts a new empty row* at the end of the table and places the insertion point in the first cell of this row. The new bottom row is given the same number of cells and the same cell widths as the row above it. To enter an actual tab character while you are in a table, you must press the Ctrl-Tab key combination.

Since it is so easy to add new rows to the end of a table, when you create a new table you might want to specify the full number of columns but only a single row. You can then simply add rows as they are needed.

Table 8.1 summarizes the keystrokes discussed in this section, as well as several other keystrokes for quickly moving the insertion point within a table.

Table 8.1: Keystrokes for Navigating through a Table

PRESS THIS KEY:	TO MOVE TO:
↑, ↓, ←, or →	Next character position
Tab	Next cell; if in last cell of table, adds a new row
Shift-Tab	Previous cell
Alt-Home	First cell in current row
Alt-End	Last cell in current row
Alt-PgUp	Top cell in current column
Alt-PgDn	Bottom cell in current column

PARAGRAPHS WITHIN A TABLE

The text within a single table cell consists of one or more complete paragraphs. If you make paragraph marks visible by selecting the Paragraph Marks option of the View/Preferences menu command, you will see a sun-shaped character, known as an *end-of-cell mark*, at the end of each cell of a table. This mark indicates both the end of a paragraph *and* the end of a cell. If you press ↵ while typing text into a single cell, Word will create a new paragraph *within the same cell.* Forexample, Figure 8.4 illustrates a table with paragraph marks enabled. The first two cells each consist of a single paragraph, with end-of-cell marks at the end of each one. The last cell, however, consists of two paragraphs, since the ◄─┘ key was pressed immediately following the word **Cells**.

As usual, pressing Shift-◄─┘ while typing text into a table cell inserts a line break at the position of the insertion point, without forming a new paragraph.

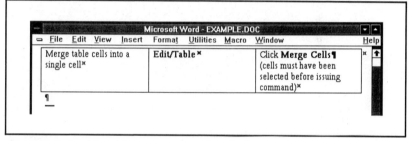

Figure 8.4: A table with paragraph and end-of-cell marks enabled

CONVERTING TEXT TO A TABLE

You also can select a block of existing document text and then convert this text to a table. Word will automatically create a table of the appropriate size and insert the text into the table cells.

When you convert text to a table, the block of text must contain the appropriate characters that will divide the text into smaller units, each of which is to be inserted into a separate table cell (unless the entire block is to be placed in a single cell!). You can divide the block of text using paragraph marks, tabs, or commas. Figure 8.5 illustrates three blocks of text ready to be converted to tables. The first block uses paragraph marks to delimit the text that is to go into each cell, the second uses tabs, and the third uses commas.

To convert a block of text to a table, first select the block, and then issue the Insert/Table menu command. When Word displays the Insert Table dialog box (which you used earlier), indicate how the block of text is divided by choosing the appropriate item in

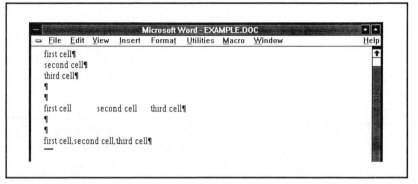

Figure 8.5: Blocks of text with characters for conversion to Word tables

the Convert From box:

Paragraphs
Tab Delimited
Comma Delimited

Once you have chosen one of these options, Word will suggest a number of rows and a number of columns, based upon the total number of cells required to contain the text, and upon the current arrangement of the text in the document. For example, if you had selected the first block of text in Figure 8.5, Word would recommend 1 column and 3 rows. If you had selected either of the second two blocks, Word would suggest 3 columns and 1 row. Figure 8.6 illustrates these three blocks after they have been converted to tables,

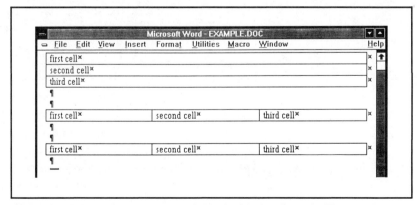

Figure 8.6: Word tables generated from the blocks of text in Figure 8.5

using the number of rows and columns recommended by Word.

Although you cannot change the total number of cells in the table, you can alter the way they are distributed among rows and columns (that is, you can change the number of rows and the number of columns provided that the *product* of these two values remains the same). For example, you could convert the first block in Figure 8.5 into a table with 3 columns and 1 row.

To remove the dialog box and generate the table, simply click the OK button.

CONVERTING A TABLE TO TEXT

You can also convert a table to normal text. When you perform this operation, Word removes the table, but preserves the text or graphics contained in the cells of the table. Word inserts this text or graphics into your document, separating the contents of each cell with a paragraph mark, a tab, or a comma (you specify which).

The first step is to select the table row or rows that you want to convert. You must select one or more entire rows. Next, issue the Insert/Table to Text menu command and choose one of the following three items within the dialog box that Word displays:

When you select one or more table rows, the Insert/Table to Text menu item replaces the Insert/Table item.

Paragraphs
Tab Delimited
Comma Delimited

If you choose Paragraphs, Word will insert the contents of each cell as a separate paragraph in your document. If you choose Tab Delimited, Word will separate the contents of each cell within a given row with a tab character, and will separate each row with a paragraph mark. If you choose Comma Delimited, Word will separate the contents of each cell with a comma, and each row with a paragraph mark. Thus, if you choose either tabs or commas as the delimiting character, the original row and column organization of the table will be maintained when it is converted to text.

When you are ready to perform the conversion, click the OK button. Once the table has been converted to text, you can restore the original table by issuing the Edit/Undo Table to Text command, or by pressing the Alt-Backspace keystroke, immediately after the conversion.

EDITING A TABLE

In this section, you will learn how to insert or delete cells within an existing table. You will also learn how to merge individual cells, and how to divide a table into two parts. Finally, you will learn how to delete text within one or more cells and how to copy or move text from one part of a table to another.

INSERTING OR DELETING CELLS

You already saw how to insert an entire row of cells at the end of a table by pressing the Tab key while the insertion point is in the last cell. This section shows you two other methods for inserting and deleting cells. The first uses the Edit/Table command, and the second requires you to select rows or columns. Let's look at both methods.

Using the Edit/Table Command

You can insert a row or column at any other position within a table by using the Edit/Table command. A new row is inserted _above_ the row containing the insertion point (or selection), and a new column is inserted to the _left_ of the column containing the insertion point (or selection). To insert a new column to the right of the table, position the insertion point just outside of the right table boundary. Keeping this pattern in mind, first place the insertion point within the appropriate row or column, and then choose the Edit/Table menu command. Word will display the Edit Table dialog box, which is illustrated in Figure 8.7.

If you are inserting a row, choose the Row option, and if you are inserting a column, choose the Column option. Then click the Insert button. A new empty row or column will be inserted. If you insert a row, the new row will have the same number of cells and the same cell widths as the row below it. If you insert a column, the new column will have the same number of cells and cell widths as the column to its left, if any (if there is no column to its left, then it will match the column to its right).

In a similar fashion, you can use the Edit/Table command to delete an entire row or column from a table. First, place the insertion point (or selection) within the row or column you want to delete.

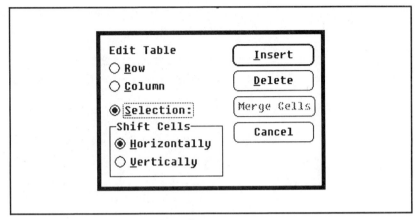

Figure 8.7: The Edit Table dialog box

Then choose the Edit/Table command, select the Row or Column option, and click the Delete button. When you delete a row, the remaining rows below move up to fill in the gap, and when you delete a column, the remaining columns to the right move to the left to fill the gap.

Deleting a row or column with the Edit/Table command removes all of the cells in the row or column, together with all of the text contained in the cells. In contrast, selecting a row or column and pressing the Del key removes all of text from the cells, but leaves the empty cells in the table.

Selecting within a Table

In addition to inserting or deleting entire rows or columns, you can also insert or delete arbitrary blocks consisting of one or more cells by selecting the cells.

To select within a table, you can use either the keyboard or the mouse. To select using the keyboard, you select one or more characters or graphics within a cell, or one or more entire cells, using the standard keyboard selection methods presented in Chapter 5 (in the section "Selecting with the Keyboard"). You can also use these methods to create a selection that includes both a table and text outside of the table.

Specifically, as explained in Chapter 5, you can use either the Shift key in conjunction with an arrow key, or press F8 and then use an

arrow key. When selecting within a table, however, there are several
unique features:

- While pressing Shift, or after pressing F8, you can use any of
  the Alt-key combinations listed in Table 8.1 to rapidly extend
  the selection.

- You can select the *entire table* by pressing the Alt-5 key combination (5 on the numeric keypad).

- You can extend the selection one character at a time only
  while the selection remains within a single cell; as soon as the
  selection is extended into a neighboring cell, each press of a
  direction key selects both entire cells.

- There is no column selection mode while in a table; pressing
  the Ctrl-Shift-F8 key combination has the same effect as
  pressing F8.

To select using the mouse, you select text or graphics within a table
using the mouse techniques described in Chapter 5, in the section
"Selecting with the Mouse." When using the mouse to select within
a table, there are several unique characteristics:

- You can extend the selection one character at a time only
  while the selection remains within a single cell; as soon as the
  selection is dragged into an adjoining cell, both entire cells
  are selected.

- There is no column selection mode within a table (the
  column selection mode is normally activated by pressing
  the right mouse button).

- Each cell has its own selection bar in the leftmost portion of
  the cell. In this area, the mouse pointer becomes an arrow
  pointing up and to the right.

Add a border to one or more
table cells

- To select an entire cell, you can click with the left mouse button in the cell's selection bar.

- To select an entire row, you can double-click with the left mouse button in *any* selection bar within the row.

- Each column has a selection area at the top of the column. In this area, the mouse pointer becomes a downward-pointing arrow.

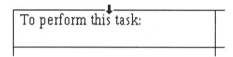

- To select an entire column, click with the left mouse button in the column selection area above the desired column. You can also select an entire column by clicking with the *right* mouse button anywhere within the column.

You also need to select portions of a table before merging table cells, copying or moving text within a table, or applying formatting commands.

To insert a block of cells, you first indicate the shape of the block you want to insert by selecting a block of existing cells within the table, as shown in Figure 8.8.

Once you have selected a group of cells to indicate the shape of the block you want to insert, issue the Edit/Table menu command and choose the Selection option. This option tells Word to match the current selection when inserting (or deleting) cells. Before clicking the Insert button, however, you must tell Word which way to move the existing table cells to make room for the inserted cells, by choosing either the Horizontally or Vertically option in the Shift Cells box. Word initially selects the Horizontally option if the horizontal dimension of the block is

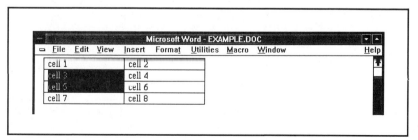

Figure 8.8: A table with a selected block of cells

less than the vertical dimension. It selects the Vertically option if the vertical dimension is less. Figure 8.9 illustrates the result of choosing the horizontal option when inserting cells into the table of Figure 8.8. Figure 8.10 shows the result of choosing the vertical option. Notice that when moving cells vertically, Word also inserts empty cells at the bottom of all other columns to make all columns the same height.

In a similar fashion, you can delete an arbitrary block of one or more table cells. First, select the block you want to remove (refer to Figure 8.8). Then, issue the Edit/Table menu command and choose the Selection option. Before clicking the Delete button, select either the Horizontally or the Vertically option to tell Word which way to shift the existing table cells to fill the gap left by the deletion. Figure 8.11 illustrates the effect of deleting the selection of cells in Figure 8.8 with the Horizontally option, and Figure 8.12 illustrates deleting with the Vertically option.

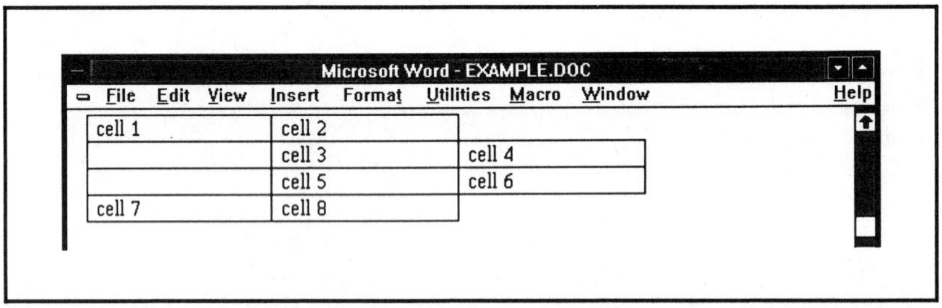

Figure 8.9: The result of inserting cells into the table of Figure 8.8 with the Horizontally option

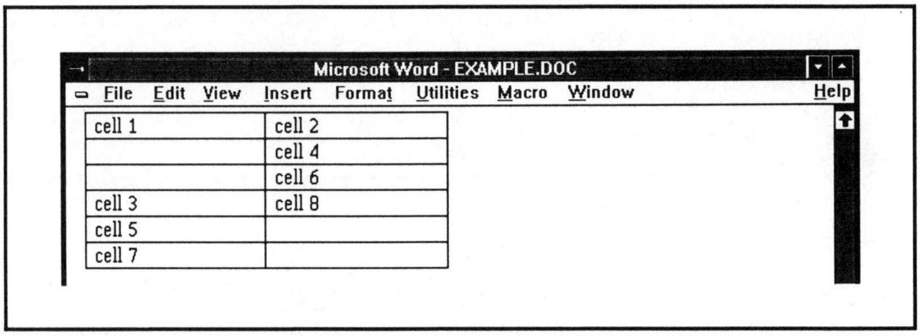

Figure 8.10: The result of inserting cells into the table of Figure 8.8 with the Vertically option

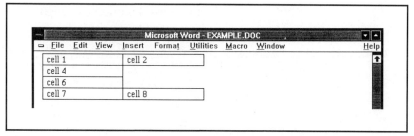

Figure 8.11: Deleting cells horizontally from the table of Figure 8.8

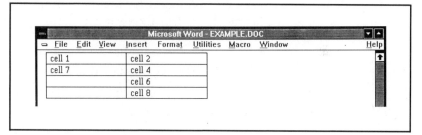

Figure 8.12: Deleting cells vertically from the table of Figure 8.8

MERGING CELLS

You cannot merge cells that are within the same column, since all cells within a given row must be the same height.

You can merge two or more adjacent cells within the same row to form a single cell. First, select the cells you want to combine. Then, issue the Edit/Table command and click the Merge Cells button.

For example, you might want to merge all of the cells within the first row of a table, so that you can place a centered title at the top of the table. The following steps would accomplish this task:

1. Place the mouse pointer within the selection bar of any cell in the first row, and double-click using the left mouse button. This step selects all cells within the first row.

2. Issue the Edit/Table command and click the Merge Cells button. The top row will become a single cell.

3. Place the insertion point at the upper left corner of the single top-row cell, and type the desired title.

4. To center the title, choose the Format/Paragraph command, select the Center option within the Alignment box, and click the OK button.

5. Delete any unnecessary paragraphs within the cell containing the title. (When Word merges cells, it inserts into the combined cell a separate paragraph for each cell that was merged.)

After you have merged a group of cells, you can later split the single resulting cell back into the same number of cells that were used to create it. Use the following steps to split a combined cell into its constituent cells:

1. Select the combined cell.

2. Issue the Edit/Table command.

3. Click the Split Cells button within the dialog box that Word displays. The combined cell will be split into its component cells.

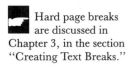

When you select a cell that was previously combined, Word replaces the Merge Cells button with the Split Cells button. Word remembers the number of cells that were merged to create the combined cell.

DIVIDING TABLES

You can split a table in order to insert standard text between any rows by placing the insertion point (or selection) within a row and pressing the Ctrl-Shift-⏎ key combination. If the insertion point is within the top row, this keystroke inserts a normal paragraph above the table. If, however, the insertion point is within any other row, this keystroke splits the table into two separate tables, with an empty normal paragraph between them. The top table in Figure 8.13 was split by placing the insertion point within cell 5 or cell 6 of this table, and pressing the Ctrl-Shift-⏎ key combination. The bottom table in the figure shows the result. In these figures, all special characters have been made visible.

Hard page breaks are discussed in Chapter 3, in the section "Creating Text Breaks."

You can also split a table by inserting a hard page break within the table. If you press the Ctrl-⏎ keystroke, Word will insert a hard page break immediately above the row containing the insertion point (or selection), splitting the table into two parts with a page break between them.

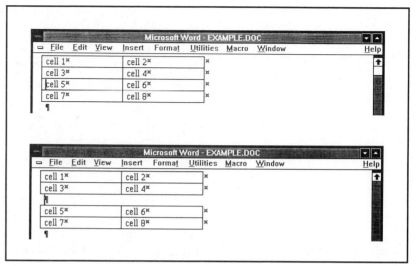

Figure 8.13: A table before and after splitting

DELETING, MOVING, AND COPYING TEXT WITHIN A TABLE

You can delete, copy, or move a block of text or graphics that is entirely *within* a cell of a table using the standard techniques explained in Chapter 5, in the section "Deleting, Moving, and Copying."

If you select one or more entire table cells and press the Del key, Word will delete the text or graphics contained within the cells, but will leave the empty cells within the table. (In contrast, when deleting cells using the Edit/Table command, the cells are completely removed from the table.) If, however, the table selection includes one or more characters outside of the table, pressing Del will remove both the selected cells and their contents.

You can also use many of the standard techniques given in Chapter 5 to move or copy a block consisting of one or more entire table cells. However, when moving or copying such a block, the following special rules apply:

- You must move or copy using the Clipboard. If you attempt to use one of the non-Clipboard techniques to move or copy a block that includes one or more entire cells, Word will display the message **Not a valid selection**.

- If you select one or more entire cells and issue the Cut command, all text and graphics will be removed from the cells, but the empty cells will remain in the table. (In contrast, when you delete cells using the Edit/Table menu command, the cells are completely removed from the table.)

- If the selection encompasses all or part of a table *and* one or more characters outside of the table, the Cut command will completely remove the selected cells and their contents. In this case, you cannot paste the Clipboard contents into a table.

- If you paste the contents of one or more entire cells into a location within a table, the new data *overwrites* the existing contents of the cells at this location. If there are not enough cells to contain the data that is being pasted, Word will add new cells as necessary. For example, if the Clipboard contains the contents of 5 cells, pasting this data will overwrite the contents of 5 table cells starting from the position of the insertion point (or the beginning of the selection). To insert new empty cells into a table, you should use the Edit/Table command, explained previously in the chapter.

- If you paste the contents of one or more entire cells into a document outside of a table, Word will create a new table to contain the pasted cell contents.

> When the Clipboard contains the contents of one or more cells, the Edit/Paste menu command is replaced with the Edit/Paste Cells command.

When you cut or copy a block consisting of one or more entire cells, and then paste these cells into another location (either inside or outside of a table), the block maintains its original shape (that is, a column of cells remains a column, a rectangular block remains a rectangular block, and so on). You can use this feature, for example, to move the contents of a column of cells within a table, as follows:

1. Select the column you want to move using any of the methods described in the section "Selecting within a Table."

2. Transfer the cell contents to the Clipboard by choosing the Edit/Cut command or by pressing Shift-Del. The cell contents will be removed from the table, but the column of empty cells will remain.

3. Place the insertion point at the top of the column to which you want to move the Clipboard contents, and issue the Edit/ Paste command, or press Shift-Ins. The contents of the cells in the Clipboard will now *replace* the current contents of the cells in the column beneath the insertion point.

USING THE TABLE FORMATTING OPTIONS

You can format any of the characters or paragraphs within a Word table using the standard formatting commands discussed in Chapters 15 and 16. Simply select text or graphics within one or more table cells, and apply the appropriate formatting command. In this section, you'll look at the special Word formatting options that can be applied specifically to tables. To implement one or more of these options, choose the Format/Table menu command. You can also open the Format Table dialog box directly from the Insert Table dialog box, described previously in the chapter, by clicking the Format button. Word will display the dialog box shown in Figure 8.14.

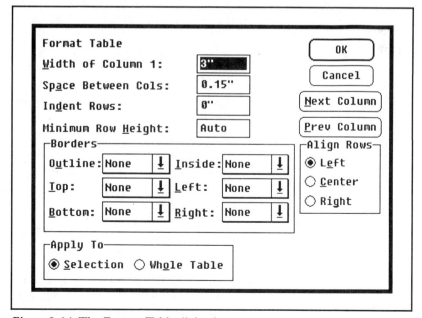

Figure 8.14: The Format Table dialog box

If you choose the Whole Table option in the Apply To area, whatever features you choose in the dialog box will be applied to the entire table. If, however, you choose the Selection option, your choices will be applied to the selected cell or cells, or to the cell containing the insertion point. Note, however, that certain features always affect the entire row or the entire column containing the selection or insertion point.

You can specify the following features through the Format Table dialog box:

- The column width

- The space between columns

- The amount the rows are indented

- The minimum row height

- The alignment of rows

- Borders placed around cells

Setting the Column Width

See Appendix B for information on specifying various units of measurement when entering values into dialog boxes.

You can adjust the width of one or more cells in the table by entering a value into the Width of Column field at the top of the Format Table dialog box (see Figure 8.14).

As you saw, you can specify an initial column width when creating a table through the Insert/Table command; this width applies uniformly to all cells in the table. The Format Table dialog box, however, allows you to specify the width of individual cells or groups of cells.

If you choose the Whole Table option in the Apply To box, the specified width will apply to all cells in the table. If, however, you choose the Selection option, the specified width will apply only to the selected cell or cells, or to the cell containing the insertion point. If you selected one or more cells in a particular column, you can assign the specified column width to these cells, and then move the selection to the next or previous column *without removing the dialog box*. After you have entered the value for the current column, simply click the Next Column button to apply the value and then move the selection to the column to the right, or click the Prev Column button to apply the value and then move the selection to the column to the left. By using the Next Column and Prev Column buttons you can move through a table, assigning different column widths to the selected cells in each column.

As you will discover in Chapter 15, you can use also use the Word *ruler* to rapidly adjust the width of one or more cells in a table. The ruler is a collection of icons that you can optionally display and use to apply paragraph formatting commands.

Setting the Column Spacing

You can adjust the amount of horizontal space Word leaves between text in adjacent table cells by entering a value into the Space Between Cols field. If you do not enter a value, Word will use the default spacing of 0.15 inches.

Sp<u>a</u>ce Between Cols: | 0.15" |

Unlike setting the column *width* as described in the previous section, adjusting the column *spacing* does not change the width of the cells or the overall width of the table as indicated by the gridlines. The column spacing does, however, affect the amount of space Word maintains between the text in a cell and the left and right edges of that cell.

If you choose the Whole Table option, the specified column spacing is assigned to all cells in the table. If you choose the Selection option, the spacing is applied to all cells within any row included in the current selection, or to all cells in the row containing the insertion point.

Setting the Row Indent

You can indent one or more rows in a table by entering the amount of the indent into the Indent Rows field (the default value is 0).

In<u>d</u>ent Rows: | 0" |

The indent is the amount of space between the left margin of the page and the beginning of the first cell in a row. By default, the indent is 0, meaning that the first cell is aligned evenly with the left margin. If you assign a positive value, the cells are moved right, toward the center of the page. If you assign a negative value, the cells are moved left, out into the margin area. Figure 8.15 illustrates positive and negative row indents.

If you choose the Whole Table option, the specified indent affects all rows in the table. If you choose the Selection option, the indent affects the row or rows included in the current selection, or the row containing the insertion point.

As explained in Chapter 15, you can also use the Word ruler to set the indent of one or more rows in a table.

Setting the Minimum Row Height

You can adjust the height of all cells in one or more rows by entering a value into the Minimum Row Height field.

```
Minimum Row Height:     Auto
```

All cells in a given row have the same height.

The default value is Auto, which makes the row just high enough to accommodate the text contained in the tallest cell in that row. If you specify a numeric value, Word will make the row at least as high as this value. However, if the value you enter is too small to contain the text, Word will automatically increase the height to accommodate the text.

If you choose the Whole Table option, the height you specify will be assigned to all cells in the table. If you choose the Selection option,

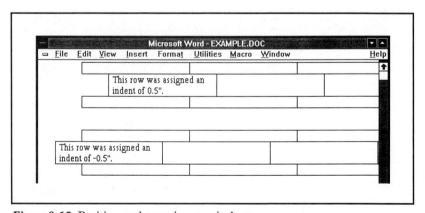

Figure 8.15: Positive and negative row indents

the height will be assigned to all cells in the row or rows included in the current selection, or to the row containing the insertion point.

Setting the Row Alignment

Row alignment affects the horizontal position of a table row with respect to the page margins. You can pick one of three alignment styles from the Align Rows area of the Format Table dialog box.

The Left option is selected by default; it aligns the left edge of the row with the left page margin. The Right option aligns the right edge of the row with the right margin, and the Center option centers the row between the left and right margins.

Remember that when you create a table through the Insert/Table command, it normally fills the entire space between the left and right margins. In this case, the row alignment style will have almost no effect. However, if you create a table with a column width other than Auto, or if you later change the width of one or more columns, you may want to specify the row alignment.

Setting the alignment through the Align Rows field shifts the horizontal position of the *entire row*. In contrast, you can set the alignment of paragraphs within specific cells by using the ruler or the Format/Paragraph command, as discussed in Chapter 15.

Choosing the Whole Table option will apply the specified alignment to all rows in the table. Choosing the Selection option will apply the alignment to the row or rows included in the current selection, or the row containing the insertion point.

Placing Borders around Cells

The options within the Borders box of the Format Table dialog box permit you to place borders around one or more cells within a table. Do not confuse table borders with table gridlines. Gridlines are optionally displayed on the screen to mark the edges of the cells so that it is easier to work with the table; they do not appear on the printed copy of the document. Borders, however, are lines that appear both on the screen and on the printed copy. Borders are placed directly on top of the edges marked by gridlines.

The options for borders are flexible. You can choose from a variety of line styles, and you can place borders on *any combination* of the cell edges that are marked with gridlines.

The Border options allow you to place borders at various positions within the table. By default, all of these options have the value None, which means that *no* borders are initially assigned to the table. To choose a border for a particular position, open the pull-down list box and select a line style.

The effect of the Border options depends upon whether you have selected a single cell (or the insertion point is within a cell), or you have selected a group of two or more cells. When specifying borders, choosing the Whole Table option within the Apply To box has the same effect as selecting the entire table and then choosing the Selection option.

You can place a border with the desired line style on any or all of the four sides of a single cell. First, you select the side you want the border on by choosing the Top, Bottom, Left, or Right box. To place a border on all four edges of the cell, first select the Outline box. (When you have selected a single cell, the Inside option has no effect.) You then see the available line styles. If you choose Top, Bottom, Left, or Right, you can choose one of the following line styles from any of these boxes:

Single
Thick
Double

When choosing the Outline box, you can also select the Shadow style, which assigns the Single style to the top and left edges, and the Thick style to the right and bottom edges. The various line styles are illustrated in Figure 8.16.

If you select two or more cells prior to opening the Format Table dialog box (or if you choose the Whole Table option), specifying a

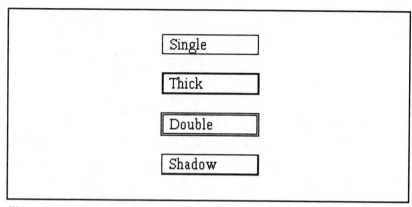

Figure 8.16: Border line styles

line style in the Outline, Top, Bottom, Left, or Right box places a border on one or more of the *outside edges* of the selection.

The table at the top in Figure 8.17 illustrates the effect of selecting the entire table, and then choosing the Thick line option from the Outline box; the inner lines seen in this figure are gridlines, not borders. If you choose a line style from the Inside box, Word will place a border on all of the inner edges within the selection. The second table

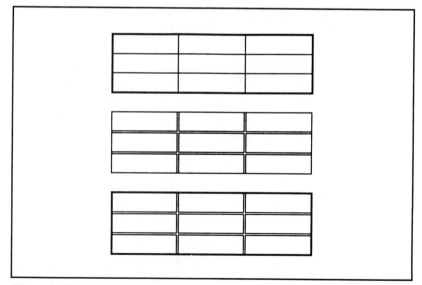

Figure 8.17: Borders assigned after selecting an entire table

in Figure 8.17 shows the effect of choosing the Double line style from the Inside box. The bottom table in this figure shows the result of choosing the Thick style from the Outline box and the Double style from the Inside box.

CALCULATING AND SORTING IN A TABLE

Using Word, you can perform calculations on numeric data contained within a document. You can also sort text within a specified document area. Calculating and sorting can be performed on data either within tables, or in any other part of a document. These operations are included in this chapter, however, because they are especially useful when working with tables.

CALCULATING

You can perform a calculation on numeric data within a Word document either by selecting the data and issuing the Calculate command, or by using a Word field.

Calculating with a Selection

To perform a calculation, first enter the appropriate numbers and *mathematical operators* (such as + , – , and so on) into your document. Then, select this data and issue the Calculate command. Word will evaluate the numbers and operators within the selection, starting from the beginning of the selection and proceeding character-by-character to the end of the selection. Characters that are neither numbers nor operators are simply ignored. The result of the calculation is placed in the Clipboard and displayed in the status bar; it can then be pasted into the desired document location.

Table 8.2 lists the mathematical operators that are recognized by the Calculate command.

In general, you should place an operator between every two numbers. For example, the expression

2 * 3

Table 8.2: Operators You Can Use in a Word Calculation

OPERATOR:	DESCRIPTION:
^	Exponentiation (raising a number to a power)
%	Percentage
*	Multiplication
/	Division
+ (or no operator)	Addition
–	Subtraction

would cause Word to multiple 2 times 3, and the expression

$$2 \char`\^ 3$$

would raise 2 to the third power (the result would be 8). There are two exceptions to this rule:

- If there is no operator in front of a number, Word will *add* the number to the result. For example, the expression

    53

    would cause Word to add 5 and 3.
- You should place the percentage operator (%) *after* a number. For example, the expression

    8 * 50%

    causes Word to multiply 8 by 50 percent; the result would be 4.

Although the Calculate command normally ignores characters that are neither numbers nor operators, you should not include an exclamation mark in your expression. It may cause the calculation to fail (Word will display the **Syntax Error** message in the status bar).

When you combine more than one operator in a single expression, you may have to specify the order in which the operations are to be

performed. For example, you might think that Word would evaluate
the expression

3 + 5 / 2

by adding 5 to 3 and then dividing the result by 2, arriving at a final
result of 4. Word, however, always performs division *before* addition.
Therefore, it would first divide 5 by 2, and then add the result to 3,
obtaining a final value of 5.5. To force Word to perform the addition
first, you can use parentheses as follows:

(3 + 5) / 2

In this case, Word treats the **3 + 5** as a single unit to be evaluated
first, and then divided by 2 (the final result would be 4).

The operators in Table 8.2 are listed in the order in which Word
performs the corresponding operations. Specifically, Word first performs any exponentiation (raising a number to a power) or percentage (that is, dividing the number preceding the % by 100). It then
performs any multiplication or division (moving from left to right).
Finally, it performs any addition or subtraction (also moving from
left to right).

You can change the normal order of precedence by grouping the
appropriate numbers and operators with parentheses, as shown in
the preceding example. Placing parentheses around a single number,
however, causes Word to treat the number as negative. For example,
the expression

5 + (3)

would yield the result 2. Similarly, Word displays a negative result in
the status bar by enclosing the number in parentheses.

Also, if you place a dollar sign ($) in front of any number in the
selection, Word will format the final result as a monetary amount.

Once you've entered the numbers and operators into your document, you should select them using either the normal or column selection mode. Extraneous nonnumeric characters are simply ignored. The
selected characters can be inside or outside of a Word table.

Next, issue the Utilities/Calculate menu command. Word will
place the result of the calculation in the Clipboard, and will also display it within the status bar. If desired, you can then paste the result

Selection methods
are discussed in
Chapter 5.

into any document location by positioning the insertion point and issuing the Edit/Paste menu command or pressing Shift-Ins.

Figure 8.18 illustrates a simple Word table. To obtain the total in the last row, the right column was selected, the Calculate command was issued, and the result was pasted into the bottom right cell.

Calculating with a Field

As you saw in Chapter 3, a field is a special instruction to the Word program that is embedded in your document. Word provides many different types of fields. You can use the *expression* field to perform a calculation within your document. The following simplified steps illustrate how to use the expression field to perform a calculation. (For complete information on how to use this field, see the "Fields" topic in the *Microsoft Word for Windows Technical Reference*.)

1. Place the insertion point where you would like to insert the result of the calculation.

2. Issue the Insert Field command by pressing the Ctrl-F9 keystroke. Word will insert the following special brace characters

   {}

   and will place the insertion point between them.

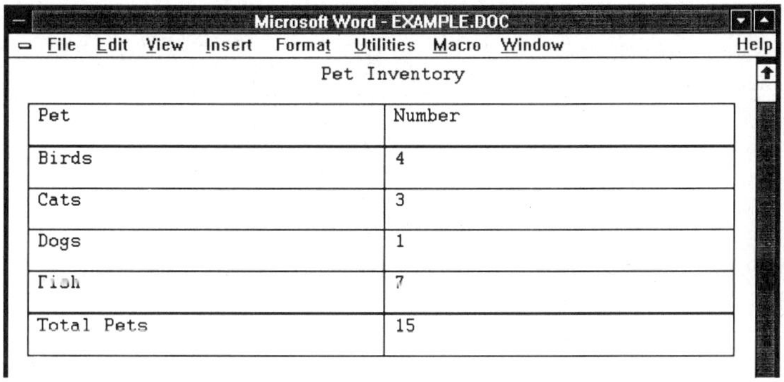

Pet	Number
Birds	4
Cats	3
Dogs	1
Fish	7
Total Pets	15

Pet Inventory

Figure 8.18: Using the Calculate command in a Word table

3. Now type

   = *expression*

   inside the brace characters, where *expression* consists of a valid combination of numbers and operators conforming to the rules outlined in the previous section.

The following is an example:

   { = \$231.79 * 6.25%}

> If you have included fields in your document, you should choose the Update Fields option when you make a printed copy (using the File/Print command), so that the values printed are as up-to-date as possible.

4. While the insertion point is still between the brace characters, press the F9 key to update the field. Word will instantly replace the brace characters and the expression they contain with the *results* of the expression.

The example field just given would be replaced with the following:

   \$14.4869

To see the results of updating a field, the Field Codes option on the View menu must *not* be selected. If you need to change the contents of a field after it has been first updated, you can temporarily enable the View/Field Codes option.

In addition to the operators recognized by the Calculate command (described in the previous section), you can use the following elements in an expression field:

> Bookmarks are described in Chapter 4, in the section "Go to a Bookmark."

- Bookmark names. The bookmark must have been assigned to a block of text within the document that contains a number or numeric expression conforming to the rules given in the previous section.

- References to table cells. You can specify a row and column in the current table by the expression

   [R*m*C*n*]

   where *m* is the number of the row and *n* is the number of the column. You can express a *range* of cells as follows:

   [R*a*C*x*:R*b*C*y*]

See the *Microsoft Word for Windows Technical Reference* for a description of all of the operators and functions that you can use in an expression field.

where *a* and *b* are the starting and ending rows, and *x* and *y* are the starting and ending columns. References to cells can be used for functions, such as the SUM function.

- A wide variety of other operators and functions. For example, the SUM operator adds the values that are specified.

As an example, consider the table illustrated in Figure 8.18. Rather than selecting the right column and issuing the Calculate command, you could include the following expression in the lower right cell:

{ = SUM([r2C2:r5C2])}

Remember that you do *not* type the brace characters. Rather, they are inserted by Word when you press the Ctrl-F9 key combination. When you update this field (by pressing F9), the field will be replaced by its result, 15. The advantage of using a field rather than the Calculate command is that if you change the numbers in any of the cells, or if you insert new cells, the sum in the bottom row will reflect the change whenever you update the field (when you print, you should update all the fields in the document by choosing the Update Fields printing option).

SORTING

Using the Word Sort command, you can sort groups of paragraphs, rows in a table, or the contents of a single column in the document. When performing a sort, you can also choose among several options that affect the *way* the items are sorted; these options are as follows:

- The *type* of sort key used to sort the items (alphanumeric, numeric, or date).
- Sensitivity to *case* when sorting.
- The position of the sort key (that is, you can sort using a specific *field*).
- The sorting *order* (ascending or descending).

Specifying the Items to Sort

Before issuing the Sort command, you must select the collection of items you want Word to sort. Each of these items is known as a *sort record*. The following are the different types of sort records you can select:

- Entire paragraphs.

- Entire rows in a table.

- The lines of text, or rows of a table, within a single column.

When performing a sort, Word rearranges the relative positions of the sort records. The sort records are treated as single units; Word does not perform any sorting within them.

To sort a group of entire paragraphs (that is, to use paragraphs as the sort records), perform the following steps:

If you do not make a selection prior to issuing the Sort command, Word automatically selects the entire document, and sorts the document paragraphs.

1. Select the paragraphs you want to sort.

2. Issue the Utilities/Sort menu command. Word will display the dialog box illustrated in Figure 8.19.

3. Choose the desired sort options, which are described in the following sections. Make sure, however, that you have not selected the Sort Column Only option (this option is not available unless you have made a column selection).

4. Click the OK button. Word will sort the selected paragraphs.

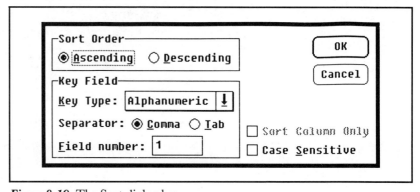

Figure 8.19: The Sort dialog box

You can undo a sort by issuing the Edit/ Undo command *immediately after the sort operation.*

.If you are in outline view (described in Chapter 24), and if your selection *begins* with a heading, Word uses entire headings as the sort records. That is, rather than rearranging individual paragraphs, it rearranges entire headings. Each heading is treated as a unit, and is moved with all of its subheadings and subtext. Furthermore, Word sorts only a single level of heading; specifically, it sorts only the heading level that is at the beginning of the selection. If it encounters a higher-level heading later in the selection, it stops the sort at this point, without including the higher level.

To sort rows in a Word table, simply select one or more *entire rows*, and then follow steps 2 through 4 described above.

As you will see in subsequent sections, by selecting only one or more columns of the desired rows, you can confine the sort to selected columns, or you can specify an alternative sort key.

You can sort a single column of items, either outside or inside of a Word table. When you perform a column sort, only the text within the selected column is rearranged; text outside of the selection is left unaltered. You cannot sort a column in outline document view.

To select a column, either press Ctrl-Shift-F8 and extend the selection with the arrow keys, or press the right mouse button and drag the highlight over the desired text. See Chapter 5 for details.

To sort a column outside of a table, select the desired text using a column selection mode. When you open the Sort dialog box, you must choose the Sort Column Only option. When sorting within a column, each *line* is treated as a separate sort record, even if the lines belong to the same paragraph. Figure 8.20 illustrates a column of text before and after sorting.

You can also use column sorting to sort complete lines belonging to one or more paragraphs. Simply select *entire rows* belonging to one or more paragraphs using a column selection mode, and choose the Sort Column Only option in the Sort dialog box.

The *User's Reference* erroneously states that you must turn off the Sort Column Only option to sort the lines within a paragraph. Actually, this option must be enabled.

To sort one or more columns within a Word table, select the desired column or columns and choose the Sort Column Only option in the Sort dialog box. The sort will be confined to the selected column or columns. The sort record will consist of the cell or cells within each row of the selected column. (That is, the cells will be rearranged as blocks; no sorting will be performed inside of the cells.)

Sorting Key Types

When performing a sort, you can specify the type of data that is being sorted. Specifically, you can specify the type of data contained

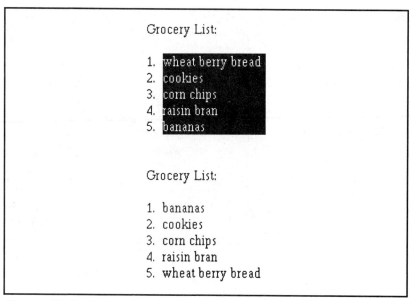

Figure 8.20: Sorting a column of text

in the *sort key*. The sort key is the portion of the sort record used to make the comparisons between the different sort records. Normally, Word uses the first 65 characters of the sort record as the key; however, in the section "Sorting by Field," you will see how to use a different portion of the sort record as a key.

To specify the sort key type, choose one of the options from the Key Type box within the Sort dialog box:

- Alphanumeric

- Numeric

- Date

When comparing sort keys, Word ignores quotation marks, spaces, tabs, and diacritical marks.

If you choose the Alphanumeric item, Word will sort the records alphabetically. Technically, the sort is based upon a special sorting table, which is listed in Appendix C of the *Microsoft Word for Windows User's Reference* (the second table, which is labeled "Alphanumeric Sorting Order"). In this table, punctuation marks precede numbers, and numbers precede letters. For each letter, the uppercase letter precedes the lowercase letter (later, in the section "Case Sensitivity," you will see how to cause Word to ignore the case of letters when sorting).

If you choose the Numeric sort key type, Word will base its comparisons on the *numeric value* of the sort keys. To determine the numeric value of a given key, Word evaluates all numbers and mathematical operators it finds within the key, according to the rules used by the Calculate command (presented in the section "Calculating with a Selection"). Thus, for example, the character 9 would come before 10. As with the Calculate command, nonnumeric characters are ignored.

If you choose the Date sort key type, each sort record must contain a date. Word will sort the records chronologically according to these dates, ignoring all characters not in date format.

Case Sensitivity

The Case Sensitive option in the Sort dialog box is available only when you have chosen the Alphanumeric sort key type. If you choose this option, the uppercase version of a letter will precede the lowercase version of the same letter. If this option is off, the case of all letters will be ignored.

Table 8.3 illustrates a list of items sorted with and without the Case Sensitive option enabled.

Table 8.3: Alphanumeric Sorting with and without the Case Sensitive Option

CASE SENSITIVE OPTION SELECTED:	CASE SENSITIVE OPTION *NOT* SELECTED:
Acme	ace
ace	Acme
Partridge	paragon
paragon	Partridge
Somali	siamese
siamese	Somali

Sorting by Field

As you saw previously, the sort key is the portion of the sort record used to make the comparisons between the different records. Normally, Word uses the first 65 characters of the sort record (or the entire record if it is shorter than 65 characters) as the sort key. You can, however, have Word use a *specific portion* of the sort record, known as a *field*, as the sort key. The manner for specifying a field depends upon whether the sort is being performed outside or inside of a table.

To have Word use a sort key other than the first 65 characters of the sort record, each record must be divided into separate fields using either commas or tab characters. You must specify the following two options within the Sort dialog box:

- Select either the Comma or Tab option (following the Separator label) to indicate the type of separator used to divide the fields in your selection.

    Separator: ◉ Comma ○ Tab

    Field number: | 1 |

- Enter the number of the field to be used for the sort key. If you are performing a regular sort (that is, a noncolumn sort), fields are counted starting with 1 at the beginning of the sort record. If you are performing a column sort (that is, Sort Column Only is selected), fields are counted from the beginning of the selection.

Figure 8.21 illustrates sorting on a specified field; it shows a sequence of lists before (shown in the top figure) and after (in the bottom figure) sorting the lists using the second field as the sort key. To create this example, the following values were specified in the Sort dialog box:

    Separator: ◉ Comma ○ Tab

    Field number: | 2 |

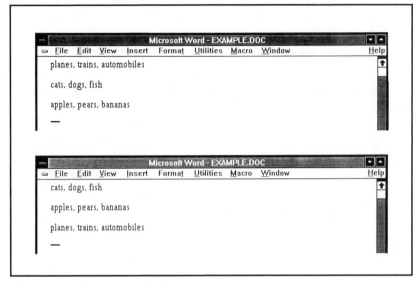

Figure 8.21: Sorting on a field

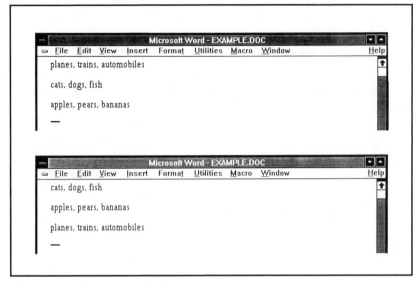 Word uses the text within only a single cell as the sort key.

Word considers each cell within a table row to be a separate field. Therefore, when you perform a sort within a table, the Separator item is not available. You need only enter a number into the Field number box to indicate the number of the cell to be used for the sort key. Cells are numbered starting with 1 *at the beginning of the selection.* Therefore, for example, you could use the second column as the sort key either by selecting the second column prior to the sort and accepting the default field number of 1, or by selecting the entire table and then specifying a field number of 2.

Sorting Orders

Finally, you can specify the sorting order by choosing either the Ascending or Descending option within the Sort Order area of the Sort dialog box.

If you choose the Ascending option, Word will arrange records in an alphanumeric sort in alphabetical order, records in a numeric sort from smaller to larger, and records in a date sort from past to present.

If you choose the Descending option, Word will arrange records in an alphanumeric sort in reverse alphabetical order, records in a numeric sort from larger to smaller, and records in a date sort from present to past.

SUMMARY

- A Word table consists of a collection of cells, which are arranged in an array of rows and columns. You can enter text or graphics into each cell.

- Using the Table feature to create tables of data in your document is generally easier than employing tab characters.

- To create a new empty table, issue the Insert/Table menu command and specify the initial number of rows and columns.

- You can type one or more paragraphs, or insert graphics, into a table cell. Word will automatically adjust the cell height as necessary.

- You can move from cell to cell within a table by pressing Tab to move to the next cell, or Shift-Tab to move to the previous cell. If you press Tab while in the last table cell, Word adds another row to the bottom of the table.

- To convert existing document text to a table, select the text and then issue the Insert/Table menu command.

- You can also convert one or more table rows to normal text by selecting the rows and choosing the Insert/Table to Text menu command.

- You can insert one or more new empty cells into a table by placing the insertion point at the appropriate position, or by selecting the appropriate block of cells, and then using the Edit/Table menu command.

- You can completely remove one or more table cells and their contents by selecting the cells and using the Edit/Table menu command.

- You can select one or more characters or cells within a table using conventional keyboard selection methods. You can also select an entire table by pressing Alt-5 (numeric keypad 5).

- To select a cell with the mouse, you can click the left edge of the cell. To select an entire row, you can double-click the left edge of any cell in the row.

- You can select an entire column by clicking the top edge of the column, or by clicking with the *right* mouse button anywhere within the column.

- To merge table cells that are within a single row, select the cells, issue the Edit/Table menu command, and click the Merge Cells button. You can later split a combined cell back into its constituent cells by selecting it, issuing the Edit/Table command, and clicking the Split Cells button.

- You can split a table into two parts by pressing the Ctrl-Shift-◄┘ keystroke. You can insert a page break into a table by pressing the Ctrl-◄┘ keystroke.

- To delete, copy, or move the contents of one or more cells, use the Clipboard techniques described in Chapter 5. When you paste the contents of one or more entire cells into another table position, the cell contents at the insertion point are overwritten.

- You can adjust the following table features by issuing the Format/Table command (the features can be applied to the entire table or to the current selection within the table): the column width, the space between columns, the row indent, the minimum row height, the row alignment, and the borders placed around the cells.

- You can perform a calculation on numeric data either inside or outside of a Word table. The data can consist of one or more numbers combined with mathematical operators. The recognized operators are listed in Table 8.2.

- To perform a calculation, first select the data and then issue the Utilities/Calculate menu command. The result will be displayed within the status bar and copied to the Clipboard, from which it can be pasted into the document.

- You can also perform a calculation using an *expression field*.

- With the Sort command you can sort groups of paragraphs, rows in a table, or lines or rows within a single column.

- The general method for sorting text is to select the text and then issue the Utilities/Sort menu command. Word will display the Sort dialog box.

- You can specify the following options within the Sort dialog box: the type of sort key (alphanumeric, numeric, or date), sensitivity to the case (alphanumeric) in the sort key, the position of the sort key within each sort record, and the sorting order (ascending or descending).

9

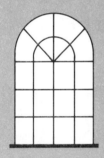

INCLUDING GRAPHICS
IN YOUR DOCUMENT

SO FAR IN THIS BOOK YOU HAVE SEEN HOW TO ENTER *text* into a Word document. Document text is composed of *characters*; as explained in Chapter 3, a character can be a letter, a punctuation mark, or another symbol. Characters are available in a wide variety of styles and sizes; a given character, however, always belongs to a fixed set of symbols, known as a *font*, which is installed in your computer.

In this chapter, you will learn how to enter *pictures*, or graphic images, into your Word documents. Unlike characters, pictures can consist of *any* shape or pattern. You can design a picture yourself or obtain it from a variety of other sources. Also, unlike a character, after a picture is inserted into a document, you can freely adjust its size and proportions.

Pictures are not created in Word; rather, they must be copied from another Windows application or imported from a disk file that contains a graphic image in a suitable format. For example, a picture might be derived from a freehand sketch produced in a Windows drawing program (such as Paintbrush), from a chart generated by a spreadsheet application (such as Excel), or from a printed image copied with a scanner.

With Word, you can smoothly integrate pictures and text in your document to create a carefully designed page layout. For example, you can include both a picture and text on the same line, and you can have Word automatically flow text around a picture. In Part III, you will learn much more about designing the layout of the pages in your document. Figure 9.1 illustrates a full printed page that includes a picture.

In this chapter, you will learn how to insert a picture into a document. You will then learn how to manipulate the picture within the document; specifically, you will see how to adjust the size and proportions of the picture, how to copy or move the picture, and how to specify the exact position of the picture on the printed page.

Note that to print a document containing pictures, you must have installed in Windows a printer that is capable of printing graphics. Also, the amount of graphic detail that can be printed depends upon your printer's resolution (that is, the maximum number of dots per square inch that the printer can generate). See Chapter 17 for more information on printing.

INSERTING PICTURES

Word provides three basic methods for inserting a picture into a document. The first and most common method is to paste it from the Clipboard. The second method is to use the Paste Link command to paste it from the Clipboard *and* establish a link with the program that is the source of the graphic data. The third method is to use the Insert/Picture command to import the picture from a disk file.

To transfer a graphic image from another application, you must have the full Windows version rather than the run-time version. These versions are described in Chapter 1.

PASTING A PICTURE FROM THE CLIPBOARD

You can use the Clipboard to capture a graphic image from another Windows program and then insert the image as a picture into a Word document. (The Windows Clipboard is described in Chapter 5.) The source for the image could, for example, be a simple

I created this page to illustrate how you can combine both text and graphics within a Word document. First, I designed the picture using Paintbrush, a Windows drawing program. When I judged that the sketch was about as good as it was going to get, I selected the rectangular area of the drawing that I wanted to use, and copied it into the Clipboard using the Paintbrush Copy command.

Next, I switched into Word, opened a new document, and inserted the picture at the beginning of the document using the **Edit/Paste** menu command. I made sure that the **Display as Printed** option was selected within the **View/Preferences** dialog box, so that the relative size of the picture on the screen would be close to the actual printed size. I decided *not* to change the size of the picture (by cropping) or the proportions of the picture (by scaling).

I then specified the exact position on the page where I wanted the graphic to be placed, by performing the following steps:

1.   I selected the picture by clicking it.

2.   I opened the **Format/Position** dialog, and chose the **Top** item from the list of alignment styles within the **Vertical** list box. This option forced Word to align the top of the picture with the upper margin on the page.

Positioning the picture not only caused Word to place it at the specified location on the page, but it also caused it to place text to the right of the picture. (The picture is contained in its own paragraph. If it were not positioned, it would be treated as a normal paragraph; that is, it would occupy the entire column width and the text in the following paragraph would be placed beneath it.)

Before entering the text, I turned off the **Pictures** option within the **View Preferences** dialog box, so that scrolling would be faster. I then typed in the document text.

Finally, before printing the document, I entered the Print Preview document view (**File/Print Preview** menu command) to check the final page layout. The picture was positioned correctly; I therefore did not have to adjust is position within Print Preview.

Figure 9.1: A document page with a picture

drawing program such as Windows Paintbrush, a spreadsheet application such as Microsoft Excel, or a full-featured illustration program such as Micrografx Designer or Corel Draw.

The following are the basic steps for transferring graphic data from another Windows program to a Word document:

1. While running the other Windows application, copy the desired graphic image into the Clipboard using the procedures provided by that application. Since most Windows programs employ a common user interface, the methods for cutting or copying data into the Clipboard should be the same as, or similar to, the Word commands described in Chapter 5.

2. Switch into the Word for Windows program, and place the insertion point at the position in the document where you want the picture. Since the graphic data is contained in the Clipboard, it is not necessary to run both applications at the same time; you can exit from the source program before switching to Word.

3. Choose the Edit/Paste menu command or press the Shift-Ins keystroke. The graphic image in the Clipboard will be inserted into the document.

Word treats a picture as if it were *a single character*. Thus, you can insert a picture into its own paragraph, or you can insert it anywhere within a paragraph already containing text. After you paste a picture, the insertion point is moved to the immediate right of the picture and assumes the full picture height. If you press the ← key, for example, the insertion point jumps to the left of the picture with a single key press. Figure 9.2 illustrates a picture that has been inserted at the beginning of a line of text in a Word document.

The maximum size of a picture that you can insert is approximately 22 inches on a side. If a picture is larger than the document window, you may have to scroll using the vertical or horizontal scroll bar to see various parts of the picture. If the picture is larger than the computer paper, the appearance of the printed copy will be unpredictable. Later in the chapter, you will see how you can easily adjust the size and proportions of a picture after it has been inserted into a document.

As you scroll through a document, Word must redraw a picture each time it comes into view in the window. Redrawing is a time-consuming process and can significantly slow the speed of scrolling.

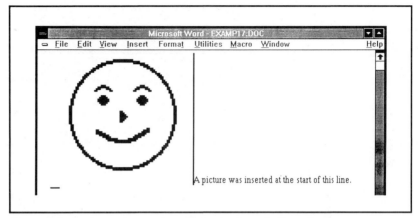

Figure 9.2: A picture inserted at the beginning of a line of text

You can, however, increase the scrolling speed by turning off the Pictures option within the View/Preferences dialog box; once this option is disabled, Word will display each picture in the document as an empty box rather than drawing the actual graphic image. You might want to disable the Pictures option while you are entering text, and then enable it when you are ready to examine the final printed appearance of your document. Pictures are also displayed as blank boxes in the draft document view, which was described in Chapter 4 (you can activate the draft view by choosing the View/Draft menu item).

PASTING FROM THE CLIPBOARD AND LINKING

Under certain circumstances, you can use the Paste Link command (on the Edit menu), rather than the normal Paste command, to insert a graphic image from the Clipboard into your document. The Paste Link command not only inserts the picture into the document, but also establishes a link between the picture and the original graphic image in the source application. This link allows you to quickly update the picture whenever the original image in the source application is altered, without retransferring the image with the Clipboard.

To use the Paste Link command, the following conditions must be met:

- You must have the full version of Windows rather than the run-time version.

- The application that is the source of the graphic image must be running at the same time as Word.

- The source application must support *dynamic data exchange* (DDE), which is a standard for data exchange among Windows programs. Microsoft Excel is an example of an application that supports DDE.

Unless all of these conditions are met, the Paste Link item on the Edit menu is displayed in gray letters and cannot be chosen.

Follow these steps for using the Paste Link command:

1. While running the source application, copy the desired graphic image into the Clipboard, following the procedures provided by that application.

2. *Without terminating the source application*, switch into Word for Windows and place the insertion point at the position in the document where you want the picture.

3. Choose the Edit/Paste Link menu command. Word will display a dialog box, indicating the name of the source application. Check the Auto Update item in this dialog box if you want Word to automatically update the picture in your document whenever the original graphic image is altered in the source application. Leave the Auto Update item unchecked if you want Word to update the picture only at your request. Click the OK button to remove the dialog box and insert the picture.

The Paste Link command inserts a picture in the same manner as the Paste command. However, the picture remains linked to its source to facilitate updating the picture if the source is altered. *Updating* a picture means making it identical to the current version of the original graphic image within the source application. If you chose the Auto Update option, Word will automatically update the picture whenever you modify the original graphic image in the source application (both applications must be running at the same time). If you did *not* choose Auto Update, you can have Word update the picture at any time by selecting the picture (as described later in the chapter) and pressing the F9 key.

When you have inserted a picture with the Paste Link command, you can later remove the link by selecting the picture and pressing the Ctrl-Shift-F9 key combination. Once the link is removed, the picture is no longer associated with its source; it becomes just like a picture inserted through the normal Paste command.

> Word fields were initially described in Chapter 4. They are fully explained in the Word *User's Reference* and *Technical Reference*.

You can also insert a picture and create a link with the picture's source by using a Word *field*. Specifically, use the DDEAUTO field to establish a link that is automatically updated, or the DDE field to establish a link that is manually updated. Using the DDEAUTO field has the same effect as choosing the Edit/Paste Link command and selecting the Auto Update option; using the DDE field has the same effect as choosing the Edit/Paste Link command without selecting the Auto Update option. For more information on employing these fields, see the *User's Reference* (under the "Linking Fields" topic) or the *Technical Reference* (under the "Fields" topic).

Once inserted, a picture linked to another application can be manipulated—as described later in the chapter—in the same manner as one simply pasted from the Clipboard.

INSERTING A PICTURE FROM A DISK FILE

> A scanner is a device that allows you to convert an image, such as a drawing or photograph, on a piece of paper to graphic data that can be stored in a disk file, which can then be displayed, edited, or printed by a computer program.

You can also insert a picture into your document by importing the graphic data from a disk file rather than pasting the image from the Clipboard. The graphic data must normally be contained in a specific type of file known as a *tagged image file format* (TIFF) file. TIFF files are typically created using scanners, and are named with the .TIF extension.

You can also import pictures from files that have other formats. However, for each format you want to import, you must install an appropriate *graphic filter*. A graphic filter is an addition to the Word program that allows it to import a specific type of graphic data. When you run the Word for Windows setup program, you can install one or more of the filters provided with the Word program; simply follow the instructions displayed on the screen. You may also be able to obtain one or more graphic filters from other software vendors; in this case, installation instructions should be provided with the filter.

The following are the steps for importing a picture from a disk file:

1. Place the insertion point at the position in the document where you want to insert the picture.

2. Choose the Insert/Picture menu command. Word will display the dialog box illustrated in Figure 9.3.

The Insert/Picture dialog box allows you to view and select the names of files within any directory in your file system. The techniques are the same as those used for the File/Open command, described in Chapter 3, in the section "Opening a Document within Word."

If you type in the name of a file not in the current disk directory, you must specify the full path name. See Appendix A for instructions on specifying path names.

3. Type the name of the file into the Picture File Name box, or select a name from the Files list box. You must specify a TIFF file or file having a format for which you have installed a graphic filter.

Once it has been inserted, a picture imported from a file can be manipulated in the same manner as one pasted from the Clipboard.

INSERTING A BLANK PICTURE FRAME

You can also use the Insert/Picture menu command to insert a *blank frame* into your document. A blank frame is used simply to

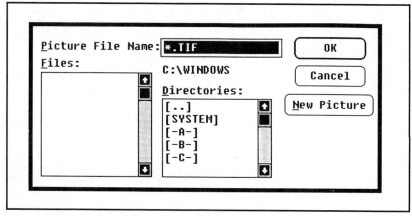

Figure 9.3: The Insert/Picture dialog box

reserve and mark an area on the printed document page. When you print your document, a blank frame will appear on the page as an empty area surrounded by a border. You can then manually paste an illustration, photograph, or other object onto this area. A blank picture frame is meant to be left blank until you physically paste an object on the printed copy of the document. Do not attempt to insert a Word picture into a blank frame while you are working with the document in the Word program.

The following is the procedure for inserting a blank picture frame:

1. Place the insertion point at the document position where you want to insert the blank frame.

2. Choose the Insert/Picture menu command. Word will display the dialog box illustrated in Figure 9.4.

3. Click the New Picture button.

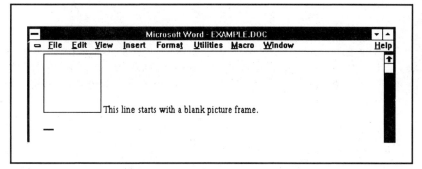

Figure 9.4: A blank picture frame with text

Initially, a blank frame is a 1-inch square with a single-line border. You can use the methods described later in the chapter to alter its dimensions, location on the page, or border style.

FORMATTING A PICTURE

Word does not provide facilities for editing graphic images. To edit a picture, you must return to the application in which the picture was created. Unless you initially inserted the picture using the Paste Link command, you must then transfer the picture back into the Word document by means of the Clipboard. However, you can alter the appearance and position of a picture through a variety of Word formatting commands. Specifically, you can perform the following formatting operations on a picture:

- You can change its size or proportions by cropping or scaling.
- You can place a border around it using one of several line styles.
- You can copy or move it to another location in the document.
- You can assign it a precise position on the printed page.

Since you must select a picture before you can format it, a brief discussion on selecting a picture is presented before describing each of these formatting operations.

SELECTING A PICTURE

Remember that Word treats a picture as if it were a single character. You can therefore select a picture using any of the basic methods for selecting characters that were described in Chapter 5. Several unique features apply when selecting a picture:

- You can select a picture simply by clicking anywhere in it.
- If you select a picture and any adjoining text characters, the entire selection is highlighted, as shown in Figure 9.5.

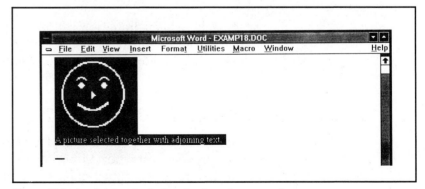

Figure 9.5: A selection including both a picture and text

- If you select *only* a picture, Word places a border around the picture rather than highlighting it. Within this border are eight small squares known as *sizing handles*, which are used for cropping or scaling the picture, as described in the next section (see Figure 9.6). While the picture is selected, the mouse pointer is an arrow rather than the usual I-beam. You can remove the selection from the picture and restore the I-beam pointer by clicking anywhere outside of the picture.

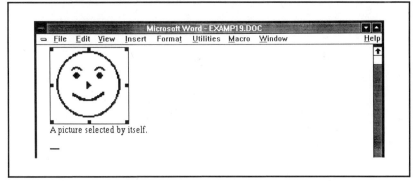

Figure 9.6: A selection including only a picture, with sizing handles

CROPPING OR SCALING A PICTURE

If you have chosen the Display As Printed option within the dialog box displayed by the View/Preferences menu command, the size of the graphic on the screen as indicated by the Word ruler (see Chapter 15) will be the same as its size on the printed page. If you have not chosen this option, the size of the graphic on the screen may be different from its printed size.

Once a picture has been inserted into a document, you can use Word to *crop* it or to *scale* it. To crop means to change the overall dimensions of the picture without changing the size of the image contained within the picture. When you reduce the original picture size by cropping, you usually lose some portion of the image (like using scissors to cut a photograph), and when you increase the size by cropping, you add white space around the image. Figure 9.7 illustrates the effect of cropping a picture. The first picture in this figure shows its original size. The second picture has been reduced in size by cropping, and the third picture has been increased in size by cropping. (Borders were added to these pictures to show their dimensions; adding borders will be explained later in the chapter.)

To *scale* means to change the overall dimensions of the picture while changing the size of the image contained in the picture. When

Word always saves the graphic data for an entire picture. If you eliminate a portion of the image by cropping, you can later restore this portion by cropping the picture to its original size.

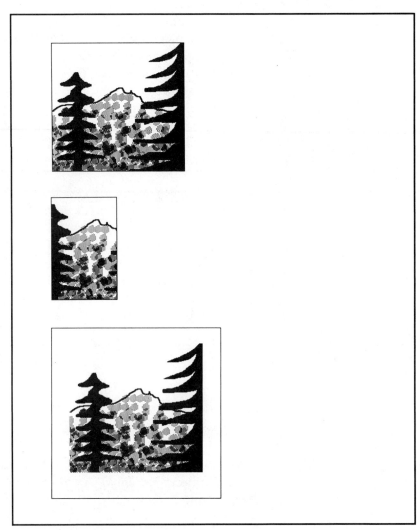

Figure 9.7: Cropping a picture

you scale a picture, you neither lose any of the original image nor do you add white space around its edges. Rather, you change the size and possibly the proportions of the graphic image. The first picture in Figure 9.8 shows the original image size. The second picture has been decreased in size by scaling, and the third picture has been increased in size by scaling.

Figure 9.8: Scaling a picture

You can crop or scale a picture either by using the mouse or by means of the Format/Picture menu command.

Cropping and Scaling Using the Mouse

To crop a picture with the mouse, first select the picture *only* (do not include text in the selection; the easiest way is simply to click anywhere inside the picture). Word will place a frame around the picture that contains the eight square sizing handles, as shown in Figure 9.6. To crop the picture, use the mouse to drag the appropriate handle either toward or away from the center of the picture. A handle in the center of a side moves only the associated side:

A handle in a corner moves both attached sides simultaneously:

Since Word always saves the graphic data for the entire picture, you can eliminate a portion of the image by dragging a side toward the center, and then restore this portion by dragging the side in the opposite direction.

To scale a picture with the mouse, hold down the Shift key while dragging the appropriate sizing handle. When scaling a picture, it makes no difference whether you drag a given side or the opposite side; the resulting size, position, and content of the picture will be the same with either handle.

While you are cropping the picture by dragging a sizing handle, Word displays (in the status bar) the current distance you have moved the side from its original position.

Cropping: 0.14" Right

See Appendix B for an explanation of the default units of measurement.

A positive measurement means that you have moved the side away from its initial position *toward* the center of the picture; a negative measurement means that you have moved the side away from its initial position in the direction *away* from the center. These measurements refer to the actual size of the picture on the printed document page, and are given in Word's current default unit of measurement.

As you change a given dimension while scaling a picture, Word also displays (in the status bar) the current size of the dimension as a percentage of the original dimension.

```
Scaling:    130% Wide
```

Cropping and Scaling Using the Format/Picture Command

You can also crop or scale a picture using the Format/Picture menu command. You might want to use this command under the following circumstances:

- You want to specify an exact measurement in inches (or some other unit).

- You do not have a mouse.

- You want to reverse the effect of all cropping and scaling that has been applied to the picture.

- You want to place a border around the graphic.

The first step is to select the picture alone (do not include any text in the selection). Next, choose the Format/Picture menu command. Word will display the dialog box shown in Figure 9.9. Notice that this dialog box indicates the original size of the picture in the default units.

See Appendix B for information on entering measurements into Word dialog boxes.

To crop the picture, you direct Word to move one or more of the four sides of the picture. First enter the distance you want the side to move *from its original position* into the appropriate box within the Crop From area of the dialog box. Enter a positive number to move the side toward the center of the picture, or enter a negative number to move the side away from the center of the picture.

For example, to crop a selected picture by moving the right side ¼″ toward the center (in other words, to crop ¼″ off the right side of the picture), enter **0.25** into the Right box.

Since Word always saves the graphic data for the entire picture, you can eliminate a portion of the image by having Word move a side

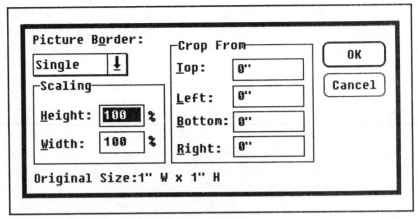

Figure 9.9: The Format/Picture dialog box

toward the center, and then restore this portion by having Word move the side away from the center.

You can scale the selected picture by entering a value into one or both of the boxes within the Scaling box. To scale the picture vertically, enter the new vertical dimension—as a percentage of the original height—into the Height box. To scale the picture horizontally, enter the new horizontal dimension—as a percentage of the original width—into the Width box.

For example, to scale the picture so that it is 50 percent taller than its original height, but only 90 percent as wide, you would enter the following values:

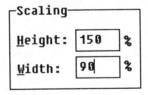

To close the dialog box and have Word apply the dimensions you have specified, click the OK button.

PLACING A BORDER AROUND A PICTURE

You also use the Format/Picture dialog box to have Word place a border around the picture. Simply choose one of the line styles from the Picture Border list box before clicking the OK button.

Picture Border:

The four available line styles, applied to empty picture frames, are illustrated in Figure 9.10.

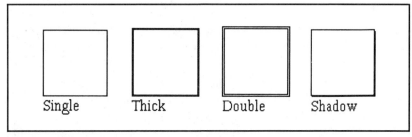

Figure 9.10: The line styles that can be used for a picture border

DELETING, MOVING, OR COPYING A PICTURE

Since Word treats a picture like a single character, you can delete, move, or copy it using the block-editing techniques discussed in Chapter 5, in the section "Deleting, Moving, and Copying." To perform one of these operations, you can select the picture alone, or select the picture in conjunction with one or more adjoining characters. Note, however, that you cannot delete a picture by backspacing over it (Word merely beeps if you press the Backspace key when the insertion point is placed immediately after a picture).

POSITIONING A PICTURE

Normally, when you print a document, a picture is simply printed at the position within the text where you inserted it; also, the position

For detailed information on positioning, see the section in Chapter 15 entitled "Positioning a Paragraph."

of the picture on the page usually changes as you insert or delete text that comes before it.

Word, however, allows you to specify the exact position on the page where it prints a given paragraph. This paragraph can contain text, a picture, or both. The basic procedure for assigning an exact position to a picture is as follows:

1. Select the picture.

2. Choose the Format/Position menu command.

3. Specify the horizontal and vertical position on the page where you want the picture to be printed, as described in Chapter 15.

To view a positioned picture in its specified location on the page, you must print the document or switch into the Page View or Print Preview document view, described in Chapter 17.

The document illustrated in Figure 9.1 contains a picture that was assigned a specific position on the page through the Format/Position command. Specifically, it was aligned with the top margin by selecting the Top item from the Vertical list box within the Format/Position dialog box (all other settings in the dialog box were left with their default values).

When you apply the Format/Position command to a picture, it becomes a *positioned object*. A positioned object has several special properties:

- It is printed at a fixed position on the page.

- It can be moved by dragging it in the Print Preview mode.

- Unpositioned text will automatically flow around it.

Positioning the picture in Figure 9.1 not only forced Word to print it at a specific position on the page, but also caused it to place text *alongside* the picture. If the picture were not positioned, it would be treated as a normal paragraph; that is, it would occupy the entire column width and the text in the following paragraph would be placed *beneath* it.

In addition to applying the Format/Position command, you can use several other methods for adjusting the position of a picture.

When you use these methods, the picture does *not* become a positioned object.

First, since a picture is treated as a single character, you can use the Format/Character menu command to assign it a superscript or subscript value to raise or lower it from its current position. The following is the basic procedure:

1. Select the picture.

2. Choose the Format/Character menu command. Word will display a dialog box.

3. In the Position box, choose either the Superscript option (to raise the picture), or the Subscript option (to lower it).

```
┌Position────────────────────────┐
│ ◉ Normal                        │
│ ○ Superscript By:               │
│ ○ Subscript    ┌─────────────┐  │
│                └─────────────┘  │
└─────────────────────────────────┘
```

See Appendix B for an explanation of points and other units of measurement.

4. Enter into the By box the amount you want to raise or lower the picture. Unless you specify another unit, the number you enter into the box will be interpreted as points (the default amount is 3 points).

You can also apply a superscript or subscript value using keystrokes or the Word *ribbon*, as described in Chapter 16.

Second, you can use standard paragraph formatting commands to adjust the relative position of a picture (together with any characters that happen to be in the same paragraph). For example, you can have Word align the picture in the center of the column, or you can have it add space before or after the picture. For a description of paragraph formatting commands, see Chapter 15.

Adding Captions to Positioned Pictures

If you want to add a caption to a picture that is *not* a positioned object (that is, you have not applied the Format/Position command to it), you can simply type the caption at the desired position near the picture.

If two adjacent paragraphs are assigned the same position through the Format/Position command, they will always be printed together, one before the other (in the same order they have been entered into the document).

If you want to add a caption to a picture that is a positioned object, use the following procedure to make sure that the caption is printed next to the picture:

1. Type the caption into a separate paragraph, either immediately before or immediately after the picture.

2. Select *both* the picture and the caption.

3. Choose the Format/Position menu command, and specify the desired position for the picture and caption.

If you want to place the caption to the side of the picture, or in some other location, you can assign the picture and caption appropriate *different* positions.

SUMMARY

- You can enter both characters and pictures into your documents. Characters belong to fixed sets of symbols known as *fonts*, which are installed in the computer. Pictures, however, can consist of any pattern; you can create them yourself.

- You cannot create pictures within the Word program. Rather, they must be obtained from another Windows application, such as a drawing program or a spreadsheet. Alternatively, you can import a picture from a disk file that stores a graphic image in an appropriate format.

- To insert a picture into a Word document, you must first run the application that is the source of the picture, and cut or copy the desired image into the Clipboard using the appropriate commands. Then, switch to Word and paste the image into the target location in the document.

- If the source application supports dynamic data exchange (DDE), you can use the Edit/Paste Link command to transfer the image with the Clipboard and establish a link between the original image and the picture in the document. The link is used to update the picture after the original image is modified in the source program.

- Alternatively, you can import a picture from a disk file by issuing the Insert/Picture menu command and entering the name of the file.

- You can also enter a blank frame into your document to reserve space for manually pasting an illustration or other object onto the printed document page. Choose the Insert/Picture menu command and click the New Picture button.

- Once a picture has been inserted into a document, you can alter its dimensions by cropping or scaling it. Cropping changes the picture size by either cutting away a portion of the image or by adding white space around it. Scaling changes the picture size by expanding or contracting the entire image itself.

- To change the image size with the mouse, first select the image by clicking anywhere within it; a frame with eight sizing handles will appear around the picture. To crop, simply drag a sizing handle in the desired direction. To scale, drag a sizing handle while pressing the Shift key.

- You can also crop or scale a picture by selecting it and choosing the Format/Picture menu command. Enter the desired dimensions into the dialog box that is displayed.

- While the Format/Picture dialog box is open, you can place a border around the selected picture by selecting the desired line style from the Picture Border list box.

- Since Word treats a picture like a single character, you can delete, move, or copy it using the standard techniques discussed in Chapters 3 and 5. You cannot, however, delete a picture by backspacing over it.

- You can have Word print a picture at a precise location on the page by selecting it and then issuing the Format/Position menu command. Fill in the appropriate values in the dialog box according to the instructions given in Chapter 15.

- You can also adjust the position of a picture by selecting it and applying the appropriate character formatting (see Chapter 16) or paragraph formatting (Chapter 15).

10

ADDING HEADERS, FOOTERS, AND FOOTNOTES

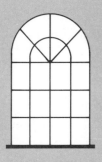

IN THIS CHAPTER, YOU WILL LEARN TWO IMPORTANT ways you can use Word to automate your work. First, you will learn how to create headers and footers; a header is text that is printed at the top of each page of a document, and a footer is text that is printed at the bottom of each page. Second, you will learn how to add footnotes to your documents, and have Word automatically keep them in the correct order and print them in the appropriate locations.

WORKING WITH HEADERS AND FOOTERS

Once you have entered a header or footer, Word will automatically print it on each page of the document. You can enter either a header or a footer, or both. Headers and footers typically contain such information as the page number, the title, and the author's name. As you will see, with Word you can also easily add the time or date when you print the document.

When you create a header or a footer, it is applied to the current document *section*. A section is a division of a document that can be assigned certain formatting values, such as a specific number of columns. (In Chapter 14, you will see how to divide a document into sections, and how to format each section.) If you have divided your document into sections, you can specify a different header or footer for each section. If you have *not* divided your document into sections, the header or footer you specify will be printed throughout the entire document.

Accordingly, if your document is divided into sections, the first step in assigning a header or footer is to place the insertion point within the appropriate section. As you will see, if you want all sections to have the same header or footer, you can simply assign the header or footer to the *first* document section and Word will automatically copy it to all remaining sections.

You can create either a header or footer that consists of a page number only, or a full header or footer that can contain any text and graphics in addition to the page number and other information.

CREATING A SIMPLE PAGE NUMBER HEADER OR FOOTER

If you want a header or footer that consists of the page number only, you can save time by choosing the Insert/Page Numbers menu command rather than the Edit/Header/Footer command described in the next section.

If you have previously added a header or footer, issuing the Insert/Page Numbers command will *replace* it. In this case, Word will ask you whether you want to replace the existing header or footer.

When you issue the Insert/Page Numbers command, Word will display the dialog box illustrated in Figure 10.1. You can now specify the position of the number on the page. First, choose either the Top option if you want to create a header, or the Bottom option if you want to create a footer. Then choose either the Left, Center, or Right option to specify the alignment of the number between the left and right margins. Click the OK button to create the header or footer and remove the dialog box. To see the page number at the specified position on

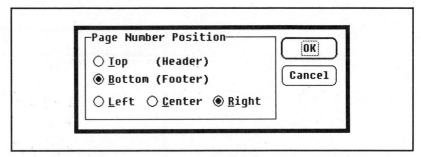

Figure 10.1: The Insert/Page Numbers dialog box

each page, you must print the document or activate the Page View or Print Preview mode (explained in Chapter 17).

A header or footer you create with the Insert/Page Numbers command has the following features:

- The header or footer consists of a page number only; no other text is included.

- The page numbers are Arabic numerals (2, 3, 4, and so on), unless you have specified a different number style through the Edit/Header/Footer command, described later in the chapter.

- The first page in the document is assigned number 1, the second page number 2, and so on throughout the entire document. Numbering does *not* start over again for each document section.

- No number is printed on the first document page. The first number printed is 2, on the second page.

You can later change any of these default features using the methods described in the next section.

CREATING AND FORMATTING COMPLETE HEADERS OR FOOTERS

To enter a full header or footer for the current document section, choose the Edit/Header/Footer menu command. Word will display the dialog box shown in Figure 10.2.

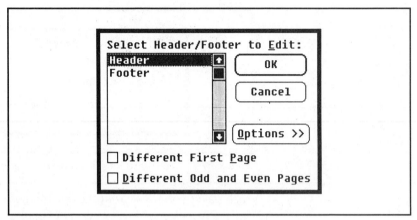

Figure 10.2: The Edit/Header/Footer dialog box

You must tell Word the type of header or footer you want to create by selecting an item from the Select Header/Footer to Edit list box. Initially, this list contains only two items, Header and Footer (unless you have previously issued the Insert/Page Numbers command). As you will see later, additional items may be added to the list as you choose various options within the dialog box.

If you want to create a standard header or footer that is the same on all document pages, you can simply choose the Header or Footer option, click the OK button, and begin entering text. However, you first may want to use the options offered in this dialog box to create a header or footer that suits the needs of your particular document. These options are explained later in the section "Using Header and Footer Options."

See Chapter 9 for information on entering graphics.

Once you click the OK button, Word splits the window horizontally into two divisions, which are known as *panes*. (See Chapter 26 for complete information on managing split windows.) Figure 10.3 illustrates a window just after clicking the OK button; it shows the document pane and the newly opened header/footer pane below it.

Notice that at the top of the header/footer pane, Word displays the type of header or footer that is being edited (for example, Header), followed by the number of the current document section—for example, (S1), indicating the first section. The icons and buttons displayed at the top of the pane are described later.

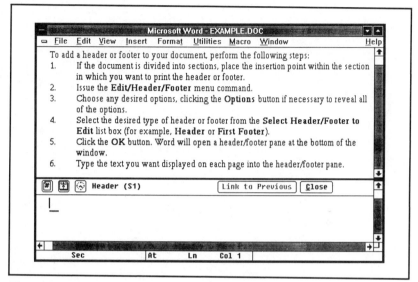

Figure 10.3: A window split into a document pane and a header/footer pane

Word places the insertion point within the header/footer pane, so that you can immediately start entering text for the header or footer. Note that you do *not* have to finish entering this text and close the header/footer pane to resume editing the document; rather, you can leave the header/footer pane open and simply move the insertion point back to the document pane. You can later return to the header/footer pane to further edit the header or footer text. To switch between panes, simply click in the desired pane with the mouse, or press the F6 key. You can also adjust the size of the header/footer pane by dragging the split bar in the desired direction (the split bar is labeled in the illustration of the Word window on the inside front cover of the book and in Figure 1.1).

If you have previously entered a header or footer through the Insert/Page Numbers or Edit/Header/Footer command, the text will appear in the header/footer pane and you can now edit it.

If you are in the galley, draft, or outline document view, Word does not display headers or footers at their designated positions on the pages of the document. Rather, they are visible only within the header/footer window pane. However, headers or footers will be displayed at their appropriate positions on the printed copy of the document, as well as in the Page View and Print Preview modes.

See Chapter 17 for a summary of all of the document views provided by Word.

If you issue the Edit/Header/Footer command while in the Page View mode, Word will simply place you at the position of the header or footer displayed within the document window, rather than opening a separate window pane. Entering or changing a header or footer on *any* page within a section will affect the headers or footers throughout the entire section.

While you are entering the text for a header or footer in the header/footer pane, you can also insert one or more of the following items of information anywhere within the text:

- The page number
- The date when the document is printed
- The time when the document is printed

The first step is to place the insertion point at the position in the text where you want to insert the item of information. For example, if you wanted to place the page number in the header, your screen might look like this:

Page:|

You can then use either the mouse or the keyboard. To insert the page number with the mouse, click the first icon at the top of the header/footer pane

To insert the date, click the second icon. To insert the time, click the third icon.

While you are in the header/footer pane, you also can insert any of these items with the keyboard by first pressing the Shift-F10 keystroke to enter the *icon bar mode*. Once you are in this mode, you can press one of the following keys to enter the desired information:

KEY   **INFORMATION ITEM**

p   Page number

d   Date

t   Time

If you entered the page number into a header or footer through the Insert/Page Numbers menu command, the page number may not be visible within the header/footer pane. To make it visible, select the entire header or footer and press the F9 key.

When you insert a page number, the number that Word displays in the header/footer pane has no particular significance; the correct page number, however, will be displayed on each page when you print the document, or when you preview the document in Page View or Print Preview. To see the actual number, date, or time, as illustrated in this chapter, make sure that the View/Field Codes menu item is *not* selected. When you insert the date or time, Word displays the *current* date or the *current* time; however, when you print the document, it replaces these with the date or time *when the document is printed*. Figure 10.4 illustrates a header containing the page number, date, and time.

When you insert the page number, date, or time, you are actually inserting a Word *field*. You can use fields to insert other information into a header or footer, such as the document title or author's name. For information on fields, see the Word *User's Reference* and *Technical Reference*, under the topic "Fields."

Linking Headers or Footers to Sections

The information in this section applies only if you have divided your document into two or more sections.

Initially, the headers or footers within all sections of a document are *linked*. This means that a header or footer you assign to a given section is automatically copied to all of the *following* sections in the document. For example, if a document consists of three sections, and you enter a header for section 1, sections 2 and 3 will automatically be

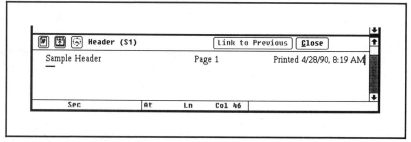

Figure 10.4: A header containing the page number, date, and time

assigned the same header. Furthermore, if you change the header for section 1, the headers for sections 2 and 3 will also be changed.

However, as soon as you change or add header or footer text for a section other than section 1, Word removes the link with the previous section. If, in the example just given, you change the header text for section 2, sections 1 and 2 will still have different headers, and the new header for section 2 will no longer be affected by changes to the header for section 1.

You can, however, restore the link between a header in a given section and that belonging to the previous section by clicking the Link to Previous button at the top of the header/footer pane

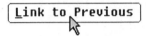

or by pressing Shift-F10 and then L. This will cause Word to replace the header or footer for the current section with that belonging to the previous section. Before doing so, however, it will display the message

Delete this header/footer and link to previous section?

In the same example, if you click the Link to Previous button while editing the header for section 2, the contents of the header for section 1 will be copied into that for section 2, and these two headers will once more be linked.

Formatting Headers or Footers

Headers are automatically assigned the header style and footers the footer style. You can change the default formatting used for all headers and footers in one or more documents by redefining this style, as described in Chapter 20.

You also can apply either character or paragraph formatting to the text for a header or footer in the same way you would format text within the body of a document. The following are some examples of formatting features that you might want to assign a header or footer (these features are discussed in Chapters 15 and 16):

Do not assign the Keep Paragraph with Next paragraph formatting feature to a header or footer.

- Boldface characters

- Centered paragraph alignment

- A line above or below the text

You might also want to adjust the tab stops within a header or footer. Initially, a header or footer has only two tab stops, one in the center of the page and one at the right margin.

Adjusting the Position of Headers and Footers

When you first enter a header or footer through the Edit/Header/ Footer command, Word assigns an initial position to a header near the top of each page, or to a footer near the bottom of each page. Table 10.1 describes these initial positions, and Figure 10.5 illustrates a header in its initial position near the top of a page (this figure depicts Word in Page View mode, which displays headers and footers in their actual positions on the printed page).

Once you have added a header or footer, you can adjust either its horizontal position or its vertical position on the page. To adjust the horizontal position, you can use appropriate paragraph formatting commands, which are described in Chapter 15. For example, you could assign the header or footer a negative left or right indent to move it out into the left- or right-margin area of the page. Also, you could assign the

Table 10.1: The Initial Positions of Headers and Footers

	HEADER:	**FOOTER:**
Initial horizontal position:	Aligned with the text margins	Aligned with the text margins
Initial vertical position:	Distance from top of page set in Header box* (by default 0.5 inches from the top)	Distance from bottom of page set in Footer box* (by default 0.5 inches from the bottom)
*Within the Edit/Header/Footer dialog box		

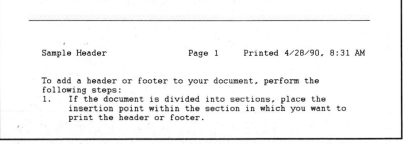

Figure 10.5: A header in its initial position on the page

centered alignment style to center a header or footer between the right and left margins.

You can easily adjust the vertical position of a header or footer by switching into the Print Preview mode, and using the methods described in Chapter 17 to drag a header or footer to the desired vertical position within the margin area.

Finally, you can place a header or footer at any position on the page by using the Format/Position menu command, which is explained in Chapter 15.

Print Preview was introduced in Chapter 2, and is fully described in Chapter 17.

Closing the Header/Footer Pane

You can close the header/footer pane at any time by clicking the Close button at the top of the pane or by pressing the Shift-F10 keystroke and then typing **C**. You can also close it by dragging the split bar all the way to the top or the bottom of the window.

Word saves all text you have entered into the header/footer pane, and you can resume editing this text later by reissuing the Edit/Header/Footer menu command.

If you want to enter a different type of header or footer, or if you want to enter a header or footer for another document section, you do *not* need to close the header/footer pane. Rather, you can simply reissue the Edit/Header/Footer command; the pane for the new header or footer will overlay the existing pane.

USING HEADER AND FOOTER OPTIONS

Before clicking the OK button to begin entering the text for the header or footer, you can specify one or more of the following options within the Edit/Header/Footer dialog box:

- Different First Page
- Different Odd and Even Pages
- Page Numbers
- Distance From Edge

Different First Page

Choosing the Different First Page option allows you to create a separate header or footer for the first page of the current section, or to eliminate the header or footer from the first page.

`Different First Page`

When you choose this option, the following two items are added to the Select Header/Footer to Edit list box:

First Header
First Footer

You must issue the Edit/Header/Footer command for *each* type of header or footer you want to enter. Whenever you issue this command, you must select the appropriate item from the list box before clicking OK.

To enter text for the header or footer on the first page of the section, select the First Header or First Footer item before clicking the OK button. If you don't enter text for the header or footer on the first page, Word will *not print* a header or footer on this page.

Different Odd and Even Pages

If you select the Different Odd and Even Pages option, you can enter separate headers or footers for odd and even pages. This feature would be useful, for example, if you wanted the page number always printed on the *outside* edge of the page (in other words, you wanted it printed on the left side of even pages, but on the right side of odd pages).

When you select this option, Word *replaces* the Header and Footer items in the list box with the following:

Even Header
Even Footer

If you have also selected the Different First Page option, the list box will contain the First Header and First Footer items. In this case, choosing one of the Even or Odd items from the list box will affect pages other than the first page.

Odd Header
Odd Footer

As you have seen, you must issue the Format/Header/Footer command separately for each type of header you want to enter.

Page Numbers

Most headers or footers contain a page number; you will see later how to insert a page number into the header or footer text. Before entering the header text, however, you can specify the starting page number as well as the type of numbers that Word displays. To set either of these options, you must first click the Options button

to expand the Edit/Header/Footer dialog box. The expanded dialog box is illustrated in Figure 10.6.

The page numbering options are set within the Page Numbers area of this dialog box. The starting page number is entered into the Start at box. The default value is Auto. If you are entering a header or footer for the first document section (or if the document isn't divided into sections), the Auto value causes Word to start numbering the pages with 1. If you are entering a header for a section other than the first one, the Auto value causes Word to start with a number

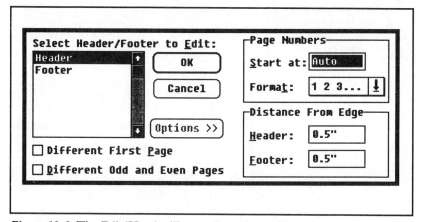

Figure 10.6: The Edit/Header/Footer dialog box with options

Once the document has been paginated, as described in Chapter 17, the page number that would be printed in a header or footer for the current page is displayed within the status bar, following the **Pg** display.

that is 1 greater than the number of the last page of the previous section. Thus, if all sections in a document are numbered with the Auto option, the pages will be numbered consecutively, beginning with 1.

If, however, you want the numbering for the current section (or the entire document, if it is not divided into sections) to begin with a specific number, enter this number into the Start at box. If, for example, the insertion point was in the second document section at the time you issued the Edit/Header/Footer command, and you enter **100** into the Start at box, when Word reaches the second section, it will start numbering the pages 100, 101, and so on.

You can also specify whether to use Arabic, roman, or alphabetic characters for numbering pages by selecting an item from the Format list box, as shown in Figure 10.7.

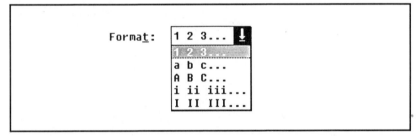

Figure 10.7: The Format list box

Table 10.2 describes the different styles you can choose from this list box. By default, Word uses Arabic numerals.

Table 10.2: The Types of Numbers You Can Choose for Numbering Pages

ITEM IN FORMAT LIST BOX:	TYPE OF NUMBER USED FOR NUMBERING PAGES:
1 2 3 . . .	Arabic numerals
a b c . . .	Lowercase alphabetic
A B C . . .	Uppercase alphabetic
i ii iii . . .	Lowercase roman
I II III . . .	Uppercase roman

If you place a header or footer closer than 0.5 inches from the top or bottom edge of the page, some laser printers may not be able to print the headers or footers.

Distance from Edge

You can also specify the distance between a header and the top of the page, or the distance between a footer and the bottom of the page. To do so, first expand the Edit/Header/Footer dialog box by clicking the Options button, then enter the desired value into the Distance From Edge area of the Edit/Header/Footer dialog box. By default, both distances are 0.5 inches. If you place the header or footer within the area of the page normally occupied by the text, Word will move the text toward the center of the page, so that the header or footer and the text will not overlap (in other words, the top or bottom margin is automatically increased). As you have seen, you can easily adjust the position of headers or footers using either the Format/Position menu command or the Print Preview mode.

Changing Options

You normally set all required options before entering the text for a header or footer. You might, however, decide to change one or more options after entering the text. In this case, it may not be obvious exactly how Word processes the existing text. Table 10.3 summarizes the effects of changing the Different First Page or Different Odd and Even Pages option after you have entered header or footer text.

Table 10.3: The Results of Changing Options after Entering Header or Footer Text

CHANGE IN OPTION:	EFFECT:
Turn on Different First Page option	Header or footer on first page of the section is left blank.
Turn off Different First Page option	Text for header or footer on first page of the section is discarded
Turn on Different Odd and Even Pages option	Existing header or footer text is copied to both odd and even headers or footers
Turn off Different Odd and Even Pages option	Text from *odd* header or footer is used for both odd and even pages.

USING FOOTNOTES IN YOUR DOCUMENT

Word greatly simplifies the task of adding footnotes to your documents. It allows you to insert footnote references into the document and to type the corresponding footnote text into a separate window pane. It automatically numbers the references (if desired) and prints the footnote text in the correct order and at the appropriate positions within the document.

Figure 10.8 illustrates the three basic components of a footnote: the footnote reference, the footnote text, and the footnote separator.

The reference is embedded with a Word command within the document text and usually consists of a superscript number that is assigned by Word; these references are automatically kept in numeric order. Alternatively, you can specify another reference mark, such as an asterisk.

The footnote text begins with the same mark used for the reference. Word normally prints the text for each footnote at the bottom of the page on which the reference occurs. Alternatively, however, footnotes can be placed at the end of the section or at the end of the document.

In this section, you will learn how to insert a footnote reference and type in the corresponding footnote text. You will then learn how to delete, move, or copy a footnote. You will also learn how to specify the separator used to divide the footnote text from the document text (by default, Word uses a simple line). Finally, you will learn how to designate the position of the footnote text within the document, and the numbering scheme used for automatically numbered footnote references.

Later in the chapter, you will learn how to specify the type of separator used to divide the footnotes from the document text.

```
This sentence contains a footnote reference.¹


───────────────────

¹ This is the footnote text.
```

Figure 10.8: A footnote reference and the corresponding text

INSERTING A FOOTNOTE

To insert a footnote reference, place the insertion point at the desired position in your document, and choose the Insert/Footnote menu command. Word will display the dialog box shown in Figure 10.9.

Once the dialog box is displayed, you first specify the type of footnote reference mark you want, and then click the OK button to begin entering the footnote text.

Specifying the Footnote Reference

You can either check the Auto-numbered Reference box to have Word insert an automatically numbered footnote reference, or you can enter any reference symbol into the Footnote Reference Mark box.

You can change the formatting of footnote references. For example, you could assign a different font, character size, position, or other feature (see Chapters 15 and 20).

The Auto-numbered Reference option, which is selected by default, causes Word to use a number as a reference mark; this number is normally formatted as a small superscript character. Usually, the first footnote reference in the document is assigned number 1, the second footnote reference is assigned number 2, and so on. If you insert a footnote reference before an existing reference, Word automatically renumbers the references to keep them in correct numerical order. Later in the chapter, you will learn how to specify a starting number other than 1 (in the section "Specifying the Footnote Position and Numbering Scheme").

You can enter both automatically numbered footnote reference marks *and* reference marks specified in the Footnote Reference Mark box into the same document.

Alternatively, you can have Word use a specific footnote reference mark by entering the desired character or characters into the

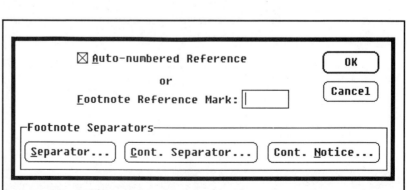

Figure 10.9: The Insert/Footnote dialog box

Footnote Reference Mark box (Word will automatically remove the check from the Auto-numbered Reference option). You might, for example, enter an asterisk.

Footnote Reference Mark: `*`

If you type a *number* into the Footnote Reference Mark box, Word will use this number as a footnote reference. It will not, however, treat the number like an automatically numbered footnote reference. Specifically, it will not change the number to keep it in sequence with surrounding numbers, and the number will not affect the numbering of any nearby automatically numbered references.

Typing the Footnote Text

When you have specified the type of footnote reference and you are ready to begin entering the footnote text, click the OK button in the Insert/Footnote dialog box or press ←. Word will split the window into a document pane and a footnote pane, and will insert the footnote reference both into the document and into the footnote pane, as illustrated in Figure 10.10.

You can format footnote text in the same manner as formatting other text in the document, as explained in Chapters 15 and 16. As you will see in Chapter 20, footnote references are assigned the footnote reference style, and footnote text the footnote text style.

Word places the insertion point immediately following the reference in the footnote pane so that you can begin typing the footnote text (see Figure 10.10).

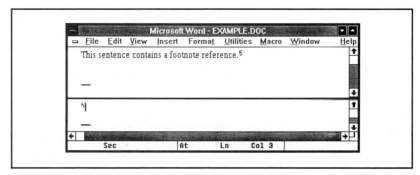

Figure 10.10: A window divided into a document pane and a footnote pane

You can use the Word Go To command (discussed in Chapter 4) to move the insertion point to a specific footnote reference in your document. First, press the F5 key or choose the Edit/Go To menu command. Then, at the prompt, type **f** followed by the number of the footnote. The Go To command counts all footnote references from the beginning of the document, ignoring the actual numbers (if any) contained in the reference marks. For example, if the first four reference marks in your document are as follows:

    1, *, a, 2

the Go To command would consider these to be footnotes 1, 2, 3, and 4. If you enter **f** or **f +** (without a number), Word will take you to the *next* footnote. If you enter only **f −** , Word will take you to the previous footnote.

To move the insertion point back and forth between the two panes, click within the desired pane or press F6. To adjust the size of the footnote pane, drag the split bar up or down (the split bar is labeled in the illustration of the Word window on the inside front cover of the book and in Figure 1.1).

Document views are summarized in Chapter 17.

When you are in the galley, draft, or outline document view, Word does not display footnotes within the document; rather, they are displayed only within the footnote pane. Footnotes will appear in their appropriate positions on the page on the final printed copy, as well as in the Page View and Print Preview modes.

If the Page View mode is active when you issue the Insert/ Footnote command, Word does not open a footnote pane. Rather, it simply places the insertion point at the position on the page where the footnote text will be printed. In Page View, you can edit a footnote at any time by going directly to the footnote text on the page and making the desired changes.

EDITING A FOOTNOTE

Once Word has opened the footnote pane, you can edit any of the footnotes that have been entered for the current document. You can scroll through the footnotes and position the insertion point using the same methods employed within a normal document window. Notice that when you place the insertion point within the text for a particular footnote, the document pane automatically scrolls, if necessary, to reveal the corresponding footnote reference in the document. Likewise, when you place the insertion point within a line containing a footnote reference in the document, the footnote pane automatically scrolls, if necessary, to reveal the corresponding footnote text.

You can close the footnote window at any time using one of the following three methods:

- Drag the split bar all the way to the top or bottom of the window.

- Double-click a footnote reference within the footnote pane.

- Choose the View/Footnotes menu item. Choosing this item will remove the check mark from it and will disable the option.

If you close a footnote window and later reissue the Insert/Footnote command, Word will again open the footnote pane, and you can resume editing the footnote text.

You can also open the footnote pane at any time using one of the following three methods:

- Hold down the Shift key while dragging the split bar down to the desired position.

- Double-click any footnote reference within the document.

- Choose the View/Footnotes menu item. Choosing this item will add a check mark in front of it, and will enable the option.

DELETING, MOVING, OR COPYING A FOOTNOTE

You can delete, move, or copy a footnote reference together with its associated text by performing a single operation on the footnote reference.

To delete both a footnote reference and the corresponding footnote text, select the footnote reference in the document and press the Del key or the Shift-Del key, or issue the Edit/Cut menu command. You cannot delete an automatically numbered footnote reference by simply backspacing over it, or by placing the insertion point in front of it and pressing Del.

If you delete an automatically numbered footnote, Word automatically renumbers the remaining footnotes.

If you move a footnote reference within the document using one of the standard moving techniques presented in Chapter 5, Word will move both the reference and its associated text. If the footnote has an automatically numbered reference, Word will renumber the footnotes appropriately.

Finally, if you copy a footnote reference using one of the standard copying methods given in Chapter 5, Word will insert a new footnote reference at the target position of the copy operation, and will insert a copy of the footnote text at the corresponding position within the footnote area. Again, Word will automatically maintain correct numbering.

SPECIFYING FOOTNOTE SEPARATORS

You can specify the characters that Word uses to separate the footnote text from the document text on each page where footnotes are printed. You can also specify the message that Word prints whenever footnotes are continued on the next page.

To specify one of these items, issue the Insert/Footnote menu command and click the appropriate button within the Footnote Separators area of the dialog box.

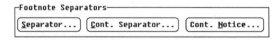

Whichever button you select, Word will open a separate pane. As usual, you can move the insertion point between panes by clicking within the desired pane, or by pressing F6.

You can adjust the size of the separator pane by dragging the split bar, and you can close the pane using one of the following methods:

- Click the Close button.

- Press Shift-F10 and then C.

- Drag the split bar all the way to the top or bottom of the window.

If you click the Separator button, the pane will contain the current separator used to divide the document text from the footnotes at the bottom of the page. By default, this separator is a single line extending approximately a third of the way across the text column; it is illustrated in Figure 10.8. You can replace this separator with one or more other characters, or you can add characters to it. Notice that Word treats the separator line as a single character; you can therefore delete or copy it in its entirety, but you cannot change its length.

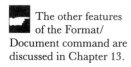
Continuation separators and notices are not used if you place footnotes at the end of each section or at the end of the document.

If you click the Cont. Separator button, you can edit the separator Word uses to divide the document text from footnotes *that have been continued from the previous page*. Normally, all footnote text is printed at the bottom of the page on which the reference occurs. Occasionally, however, there is insufficient room on this page; in this case, Word will continue the footnotes on one or more following pages. On these following pages, Word will use the special continuation separator to divide the document text from the footnote text. By default, the continuation separator is a line extending across the entire text column. This line is also treated as a single character; you can replace it or add characters to it.

If you click the Cont. Notice button, you can type in the message you want Word to display at the bottom of the page when footnotes are continued on the next page. By default, there is no message. You might want to enter a message such as

Footnotes continued on next page...

Word does not display the continuation message if the page break falls *between* footnotes. It is displayed only when Word must divide the text for a single footnote between two pages.

While any one of these three footnote separator panes is open, you can restore the original separator or message defaults by clicking the Reset button, or by pressing Shift-F10 and then R.

SPECIFYING THE FOOTNOTE POSITION AND NUMBERING SCHEME

The other features of the Format/Document command are discussed in Chapter 13.

To specify either the position of footnotes within the document, or the numbering scheme used for automatically numbered footnote references, issue the Format/Document menu command. These features are set through the Footnotes area of the dialog box that Word displays (Figure 10.11).

```
┌Footnotes──────────────────────────┐
│ Print at: │Bottom of Page   │ ↓ │ │
│                                    │
│ Starting Number: │1            │   │
│ ☐ Restart # Each Section           │
└────────────────────────────────────┘
```

Figure 10.11: The Footnotes box

Specifying the Footnote Position

You can tell Word where to place the footnotes within your document by choosing the appropriate item from the *Print at* list box (see Figure 10.12), which is located within the Footnotes area of the Format/Document dialog box.

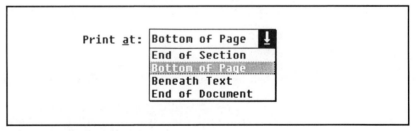

Figure 10.12: The Print at list box

Bottom of Page is the default option. It causes Word to print the footnote text at the bottom of the page containing the corresponding footnote reference. With this option, the footnote text is always printed at the lowest possible position within the text area of the page. Therefore, if there is not enough text on the page to fill the area above the footnotes, Word will leave a gap between the document text and the footnote text. This situation is illustrated in Figure 10.13.

Figure 10.13: A page illustrating the Bottom of Page footnote placement
option

The Beneath Text option also causes Word to print the footnote
text at the bottom of the page containing the corresponding footnote reference. With this option, however, the footnote text is printed
immediately below the text on the page. For pages with sufficient text
to fill the entire available space, this option has the same effect as Bottom of Page. However, if there is too little document text on a page to
fill the available space, the Beneath Text option prevents Word from
leaving a gap between the document text and the footnote text. Figure 10.14 illustrates the same page shown in Figure 10.13, with the
Beneath Text option chosen.

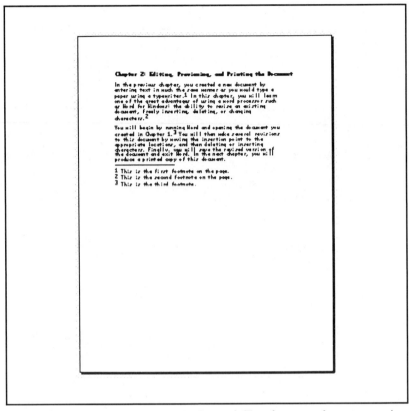

Figure 10.14: A page illustrating the Beneath Text footnote placement option

Document sections are described at the beginning of the chapter. Sections, and the Format/Section command, are fully explained in Chapter 14.

The End of Section option causes Word to place each footnote at the end of the document section that contains the corresponding reference. Normally, when you select this option, each section that has one or more footnote references will have the corresponding footnote text at the end. However, you can disable footnote text for a specific section; in this case, Word will move the text to the end of the *next* section for which footnote text is enabled. To disable footnote text for a specific section, perform the following three steps:

1. Place the insertion point within the section.

2. Choose the Format/Section menu command. Word will display a dialog box.

3. The Include Footnotes option will initially be selected. Click within the check box (or press Alt-F) to remove the check mark and disable this option.

Finally, you can select the End of Document option to have Word place all footnote text at the end of the document. Such footnotes are sometimes called *end notes*.

Specifying the Numbering Scheme

As you saw previously in the chapter, Word automatically numbers all footnotes inserted with the Auto-numbered Reference option. Word normally starts numbering these footnotes with 1. If you want to use a different starting number, enter the desired number into the Starting Number field in the Footnotes area of the Format/Document dialog box.

$\underline{S}$tarting Number: `1`

Also, Word usually numbers footnotes continuously throughout the document. It assigns the specified starting number to the first footnote and increments the number for each subsequent footnote. You can, however, have Word restart the numbering with the specified starting number *at the beginning of each section* by checking the Restart # Each Section option (by default, this option is *not* selected).

For example, if you entered **10** into the Starting Number field, and checked the Restart # Each Section item in the Format/Document dialog box, Word would number the footnotes *within each section* using the numbers 10,11,12, and so on.

SUMMARY

- A header is text or graphics that Word prints at the top of each page in a document. A footer is text or graphics that Word prints at the bottom of each page.

- You can specify a separate header or footer for each document section. If your document consists of more than one section, first place the insertion point within the desired section. If you want all sections to have the same header or footer, place the insertion point within the *first* section and Word will automatically copy the header or footer you enter to all remaining sections.

- If you want a header or footer than consists of only a page number, choose the Insert/Page Numbers menu command.

- To insert a full header or footer containing text as well as the page number or other information, choose the Edit/Header/Footer menu command. Word will display a dialog box.

- If you want a different header or footer (or *no* header or footer) on the first page, select the Different First Page option. If you want different headers or footers on odd and even pages, select the Different Odd and Even Pages option.

- Click the Options button in the Edit/Header/Footer dialog box if you want to specify the starting page number, the style of the page numbers, or the distance of the header or footer from the top or bottom of the page.

- To begin entering text for the header or footer, choose the desired type of header or footer from the Header/Footer to Edit list box within the Edit/Header/Footer dialog box, and click the OK button. Word will open a header/footer pane at the bottom of the document window.

- Enter and format the header or footer text into the newly opened pane. You can use the icons at the top of this pane to insert the page number, the date, or the time into the header or footer text.

- To enter a different type of header or footer, or a header or footer for a different section, reissue the Edit/Header/Footer menu command for each one. You don't need to close the header/footer pane before choosing this command.

- When you are done with the header/footer pane, you can close it by clicking the Close button, or by dragging the split bar all the way to the top or bottom of the window.

- Word also automates the task of inserting footnotes into your documents. A footnote consists of three parts: the reference (usually a superscript number) embedded in the document text; the footnote text, usually printed at the bottom of the page; and the footnote separator, which divides the footnote from the document text.

- To insert a footnote, place the insertion point at the desired position in your document and choose the Insert/Footnote menu command. Word will display a dialog box.

- In the Insert/Footnote dialog box, choose the Auto-numbered Reference to have Word insert an automatically numbered footnote reference, *or* enter one or more characters as an alternative reference into the Footnote Reference Mark box.

- Next, click the OK button and type the desired footnote text into the footnote pane that Word opens at the bottom of the document window. While the footnote pane is open, you can also edit any other footnotes that have been entered into the document, using standard editing techniques.

- If you want to close the footnote pane, choose the View/Footnotes menu option. You can later reopen the pane by choosing this same menu option again.

- You can delete both a footnote reference and its corresponding text by selecting the reference and pressing Del. You move or copy both a footnote reference and its corresponding text by performing a move or copy operation on the reference alone, using one of the standard techniques presented in Chapter 5.

- You can specify the separator that Word uses to divide the document text from the footnote text at the bottom of each page. You can also specify the message that Word prints whenever a footnote is continued on the next page. To specify one of these options, click the appropriate button at the bottom of the Insert/Footnote dialog box.

- You can have Word place footnote text at the bottom of the page on which the reference occurs, immediately below the document text on this page, at the end of the section, or at the end of the document. You can also tell Word the starting footnote number to use, and whether to restart footnote numbering with each document section. These options are all selected within the Footnotes area of the Format/Document dialog box.

11

CREATING INDEXES AND
TABLES OF CONTENTS

IN THIS CHAPTER, YOU WILL LEARN HOW TO USE
Word to automatically create indexes, tables of contents, and other
tables of items for your documents.

An *index* is a list of important words and topics contained in a document, together with the page number or numbers on which each
word or topic is found. Rather than manually going through a
finished document and typing each item into an index, you can have
Word automatically compile an index from entries you insert while
you are writing the document. Not only does Word's indexing feature save you the time required to type and format an index, but also
you can have Word automatically *update* the index whenever the position of one or more page breaks in the document changes.

In this chapter, the general term *table of contents* is used to refer to all
types of lists created using the Word table of contents feature. You can
use Word to automatically create tables of contents, as well as other

lists, such as lists of figures, tables, photographs, or illustrations. As you will see, you can include more than one table of contents within a single document.

CREATING INDEXES

Using the Word indexing feature consists of two main steps:

1. Specifying each item that is to be included in the index by inserting an *index entry* directly into the document text at the point where the word or topic is discussed.

2. Inserting the index itself. When you insert an index, Word generates an index based upon the entries that you inserted.

In this section, you will learn how to insert index entries, and how to insert and update the index itself.

INSERTING INDEX ENTRIES

> Be sure to place the index entry immediately *after* the document text you are indexing; otherwise, Word may insert a page break between the index entry and the text, resulting in the index containing the wrong page number.

For each item you want Word to include in the index, you must insert an index entry into the document text. To insert an index entry, perform the following steps:

1. Place the insertion point immediately after the discussion of the word or topic within the document. For example, to index the topic "watering" in a book on house plants, you might place the insertion point after the following sentence, assuming that this sentence concludes the discussion on watering:

   Thus, the importance of regular watering cannot be overemphasized.

2. Choose the Insert/Index Entry menu command. Word will display the dialog box shown in Figure 11.1.

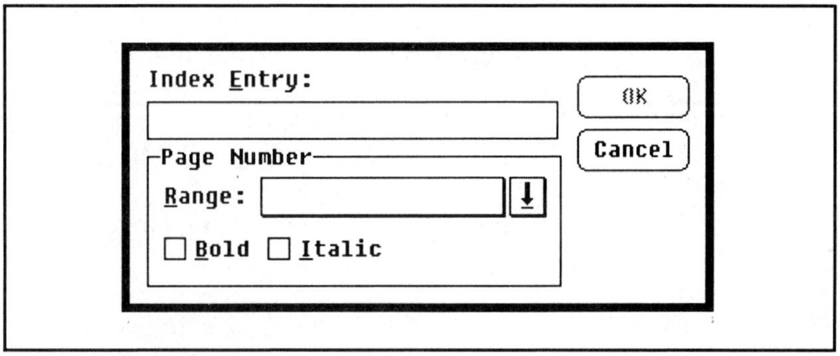

```
┌─────────────────────────────────────────────────────┐
│                                                       │
│   Index Entry:                          ┌────────┐    │
│                                         │   OK   │    │
│   ┌─────────────────────────────┐       └────────┘    │
│   │                             │       ┌────────┐    │
│   ┌─Page Number─────────────────┐       │ Cancel │    │
│   │ Range: ┌───────────────┐ ┌─┐│       └────────┘    │
│   │        │               │ │↓││                     │
│   │        └───────────────┘ └─┘│                     │
│   │  ☐ Bold  ☐ Italic           │                     │
│   └─────────────────────────────┘                     │
│                                                       │
└─────────────────────────────────────────────────────┘
```

Figure 11.1: The Insert/Index Entry dialog box

If you selected by highlighting before going to the Insert/Index Entry dialog box, only the first 64 characters of selected text would be displayed in the box.

3. Type the description you want to appear in the index into the Index Entry box, as in the following example:

Index Entry:

```
watering|
```

The maximum number of characters you can enter is 253.

4. Click the OK button or press ⏎.

Word will insert an index entry into the document at the position of the insertion point. In the example just given, the index entry would be placed at the end of the sentence and would look like this on the screen:

Thus, the importance of regular watering cannot be overemphasized.{XE "watering"}|

The meaning of the various parts of the index entry will be described shortly.

If the example index entry were located on page 12 of the document, Word would include the following item in the index when you compiled the index as described later in the chapter:

watering, 12

In this example, since the description of the topic (**watering**) *is included* *in the document text,* you could save typing using the following alternative method for inserting an index entry:

1. *Select* the word or the description of the topic within the document text, as in the following example:

Thus, the importance of regular **watering** cannot be overemphasized.

> If the current selection contains more than 64 characters, Word will show only the first 64 characters.

2. Choose the Insert/Index Entry menu command. Notice that the selected text already appears in the Index Entry box within the Insert/Index Entry dialog box.

Index Entry:

```
watering
```

3. Click the OK button or press ↵. You can choose several options; see the section "Using Options in the Insert/Index Dialog Box" below.

If you insert more than one index entry with the same description (that is, the text entered into the Index Entry box is the same for two or more entries), Word will combine these entries into a single item in the index. For instance, if you inserted the example entry on pages 12 *and* 25, the resulting index item would be as follows:

watering, 12,25

The text that is inserted into your document when you issue the Insert/Index Entry command is a particular type of Word *field*. Fields are displayed in this way on your screen:

{XE "watering"}.

A field is an instruction to the Word program that is embedded in a document. It is *not* part of the normal text that is printed; rather, it instructs Word to insert some item or perform some action.

The braces ({ and }) surrounding the field are special characters that indicate the boundaries of the field. You cannot type in these characters using the keyboard; rather, you must insert them into your document through an appropriate command, such as Insert/ Index Entry. (You can, however, type or edit text *between* the braces.) The letters **XE** tell Word that the field is an index entry. The quote characters enclose the exact text that is to appear in the resulting index item.

Once you have inserted an index entry through the Insert/Index Entry command, you do not need to reissue this command if you want to alter the text for the index item. Rather, you can simply edit the characters inside the quote characters using standard editing methods.

See Chapter 16 for information on hidden text.

Notice that the entire index entry field is underlined with a dotted line. This marking indicates that the characters are formatted as *hidden text*. Hidden text is visible on the screen only when the Hidden Text item is selected within the View/Preferences dialog box. Also, hidden text is visible on the printed copy of the document only when the Hidden Text item in the File/Print dialog box is selected at the time you print the document. Because index entries are formatted as hidden text, you should observe the following guidelines while working with a document containing index entries:

- Enable the Hidden Text item in the View/Preferences dialog box while entering text into your document, so that you can see where index entries have been inserted and you can edit the entries if desired.

- Disable the Hidden Text item in the View/Preferences dialog box when previewing the printed appearance of the document and making final formatting changes (as discussed in Chapter 17). If hidden text is visible, it may change the position of page breaks and other elements of the page layout.

- When you print the document, make sure that the Hidden Text item within the Include area of the File/Print dialog box is turned off so that the index entries are not printed.

Note finally that you can delete, move, or copy an index entry field that has been inserted into your document, using the standard

CH. 11

To delete, move, or copy the index entry, make sure that you select the entire field before performing the operation.

operations presented in Chapter 5. Since, however, an index entry is a field, when performing these operations, you will notice the following characteristics:

- You cannot delete any portion of the index entry by placing the insertion point in front of it and pressing Del, nor can you delete it by placing the insertion point after the field and pressing Backspace.

- If you place the insertion point in front of the index entry and press Shift-→, or if you place the insertion point after the index entry and press Shift-←, Word will select the *entire index entry* with a single keystroke. If, however, you place the insertion point inside the index entry field, you can select one or more individual characters.

Since index entries are Word fields, an alternative method for entering one into your document is to press Ctrl-F9 to insert an empty field, and then manually type in the contents of the field. You could also use the Insert/Field menu command. For information on these alternative techniques, see the "Fields" topic in the Word *User's Reference* or *Technical Reference*.

Specifying Multiple-Level Index Items

Index items can contain two or more levels. For example, the following index items are displayed on two levels:

    bugs
        eliminating, 24
        identifying, 20
        on orchids, 115

To insert an actual colon character into the text for an index item—without creating an additional level—type a backslash character immediately in front of the colon (that is, type \:).

To create an index item that consists of two or more levels, simply insert a colon character (:) into the entry text to separate each level. For example, to create the first of the example index items shown above, you would type the following text into the Index Entry box:

    bugs:eliminating

Using Options in the Insert/Index Entry Dialog Box

Before clicking the OK button to insert an index entry, you can select one or more options within the Insert/Index Entry dialog box. These options affect the page number printed within the resulting index item. They are located within the Page Number area of the dialog box.

```
┌─Page Number──────────────────────────┐
│ Range:  [                        ] [↓]│
│                                       │
│ ☐ Bold  ☐ Italic                      │
└───────────────────────────────────────┘
```

First, you can specify a page number *range* by typing the name of a bookmark into the Range list box, or by selecting the name of a bookmark from the pull-down list.

```
Range: [|                        ] [↓]
       │ w                        │ [↑]
       │                          │ [ ]
       │                          │ [↓]
```

As you have seen, when Word compiles an index, it normally displays only a single page number for each index entry in the document (which is the number of the page containing the index entry field). However, the text you want to index may be located on more than one page. To have Word display the correct range of pages in the index, use the following procedure:

1. Select the entire block of text that you want to index. For example, if you were entering an index entry for the word **watering**, you would select the entire discussion on this topic.

2. Choose the Insert/Bookmark menu command, type a name for the bookmark into the Bookmark Name box

   Bookmark Name:
   ```
   [w|                        ]
   ```

and then click the OK button. Alternatively, you can press

As explained in Chapter 4, a bookmark is a label you can assign to a position in a document or to a block of one or more characters.

the Ctrl-Shift-F5 key combination and type a name for the bookmark at the prompt within the status bar.

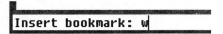

3. Choose the Insert/Index Entry menu command.

4. Type the word or description for the index item into the Index Entry box.

5. Type the name of the bookmark assigned in step 2 into the Range box, or select this name from the pull-down list

and click the OK button. Word will insert the appropriate index entry field into the document.

{XE "watering" \r "w"}

Although defining and specifying a bookmark adds a lot of work to inserting an index entry, it is the safest general method to use, since it is difficult to know in advance whether the indexed text will span more than one page. If you specify a bookmark and the corresponding text ends up on only a single page, then Word will display only a single page number.

While the Insert/Index Entry dialog box is open, you can also select the Bold option, the Italic option, or both. The Bold option causes Word to use bold text for the number, and the Italic option causes Word to use italic text for the number.

Using Switches to Specify Index Entry Options

You can specify one or more additional options that affect the way Word processes an index entry by using switches. A *switch* is a backslash

(\) followed by a letter and possibly some text; it is inserted directly into the index entry field. For example, the switch \b that is a part of the following index entry would cause Word to use boldface letters for the page number in the index entry (it has the same effect as choosing the Bold option within the Insert/Index Entry dialog box):

{XE "fertilizers" \b}

Use the following general procedure to specify an index entry option with a switch:

1. Place the insertion point at the position where you would like to insert the index entry, and issue the Insert/Index Entry menu command.

2. Type the text for the index entry into the Index Entry box in the dialog box. Do *not,* however, include the switch or any of the text that follows the switch.

3. Click the OK button. Word will insert an index entry field.

4. Type the switch and any following text directly into the field. You can include more than one switch in a single index entry field.

Word inserts all text entered into the Index Entry box between quotation marks in the resulting field; switches must *follow* the closing quote mark.

Table 11.1 lists the switches you can include in an index entry field.

Notice that each of the switches in Table 11.1, except \t, produces the same effect as an option within the Insert/Index Entry dialog box. (These options were explained in the previous section.)

You can use the \t switch to create cross-references. Specifically, you can create an index item that refers to another item rather than including the page number(s). To use this switch, type the following four items into the index entry field immediately after the entry text (in the order given): a space, the \t switch, another space, and the text for the cross-reference. If the text for the cross-reference contains one or more spaces, the entire text must be enclosed in quotes. For example, the index entry field

{XE "moisture" \t "see watering"}

Table 11.1: Switches You Can Use in an Index Entry Field

SWITCH:	EFFECT:
\b	Specifies bold page number (same as Bold option in Insert/Index Entry dialog box).
\i	Specifies italic page number (same as Italic option in Insert/Index Entry dialog box).
\r *bookmark*	Prints the range of page numbers that contain the specified bookmark (same as Range option in Insert/Index Entry dialog box).
\t *"text"*	Prints *text* rather than a page number (must enclose *text* in quote characters if it consists of more than one word).

would generate this item in the index:

moisture, see watering

INSERTING THE INDEX

The different options you can choose are discussed in the next section, "Using Options in the Insert/ Index Dialog Box."

Once you have completed writing your document and inserting all desired index entries, you can have Word compile an index from these entries and insert it into the document. Use the following steps for creating an index:

1. Place the insertion point at the position in the document where you want the index. Although an index is normally placed near the end of a document, Word allows you to insert an index at any desired location.

If the View/Field Codes menu option is enabled, you will see the field code {INDEX} rather than seeing the index itself. Therefore, to see the index on the screen, make sure that this option is not selected.

2. Issue the Insert/Index menu command. Word will display the dialog box shown in Figure 11.2.

3. Choose the desired options.

4. Click the OK button.

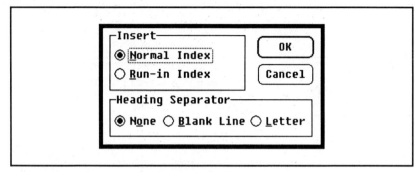

Figure 11.2: The Insert/Index dialog box

Word will insert an up-to-date index based upon the index entries it finds in the document. When Word creates an index, it automatically paginates the document, as described in Chapter 17.

If you later delete, add, or change one or more index entries, or make any editing or formatting change to the document that changes the position of page breaks, you must *update* the index. To update the index, place the insertion point anywhere within the index—or select the index—and press the F9 key. Alternatively, you can update an index by choosing the Update Fields option when printing the document (see Chapter 17).

You can also delete, move, or copy an index using the standard operations presented in Chapter 5. Like an index entry, an index is actually a Word field. Therefore, when performing these operations, you will notice the following characteristics:

- You cannot use the Del key to delete any portion of an index when the insertion point is in front of it, nor can you delete text from an index by placing the insertion point after the field and pressing Backspace.

- If you place the insertion point in front of the index and press Shift-→, or if you place the insertion point after the index and press Shift-←, Word will select the *entire index* with a single keystroke.

Using Options in the Insert/Index Dialog Box

While the Insert/Index dialog box is open, you can choose one or more options that affect the appearance of the index that Word

---

You can freely edit text within an index. However, your editing changes will be lost if the index is subsequently updated.

To delete, move, or copy the index, make sure that you select the entire field before performing the operation.

Creating multiple-
level index items is
discussed in the section
"Specifying Multiple-
Level Index Items."

compiles. First, within the Insert box you can choose either the Normal Index option or the Run-in Index option. These options determine the way Word formats multiple-level index items.

Normal Index is the default option, and causes Word to start each index subitem on a new line, and to indent each subitem. For example, the following index item contains three levels and was created with the Normal Index option:

```
plants
    carnivorous
        feeding, 78
```

The Run-in Index option causes Word to place all subitems within the same paragraph. Also, Word will separate the first two subitems with a colon (:), and will separate the remaining items with semicolons (;), rather than separating them with line breaks. If the index item shown in the example just given were created with the Run-in Index option, it would be formatted as follows:

```
plants: carnivorous; feeding, 78
```

You can also choose one of the three options in the Heading Separator box:

```
┌─Heading Separator──────────────┐
│ ◉ None  ○ Blank Line  ○ Letter │
└────────────────────────────────┘
```

These options specify how Word divides the index items for each letter of the alphabet (that is, how it divides the items starting with the letter **a** from those starting with the letter **b**, and so on).

The default option is None, which leaves no separator or lines between groups of index items. The following is a portion of an index formatted with the None option:

```
African violet, 214
Amaranthus, 267, 315
Aphids, 38
Avocado, 239–241
Banana, 189, 218
Begonia, 146–148
```

The Blank Line option causes Word to leave a blank line between sections, as in the following example:

African violet, 214
Amaranthus, 267, 315
Aphids, 38
Avocado, 239–241

Banana, 189, 218
Begonia, 146–148

Finally, the Letter option causes Word to label each section with the appropriate letter, as illustrated by the following index items:

A
African violet, 214
Amaranthus, 267, 315
Aphids, 38
Avocado, 239–241
B
Banana, 189, 218
Begonia, 146–148

Using Switches to Specify Index Options

Switches are explained in the section "Using Switches to Specify Index Entry Options."

You can use switches to specify several options that affect the way Word compiles an index. The switches used for specifying index options, however, are different than the ones to specify index entry options. When you use switches for compiling an index, however, it is easier to manually enter the entire field contents using the Insert Field key (Ctrl-F9), rather than using the Insert/Index menu command.

You could also enter an index field by using the Insert/Field menu command. See the topic "Fields" in the Word *User's Reference* or *Technical Reference.*

Use the following general method to specify an option with a switch when you create an index:

1. Place the insertion point at the position in the document where you want the index.

2. Press the Ctrl-F9 keystroke (the Insert Field key) to insert an empty field at the position of the insertion point.

{}

You can include more than one switch in a single index field.

3. Type the following items into the field (in the order given): the word **index**, a space, and one or more switches together with any accompanying text (the text for each switch should follow that particular switch). For example, the following field would create an index containing only those entries beginning with the letters **a** through **g**:

{index \p A-G}

4. When you have completed typing in the contents of the field, press the F9 key while the insertion point is still within the field. Word will compile the index, and replace the field with the actual index.

Make sure that the View/Field Codes item on the menu is turned off; otherwise, you will see the field code rather than the index.

5. If you need to edit the field contents, you can temporarily remove the index and restore the field by pressing the Shift-F9 key combination while the insertion point is within the index. When you have completed editing the field, press F9 again to display the latest version of the index.

Table 11.2 lists the most important switches you can use within an index field.

Table 11.2: Some Switches That You Can Include in an Index Field

SWITCH	EFFECT
\b *bookmark*	Compiles index using only entries found in the block of text labeled by *bookmark*.
\e *chars*	Specifies separator between description and page number in index item (default is a comma followed by a space). You can use a tab character, but be sure to enclose it in quotes.
\g *chars**	Specifies separator between the two page numbers in a range (default is a hyphen; for example, **23–28**).
\h *chars**	Specifies characters to be used as headings for each group of index items beginning with a given letter. (See Table 11.3.)

Table 11.2: Some Switches That You Can Include in an Index Field
(continued)

SWITCH	EFFECT
\l *chars***	Specifies characters to be used to separate individual numbers in a list of page numbers for an index item.
\p *letter–letter*	Includes only index items beginning with letters in the range *letter–letter*.
\r	Does not separate index subitems with line breaks (same as the Run-in Index option in Insert/Index dialog box).

* *chars* denotes one or more characters; if it includes any space or tab characters, you must enclose all of the characters in quotes.

The \b switch allows you to compile an index for a *portion* of a document. Simply assign a bookmark to the portion of the document you want to index, and type the bookmark name following the \b switch in the index field. The method for assigning bookmarks is discussed in the section "Using Options within the Insert/Index Entry Dialog Box."

The \h switch permits you specify the characters, if any, to be used as headings for each group of index items that begin with the same letter. This switch permits a finer level of control over the index headings than the three options within the Insert/Index dialog box that were described previously. Table 11.3 describes the effects of specifying different characters with this switch.

Notice in Table 11.3 that if you enter one or more alphabetic characters, Word ignores the specific letters entered and simply uses the appropriate letter for each section of index items (that is, it will use **A** for the items that begin with A, and so on).

Finally, the \p switch allows you to generate partial indexes. With this switch, Word will compile an index that contains only those entries that begin with the letters within the specified range of the alphabet. For example, the following field would create an index that

Table 11.3: Effects of Specifying Various Character Combinations with the \h Switch

CHARACTERS USED WITH \H:	EFFECT:
Any single letter (such as **A** or **x**	Headings will be **A, B, C,** and so on.
Several letters	Headings will match the *number* of letters given; for example, if you specified **xxx** or **abc,** headings would be **AAA, BBB, CCC,** and so on.
Nonalphabetic characters(s)	Character(s) printed literally in headings; for example, specifying ***x*** would result in the headings ***A*,** ***B*, *C*,** and so on.
Blank space (that is, " ")	Blank line between each group of index items (the same as Blank Line option in Insert/Index dialog box).
No character (that is, " ")	No headings (the same as None option in Insert/Index dialog box).

consists of entries beginning with letters in the range from A to M:

```
{index \p A-M}
```

Compiling a large index can cause your computer to run out of memory. Microsoft recommends that if the index contains over 4,000 entries, you should compile it a portion at a time. You can compile a complete index in sections by using the \p switch. Simply specify the different portions of the index in separate fields, placing these fields next to each other in the document. For example, the following fields would create a complete index in two sections:

```
{index \p A-M}{index \p N-Z}
```

After inserting these fields, select *all* of them and press F9 to convert them into the actual index. When Word creates the index, it will insert a blank line between each section; if desired, you can manually delete these blank lines.

CREATING TABLES OF CONTENTS

The process for creating a table of contents is similar to that for creating an index. Like an index, a table of contents is created in two basic steps:

> If you have entered outline headings into your document as described in Chapter 24, you can use them instead of entries to generate a table of contents.

1. You specify each item that is to be included in the table of contents by inserting a *table of contents entry* directly into the document text at the position of the item you want listed.

2. You insert the table of contents itself. Word will automatically compile the table either from table of contents entries or from outline headings.

In this section, you will learn how to insert table of contents entries, and how to generate a table of contents from these entries.

There is another method for creating a table of contents, not covered in this chapter. This method uses outline headings. As you will see in Chapter 24 (which discusses outlining), you can format paragraphs within your document as *outline headings*. An outline heading can be assigned any one of 9 different levels. You can generate a table of contents directly from the existing outline headings in a document. This method eliminates the need to explicitly insert a table of contents entry for each item you want to appear in the table of contents. Instead, Word will include an item in the table, together with its page number, for each outline heading (or for only those headings within a specified range).

INSERTING TABLE OF CONTENTS ENTRIES

To include an item in a table of contents, you must insert a *table of contents entry* within the document text immediately following the text in your document you want referenced. This entry tells Word the

You can also use the Insert/Field menu command to insert a table of contents entry field. See the Word *User's Reference* or *Technical Reference* for instructions.

text that is to appear in the table of contents item, as well as the page number that should be displayed for this item.

Like index entries, which were described previously in the chapter, table of contents entries are Word fields. Since Word does not provide a menu command specifically for inserting table of contents entries, you must insert them using one of the general methods for inserting fields.

The following procedure is a convenient method for inserting table of contents entries. You can use this method for creating a general table of contents or a table of other items such as illustrations. Later in the chapter, you will see how to specify entries when you are including more than one table within a single document.

1. Place the insertion point immediately after the item in your document that you want to reference in the table of contents. For example, you might place it after a heading or the title for a section.

II. Fertilizer|

2. Press the Ctrl-F9 keystroke to insert an empty field.

II. Fertilizer {|}

3. Type the following items into the field: the letters **tc**, a space, an opening quote, the exact text you want to appear in the table of contents, and a closing quote.

II. Fertilizer {tc "Fertilizer"}

When you compile the table of contents entry, the example entry just shown would generate this item in the table

Fertilizer 12

assuming that the table of contents entry was inserted on page 12 of the document.

Like index entries, table of contents entries are automatically formatted as hidden text. You should therefore observe the guidelines for working with hidden text that are listed in the section "Inserting Index Entries."

Once you have inserted a table of contents entry, you can delete, move, or copy it in the same manner as a index entry field, as described previously in the section "Inserting Index Entries."

Using Switches to Specify Table of Contents Entry Options

Switches are discussed in the section "Using Switches to Specify Index Entry Options."

You can use two different switches to specify options when inserting table of contents entries. To specify a switch, simply type it into the **tc** field following the entry text.

First, you can use the \l switch to specify the level of the table of contents item. The level effects the amount of indentation of the item. A level 1 item is flush with the left margin, a level 2 item is indented one tab stop, a level 2 item is indented two tab stops, and so on. Simply type the number of the desired level after the \l switch. You can specify levels 1 through 9; if you do not specify a level, the item will automatically be formatted as a level 1 item.

For example, if the following two table of contents entries were inserted on pages 12 and 13 of the document

{tc "Carnivorous Plants"}

{tc "Venus Fly Traps (Dionaea muscipula)" \l 2}

the following entries would be created in the table of contents:

Carnivorous Plants 12
    Venus Fly Traps (Dionaea muscipula) 13

You can use the \f switch to specify a particular table if you are including more than one table of contents in your document. For example, you might want to include both a general table of contents *and* a table of illustrations. Following the \f switch, type a single letter identifying the particular table in which you want to include the item. You should use a different letter for each table of contents.

For example, if you wanted to generate a general table of contents and a table of illustrations, you could label all entries for the general table with the letter **C**

{tc "Planting" \f C}

and all entries for the table of illustrations with **I**

{tc "A Hyacinth growing upside down in water" \f I}

Later in the chapter, you will see how to compile separate tables using the letters that you assigned to each table with the \f switch.

If you do not *include the \f flag, or if you include the switch but do not specify a letter, Word automatically assigns the letter* **C** *to the entry.*

INSERTING THE TABLE OF CONTENTS

Once you have completed entering all of the table of contents entries, you can insert the table of contents itself at any position in your document. However, if you are including more than one table of contents in your document, you must use a different method for creating a field, which is described in the next section, ''Using Switches to Specify Table of Contents Options.'' Use the following procedure to insert one table of contents:

1. Place the insertion point at the position where you would like to insert the table of contents.

2. Choose the Insert/Table of Contents menu command.

3. Select the Use Table Entry Fields option.

4. Click the OK button or press ←.

Word will compile the table of contents entries and insert the resulting table of contents at the position of the insertion point.

You can edit text within a table of contents. However, your editing changes will be overwritten if you subsequently update the table.

If you later delete, add, or change one or more table of contents entries, or make an editing or formatting change to the document that alters the position of page breaks, you must update the table of contents. To do this, place the insertion point anywhere within the table of contents—or select it—and then press F9. Alternatively, you can choose the Update Fields option when printing the document.

You can delete, move, or copy a table of contents in the same manner as an index, as described in the section "Inserting the Index."

Using Switches to Specify Table of Contents Options

Switches are discussed in the section "Using Switches to Specify Index Entry Options."

Word provides several switches that control the way it compiles a table of contents. If you want to specify a switch when compiling a table of contents, you should manually enter the field using the Insert Field key (Ctrl-F9) rather than using the Insert/Table of Contents menu command. Use the following general method:

1. Place the insertion point at the position in the document where you want the table of contents.

2. Press the Ctrl-F9 keystroke (the Insert Field key) to insert an empty field at the position of the insertion point.

3. Type the following items into the field in the order listed: the word **toc**, a space, one or more switches, and any accompanying text (the text for each switch should follow that particular switch). To compile a table of contents from table of contents entries, you must include the \f switch, which will be explained later. For example, the following field would compile a table for a portion of a document:

   {toc \f \b part1}

   where **part1** is the name of a bookmark, as explained later.

4. When you have completed typing the contents of the field, press the F9 key while the insertion point is still within the field. Word will compile the table of contents, which will replace the field within the document.

If you need to edit the field, you can temporarily remove the table of contents and restore the field by pressing the Shift-F9 key combination while the insertion point is within the table of contents. When you have completed editing the field, press F9 again to display the latest version of the table of contents.

Table 11.4 lists the most important switches you can use within a table of contents field.

Table 11.4: Some Useful Switches You Can Use within a Table of Contents

SWITCH:	EFFECT:
\b *bookmark*	Compiles table of contents using only entries found in the block of text labeled by *bookmark*.
\f *char*	Compiles table of contents using entries identified by *char*.
\o *level1–level2*	Compiles table from outline headings with levels within the range *level1–level2* (see Chapter 24).

The \b switch allows you to compile a table of contents for a *portion* of a document. Simply assign a bookmark to the portion of the document for which you want to create a table, and enter the name of the bookmark following the \b switch. The method for assigning bookmarks was presented previously in the chapter, in the section "Using Options in the Insert/Index Entry Dialog Box."

In order to compile a table of contents from table of contents entries (rather than from outline headings), you *must* include the \f flag in the field. If you do not type a character after this flag, Word will compile a table of contents from *all* entries that are not labeled or are labeled with the character **C**. As explained previously in the chapter (in the section "Using Switches to Specify Table of Contents Entry Options"), you can label a table of contents entry by using the \f flag within the *table of contents* entry field. You need to label table of contents entries if you have more than one table of contents in a single document.

If you type a character after the \f flag in the table of contents field, then Word will compile a table of contents using *only* those entries that are labeled with the same character. For example, the following field would compile a table of contents from all table of contents entries that were identified with the letter **I**:

{toc \f I}

SUMMARY

- To create an index, you must insert an index entry into your document for each item that you want to include in the index. When all entries have been inserted, you can insert the index itself.

- To insert an index entry, place the insertion point immediately after the text you want to index, choose the Insert/ Index menu command, and enter the text you want to appear in the index (into the Index Entry box within the Insert/Index Entry dialog box). Alternatively, you can select the text you want for the index, choose the Insert/Index menu command, and then *instead* of having to retype the text, just click the OK button or press ◂┘. Word will insert an appropriate field into your document.

- To create a multiple-level index item, insert a colon between the text for each level, as you type the description into the Index Entry box.

- To have Word display a *range* of page numbers in an index entry, assign a bookmark to the text you want to index, and type the name of this bookmark into the Range box within the Insert/Index Entry dialog box.

- To create bold or italic index numbers, select the Bold or Italic option within the Insert/Index Entry dialog box.

- You can specify additional options that affect an index entry by typing one or more switches directly into the index entry field. These switches are described in Table 11.1.

- Once you have completed entering the index entries, you can generate the index by placing the insertion point at the desired position in the document and issuing the Insert/ Index menu command.

- Choose the Normal Index option in the Insert/Index dialog box to create an index in which each index subitem is placed on a separate line. Choose the Run-in Index option for an index in which each subitem is separated with a colon or semicolon rather than a line break.

- You can select the type of heading placed at the top of each section of the index by choosing an option from the Heading Separator area of the Insert/Index dialog box.

- You can specify additional options that affect the index by typing one or more switches directly into the index field. These switches are described in Table 11.2.

- To create a table of contents, insert a table of contents entry into your document for each item that you want included in the table of contents. When all entries have been inserted, insert the table of contents itself.

- To insert a table of contents entry, place the insertion point immediately after the text you want to reference in the table, press the Ctrl-F9 keystroke to insert an empty field, and enter the following items into the field: the letters **tc**, a space, and the text you want to appear in the table of contents enclosed in quote characters.

- When entering a table of contents entry, you can include the \l switch to specify the level of the item, or the \f switch to specify a particular table if you are including more than one table in your document.

- When you have completed entering the table of contents entries, you can insert the table of contents itself by placing the insertion point at the appropriate position in your document and choosing the Insert/Table of Contents menu command. Select the Use Table Entry Fields option before clicking the OK button.

- When inserting a table of contents, you can enter one or more switches directly into the table of contents field (press Ctrl-F9, type **toc**, and enter the switches you want). The \b field allows you to compile a table of contents for a *portion* of a document (which is identified using a bookmark). The \f flag allows you to specify a particular table of contents in a document that has more than one table of contents.

- Alternatively, you can create a table of contents directly from outline headings. This method is discussed in Chapter 24.

FORMATTING
AND PRINTING

In Part II, you learned how to enter text and graphics into a Word document. Now that you know how to create the basic document content, this part of the book shows you how to control the printed appearance of a document and how to produce the final printed document copy. Specifically, you will learn how to format each level of a document, how to preview the printed document copy, how to print the document, and how to generate form letters. As you will see, Word takes full advantage of the graphics interface provided by Microsoft Windows, and allows you to precisely control the layout of each page of your documents. Word provides many of the features offered by dedicated **desktop publishing** programs.

12

AN OVERVIEW OF
FORMATTING AND PRINTING

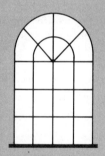

WORD FOR WINDOWS IS DESIGNED TO GIVE YOU A high degree of control over the printed appearance of your documents. This control is provided through a wide variety of *formatting* commands, which are applied to various levels of the document, ranging from individual characters to the entire document.

Working with this large and sophisticated set of commands, however, can be confusing. It may not be clear where to start and what steps to take, and it can be difficult to find the exact command required to format a particular document element (such as line numbers). Before Part III plunges into the many details of formatting, this chapter is provided to assist you in two ways.

First, to help you get started, it provides an overview of the basic steps required to format and print a document. Second, to help you find the appropriate formatting commands, it lists the document elements that are formatted by each basic command.

FORMATTING AND PRINTING YOUR DOCUMENT: THE BASIC STEPS

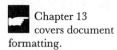 The options used for precisely formatting a document are often referred to as desktop publishing features.

Once you have entered the basic document content, as described in the Parts I and II, you are ready to adjust the printed appearance of the document and to generate the final printed copy. The following are the basic steps for formatting and printing your document:

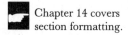 Chapter 13 covers document formatting.

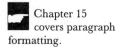 Chapter 14 covers section formatting.

1. Apply document formatting commands. They are used to set features for the *entire document*, such as the page size, the margins, and the default positions of tab stops.

2. Apply section formatting commands. They set features for the *entire document section*, such as the number of text columns and the presence of line numbering. As you will see, a document consists of one or more sections. If you want to vary any of these formatting features within a document, you should first divide the document into two or more sections, and then apply the appropriate section formatting commands to each section. For example, if you want to have one text column (the default) in one portion of a document, and two columns in another portion, you should first divide the document into two sections, and then specify the desired number of columns for each section.

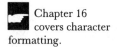 Chapter 15 covers paragraph formatting.

3. Apply paragraph formatting commands. They set features for one or more individual paragraphs, including the alignment on the page, indentations, the line spacing, and many other characteristics.

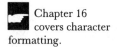 Chapter 16 covers character formatting.

4. Apply character formatting commands. They set features for one or more characters, such as the font, the character size, and the presence of enhancements such as italics.

5. If desired, perform automatic hyphenation. It must be done after you have completed editing and formatting the document so that all line breaks are at their final positions.

6. Preview the printed appearance of the document and perform any required formatting adjustments by entering the Print Preview or Page View mode.

7. Perform automatic hyphenation again if you are hyphenating the document, and if changes made in step 6 affected the positions of one or more line breaks.

8. Set the printing options and print the document.

You may not need to perform all of these steps, and you may not want to perform them in the order given, for several reasons. First, as you saw in Chapter 3, when you create a new document, it is based upon a document template that specifies a set of default formatting features. You do not need to issue a formatting command unless you want to change a default feature. For example, you may want to accept all of the default document and section formatting features. In this case, you do not need to perform steps 1 and 2 above.

Second, you may want to issue formatting commands while you are still entering text and graphics into the document. For example, while typing in the document text you might want to choose the italic character enhancement, then enter the text that is to appear in italics, and turn off the italic enhancement to resume entering normal characters.

Third, you do not need to apply the formatting commands in the order listed (in other words, steps 1 through 4 can be performed in any order). However, there may be an advantage to following this order. Notice that according to the list, the document is formatted starting with the highest level (the entire document) and proceeding toward the lowest level (characters). To specify certain document features, you must follow this order. For example, to have Word display line numbers, you must *first* specify a section formatting option to enable line numbering for the entire section; you can *then* turn line numbering off for one or more paragraphs through the appropriate paragraph formatting feature.

Finally, as you become a more experienced Word user and begin using advanced features such as document templates and style definitions, you may follow a very different series of steps when preparing a document.

FINDING THE CORRECT FORMATTING COMMAND

You choose the four basic Word formatting commands directly from the Format main menu item.

Format
Character...
Paragraph...
Section...
Document...

Each of these commands allows you to format one of the four basic levels of a document, and each command displays a dialog box that allows you to choose one or more formatting options. The dialog boxes and the options they contain will be described in detail in the following chapters.

When formatting your document, however, it may not be obvious at which level a particular document feature must be formatted. For example, if you want to add line numbers, you may wonder whether they must be enabled for the entire document using the Format/ Document command, or whether they must be enabled for one or more specific sections using the Format/Section command. Table 12.1 will help you find the appropriate command for formatting a given document element.

Table 12.1: Document Features Formatted through the Four Basic Formatting Commands

USE THE FORMAT/DOCUMENT COMMAND (CHAPTER 13) TO FORMAT:
Footnotes: position within document (bottom of page, beneath text, end of section, or end of document)
Footnotes: restart numbering with each section
Footnotes: starting number
Margins: enable mirrored margins
Margins: top, bottom, left, right, inside, or outside
Margins: gutter width (space added to left or inside margin)
Page height
Page width

Table 12.1: Document Features Formatted through the Four Basic Formatting Commands (continued)

USE THE FORMAT/DOCUMENT COMMAND (CHAPTER 13) TO FORMAT:

Tab stops: default spacing

Template attached to document

Widow control (eliminates single lines separated from rest of paragraph)

USE THE FORMAT/SECTION COMMAND (CHAPTER 14) TO FORMAT:

Columns of text: number of

Columns of text: space between

Columns of text: line between

Footnotes: enable printing at end of section

Line numbering: increment value (that is, count by 1, by 2, by 3, and so on)

Line numbering: distance between numbers and text

Line numbering: enable

Line numbering: restart position (restart on each page, section, or number continuously through document)

Line numbering: starting number

Section: starting position (on same page, on new page, and so on)

Section: vertical alignment (with top, with center, or justified)

USE THE FORMAT/PARAGRAPH COMMAND (CHAPTER 15) TO FORMAT:

Alignment: left, center, right, or justified

Border: none, box, bar, above, or below; using various patterns

Indent: left

Indent: right

Table 12.1: Document Features Formatted through the Four Basic Formatting Commands (continued)

USE THE **FORMAT/PARAGRAPH** COMMAND (**CHAPTER 15**) TO FORMAT:
Indent: left indent of first line
Line numbering: enable
Page break before paragraph
Paragraph: keep together on page
Paragraph: keep together with next paragraph
Space before paragraph
Space after paragraph
Space between lines in paragraph
Style of paragraph (see Chapter 20)
Tab stops: position and style

USE THE **FORMAT/CHARACTER** COMMAND (**CHAPTER 15**) TO FORMAT:
Color
Enhancement(s): bold, italic, small caps, hidden, underline, word underline, double underline
Font (Tms Rmn, Courier, Script, and so on)
Position: normal, superscript, or subscript
Size in points
Spacing: normal, expanded, or condensed

In addition to the four major formatting commands listed in Table 12.1, Word provides two additional menu commands for formatting paragraphs: Format/Tabs and Format/Position. Format/Tabs sets the position and style of the tab stops for one or more selected paragraphs. You can also access this command through the Format/Paragraph dialog box. Format/Position places a paragraph containing text or graphics at a specific position on the page. Since

The ruler is covered in Chapter 15, and the ribbon is discussed in Chapter 16.

both these commands affect paragraphs, they are discussed along with the Format/Paragraph command in Chapter 15.

As you will see in the following chapters, you can issue the paragraph and character formatting commands using the keyboard as well as through the menu commands described in this section. You will also see that you can format paragraphs by directly manipulating a collection of icons at the top of the screen known as the *ruler*. You will learn how to display the ruler, and how to use it with the mouse or keyboard. Similarly, you can format characters using a collection of icons known as the *ribbon*.

FEATURES FORMATTED AT SEVERAL LEVELS

If a single feature is formatted at more than one document level, you should format it first at the highest level and then proceed toward the lowest level. An example of such a feature is line numbering. You must *first* enable line number for one or more entire sections using the Format/Section command. You can *then* turn line numbering off for one or more selected paragraphs by issuing the Format/ Paragraph command.

Footnotes are another example of a feature formatted at more than one level. As you saw in Chapter 10, you determine where footnotes are placed within your document through the Format/Document command. If you choose the End of Section option, footnote text will be placed at the end of each section. You can then, however, disable footnotes for one or more specific sections through the Format/ Section command (in this case, the footnote text will be moved to the end of the next section for which footnotes are enabled).

Tab positions are also set at several document levels. First, you can set the default tab spacing for the entire document using the Format/ Document command. You can then adjust the position and type of tab stops for one or more paragraphs through the Format/Paragraph or Format/Tabs command.

SUMMARY

- To format and print your document, first proceed from the highest toward the lowest level: document, section, paragraph, and character formatting. Next, if desired, perform automatic hyphenation. Then preview the document, adjust the formatting, set the printing options, and print.

- To determine which formatting command to use for formatting a given feature, refer to Table 12.1. If a feature you want to use is formatted at more than one level, proceed from highest to lowest document levels.

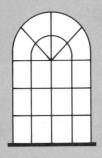

13

FORMATTING DOCUMENTS

IN THIS CHAPTER, YOU WILL LEARN HOW TO CHOOSE formatting options that affect the entire document. These options are selected through the Format/Document menu command.

When you choose the Format/Document command, Word displays the dialog box shown in Figure 13.1. You will learn how to set the following formatting options using this dialog box:

- Page size
- Margins
- Default tab stops
- Footnote placement
- Widow control
- Template attached to document

In this chapter, you will also learn how to cause Word to use your current document formatting settings as the default values, so that these settings will automatically be applied to future documents. Finally, you will see how to override the document formatting settings for one or more sections or paragraphs.

As you can see in Figure 13.1, each of the text boxes within the Format/Document dialog box displays the current setting for the option. You do not need to enter a value unless you want to *change* the current setting. To remove the dialog box and apply any changes you have entered, click the OK button. To remove the dialog box without applying changes, click the Cancel button.

SETTING THE PAGE SIZE

See Appendix B for a discussion on entering measurements into Word dialog boxes.

The page size is the first of a series of settings that allow Word to compose each page of the document. The page size is the physical

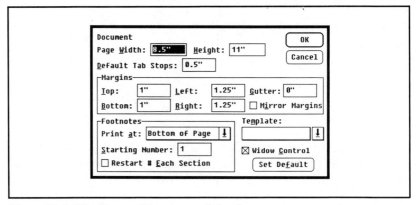

Figure 13.1: The Format/Document dialog box

size of the paper on which you are going to print the document (see Figure 13.3, in the next section). The page width is set through the Page Width box on the Format/Document dialog box, and the page height is set through the Height box. These boxes display the current values, as shown in Figure 13.1. If you want to change a value, enter the new value into the appropriate box.

Word will issue a warning if you try to print—or use Print Preview—and the page size specified in the Format/Document dialog box differs from that specified through the File/Printer Setup menu command discussed in Chapter 17. The two sizes should be the same.

SETTING THE DOCUMENT MARGINS —

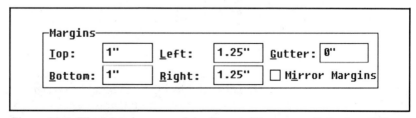 You can also set the document margins using the Word *ruler*. Since the ruler is primarily a device for formatting paragraphs, it is described in Chapter 15.

A *margin* is the distance between the document text and the edge of the paper. You can specify the document margins through the Margins area of the Format/Document dialog box. The way that Word sets the margins depends upon whether you choose the Mirror Margins option within this dialog box.

SETTING MARGINS WITHOUT *THE MIRROR MARGINS* OPTION

If you are designing a document that is to be printed on only one side of the paper, you should *not* select the Mirror Margins option. When this option is not selected, you can set the top, bottom, left, and right margins, as well as the gutter margin, which will be explained later. When Mirror Margins is not selected, the Margins area appears as illustrated in Figure 13.2.

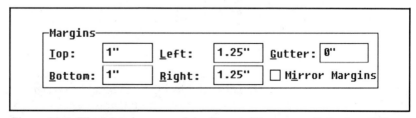

Figure 13.2: The Margins area of the Format/Document dialog box (Mirror Margins option *not* selected)

If you enter a negative value into the Top or Bottom box, Word will set the margin as if the number were positive; however, Word will *not* adjust the margin if a header or footer is too large to fit within the margin area (rather, the text and header or footer will overlap).

The Top, Bottom, Left, and Right boxes display the current margin settings. If you want to change a setting, enter the desired measurement into the appropriate box. Figure 13.3 illustrates the four page margins, as well as the page width and height.

You can also specify a gutter margin by entering the desired value into the Gutter box.

<u>G</u>utter: 0"

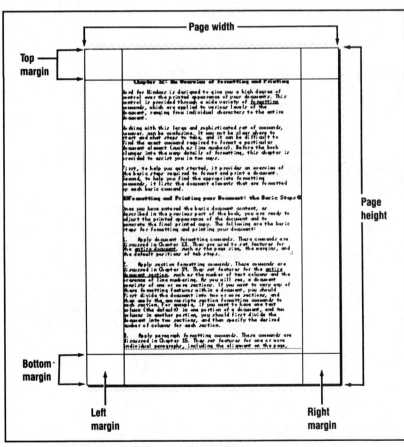

Figure 13.3: The top, bottom, left, and right document margins (Mirror Margins option *not* selected)

When the Mirror Margins option is off, the *gutter margin* is an additional space that is added to the *left margin* of each page. Note that specifying a gutter margin does not change the value displayed in the Left box; rather, when Word calculates the left margin, it *adds* the values in the Left and Gutter boxes. The purpose of a gutter margin is to allow room for binding the printed copy of the document. To add a gutter margin, enter the desired value into the Gutter box. Figure 13.4 illustrates the same document shown in Figure 13.3 after specifying a 0.5″ gutter margin (the gutter shown in Figure 13.3 is 0″).

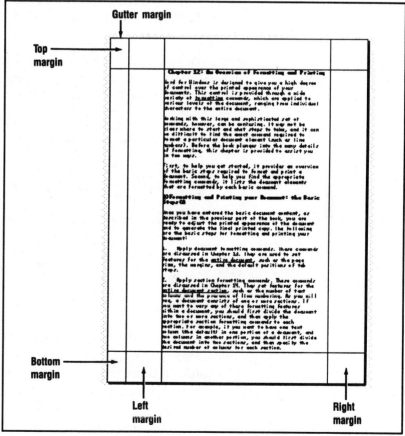

Figure 13.4: A document with a gutter margin (Mirror Margins option *not* selected)

Note that rather than specifying a gutter margin, you could simply add the desired amount to the left-margin value in the Left box. Thus, you could produce the same effect by using either of the following two procedures:

- Specifying a gutter margin of 0.5″

- Specifying a gutter margin of 0″ and adding 0.5″ to the value entered into the Left box

SETTING MARGINS WITH THE MIRROR MARGINS OPTION

If you are creating a document that is to be printed on both sides of the paper, you can choose the Mirror Margins option so that the left and right margins on facing pages will be symmetric (that is, mirror images of each other). When you select this option, the Margins area of the dialog box appears as shown in Figure 13.5.

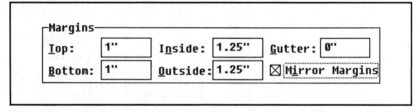

Figure 13.5: The Margins area of the Format/Document dialog box (Mirror Margins selected)

Notice that, compared to Figure 13.2, in the dialog box in Figure 13.5 the Left box is replaced with the Inside box, and the Right box is replaced with the Outside box.

The value entered into the Inside box specifies the left margin on odd-numbered pages and the right margin on even-numbered pages. If the printed document pages are bound as in a book, this margin will always be on the inside (that is, on the side near the binding).

Likewise, the value entered into the Outside box specifies the right margin on odd-numbered pages and the left margin on even-numbered pages. When the pages are bound, this margin will always be on the outside (that is, on the side away from the binding).

The Top, Bottom, Inside, and Outside boxes contain the current margin settings. If you want to change a setting, enter the desired measurement into the appropriate box. Figure 13.6 illustrates two facing pages (an even-numbered and an odd-numbered page), belonging to a document that has been assigned an inside margin of 1.75″ and an outside margin of 0.75″.

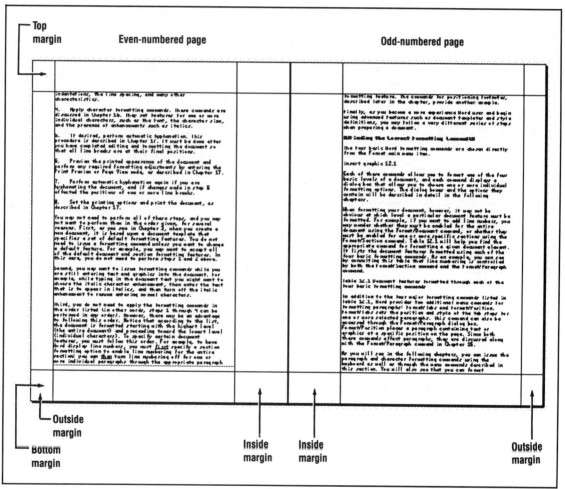

Figure 13.6: The top, bottom, inside, and outside page margins (Mirror Margins option selected)

You can also specify a gutter margin by entering the desired value into the Gutter box. When the Mirror Margins option is off, the gutter margin is an additional space added to the *inside* margin on all pages. Specifying a gutter margin does not change the value displayed in the Inside box; rather, when Word calculates the inside margin, it *adds* the values in the Inside and Gutter boxes. Figure 13.7 illustrates the same document shown in Figure 13.6 with a 0.5″ gutter margin (the gutter shown in Figure 13.6 is 0).

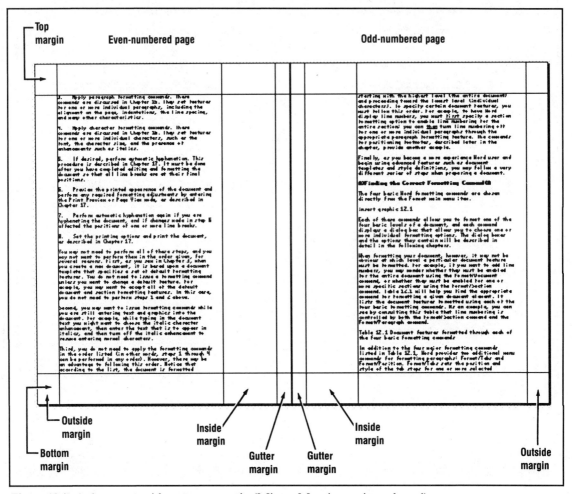

Figure 13.7: A document with a gutter margin (Mirror Margins option selected)

SETTING THE DEFAULT TAB STOPS

The Default Tab Stops box displays the current default distance between tab stops.

In Chapter 15, you will learn how to adjust the positions and types of tab stops for one or more paragraphs. The tab stops you set override the default stops.

```
Default Tab Stops: 0.5"
```

If you want to change the value, enter the desired measurement into this box (the initial value assigned by Microsoft is 0.5″).

As you have seen, each time you press the Tab key while typing in document text, Word aligns the insertion point at the next tab stop. Word automatically assigns a series of tab stops to all paragraphs in the document. The measurement entered into the Default Tab Stops box is the distance between these tab stops. For example, if this measurement is 0.5″, the first tab stop will be 0.5″ from the left margin, the second tab stop 1.0″ from the left margin, and so on until the right margin is reached.

ASSIGNING FOOTNOTE PLACEMENT

You can use the options within the Footnotes area of the Format/Document dialog box to specify the following features of the footnotes in your document:

The footnote options were fully described in Chapter 10, in the section "Specifying the Footnote Position and Numbering Scheme."

- The footnote position (bottom of page, beneath text, end of section, or end of document)
- The starting footnote number
- Whether footnote numbering restarts with each document section

ENABLING WIDOW CONTROL

If you select the Widow Control option

If a paragraph has three lines or less, the Widow Control option will have no effect.

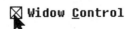 ⊠ **Widow Control**

Word will adjust the page breaks in the document so that a single line of a paragraph is never separated from the rest of the paragraph by a page break. Specifically, Word will perform the following two actions:

- If the last line of a paragraph is about to be printed alone at the top of a new page (a *widow*), Word will move the previous line to the new page, so that this page will contain the last *two* lines of the paragraph.

- If the first line of a paragraph is about to be printed alone at the bottom of a page (an *orphan*), Word will move this line to the next page, so that the entire paragraph will be printed on the next page.

Selecting the Widow Control option can cause the number of lines on each page to vary slightly. Therefore, if each page must have exactly the same number of lines (for example, certain legal documents), you should disable this option.

CHANGING THE DOCUMENT TEMPLATE

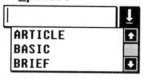 Document templates are discussed in Chapter 19.

The Format/Document dialog box also allows you to change the template associated with the document by typing the name of the desired template into the Template box, or by selecting a template name from the pull-down list.

Template:

| ARTICLE |
| BASIC |
| BRIEF |

As you saw in Chapter 3, the template is the framework upon which a document is built.

ALTERING THE DEFAULT SETTINGS

If you click the Set Default button

Word will make all of the settings currently entered into the Format/ Document dialog box the *new default settings*, which will automatically be applied to future new documents. More accurately, Word will assign all of the settings in the dialog box to the *current document template*. If you later create a new document based upon this template, this document will automatically acquire the specified settings.

OVERRIDING DOCUMENT FORMATTING

Although the options you select through the Format/Document command apply to the entire document, you can override or modify some of them for one or more sections or paragraphs. Specifically, you can override the following formatting settings:

- Default tab stops
- Footnotes
- Margins
- Widow control

Footnotes are discussed in Chapter 10.

Chapter 15 explains how to add or remove tab stops for one or more paragraphs. You can set the position and style of each tab stop.

If you have chosen the End of Section option in the Format/ Document dialog box (to place footnote text at the end of each document section), you can override this option for one or more sections by disabling footnote text through the Format/Section command. If you disable footnote text for a given section, Word places it at the end of the next section for which footnote text is enabled.

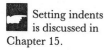
Setting indents
is discussed in
Chapter 15.

The left and right (or inside and outside) document margins specify the horizontal distance between the document text and the left or right edges of the page. You can adjust this distance (either increasing or decreasing it) for one or more individual paragraphs by setting the paragraph *indents*.

Finally, if you do not select the Widow Control option in the Format/Document dialog box, you can apply a similar option—Keep Paragraph Together—for one or more paragraphs. You set the Keep Paragraph Together option through the Format/Paragraph dialog box, which is explained in Chapter 15. Unlike the Widow Control option, the Keep Paragraph Option causes Word to always keep the *entire* paragraph together on a single page.

SUMMARY

- The Format/Document menu command lets you choose formatting options that affect the entire document.

- You can tell Word the size of the paper on which you are currently printing by entering the measurements into the Page Width and Height boxes within the Format/Document dialog box.

- The document *margins* are the distances between the text and the edges of the page. You can set the margins through the Margins area of the Format/Document dialog box.

- If you do not select the Mirror Margins option, you can specify the top, bottom, left, and right page margins. You can also specify a gutter margin, which is a space added to the left document margin.

- If your document is going to be printed on both sides of the paper, you can create symmetric margins on facing pages by selecting the Mirror Margins option. You can then specify the top, bottom, inside, and outside page margins. You can also specify a gutter margin, which is a space added to the inside document margin.

- You can specify the distance between the default tab stops by entering a value into the Default Tab Stops box.

- You can assign the position and numbering scheme used for footnotes through the Footnotes area of the Format/Document dialog box.

- By selecting the Widow Control option, you can have Word adjust the page breaks in the document so that a single line of a paragraph is never separated from the remainder of the paragraph by a page break.

- You can change the template associated with the document by entering the name of the desired template into the Template box.

- If you click the Set Default button, Word will make the current settings within the Format/Document dialog box the default values, which will automatically be applied to new documents that are based upon the same template.

- You can override the following document formatting features for one or more paragraphs: the default tab stops, the margins, and widow control. You can also prevent Word from placing footnote text at the end of specific document sections.

14

FORMATTING SECTIONS

IN THE PREVIOUS CHAPTER, YOU LEARNED HOW TO issue formatting commands that affect the entire document. In this chapter, you will learn how to apply the next level of formatting commands: those that control the appearance of document divisions known as *sections*. These commands are applied through the Format/ Section menu command.

First you will learn how to create separate sections within your document. You will then learn how to apply section formatting features to one or more specific sections.

DIVIDING A DOCUMENT INTO SECTIONS

When you first create a new document, it consists of a single section. If you select one or more formatting options through the

Format/Section menu command while the document consists of a single section, the options will be applied to the entire document (just like the options selected through the Format/Document command).

You can, however, divide a document into two or more sections. By dividing a document into sections, you can *vary* the section formatting features from one part of the document to another. For example, an important formatting feature that you can assign to a section is the number of text columns. By dividing the document into sections, you can arrange the text in a single column throughout one section of the document and arrange it in two columns throughout another section. (You can even vary the number of columns displayed on a single page.)

To create a new section within a document, you must insert a *section break* (which is analogous to a page break). The first section break you insert divides the document into two sections; all text before the break belongs to *section 1*, and all text after the break belongs to *section 2*. If you insert a second section break, the document will consist of three sections, and so on. Figure 14.1 illustrates a document that has three sections (two section breaks have been inserted).

To insert a *section* break:

1. Place the insertion point where you want the break.

2. Issue the Insert Break menu command. Word will display the dialog box shown in Figure 14.2, from which you can select a page break, a column break, or one of four types of section breaks.

3. Choose one of the four types of section breaks from the Section Break area of the Insert/Break dialog box. The option you choose will determine where Word will start printing the new section (the one following the break) in relation to the previous section (the one before the break).

4. Click OK.

If you select the Next Page option, Word will start printing the new section at the top of the next page; in other words, the section break will also create a page break.

If you select the Even Page option, Word will start printing the new section on the next *even-numbered* page, and if you select the Odd

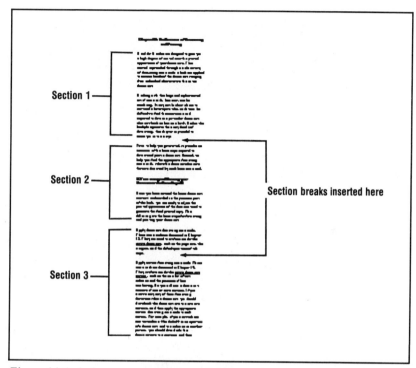

Figure 14.1: A document consisting of three sections

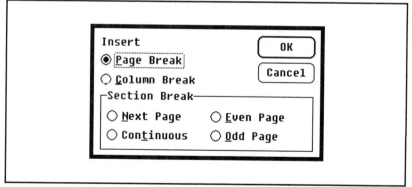

Figure 14.2: The Insert/Break dialog box

As you saw in Chapter 10, Word normally numbers pages continuously throughout the document, ignoring section breaks; however, you can force Word to start numbering a section with a specified line number.

Page option, Word will start printing it on the next *odd-numbered* page. Note that the Even Page and Odd Page options may result in either one or two page breaks. For example, if you select the Odd Page option, and the next page is odd-numbered, Word will insert a single page break. If, however, the next page is even-numbered, Word will insert two page breaks (resulting in one completely blank page).

Here's a situation in which you might want to choose the Odd Page option: You are writing a document that contains a title page in front of each chapter. Since a title page has a different page layout than the chapter text, you place each title page and each chapter in a separate document section. The document is going to be printed on both sides of the page. Because you want each chapter to start on an odd-numbered page rather than on the back of the title page, you choose the Odd Page option when inserting the breaks for the chapter sections.

Finally, if you select the Continuous option, Word will start printing the new section immediately following the previous section; in other words, it will insert *no* page breaks. You would choose this option if you wanted different section formatting options to appear on the same page. For example, through this option you can create a page that has a single column of text at the top, but two columns of text at the bottom.

As you will see later in the chapter, regardless of the starting option you chose when inserting a page break, you can later *change* the starting position through the Insert/Section menu command.

Word marks the position of a page break by displaying a double dotted line extending across the text column:

The page break mark will not appear on the printed document copy.

GOING TO A SECTION

For information on the Go To command, refer to Chapter 4 (in the section "Go to a Section").

Once you have divided a document into sections, you can move the insertion point to a particular section using the Go To command. Remember that sections are numbered beginning with 1. To go to a specific section, you can issue the Edit/Go To menu command, or press F5; at the prompt, type **s** followed immediately by the section number, and press ◄──┘. For example, to go to the third section, type the following at the prompt:

s3

Also, as you saw in Chapter 4, you can go to a particular line or page within a section. For example, to go to the top of the second page in the third section, type the following at the Go To command prompt:

s3p2

FORMATTING A SECTION

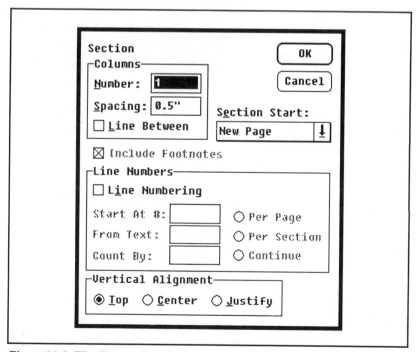

> If you select text belonging to more than one section when you choose the Format/Section command, the formatting options you choose will be applied to *all* sections selected.

To assign formatting features to a section of your document, first place the insertion point within the desired section. Remember that if you have not divided your document into sections, the document will consist of a single section; in this case, you can place the insertion point anywhere within the document, and the features you assign will be applied to the entire document.

Next, choose the Format/Section menu command. Word will display the dialog box illustrated in Figure 14.3.

Figure 14.3: The Format/Section dialog box

CH. 14

Throughout this chapter, the term *current section* refers to the section containing the insertion point or selection at the time you issued the Format/Section menu command. The formatting options you choose are applied to the current section.

The options in this dialog box allow you to assign the following formatting features to the current section:

- The section starting point
- The vertical alignment of text
- The number and spacing of text columns
- Line numbering
- The presence of footnote text at the end of the section

Notice that each text box within the Format/Section dialog box displays the current setting for the option. You do not need to enter a value unless you want to *change* the current setting. To remove the dialog box and apply any changes you have entered, click the OK button. To remove the dialog box without applying changes, click the Cancel button.

Remember from Chapter 10 that you can also assign headers or footers to each section in the document (using the Edit/Header/Footer or Insert/Page Numbers menu command). Remember also that you can assign the starting page number for a given section through the Page Numbers area of the Edit/Header/Footer dialog box.

SPECIFYING WHERE THE SECTION STARTS

See Chapter 10 for information on specifying the starting page number for a document section.

You can specify the starting position of the current section by selecting one of the options from the Section Start pull-down list within the Format/Section dialog box.

Se̲ction Start:

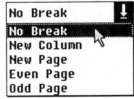

The starting option you choose here *overrides* the starting option chosen when you first created the new section through the Insert/Break command, discussed previously. Notice also that the Section Start box has an additional option—New Column—that was not found in the Insert/Break dialog box.

The New Page option (the default) causes Word to start printing the current section at the top of the next page beyond the previous section. It has the same effect as the Next Page option in the Insert/Break dialog box. (If you are formatting the first section in the document, Word will simply begin printing the section on the first page of the document, as usual.)

The Even Page option causes Word to begin printing the section at the top of the first *even-numbered* page past the end of the previous section. It has the same effect as the Even Page option in the Insert/Break dialog box. (If you are formatting the first document section, this option will cause Word to start the section on the first even-numbered page of the document, normally page 2.)

The Odd Page option causes Word to begin printing the section at the top of the first *odd-numbered* page past the end of the previous section. It has the same effect at the Odd Page option in the Insert/Break dialog box. (If you are formatting the first document section, this option will cause Word to start the section on the first odd-numbered page of the document, normally page 1.)

The No Break option causes Word to begin printing the section immediately following the previous section, with no page breaks inserted. This option is the same as the Continuous option within the Insert/Break dialog box.

Formatting text in multiple columns, and the method for inserting column breaks, is discussed later in the chapter, in the section "Setting the Number of Columns."

Finally, the New Column option causes Word to start printing the current section at the top of a new text column. In other words, Word inserts a column break before beginning the next section. This option assumes that the previous section and the current section have the same number of columns; if they have different numbers of columns, Word starts printing the current section at the beginning of a new page (as if you had chosen the New Page option). Figure 14.4 illustrates a section that has been assigned the New Column starting option (both sections use three columns per page).

Note that the Insert/Break command does not offer an equivalent to the New Column option. Therefore, to insert a section that starts on a new column, you must issue the Insert/Break command and

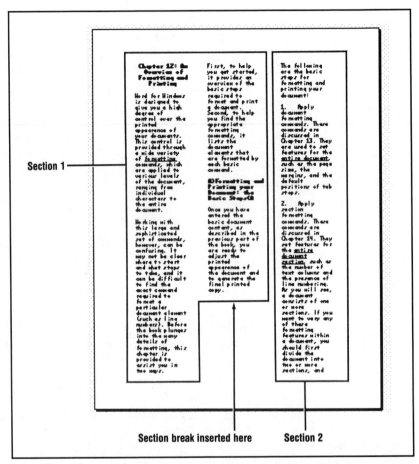

Figure 14.4: A section that starts with the New Column option

temporarily choose some other starting position option (such as Next Page). You can then issue the Format/Section command and specify the New Column option.

SPECIFYING THE VERTICAL ALIGNMENT

By choosing an option within the Vertical Alignment area of the Format/Section dialog box, you can specify the vertical alignment of the text on each page within the current section:

Top
Center
Justify

If a given page within the section contains the maximum number of lines, the vertical alignment option you choose will have no effect on the page layout. If, however, the text does not fill the entire vertical space between the top and bottom margins, the vertical alignment option affects the way that Word distributes the free white space on the page. There are several reasons why the text on a page may not fill the entire vertical space. For example, the page may contain a hard page break (inserted by pressing Ctrl-◄┘), which forces Word to begin printing text on the next page even if the current page has not been filled. Also, you may have formatted a paragraph with the Keep Paragraph Together option, which can cause Word to move the entire paragraph to the next page so that the paragraph can be kept together (see Chapter 15).

The Top option (which is the default) causes Word to align the text with the top margin. Figure 14.5 illustrates a page containing free space in the vertical direction; this page is contained in a section formatted with the Top vertical alignment option.

The Center option causes Word to align the text on the page between the top and bottom margins. Figure 14.6 illustrates the same page section shown in Figure 14.5, formatted with the Center option.

The Justify option causes Word to align the top line on the page with the top margin, and the bottom line with the bottom margin. When justifying text vertically, Word adds space evenly *between* each paragraph. It does not alter the line spacing within paragraphs. Figure 14.7 illustrates the same page shown in the previous figures, formatted with the Justify option.

Methods for aligning text in the *horizontal* direction are given in Chapter 15.

If you want to align the text on a page using a pattern not provided by these three options (for example, you might want to align the text with the bottom margin), you can use the Format/Position command, described in Chapter 15. The Format/Position command allows you to place one or more paragraphs almost anywhere on the page.

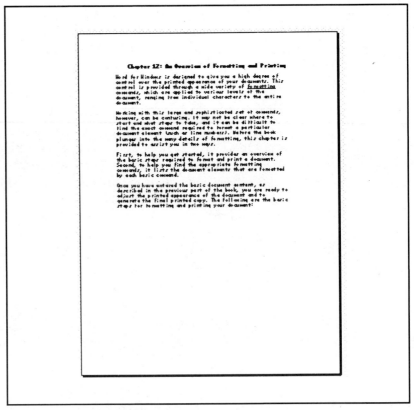

Figure 14.5: A page illustrating the Top vertical alignment option

As an example, you could center the text contained on a title page, both vertically and horizontally, through the following steps (these steps assume that you have already typed in the title text):

1. If the title page is not at the beginning of the document, place the insertion point immediately in front of it and insert a section break by choosing the Insert/Break menu command. Select the Next Page, Even Page, or Odd Page option (see the explanations of these options given previously in the chapter), and click the OK button.

2. Place the insertion point at the end of the title page and insert another section break, using the same method described in step 1. The title page is now contained in its own section.

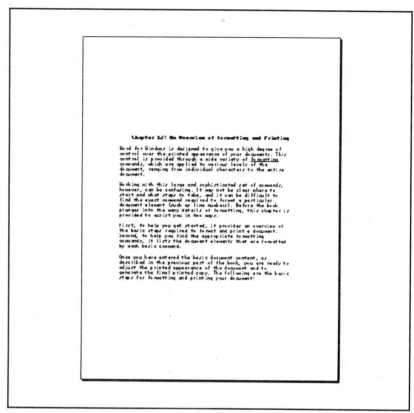

Figure 14.6: A page illustrating the Center vertical alignment option

If you are in Page View, you will not see the correct location on the page with the Center option. To see the correct location, choose Print Preview.

3. Place the insertion point anywhere within the title page and choose the Format/Section command. Select the Center option within the Vertical Alignment area of the dialog box, and click the OK button. The title page text will now be centered vertically.

4. Select all paragraphs within the title page and press the Ctrl-C keystroke to center the text in the horizontal direction.

SETTING THE NUMBER OF COLUMNS

Normally, document text is arranged in a single column on each page. You can, however, have Word arrange text in two or more

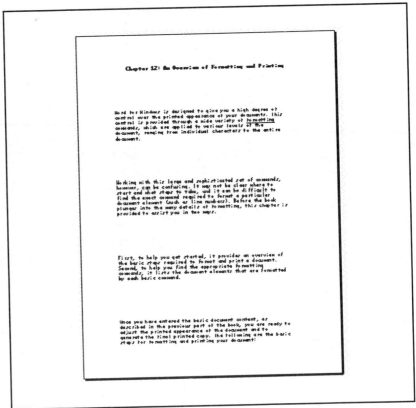

Figure 14.7: A page illustrating the Justify vertical alignment option

columns on each page. To arrange the text contained in a particular section into multiple columns, you set the appropriate options within the Columns area of the Format/Section dialog box.

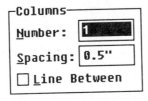

The type of columns created through the Format/Section dialog box are known as *snaking* columns, like those in a newspaper. The text

Do not confuse the snaking columns of text created through the Format/Section command with the rows and columns of cells created using Word tables, as described in Chapter 8.

on each page flows from the bottom of one column to the top of the next column to the right. Figure 14.8 illustrates the flow of text on a page with three columns.

To arrange text in snaking columns, first enter the desired number of columns into the Number box (the default is 1). The maximum number of columns you can enter depends upon the size and layout of the page; the resulting width of the text in each column must be at least 0.5″. If you enter a number of columns that would result in narrower text, Word will issue a warning.

The Spacing box specifies how much space Word places between each column. The default value is 0.5″. If you want a different amount of space, enter the desired measurement into this box.

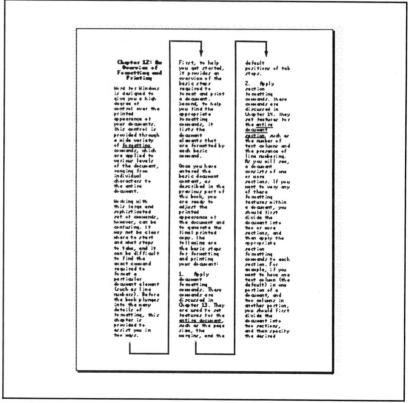

Figure 14.8: Snaking columns created through the Format/Section command

You cannot see the vertical lines between columns in Page View; you can see them in Print Preview.

If you select the Line Between option (which is *not* selected by default), Word will print a vertical line between each column. The lines will all be as long as the longest text column on the page.

Columns are displayed on the screen in their actual widths (or *close* to their actual widths, if the Display as Printed option is not selected within the View/Preferences dialog box). In galley view (normal editing view), outline view, and draft view, only a single column is shown at a time. In Page View and Print Preview, however, the columns are shown side by side, as they will appear on the final printed copy.

You can vary the column arrangement on a single page. For example, to display a single column of text on the top half of a page, but two columns of text on the bottom half, use the following procedure (this procedure assumes that the page currently contains a single column of text):

1. Place the insertion point at the position on the page where you want to begin displaying two columns.

2. Choose the Insert/Break menu command. Select the Continuous option within the dialog box, and click the OK button. Word will create a new section on the same page.

3. Place the insertion point within the new section and choose the Format/Section menu command. Enter **2** into the Number box within the Columns area of the dialog box, and click the OK button.

The resulting page is illustrated in Figure 14.9.

As Word arranges text into columns, it automatically begins placing text within the next column when it reaches the end of the current column (the *next column* is the one to the right of the current column, or the first column on the next page if the current column is the rightmost one on the page). This process is analogous to the way Word automatically places text on a new page when it reaches the end of the current page.

You can force Word to start placing text within the next column, anywhere before reaching the end of the current column, by manually

Figure 14.9: A single page containing both one column and two columns of text

inserting a column break. As with a hard page break (inserted as described in Chapter 3), Word will always begin a new column when you insert a column break. To insert a column break, first place the insertion point where you want the break, and then choose the Insert/Break menu command. Select the Column Break option and click the OK button. Alternatively, you can insert a column break at the position of the insertion point by simply pressing the Ctrl-Shift-◄━ key combination. A column break is displayed on the screen as a single dotted line (only in galley, draft, or outline view; not in Page View). Figure 14.10 illustrates a column break that has been manually inserted before the end of the second column.

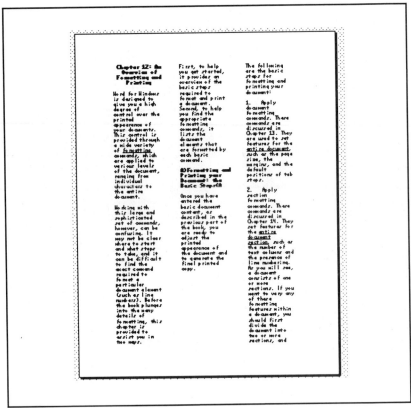

Figure 14.10: A manually inserted column break in column 2

NUMBERING LINES

Line numbers are *not* visible in galley view (normal editing view), outline view, draft view, or Page View. They are displayed only in Print Preview, and on the final printed page.

You can have Word automatically display numbers next to the lines in the current section by choosing the Line Numbering option within the Line Numbers area of the Format/Section dialog box (see Figure 14.3).

When you have enabled line numbering for a section, Word displays consecutive numbers to the left of the lines within the section. Blank lines inserted by pressing ◄┘ are numbered as well as lines that contain text. However, blank lines created by adding space before or after a paragraph through the Format/Paragraph command are *not* numbered. Figure 14.11 illustrates the beginning of the printed copy of a document section containing line numbers.

```
1   This document section contains line numbers. By choosing the Line Numbering option
2   within the Line Numbers area of the Format/Section dialog box, you can have Word
3   display numbers in front of the lines of the current section. Other options within the
4   Line Numbers area allow you to specify the starting line number, the distance between
5   the line numbers and the text, which lines you want Word to number, and where you
6   want Word to restart the numbering.
```

Figure 14.11: A portion of a printed document displaying line numbers

If you vertically justify your section with the Format/Section command, you may see extra blank space between the line numbers.

Although the Line Numbering option enables line numbering for the entire document section, you can prevent Word from numbering one or more paragraphs within the section by turning off the Line Numbering option within the Format/Paragraph dialog box (explained in Chapter 15). If you disable line numbers for a paragraph, Word neither displays numbers next to the lines of this paragraph, nor does it count the lines in the paragraph to calculate the next number that it displays. For example, if you disable line numbering for a paragraph, and if the last number displayed in the previous paragraph is **23**, the first number displayed in the next paragraph will be **24**.

The Line Numbers area of the Format/Section dialog box also allows you to choose one or more options that control the way Word numbers the lines in the current section.

The Start At # box specifies the starting line number. By default, the starting number is 1. If you would like Word to start numbering lines using another number, you can enter a positive integer into the Start At # box.

If you are formatting a section other than the first section, and you choose the Continue option, described later, the value entered into the Start At # box is ignored.

The From Text box specifies the distance between the right edge of the line numbers and the left text margin. The default value is Auto, which causes Word to use a distance of 0.25" for text arranged in a single column, or 0.13" for text in multiple columns. If you want Word to use a different distance, enter the desired measurement into this box. (Entering the number 0 has the same effect as the value Auto.)

The Count By box specifies *which* lines to number. Word will number only lines that are multiples of the number entered into this box. The default value is 1, which causes Word to number every line. If you enter 2, Word will only number every other line. For example, if the starting number entered into the Start At # box is 1, and if you enter **2** into the Count By box, Word will number lines 2, 4, 6, 8, and so on. Similarly, if you enter 3 into the Count By box, Word will number lines 3, 6, 9, and so on. Word will number lines in a similar fashion for any positive integer you enter into this box.

You can select only *one* of the following options: Per Page, Per Section, or Continue.

Selecting the Per Page option, which is the default, causes Word to restart the line numbering on every page. That is, Word will number each page in the current section starting with the number entered into the Start At # box.

Selecting the Per Section option causes Word to start numbering the current section with the number entered into the Start At # box. If you select this option, Word will *not* restart numbering with each page. If more than one section was selected when the Format/Section command was issued, Word will start numbering each section in the selection with the Start At # value.

Finally, if you select the Continue option, Word will begin numbering the lines in the section with a number that is 1 greater than the number of the last line in the previous section. Word will ignore the value entered into the Start At # box. Note, however, that if you apply this option to the first document section, Word will simply begin numbering with the number specified in the Start At # box; in this case, the Continue option will have the same effect as the Per Section option.

INCLUDING FOOTNOTES

As you saw in Chapter 10 (in the section "Specifying the Footnote Position"), if you have placed footnote text at the end of each section in the document, you can have Word move the footnote text from the end of the current section to the end of the next section for which footnotes are enabled. To move the footnote text, simply remove the check from the Include Footnotes option (this option is selected by default) of the Format/Section dialog box. To remove the check, go to the Format/Document dialog box, and select End of Section under the **Footnotes Print at** heading.

SUMMARY

- Initially, a document consists of only a single section. You can, however, divide a document into two or more sections by inserting section breaks.

- To insert a section break, place the insertion point at the position in the document where you want the new section to begin, and choose the Insert/Break menu command. Word will display a dialog box.

- Next, choose one of the options within the Section Break area of the dialog box. The option you choose tells Word where to begin the new section. Click the OK button to remove the dialog box and insert the section break.

- You can move the insertion point to a given section by pressing the F5 key or by choosing the Edit/Go To menu command. At the prompt, type s followed by the number of the desired section.

- To assign one or more formatting features to a section in your document, place the insertion point within the section and choose the Format/Section menu command. Word will display a dialog box.

- Choose one of the options within the Section Start pull-down list to specify where you want the section to start. The option you select here overrides the option chosen when you inserted the section break.

To see proper alignment, go to Print Preview. You won't see alignment changes in Page View.

- Selecting an option in the Vertical Alignment area of the Format/Section dialog box tells Word how to vertically align text on all pages within the section that have extra vertical space.

You'll be able to see the vertical line in Print Preview, but not in Page View.

- You can have Word arrange the text in two or more columns by entering the desired number of columns into the Number box in the Columns area of the Format/Section dialog box. You can also specify the distance between columns (through the Spacing box), or place a vertical line between each column (by selecting the Line Between option).

- You can have Word display numbers within the current section by selecting the Line Numbering option within the Line Numbers area of the Format/Section dialog box. The other options within this area specify the starting line number, the distance of the numbers from the text, which lines you want numbered, and where you want Word to restart line numbering.

15

FORMATTING PARAGRAPHS

IN THIS CHAPTER, YOU WILL LEARN HOW TO ASSIGN formatting features to specific paragraphs within your document. The chapter begins by defining a paragraph, and describing how to divide a document into separate paragraphs. You will then learn the three basic methods for applying paragraph formatting: the Format/ Paragraph menu command, the Word ruler, and the keyboard. Finally, you will learn how to place a paragraph containing text or graphics at a specific position on the page.

CREATING AND SELECTING PARAGRAPHS

A new Word document consists of a single paragraph. As you saw in Chapter 3, whenever you press the ◀──┘ key, you add a new paragraph to the document. Paragraphs are separated by means of paragraph marks. A *paragraph mark* is a special character that is normally invisible. You can, however, make paragraph marks visible (as ¶ characters) by selecting the Paragraph Marks option within the View/Preferences dialog box. Paragraph marks are never printed.

A single paragraph consists of all characters and pictures that come *after* the preceding paragraph mark (or after the beginning of the document, if there is no preceding mark) *up to and including* the following paragraph mark. Figure 15.1 illustrates a document that consists of three paragraphs (the Paragraph Marks option has been selected). Notice that the second paragraph consists of only the paragraph mark itself. It was inserted to create a blank line between the two paragraphs that contain text (later in the chapter, you will learn how to have Word automatically insert a blank line between paragraphs).

The first paragraph in a new document is initially assigned a set of default paragraph formatting features. This chapter refers to default settings for various features; these are the default settings initially set by Microsoft. In Part IV, however, you will learn how to *modify* the default settings that are automatically assigned to new documents. If you have performed such a modification, your defaults may not be the same as those mentioned in this chapter. You can accept the default formatting features, or you can change one or more of them for specified paragraphs, as described in this chapter.

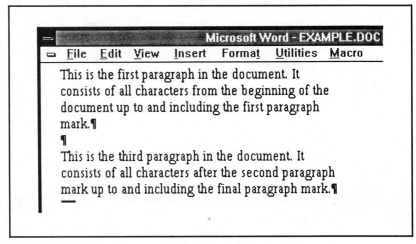

Figure 15.1: A document consisting of three paragraphs

When you insert a paragraph by pressing ◄—, the new paragraph normally gains all of the paragraph formatting features (default or assigned) possessed by the paragraph that contains the insertion point when you press ◄—. (In Chapter 20, however, you will see an exception to this rule.)

Conceptually, the paragraph formatting is contained in the paragraph mark at the end of the paragraph. If you have made paragraph marks visible (through the Paragraph Marks option in the View/ Preferences dialog box), you can delete, copy, or move a paragraph mark like any other character. If you delete a paragraph mark, you will remove the formatting from the associated paragraph, and the paragraph text becomes part of the following paragraph. (You cannot, however, delete the last paragraph mark in the document, nor can you backspace over a paragraph mark if the paragraphs before and after the mark have different formats.)

See the end of Chapter 5 ("Other Copying Techniques") for instructions on using the mouse to copy paragraph formatting.

If you move or copy a paragraph mark, the text preceding the point where you insert the mark becomes part of a new paragraph, which acquires the formatting contained in the mark. Copying a paragraph mark thus provides a method for copying a set of paragraph formatting features within a document or between documents.

Before applying paragraph formatting using any of the methods described in this chapter (the Format/Paragraph command, the ruler, or the keyboard), you must indicate the paragraph or paragraphs that you want to format. To format a single paragraph, you should select all or part of this paragraph, or simply place the insertion point anywhere within the paragraph. To format several paragraphs, select all or part of the desired paragraphs (the selection must include at least one character within the first and last paragraphs of the group of paragraphs you want to format; this character can be the paragraph symbol).

USING THE FORMAT/PARAGRAPH COMMAND

The most flexible and complete method for formatting the selected paragraph or paragraphs is to choose the Format/Paragraph menu command. In response to this command, Word displays the dialog box illustrated in Figure 15.2.

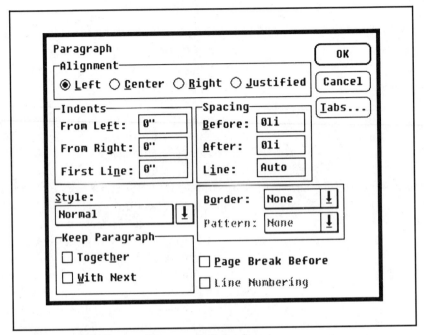

Figure 15.2: The Format/Paragraph dialog box

The Format/Paragraph dialog box displays the current paragraph formatting settings. You need enter only those values that you want to *change* from their current setting. Through this dialog box, you can set the following basic formatting features:

- The paragraph indents
- The paragraph alignment
- The spacing between paragraphs, and the spacing between lines within a paragraph
- The paragraph style
- Borders displayed around the paragraph
- The position of page breaks
- Numbering of the paragraph lines
- Tab stops (set through the Format/Tabs dialog box)

Appendix B sum-
marizes the mea-
surements used in Word.

Word can use various units of measurement in its dialog boxes: lines, inches, centimeters, points, or picas. Most options in this chapter use lines or inches as the default unit of measurement.

SETTING THE INDENTS

In Chapter 13, you learned how to set the four document margins through the Format/Document dialog box. The margins are the default distances between the text and the edges of the page that are used throughout the entire document. In this section, you will learn how to adjust the distances between the text and the left and right edges of the page for one or more individual paragraphs by setting the left and right paragraph *indents*. An indent is the distance between the edge of the paragraph and the margin.

By default, the left and right paragraph indents are 0 (in other words, a paragraph initially fits within the document margins). If you assign a positive indent, the distance between the edge of the page and the paragraph text is increased (in other words, the edge of the text is moved toward the center of the page by the amount of the indent). If you assign a negative indent, the distance between the edge of the page and the paragraph text is decreased (in other words, the edge of the text is moved away from the center of the page by the amount of the indent; a negative indent acts like a margin release on a typewriter).

The indents are set in the Indents area of the Format/Paragraph dialog box. To set the left indent, enter into the From Left box the distance you want to move the left edge of the paragraph away from the left margin. A positive measurement will move it toward the center of the page, and a negative measurement will move it toward the left edge of the page.

To set the right indent, enter into the From Right box the distance you want to move the right edge of the paragraph away from the right margin. A positive measurement will move it toward the center of the page, and a negative measurement will move it toward the right edge of the page.

The position and width of the paragraph text depends upon the page width, the document margins, and the paragraph indents. Figure 15.3 illustrates both positive and negative paragraph indents in relation to the page width and document margins.

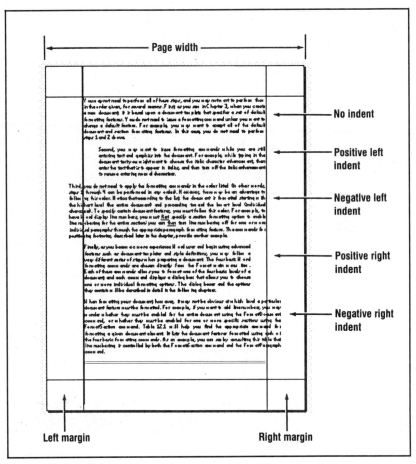

Figure 15.3: Positive and negative paragraph indents

You can also adjust the left indent of the first line of the paragraph by entering a measurement into the First Line box. The measurement you enter into this box is *not* the actual value of the left indent for the first line; rather, it is an *offset from the left indent for the whole paragraph that was entered into the From Left box*. A positive value moves the beginning of the first line to the right, and a negative value moves it to the left. If, for example, you enter **0.5** into the From Left box, and **0.25** into the First Line box, the first line will be assigned a left indent of 0.75″ and the remaining lines will be assigned a left indent of 0.5″.

As another example, if you enter **0** into the From Left box (or leave it blank) and **– 0.5** into the First Line box, the first line will have a negative indent of 0.5″ (it will project ½ inch into the left margin), and the remaining lines in the paragraph will have *no* indent.

Figure 15.4 illustrates two paragraphs for which the first line indent has been adjusted. Both paragraphs have been assigned a From Left indent of 0. The first paragraph has a First Line indent of 0.5, and the second paragraph has a First Line indent of – 0.5.

Setting Indents for Multiple-Column Text

> Formatting text in multiple columns is discussed in Chapter 14, in the section "Setting the Number of Columns."

The discussion on indents given so far has assumed that the paragraph text is arranged in a single column. You can also assign paragraph indents to text formatted in two or more columns. With multicolumn text, an indent is the distance between the edge of the text and *a column boundary.* The column boundaries are the edges of the columns of text; the positions of the boundaries are assigned when you format the document section (you will see later in the chapter how they can be directly adjusted using the Word ruler).

> The left boundary of the leftmost column is at the position of the left document margin, and the right boundary of the rightmost column is at the position of the right document margin.

If you assign a positive indent, the edge of the text in the column is moved toward the center of the column. If you assign a negative indent, the edge of the text is moved away from the center of the column. Figure 15.5 illustrates text arranged in two columns; the figure shows the column boundaries and several types of indents.

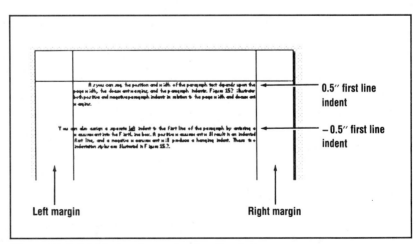

Figure 15.4: Positive and negative first line indents

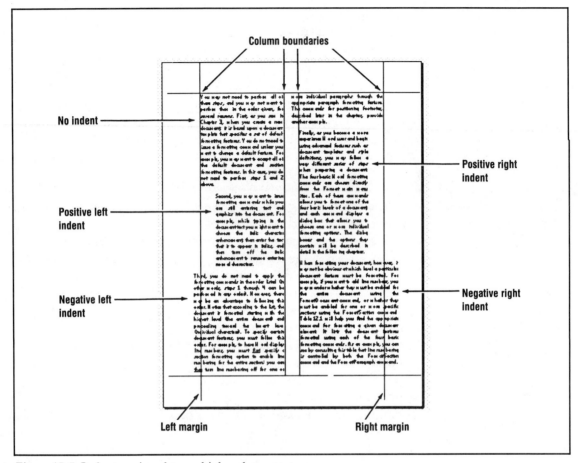

Figure 15.5: Indents assigned to multiple-column text

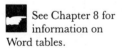 See Chapter 8 for information on Word tables.

Note that you can also assign indents to a paragraph of text within a Word table. In this case, the indent moves the text away from the edges of the cell. However, you should not attempt to assign a negative indent to a paragraph in a table, since this can make a portion of the text disappear.

SETTING THE ALIGNMENT

In the previous section, you saw how to adjust the horizontal limits of a column of text by setting paragraph indents. In this section, you will learn how to specify the alignment of the paragraph text *within* the paragraph indents. To specify the paragraph alignment, choose one of the options within the Alignment area of the Format/Paragraph dialog box.

The Left option (the default) causes Word to align the left end of each line of the paragraph with the left indent. The right edge of the paragraph is *ragged* (that is, uneven).

The Center option centers each line of the paragraph between the left and right indents. With this option, both the left and right edges of the paragraph are ragged.

The Right option aligns each line with the right indent. With this option, the left edge of the paragraph is ragged.

The Justified option causes Word to align the left ends of the lines with the left indent and the right ends with the right indent. With this option, neither the left nor the right edge of the paragraph is ragged. Word achieves the justified alignment by adding space as necessary between words. You can minimize the amount of space Word must add between words by hyphenating the paragraph, as described in Chapter 17.

Figure 15.6 illustrates each of the four paragraph alignment styles applied to the same paragraph.

Remember that the first line may have a different left indent than the remaining lines of the paragraph.

Word does not attempt to justify the *last* line of the paragraph; it is simply left-aligned.

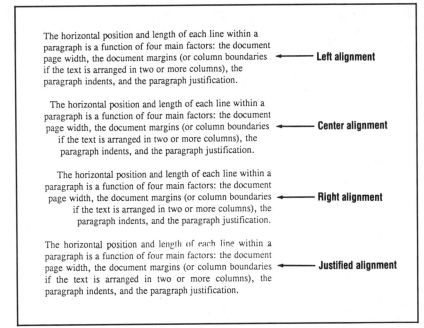

Figure 15.6: The four paragraph alignment styles

SETTING THE SPACING

If you have added a border above the paragraph (as described shortly), the additional space is inserted above the border.

A *line* refers to a fixed amount of space, which is equivalent to ⅙″, or 12 points. If the line consists of 12-point characters (see Chapter 16), entering a line spacing of **1** will result in single-spacing, entering **2** will result in double spacing, and so on.

You can set the amount of vertical space Word places between lines and paragraphs by entering the desired measurements into the Spacing area of the Format/Paragraph dialog box.

To add additional space *before* the paragraph, enter the desired amount of space into the Before box. The default value is 0; by entering a nonzero measurement, you can have Word insert additional space between the current paragraph and the preceding paragraph. Unless you specify a unit of measurement, Word assumes that the value you enter is the number of lines. For example, if you enter **1.5**, Word will add one and a half lines of extra space.

In a similar fashion, you can add additional space *after* the current paragraph by entering a measurement into the After box. If you have added a border below the paragraph (as described shortly), the additional space is inserted below the border.

You can also specify the line spacing within the paragraph by entering a measurement into the Line box. The default value is Auto; this value causes Word to use for each line the minimum amount of vertical space necessary to accommodate the tallest character on the line (as you will see in Chapter 16, you can assign characters different heights). Like the other measurements in the Spacing area, the default unit is *lines*.

Entering a *positive* measurement into the Spacing box specifies the *minimum* line spacing. For example, if you enter **2**, Word will set the line spacing to 2 lines (⅓″); however, if the line contains one or more characters that are too tall to fit within this space, it will automatically increase the line height to accommodate the tallest character. Use this setting if you do want spacing to be automatically adjusted.

Entering a *negative* measurement into the Spacing box specifies an absolute line spacing, which is not automatically adjusted. If a character on a line is too tall to fit within this space, Word does not adjust the space; rather, it simply allows the characters to overlap the line above on the printed copy (on the screen, the characters appear cut off at the top). Entering **0** into the spacing box has the same effect as the value Auto.

ASSIGNING THE STYLE

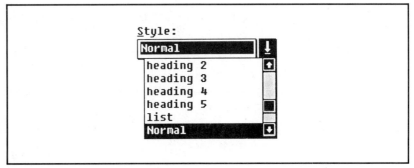

For more information on styles, see Chapter 20.

As you will learn in Chapter 20, a style is an entire set of paragraph and character formatting features that you can assign to one or more paragraphs. Styles are identified by name. By default, paragraphs are assigned the Normal style.

The Style box in the Format/Paragraph dialog box displays the name of the style currently assigned to the selected paragraph (unless you have selected more than one paragraph and the selected paragraphs do not all have the same style; in this case, the Style box will be blank). You can type in the name of another style, or select it from the pull-down list (Figure 15.7).

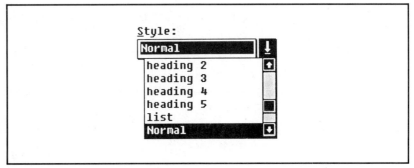

Style:

Normal

heading 2
heading 3
heading 4
heading 5
list
Normal

Figure 15.7: The Style pull-down list

ADDING BORDERS

If you assign the Box border style to several adjacent paragraphs, Word will place a single box around the entire group of paragraphs, rather than placing a box around each paragraph separately.

You can add a border to one or more sides of the current paragraph by choosing a border style from the Border pull-down list in the Format/Paragraph dialog box. Each of the border styles you can choose is illustrated in Figure 15.8.

Once you have selected a border style other than None, you can choose the line pattern used for drawing the border from the Pattern pull-down list, shown in Figure 15.9.

Figure 15.10 illustrates the line patterns, applied to the Box border style. Note that the Shadow pattern is not available if you have selected the Bar or Above border style.

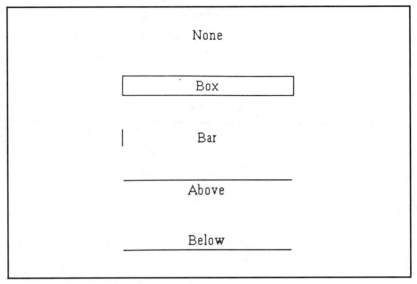

Figure 15.8: The border styles you can assign to a paragraph

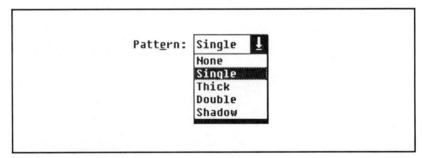

Figure 15.9: The Pattern pull-down list

CONTROLLING PAGE BREAKS

The Format/Paragraph dialog box provides three options that control the position of page breaks with respect to the paragraph.

The Keep Paragraph Together option prevents Word from inserting a page break anywhere within the paragraph. If the paragraph does not fit completely on the current page, Word will move the entire paragraph to the next page.

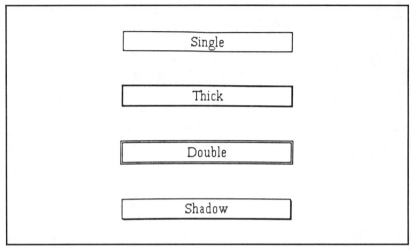

Figure 15.10: The line patterns you can use for a paragraph border

You must have at least two lines of each paragraph on the same page to use Keep Paragraph With Next.

The Keep Paragraph With Next option forces Word to print the paragraph on the same page as the beginning of the following paragraph. In other words, it will not insert a page break *between* a paragraph assigned this feature and the following paragraph. As an example, you could format the paragraph containing a heading with this option so that Word does not insert a line break between the heading and the body of text that follows it.

Finally, the Page Break Before option causes Word to insert a page break immediately before the paragraph. You can select this option to make sure that the paragraph is printed at the top of a page.

Note that in addition to assigning the three options discussed in this section to one or more individual paragraphs, you can also assign the Widow Control option to all paragraphs in the document, through the Format/Document menu command. As you saw in Chapter 13, the Widow Control option prevents Word from inserting a page break between the first or last line of a paragraph and the remainder of the paragraph.

ENABLING LINE NUMBERING

As you saw in Chapter 14, if you have enabled line numbering for a document section, you can prevent Word from numbering a selected paragraph within this section by turning off the Line Numbering option within the Format/Paragraph dialog box.

SETTING TAB STOPS

If you are creating tables of text or graphics, it is generally much easier to use the Table feature discussed in Chapter 8, rather than using tab characters.

As you saw in Chapter 3, pressing the Tab key causes Word to move the insertion point to the next tab stop. When you press the Tab key, Word inserts a tab character. If you have selected the Tabs or Show All * option within the View/Preferences dialog box, a tab character is displayed as an arrow pointing to the right. If neither of these options is selected, a tab character is invisible. On the screen and on the printed copy of the document, a tab character creates just enough white space to align the following text at the position of the next tab stop.

Each paragraph is assigned a set of tab stops (the tab stops can vary from one paragraph to another). A given tab stop can be placed at any horizontal position on the page, and can be assigned one of several alignment styles and leader character styles (these styles will be explained later). Initially, a paragraph is assigned the *default tab stops* that have been defined for the entire document. As you saw in Chapter 13, the original default tab stops are placed 0.5″ apart; however, you can change the spacing of the default tab stops for the entire document by entering another value into the Default Tab Stops box within the Format/Document dialog box. The default tab stops are also left-aligned and have no leader character.

In this section, you will learn how to define *custom* tab stops for one or more paragraphs. Custom tab stops replace the default tab stops. When you define a custom tab stop, Word automatically removes all default tab stops to the left of the custom stop.

To define custom tab stops for the selected paragraph or paragraphs, click the Tabs button within the Format/Paragraph dialog box. Word will apply the formatting features specified in the Format/Paragraph dialog box, remove this dialog box, and then display the Format/Tabs dialog box, which is illustrated in Figure 15.11. Alternatively, if the Format/Paragraph dialog box is not currently open, you can open the Format/Tabs dialog box immediately by choosing the Format/Tabs menu command.

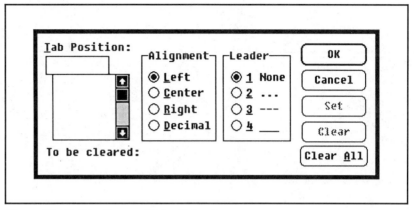

Figure 15.11: The Format/Tabs dialog box

Once the Format/Tabs dialog box is open, you can define a new custom tab stop, remove or modify an existing custom tab stop, or remove all custom tab stops. You can define, remove, or modify an entire series of custom tab stops while the dialog box remains displayed, using the methods described in this section. Once you have completed performing all desired tab operations, click the OK button to remove the dialog box and assign your changes. To remove the dialog box without applying changes, click the Cancel button.

Defining a New Custom Tab Stop

To define a new tab custom stop, first enter the position of the tab stop into the Tab Position box. The numeric value you enter into this box specifies the distance between the left margin and the tab stop. You can place the tab stop either inside or outside of the document margins. If you enter a negative measurement, the tab will be placed the specified distance to the left of the left margin.

To specify the tab alignment style, choose one of the options within the Alignment area: Left, Center, Right, or Decimal.

The Left alignment style is the default. With this style, the text you type immediately after inserting the tab character extends to the right of the tab stop.

If you choose the Center style, the text you type immediately after inserting the tab character will extend equally in the left and right directions (in other words, this text is automatically centered on the tab stop). The text will stop extending in the left direction, however, if it is about to overlap an existing character.

Assigning the Right alignment style causes the text you type after inserting the tab character to extend to the left of the tab stop. The text will stop extending in the left direction, however, if it is about to overlap an existing character; it will then extend in the right direction.

Finally, if you assign the Decimal alignment style to a tab stop, the text you type immediately after inserting the tab character extends to the left (until encountering an existing character); however, once you type a decimal point (that is, a period character), the text begins extending to the right. The result is that the decimal point is positioned at the tab stop. If you enter a column of numbers centered on the same decimal tab stop, the decimal points within the numbers will be aligned vertically.

Figure 15.12 illustrates the four tab stop alignment styles.

You can also add a *leader* to a custom tab stop. A leader is a series of characters that Word automatically inserts between the position where you press the Tab key and the text that you enter after pressing Tab (in other words, the leader fills the white space created by the tab character). The leader is specified through the Leader area of the Format/Tabs dialog box.

By default, the 1 None option is selected, which causes Word not to use a leader. To add a leader, select one of the other three options. The second, third, and fourth options cause Word to use periods,

> To use the Decimal style, the period character must be surrounded by numeric characters; otherwise, Word will continue moving characters to the left and will not center the period.

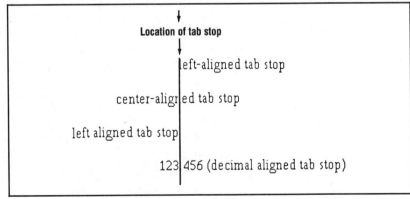

Figure 15.12: The four alignment styles of tab stops

hyphens, or underline characters, respectively, as the leader character. The following line illustrates the second leader style:

Total number of birds............................27

In this line, the tab stop immediately in front of the **27** was assigned the second leader style. The Tab key was pressed after typing the word **birds**.

When you have finished defining the tab stop, click the Set button to add the tab stop to the paragraph (or just click the OK button if you are making no further changes). Clicking the Set button does *not* remove the dialog box and add the tab stop. Rather, Word leaves the dialog box open so that you can continue to format tab stops, and adds the measurement for the tab you defined to the Tab Positions list box. All tab stops you have defined will actually be added to the paragraph when you remove the dialog box by clicking the OK button. You can define up to 50 tab stops.

Removing or Modifying a Custom Tab Stop

To remove or modify a custom tab stop, first select the measurement for this tab stop from the Tab Position list box.

As soon as you select the measurement from the list box, Word copies it to the Tab Position text box above the list.

To remove the custom tab stop at the measurement currently contained in the Tab Position box, click the Clear button in the Format/ Tabs dialog box. Clicking the Clear button does *not* remove the dialog box and immediately clear the indicated tab stop. Rather, the dialog box remains open so that you can continue to perform tab operations, and Word displays the tab stop measurement following the **To be cleared** label at the bottom of the dialog box. If you delete additional tab stops, their measurements will be added to this list.

To be cleared: 1.75″, 3″, 4.5″

When you remove the dialog box by clicking the OK button, all tab stops in the list will actually be removed. If, however, you remove the dialog box by clicking the Cancel button, none of the indicated tabs will be cleared.

As you saw, when you add a custom tab stop, Word automatically removes all default tab stops to its left. If you later delete a custom tab stop, Word restores any default tab stops that is to its left but not to the left of a remaining custom tab stop.

You can instruct Word to remove *all* custom tab stops you have added to the paragraph by clicking the Clear All button within the Format/Tabs dialog box. Word will then display **All** following the **To be cleared** label at the bottom of the dialog box. When you click the OK button to remove the dialog box, all custom tab stops will be removed and all default tab stops will be restored.

To modify the alignment or leader for the tab stop currently displayed in the Tab Position box, simply select the desired options from the Alignment or Leader areas of the dialog box, and then click the Set button (or just click the OK button if you are making no further changes). The changes will be implemented when you remove the dialog box by clicking OK.

USING THE RULER

The Word ruler is a collection of icons that you can display at the top of the window. You can use the ruler either with the mouse or with the keyboard to apply the following paragraph formatting features to the selected paragraph or paragraphs:

- Paragraph indents
- Paragraph alignment
- Space before the paragraph (0 or 1 line)
- Line spacing (1, 1.5, or 2 lines)

- Style assigned to the paragraph
- Custom tab stops

Each of these paragraph formatting features was explained previously in the chapter, in the section "Using the Format/Paragraph Command." See this section for information on the *effect* of each feature. The following sections focus on the methods for *applying* the features using the ruler.

You can also use the ruler with the mouse to set the following two features (which are not *paragraph* formatting features):

- Document margins and inner column boundaries
- Cell widths in tables

USING THE RULER WITH THE MOUSE TO FORMAT PARAGRAPHS

If the ruler is not currently displayed, you can display it by choosing the View/Ruler menu option (when the ruler is displayed, Word places a check mark next to the option). You can later remove the ruler by selecting this same option again. The ruler is illustrated in Figure 15.13.

The Word ruler can be in one of three different views: paragraph view, margin view, or column view (column view is available only when the selection is within a Word table). You can switch from view to view by clicking the *ruler view icon* at the right end of the ruler.

You will learn about margin view in the section "Using the Ruler to Set Document Margins and Inner Column Boundaries," and you will learn about column view in the section "Using the Ruler to Set Cell Widths in Tables."

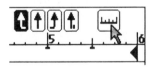

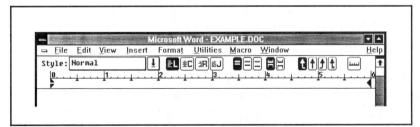

Figure 15.13: A document window with the Word ruler

To apply paragraph formatting features, the ruler should be in paragraph view, which is illustrated in Figure 15.13. In this view, the 0 on the numeric scale is even with the left margin and the scale contains a series of small inverted **T**s indicating the positions of the default tab stops. If the ruler is not in paragraph view, click the *ruler view icon* at the right end of the ruler once (or twice, if necessary) to switch it into paragraph view.

Setting the Indents

You can set a paragraph *indent* by dragging the appropriate triangular icon to the desired position. To drag one of these icons, place the mouse pointer over the icon, press the left mouse button, and, while holding down the button, move the icon left or right to the desired position and then release the button. To set the *right* indent, drag the triangular icon at the right end of the ruler scale.

You can drag this icon to the left to create a positive right indent, or to the right to create a negative right indent.

To set the *left* indent, drag the *two* triangular icons at the left end of the ruler. To drag both of these icons simultaneously, *you must place the pointer on the lower icon.*

To set the left indent for the first line only, drag the *upper* triangular icon.

Notice that the upper icon moves independently of the lower one.

You can also adjust the left indent of all lines in the paragraph *except the first line,* by dragging only the lower icon. To drag the lower icon alone, you must press the Shift key while you are dragging it.

To set a negative left indent, you must drag the upper, lower, or both left indent icons to the left. To drag one of these icons to the left, you must follow these two steps:

1. While holding down the Shift key, drag either the upper or lower triangular icon a little to the right, and then drag it to the left of the margin. Word will immediately extend the ruler scale to the left of the margin.

2. Once Word has extended the ruler scale into the margin area, you can drag to upper or lower triangular icon to the desired position as described previously.

You can also use the ruler to set the indents of paragraphs within Word tables. Setting the indents with the ruler has the same effect as setting the indents through the Indents area of the Format/Paragraph dialog box.

Setting the Alignment

You can set the paragraph alignment by clicking one of the four icons near the center of the ruler.

The effects of these icons are shown in Figure 15.14. These icons have the same effect as the options within the Alignment area of the Format/Paragraph dialog box.

Setting the Spacing

You can adjust the amount of space Word leaves before the selected paragraph by clicking one of the following two icons:

Icon	Alignment Style
⊟L	Left
⊟C	Center
⊟R	Right
⊟J	Justified

Figure 15.14: Paragraph alignment icons

These icons, which have the effects shown in Figure 15.15, allow you to choose one of only two values; to specify *any* amount of space before the paragraph, you can enter the desired measurement into the **Spacing, Before** text box within the Format/Paragraph dialog box, as described previously in the chapter.

Icon	Space before paragraph
⊟	0 lines (close space)
⊟	1 line (open space)

Figure 15.15: Paragraph spacing icons

You can also specify one of three paragraph line spacings by clicking one of the following icons:

These icons adjust the line spacing as shown in Figure 15.16. To specify a line spacing value other than one of these (or to enter an absolute spacing, which is not automatically adjusted), you can enter the desired measurement into the **Spacing, Line** text box within the Format/Paragraph dialog box, as described previously in the chapter.

Icon	Line spacing
⊟	1 line
⊟	1.5 lines
⊟	2 lines

Figure 15.16: Line spacing icons

Assigning the Style

See Chapter 20 for information on styles and on assigning or defining a style using the ruler.

You can assign a style to the selected paragraph or paragraphs by typing the name of the style into the Style box at the left of the ruler or by selecting a style name from the associated pull-down list (see Figure 15.17).

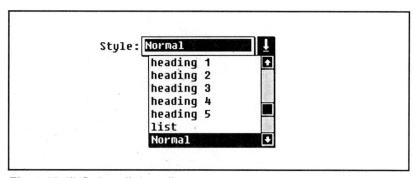

Figure 15.17: Style pull-down list

Assigning a style using the ruler has the same effect as specifying a style through the Style box within the Format/Paragraph dialog box. However, as you will see in Chapter 20, the ruler also allows you to define a new style or change an existing style based upon the current selection.

Setting Tab Stops

When the ruler is in paragraph view, the scale contains a mark for each tab stop, as shown in Figure 15.18.

Tab stops were explained previously in this chapter in the subsection "Setting Tab Stops," under the section "Using the Format/ Paragraph Command."

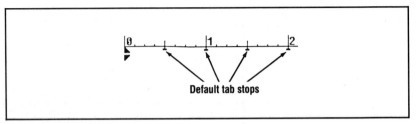

Default tab stops

Figure 15.18: Ruler with four tab stops

You can use the ruler to assign or remove one or more custom tab stops for the selected paragraph or paragraphs. To assign a custom tab stop, perform the following two steps:

1. Click one of the following four icons to choose the desired alignment style for the tab stop:

   These icons correspond to the alignment styles shown in Figure 15.19 (see the section "Defining a New Custom Tab Stop" for an explanation).

2. Click the desired position on the ruler scale where you want to place the tab stop. Word will place a marker on the scale indicating the new custom tab stop

   (in this case, a centered tab), and will remove any default tab stops to its left.

If you want to assign a leader character to a custom tab stop, you will have to use the Format/Tab dialog box, as described previously in the chapter.

To remove a custom tab stop, simply drag the marker for the stop either above or below the ruler scale.

Icon	Tab stop alignment
⬆	Left
⬆	Center
⬆	Right
⬆	Decimal

Figure 15.19: Tab alignment options

USING THE RULER WITH THE KEYBOARD TO FORMAT PARAGRAPHS

You do not need to use the mouse to apply paragraph formatting commands with the ruler. Rather, you can apply most of these features using keyboard commands.

You can set the paragraph alignment, the space before the paragraph, the paragraph line spacing, and the paragraph style using the keyboard commands described later in the chapter (in the section "Using the Keyboard" and in Table 15.2). To perform these commands, you do *not* need to display the ruler.

You can set the paragraph indents and format custom tab stops by using the ruler with the keyboard. To control the ruler with the keyboard, you must first activate *ruler mode.*

Ruler Mode

When you are in ruler mode, you can use the keyboard to assign paragraph indents or format custom tab stops for the selected paragraph or paragraphs.

If the ruler is not currently visible, pressing the Ctrl-Shift-F10 key combination displays the ruler *and* activates ruler mode. If you then press Ctrl-Shift-F10 again, or press Esc, ruler mode is deactivated; the ruler, however, remains visible within the window and may be used with the mouse as described previously. If the ruler is visible and ruler mode is not active, you can activate it by pressing Ctrl-Shift-F10.

When ruler mode is active, Word displays a rectangular cursor below the ruler scale.

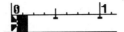

You can move this cursor along the ruler scale to indicate the position where you want to place a paragraph indent or insert or delete a tab stop. Table 15.1 summarizes the keystrokes you can use to move the ruler cursor.

Table 15.1: Keystrokes for Moving the Ruler Cursor

TO MOVE RULER CURSOR:	PRESS:
Left (small distance)	←
Left (larger distance)	Ctrl-←
Left, beyond left margin	Shift-←
Right (small distance)	→
Right (larger distance)	Ctrl-→
To 0″ mark on scale	Home
To right margin	End

Setting the Indents

To set a paragraph indent, first place the ruler cursor at the position where you want to set the indent, and then press one of the following keys:

KEY	INDENT
L *or* l	Left indent
R *or* r	Right indent
F *or* f	First line left indent

The indent you set will be immediately applied to the paragraph. While you are in ruler mode, you can set one or more indents (*and* one or more tab stops, as described in the next section). If, however, you press Esc, ruler mode will be terminated and all settings you made in ruler mode will be canceled. If you press Ctrl-Shift-F10 or ←┘, ruler mode will be terminated, but all settings will remain in effect.

Setting Tab Stops

While you are in ruler mode, you can add or remove one or more custom tab stops. To add a tab stop, first press one of the following keys to choose the alignment style of the tab:

KEY	ALIGNMENT STYLE
1	Left
2	Centered
3	Right
4	Decimal

Next, move the ruler cursor to the position where you want to place the tab stop and press the Ins key.

To delete a custom tab stop, place the ruler cursor over the tab and press Del.

While you are in ruler mode, you can add or remove one or more tab stops. If you press Esc, ruler mode will be terminated and all tab settings made in ruler mode will be canceled. If you press Ctrl-Shift-F10 or ←┘, ruler mode will be terminated and the tab settings will be applied to the selected paragraph or paragraphs.

USING THE RULER TO SET DOCUMENT MARGINS AND INNER COLUMN BOUNDARIES

You must use the mouse to set the document margins and inner column boundaries with the ruler.

In addition to the paragraph formatting features described so far, you can also use the ruler to set the document margins and inner column boundaries. The term *document margins* refers to the left and right document margins explained in Chapter 13; in Chapter 13, you saw how to set them through the Format/Document dialog box. The term *inner column boundaries* applies only to text formatted in two or more columns, and it refers to the inner edges of the text columns.

CH. 15

The column boundaries are normally set when you specify the number of columns and column spacing in the Format/Section dialog box, as described in Chapter 14. The document margins and inner column boundaries are illustrated in Figure 15.20.

To set the document margins or inner column boundaries, the ruler must be in *margin view*. In this view, the **0** on the ruler scale is aligned with the left edge of the page, and Word displays a bracket ([or]) at the position of each margin or inner column boundary. Figure 15.21 illustrates the ruler in margin view. In this figure, the selected text was arranged in two columns; notice that the left and

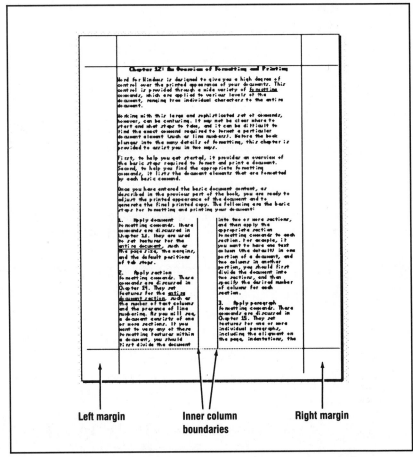

Figure 15.20: The document margins and inner column boundaries

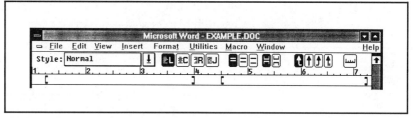

Figure 15.21: The ruler in margin view

right margins as well as the two inner column boundaries are marked with brackets.

To switch the ruler into margin view, click the ruler view icon once or twice until the ruler appears as shown in Figure 15.21. You can adjust the left or right margin by simply dragging the appropriate bracket on the ruler.

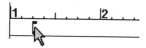

The Mirror Margins option is discussed in Chapter 13.

If you have selected the Mirror Margins option within the Format/ Document dialog box, moving the left bracket sets the *inside* margin on all pages in the document, and moving the right bracket sets the *outside* margin on all pages.

To set the inner column boundaries, drag *any one* of the brackets marking an inner column edge.

When text is divided into multiple snaking columns, each of the columns is given the same width, and the spacing between the columns is kept equal.

Whichever of these brackets you move, Word will automatically move all of the other inner brackets in order to give all columns the same width and spacing.

USING THE RULER TO SET CELL WIDTHS IN TABLES

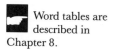

Word tables are described in Chapter 8.

You can also use the ruler to adjust the position of the edges of one or more cells within a Word table. First, you should select the cell or cells you want to adjust. Then, click the ruler view icon once or twice to switch into *column view*. In column view, the positions of edges of the selected cell or cells are indicated with **T**-shaped markers. The ruler in column view is illustrated in Figure 15.22.

You must use the mouse to set the cell widths with the ruler.

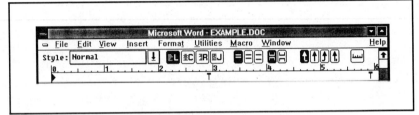

Figure 15.22: The Word ruler in column view

To adjust the position of a cell edge, simply drag the **T** icon to the desired position.

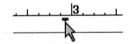

Dragging cell edges with the ruler has the same effect as entering values into the Width of Columns and Indent Rows boxes within the Format/Table dialog box, described in Chapter 8.

USING THE KEYBOARD

You can also use the keyboard to format a paragraph by means of the Format/Paragraph dialog box or the Word ruler. The keyboard commands described in this section are applied directly, without the need to open a dialog box or display the ruler.

You can also assign many paragraph formatting features by issuing direct keyboard commands. In the same manner as employing the Format/Paragraph menu command or the ruler, you must first select the paragraph or paragraphs you want to format, and then issue the command. Using a keyboard formatting command can be more efficient than using the Format/Paragraph command or the Word ruler. It may be worth the effort to learn some of the more commonly used ones. The keyboard commands are described in Table 15.2.

Table 15.2: Keyboard Commands for Formatting Paragraphs

FORMATTING FEATURE:	FORMAT/PARAGRAPH DIALOG BOX METHOD:	KEYSTROKE:
Centered paragraph alignment	Choose Alignment Center option	Ctrl-C
Indent: decrease left indent to previous tab stop (first line keeps its same offset)	Enter appropriate value into **Indents, From Left** box	Ctrl-M
Indent: decrease left indent to previous tab stop; adjust first-line offset to keep first line at its current position (reduce hanging indent)	Enter appropriate values into **Indents, From Left** and **Indents, First Line** boxes	Ctrl-G
Indent: increase left indent to next tab stop (first line keeps its same offset)	Enter appropriate value into **Indents, From Left** box	Ctrl-N
Indent: increase left indent to next tab stop; adjust first-line offset to keep first line at its current position (increase hanging indent)	Enter appropriate values into **Indents, From Left** and **Indents, First Line** boxes	Ctrl-T
Justified paragraph alignment	Choose **Alignment, Justified** option	Ctrl-J
Left paragraph alignment	Choose **Alignment, Left** option	Ctrl-L
Reset all features to defaults defined by style	Set each option in dialog box back to default	Ctrl-X
Right paragraph alignment	Choose **Alignment, Right** option	Ctrl-R
Spacing: add 1 line of space before paragraph	Enter **1** into **Spacing, Before** box	Ctrl-O
Spacing: apply double line spacing (for 12-point characters)	Enter **2** into **Spacing, Line** box	Ctrl-2
Spacing: apply 1.5-line spacing (for 12-point characters)	Enter **1.5** into **Spacing, Line** box	Ctrl-5

Table 15.2: Keyboard Commands for Formatting Paragraphs (continued)

FORMATTING FEATURE:	FORMAT/PARAGRAPH DIALOG BOX METHOD:	KEYSTROKE:
Spacing: apply single line spacing (for 12-point characters)	Enter **1** into **Spacing, Line** box	Ctrl-1
Spacing: remove space before paragraph	Enter **0** into **Spacing, Before** box	Ctrl-E
Style: apply a new style	Enter name into **Style** box	Ctrl-S, then type style name and press ⏎

Notice that for each command, Table 15.2 describes the equivalent method that you would use with the Format/Paragraph dialog box. Each formatting feature was described previously in the chapter, in the section "Using the Format/Paragraph Command."

The Ctrl-X keyboard command is especially useful. With this single keystroke, you can restore all of the paragraph formatting features of the selected paragraph back to the default values defined by the paragraph's style.

POSITIONING A PARAGRAPH

So far in this chapter, you have seen how to adjust the position of a paragraph relative to the document margins and the surrounding paragraphs (by setting the indents, the alignment, and the space before and after the paragraph). In this section, you will learn how to place a paragraph containing text or graphics at a specific position on the printed page, through the Format/Position menu command. This command provides you a high level of control over the layout of each page of your documents. In Chapter 9, Figure 9.1, you saw an example of a paragraph containing a picture that was assigned a specific position on the page through the Format/Position command.

A paragraph that has been assigned a specific position through the Format/Position command is known as a *positioned object*. A positioned object has the following important properties:

- It is printed at a specific location on the page (for example, the paragraph containing the picture in Figure 9.1 was aligned with the upper and left document margins).

- You can assign the paragraph a specific width.

- Word will flow unpositioned text around the positioned object (for example, Word automatically filled in the space to the right of the picture in Figure 9.1 using unpositioned text).

- You can directly move the paragraph on the page in the Print Preview mode.

Print Preview mode is described in Chapter 17.

In galley view (normal editing view), draft view, and outline view, a positioned object is *not* displayed at its assigned position on the page. Rather, it appears at the location where you entered it into the document, as if it were not positioned. However, in the Page View and Print Preview modes, the paragraph will appear at its assigned position.

If you select two or more paragraphs before assigning a position, the paragraphs will be printed together on the page in the same order that they have been entered into the document.

To assign a position to the selected paragraph or paragraphs, choose the Format/Position menu command. Word will display the dialog box shown in Figure 15.23. If you accept all of the default values in this dialog box, the paragraph will remain unpositioned. If, however, you change one or more default values, the paragraph will become a positioned object, with all of the properties listed previously in this section. If you later want to restore all of the default values (making the paragraph no longer a positioned object), click the Reset button.

To specify the *horizontal* position of the paragraph on the page, you must first select one of the three reference points following the **Relative to** label within the Horizontal area of the Format/Position dialog box. The Margin option positions the paragraph relative to the left or right document margins, the Page option positions it relative to the left or right edges of the page, and the Column option positions it relative to the left or right edges the text column. If the paragraph is in a section formatted as a single column, the Column option will have

If you apply the Format/Position command to one or more cells in a Word table, Word keeps the entire table together, and prints it at the specified page position.

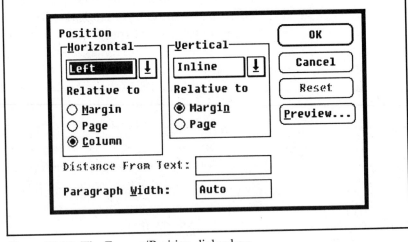

Figure 15.23: The Format/Position dialog box

When specifying page positions, remember that most laser printers cannot print closer than 0.5″ from the edge of the page.

the same effect as the Margin option, since the edges of the column coincide with the document margins; however, if the text is arranged in two or more columns, these two options may have different effects.

Once you have specified a horizontal reference point, you should specify the placement of the paragraph with respect to this reference point. You can specify the placement in one of two ways. First, you can type an exact measurement into the Horizontal text box. For example, if you enter **1.5″**, and if you have chosen the Margin option, Word will place the left edge of the paragraph exactly 1.5″ from the left document margin. Second, you can choose one of the alignment options from the Horizontal pull-down list, as shown in Figure 15.24.

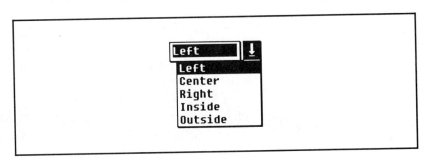

Figure 15.24: Horizontal alignment options

The Left option aligns the paragraph flush with the left margin, left edge of the page, or left edge of the column (depending upon your choice of reference point). The Center option aligns the paragraph midway between the left and right margins, page edges, or column edges. The Right option aligns the paragraph flush with the right margin, right edge of the page, or right edge of the column.

The Inside option aligns the paragraph flush with the inside margin, inside edge of the page, or inside edge of the column. The *inside* is on the left of odd-numbered pages, and on the right of even-numbered pages.

Finally, the Outside option aligns the paragraph flush with the outside margin, outside edge of the page, or outside edge of the column. The *outside* is on the right of odd-numbered pages, and on the left of even-numbered pages.

In a similar manner, to specify the *vertical* position of the paragraph on the page, you must first select the Margin or the Page option within the Vertical area of the Format/Position dialog box. The Margin option positions the paragraph relative to the top or bottom document margins, and the Page option positions it relative to the top or bottom edges of the page.

After specifying the vertical reference point, you should either enter an absolute measurement into the Vertical text box

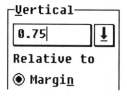

or select an alignment option from the Vertical pull-down list.

The Inline option does *not* place the paragraph at a specific vertical position on the page; rather, the paragraph is printed at its normal vertical position (that is, between the paragraphs of unpositioned text that surround it within the document).

The Top option aligns the paragraph flush with the top margin or top of the page. The Center option aligns the paragraph midway between the top and bottom margins or top and bottom edges of the page. The Bottom option aligns the paragraph flush with the bottom margin or bottom edge of the page.

You can also specify the distance between a positioned paragraph and any nonpositioned text that surrounds it by entering the desired measurement into the Distance from Text box. If you have not changed any of the default options in the Format/Position dialog box, you will not be able to enter a value into the Distance From Text box (the box will be displayed in gray; since such a paragraph is *not* a positioned object, Word will not flow text around it). The default distance is 0.13″.

Finally, you can specify the width of a positioned paragraph by entering a measurement into the Paragraph Width text box. The default width is Auto. This value assigns a text paragraph the normal width of the column that contains it in the document. The Auto value assigns a picture the width it was given when it was inserted into the document or formatted with the Format/Picture command.

The default settings in the Format/Position dialog box (that is, the settings of a nonpositioned paragraph) are as follows:

- The Horizontal reference point is Column.

- The Horizontal distance is Left alignment.

- The Vertical reference point is Margin.

- The Vertical distance is Inline.

- The Distance From Text has no value, since this setting applies only to positioned objects.

- The Paragraph Width is Auto.

In contrast, the picture in Figure 9.1 was assigned the following settings:

- The Horizontal reference point is Margin.
- The Horizontal distance is Left alignment.
- The Vertical reference point is Margin.
- The Vertical distance is Top.
- The Distance From Text is 0.13".
- The Paragraph Width is Auto.

For more information on Print Preview mode, see Chapter 17.

You can accept the changes entered into the Format/Position dialog box and immediately activate the Print Preview mode by clicking the Preview button. As you will see in Chapter 17, the Print Preview mode not only allows you to view the layout of the page containing a positioned object, but also allows you to directly move a positioned object to any location on the page.

SUMMARY

- You divide a document into paragraphs by pressing the ⏎ key. Each time you press this key, you create a new paragraph.

- Each paragraph is terminated with a paragraph mark. Paragraph marks are normally invisible. You can, however, have Word display them as ¶ characters by choosing the Paragraph Marks option within the View/Preferences dialog box. If you move or copy a paragraph mark, the paragraph's formatting is applied to the text that precedes the new location of the mark.

- Before issuing any of the formatting commands discussed in this chapter, you must select the paragraph or paragraphs you want to format.

- The most flexible and complete method for formatting the selected paragraph or paragraphs is to choose the Format/Paragraph menu command.

- You can set the following formatting features through the dialog box displayed by the Format/Paragraph command: the paragraph indents, the paragraph alignment, the paragraph spacing, the paragraph style, borders displayed around the paragraph, the position of page breaks, numbering of paragraph lines.

- You can define custom tab stops for the selected paragraph or paragraphs through the Format/Tabs dialog box (opened by issuing the Format/Tabs menu command, or by clicking the Tabs button within the Format/Paragraph dialog box).

- The ruler is a set of icons that enables you to directly apply many paragraph formatting features using the mouse or keyboard. You can display the ruler (or hide it if it is already displayed) by choosing the View/Ruler menu option.

- Using the ruler in conjunction with the mouse or keyboard, you can assign the following features to the selected paragraph or paragraphs: paragraph indents, paragraph alignment, space before the paragraph (0 or 1 line), line spacing within the paragraph (1, 1.5, or 2 lines), the paragraph style, and custom tab stops.

- Using the ruler in conjunction with the mouse, you can also set the document margins and inner column boundaries, and the width of the selected cells in a Word table.

- You can also apply many formatting features directly to the selected paragraph or paragraphs by issuing keyboard commands. These commands are described in Table 15.2.

- You can use the Format/Position menu command to place a paragraph containing text or graphics at an exact position on the printed page.

16

FORMATTING CHARACTERS

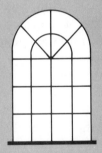

See Chapter 5 for information on copying character formatting from one block of characters to another. Also, see Chapter 6 for a discussion on searching for or replacing character formatting.

THIS IS THE FINAL CHAPTER ON FORMATTING A Word document. In it, you will learn how to apply formatting to individual characters. Character formatting controls the appearance of characters both on the screen and on the final printed copy of the document.

The chapter first explains how to select characters prior to formatting and how to adjust the appearance of character formatting features on the screen. It then describes the three basic methods for applying character formatting: the Format/Character command, the Word ribbon, and the keyboard commands. You should read the section on the Format/Character command even if you are primarily interested in the ribbon or keyboard methods, since this section includes more thorough explanations of each of the formatting features.

See Chapter 20 for information on defining and assigning styles.

As you read through the chapter, keep in mind that you do not need to issue a character formatting command unless you want to *change* the default character formatting for one or more characters. The default character formatting depends upon the *style* currently assigned to the paragraph containing the characters.

SELECTING CHARACTERS

If you *select* one or more characters in your document prior to assigning character formatting, the formatting features you choose will be applied to the selected characters. If the document does *not* contain a selection at the time you assign character formatting, the features you choose will be applied to the characters you subsequently type at the insertion point. (In the second case, the formatting is conceptually applied to the insertion point itself.)

Prior to formatting, you can select a block of characters using the normal selection mode or the column selection mode, as explained in Chapter 5.

For example, if you select a block of text and then assign the Bold character enhancement, the selected characters will instantly become bold. If, however, you assign the Bold character enhancement *without* previously selecting one or more characters, you will see no immediate change. However, all characters you then type at the insertion point will be bold (until you move the insertion point to some other position in the document, or switch off the bold feature).

In general, when you type a character into your document, the character will be assigned the same formatting as the existing character immediately *before* the insertion point, *plus* all formatting you assign through one of the commands presented in this chapter. There is one exception: If the insertion point is at the *beginning* of a paragraph, any characters you type will acquire the formatting of the first character in the paragraph plus any assigned formatting.

VIEWING CHARACTER FORMATTING

See Chapter 17 for information on installing and selecting printers within the Windows environment.

The printer that is currently selected to receive output from Word may not be able to print all character formats. For example, a printer can typically print only a limited range of character fonts and sizes. It may also not be able to print certain character enhancements, such as italics.

The Display as Printed option also causes Word to insert line breaks at the actual positions where they will occur on the printed copy.

If you select the Display as Printed option within the View Preferences dialog box, Word will display on the screen *only* those character formatting features that the current printer can actually print.

Consider, for example, formatting a group of characters as italic when the Display as Printed option is selected. If the current printer can print italics, then the characters will be displayed on the screen in italic, just as they will appear on the final printed copy produced by this printer. If, however, the printer cannot generate italic characters, then the characters will appear on the screen and on the printed copy in nonitalic type. Note that even though the italics do not *appear* on the screen, this formatting feature is nevertheless assigned to the characters; if you later turn off the Display as Printed option *or* change to a printer that can generate italics, the characters will immediately be converted to italics on the screen.

If the Display as Printed option is *not* selected, then the characters will appear in italics regardless of the printing capabilities of the current printer.

The following sections will describe the effects of the current printer selection and the Display as Printed option on the appearance of specific formatting features.

USING THE FORMAT/CHARACTER COMMAND

Once you have selected one or more existing characters that you want to format, or have placed the insertion point where you want to insert new characters, choose the Format/Character menu command. Word will display the dialog box shown in Figure 16.1.

Through this dialog box, you can specify the following character formatting features:

- The character font
- The character size
- The character color
- Character enhancements

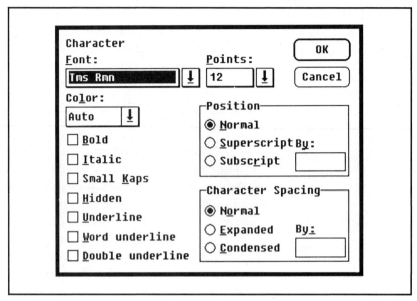

Figure 16.1: The Format/Character dialog box

- The vertical position of characters (superscript or subscript)
- The character spacing

For each of these features, the Format/Character dialog box displays the value currently assigned to the selection or insertion point. Note, however, that if the current selection includes characters with *different* formatting features (for example, if the selection includes two different character sizes), then the area specifying the feature will be left blank or will be filled with gray shading (the exact situation will be described for each feature). In any case, you need enter a value only if you want to *change* the current setting.

Clicking the OK button removes the dialog box and applies the formatting features you selected. Clicking the Cancel button removes the dialog box without applying the specified formatting.

CHOOSING THE FONT

The character *font* specifies the general shape or style of the characters. A specific font is identified by name, such as Tms Rmn or

Courier. The Font text box within the Format/Character dialog box contains the name of the font currently assigned to the selection or insertion point. Note, however, that if the selection contains more than one character font, the Font box will be empty.

To assign a specific font, choose the name of the desired font from the Font pull-down list (Figure 16.2). This list contains the names of the fonts that can be printed on the printer that is currently selected. The list that appears on your system will probably be different from that shown here. Figure 16.3 illustrates the printed appearance of several different fonts (these fonts may not be available for your printer).

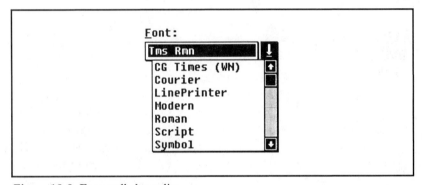

Figure 16.2: Font pull-down list

Figure 16.3: Several fonts

See the Windows manual for a list of the names of the fonts that can be displayed on the screen.

Alternatively, if you know the name of a Windows font that is *not* included in the list, you can type the name into the Font box in the Format/Character dialog box. If the Display as Printed option is *not* selected, then Word will display the specified font on the screen even though the current printer cannot produce it. When Word prints the document, it will use the printer font that is closest in appearance to the specified font. If you later change the printer to one that can generate the specified font, this font will be printed.

If the Display as Printed option *is* selected, then Word will display the characters on the screen *and* print the characters using the printer font that is closest to the specified font.

SETTING THE CHARACTER SIZE

See Appendix B for an explanation of points and other units of measurement.

The current character size is displayed in the Points box of the Format/Character menu. The character size in this box is the *height* of the characters in points. Note, however, that if the current selection contains more than one character size, the Points box will be empty.

If you want to specify another size, choose the desired number of points from the Points pull-down list (Figure 16.4). This list contains the character sizes that the selected printer can print using the font currently specified in the Font box. To obtain an accurate list of sizes, you should therefore select the font *before* selecting the size.

Figure 16.5 illustrates the printed appearance of a given font (CG Times [WN]) printed in several different sizes. Notice that as the

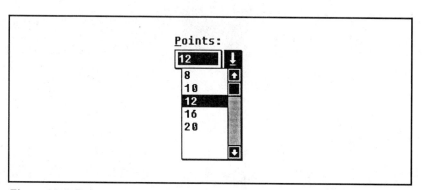

Figure 16.4: Points pull-down list

This is 8 points.

This is 10 points.

This is 12 points.

This is 16 points.

This is 20 points.

Figure 16.5: Characters in several sizes

character height is changed, the character width is also changed, so that the characters maintain the same proportions.

Alternatively, you can type a character size not contained in the list directly into the Points box. If the Display as Printed option is *not* selected, then Word will display the specified character size on the screen even though the selected printer cannot print the current font in this size. When Word prints the document, it will use the available size that is nearest to the specified size. If the Display as Printed option *is* selected, Word will display the characters on the screen *and* print the characters using the available character size nearest to the specified size.

SPECIFYING THE CHARACTER COLOR

The current character color is displayed in the Color box on the Format/Character menu. If, however, the selection contains more than one color, this box will be empty. To specify a particular color, choose a color from the pull-down list (Figure 16.6).

The value Auto is the color you have assigned to the Window Text item through the Windows Control Panel.

See your Windows manual for information on setting the Window Text color through the Control Panel.

If the currently selected printer (or plotter) can print colors, the selected characters will be printed in the specified color; otherwise, the color assigned to the characters will be ignored. If you have a

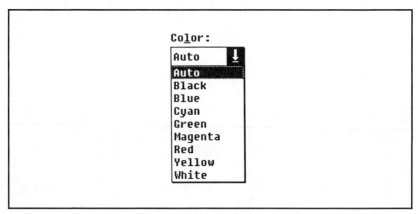

Figure 16.6: Color pull-down list

color monitor, the characters will be displayed on the screen in the designated color, *even if* you have chosen the Display as Printed option and the printer cannot print colors.

ASSIGNING CHARACTER ENHANCEMENTS

You can also assign a variety of character enhancements to emphasize the selected text. The following enhancements are available:

- Bold
- Italic
- Small Kaps
- Hidden
- Underline
- Word underline
- Double underline

An enhancement currently assigned to the selected text has an **X** in the box next to the option in the dialog box.

⊠ I̲talic

If, however, an enhancement is assigned to only a *portion* of the selected text, the box is shaded rather than being marked with an **X**.

☐ `Italic`

If an enhancement is not currently enabled (the box is empty), or is enabled for only a portion of the selected text (the box is shaded), you can enable it for *all* of the selected text by clicking the box. If an enhancement is currently enabled (the box has an **X**), you can turn it off by clicking the box. In general, you can combine enhancements; for example, you can assign both Bold and Italic to the same text. However, you can choose only a *single* underline style (Underline, Word underline, or Double underline). If you click an underline style when another underline style has been previously selected, Word automatically turns off the previous style.

Figure 16.7 illustrates various character enhancements assigned to characters having the same font (CG Times [WN]).

CG Times (WN) characters with no character enhancements.

CG Times (WN) characters with the Bold enhancement.

CG Times (WN) characters with the Italic enhancement.

CG Times (WN) characters with the Bold and Italic enhancements.

CG TIMES (WN) CHARACTERS WITH THE SMALL KAPS ENHANCEMENT.

<u>CG Times (WN) characters with the Underline enhancement.</u>

<u>CG</u> <u>Times</u> <u>(WN)</u> <u>characters</u> <u>with</u> <u>the</u> <u>Word</u> <u>Underline</u> <u>enhancement.</u>

<u>CG Times (WN) characters with the Double Underline enhancement.</u>

Figure 16.7: Selected character enhancements

If you have selected the Display as Printed option, Word will display on the screen only those enhancements that the selected printer can create.

If you assign the Hidden enhancement, the selected characters will exhibit the following features:

- If the Hidden Text option within the View/Preferences dialog box is selected, the characters will be displayed on the screen with a dotted underline.

  T̤h̤i̤s̤ ̤i̤s̤ ̤a̤ ̤l̤i̤n̤e̤ ̤o̤f̤ ̤h̤i̤d̤d̤e̤n̤ ̤t̤e̤x̤t̤.̤

- If the Hidden Text option within the View/Preferences dialog box is *not* selected, the characters will be invisible on the screen.

- If the Hidden Text option within the Include area of the File/Print dialog box is selected, hidden text will be printed; otherwise, it will not be printed.

ADJUSTING THE VERTICAL POSITION OF CHARACTERS

You can adjust the vertical placement of the selected characters by choosing one of the three options within the Position area of the Format/Character dialog box:

Normal
Superscript
Subscript

The Normal option leaves the text in its standard vertical position. The Superscript option raises the characters above the base line and decreases the character size. The Subscript option lowers the characters below the base line and decreases the size. If you select the Superscript or Subscript option, you can enter the amount the characters should be raised or lowered by entering a measurement into the By box. The default measurement is 3 points. You can enter a value between 0 points and 63.5 points, in 0.5-point increments.

By:

4.5pt|

ALTERING THE CHARACTER SPACING

You can adjust the amount of space *between* characters on the printed copy by choosing one of the options from the Character Spacing area of the Format/Character dialog box.

> Normal
> Expanded
> Condensed

If you select the Normal option, Word will neither increase nor decrease the standard amount of space printed between each character. If you select the Expanded option, Word will increase the amount of space between characters; this space is added to the right side of each character. If you select the Condensed option, Word will subtract space from the right side of each character.

If you have selected the Expanded or Condensed option, you can specify the amount of space to be added or subtracted by entering the number of points into the By box. For the Expanded option, the default amount is 3 points; you can enter a measurement between 0 and 14 points, in 0.25-point increments. For the Condensed option, the default amount is 1.5 points; you can enter a measurement between 0 and 1.75 points in 0.25-point increments.

You can adjust the amount of space between characters to add emphasis to a block of text; for example, you might want to emphasize a title by formatting it as expanded text. You can also adjust the spacing to improve the appearance of characters that don't fit well together, such as an italic character placed next to a normal character.

USING THE RIBBON

You can apply many of the character formatting features to the current selection or insertion point using the Word *ribbon* in conjunction with the mouse. The ribbon is a set of icons that you can optionally display at the top of the window. It is similar to the Word ruler, described in Chapter 15.

To display the ribbon, choose the View/Ribbon menu command. Choosing this command again will remove the ribbon. Figure 16.8 illustrates a window with the ribbon displayed at the top.

Using the ribbon, you can choose the following features:

- The character font
- The character size
- The following character enhancements: Bold, Italic, Small Kaps, Underline, Word underline, Double underline
- Superscript
- Subscript
- Visibility of special characters

At the left end of the ribbon, you will find the Font box and pull-down list, as well as the Pts box and pull-down list. You can use these to specify the character font and size, in the same manner as the Font and Points boxes and pull-down lists in the Format/Character dialog box, which were described previously in the chapter.

The remainder of the ribbon contains a series of icons that allow you to choose various character formatting features. If a given feature is already assigned to the current selection or insertion point, the corresponding icon will be highlighted. If the feature is assigned to only a *portion* of the current selection, the icon will be displayed in gray. For example, the following ribbon icons indicate that *all* characters in the selection are bold, *some* of the characters are italic, and *none*

A *gray* object in the screen normally appears in lighter type.

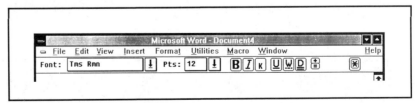

Figure 16.8: The Word ribbon

of the characters have any of the other enhancements:

If a feature is not assigned to the selection or is assigned to only a portion of the selection (the icon is gray), you can assign it to the entire selection by clicking the icon. If a feature is already assigned to the entire selection (the icon is highlighted), you can remove it from the entire selection by clicking the icon.

Figure 16.9 summarizes the effect of each icon within the ribbon. Note that selecting the icon on the far right of the ribbon

is the same as choosing the Show All * option within the View/ Preferences dialog box. It causes Word to display visible symbols for

Icon	Effect
B	Bold
I	Italic
K	Small Kaps
U	Underline
W	Word underline
D	Double underline
+	Superscript (by 3 points)
=	Subscript (by 3 points)
*	Show all special marks

Figure 16.9: The ribbon icons

characters that are normally invisible, such as spaces and tabs, as explained in Chapter 3 (in the section "Entering and Revising Text").

USING THE KEYBOARD

Each formatting feature was described previously in the chapter, in the section "Using the Format/ Character Command."

In addition to using the Format/Character menu command or the Word ribbon, you can directly apply many character formatting features using keyboard commands. The keyboard commands for formatting characters are listed in Table 16.1.

For each command, Table 16.1 describes the equivalent method that you would use with the Format/Character dialog box.

Note that when you issue the following keyboard commands, you must type a valid value at the Word prompt:

- Ctrl-V, to specify the character color
- Ctrl-F, to specify the character font
- Ctrl-P, to specify the character size

Unlike using the Format/Character dialog box, when using any of these three commands, you do not have the benefit of a pull-down list of valid choices; rather, you have to type a proper value at the prompt that Word displays at the bottom of the window. Note that if the ribbon is currently displayed when you issue the Ctrl-F or Ctrl-P command, Word will move the insertion point to the appropriate box within the ribbon rather than displaying a prompt at the bottom of the window. You can pull down the list associated with a box by typing Alt-↓.

Note also that the Ctrl-spacebar command eliminates all character formatting that you have directly applied using any of the methods described in this chapter. This command restores the default character formatting as defined by the style assigned to the paragraph(s) containing the selected character(s).

Table 16.1: Keyboard Commands for Formatting Characters

CHARACTER FORMATTING FEATURE:	FORMAT/CHARACTER DIALOG BOX METHOD:	KEYSTROKE:
Bold enhancement	Select Bold option	Ctrl-B
Color	Select color from Color pull-down list	Ctrl-V, then type desired color at prompt
Font	Type font name into Font box or select from pull-down list	Ctrl-F, then type name of desired font at prompt
Hidden enhancement	Select Hidden option	Ctrl-H
Italic enhancement	Select Italic option	Ctrl-I
Reset all features to defaults defined by style	Set each option in dialog box back to default	Ctrl-spacebar
Size of characters: select a specific point size	Type number of points into Points box, or select number from pull-down list	Ctrl-P, then type number of points at prompt
Size of characters: assign the *next larger* available point size (grow font)	Select the next larger size from the Points pull-down list	Ctrl-F2
Size of characters: assign the *next smaller* available point size (shrink font)	Select the next smaller size from the Points pull-down list	Ctrl-Shift-F2
Small Kaps enhancement	Select Small Kaps option	Ctrl-K
Subscript (3 points)	Select Subscript option and accept default amount in By box	Ctrl- = (Ctrl-equal sign)
Superscript (3 points)	Select Superscript option and accept default amount in By box	Ctrl- + (Ctrl-plus sign)
Underline enhancement	Select Underline option	Ctrl-U
Underline (double) enhancement	Select Double underline option	Ctrl-D
Underline (word) enhancement	Select Word underline option	Ctrl-W

SUMMARY

- You can format characters either by choosing the Format/Character menu command, by using the Word ribbon, or by issuing keyboard commands.

- To apply formatting to existing characters in your document, select these characters before issuing the formatting command.

- To specify the formatting of characters you are about to type, place the insertion point at the position where you want to insert the characters before issuing the formatting command.

- To have Word display only those formatting features that can be printed on the currently selected printer, select the Display as Printed option within the View/Preferences dialog box.

- By choosing the Format/Character menu command, you can apply the following character formatting features: font, size, color, enhancements (such as bold or italic), superscript, and subscript.

- To display the Word ribbon, choose the View/Ribbon menu option. To remove the ribbon, choose this option again.

- The ribbon allows you to apply the following formatting features: font, size, enhancements, superscript, and subscript. You can also show or hide special marks (such as spaces and tabs).

- You can directly apply many character formatting features using keyboard commands. These commands are listed in Table 16.1.

17

PREVIEWING AND PRINTING YOUR DOCUMENT

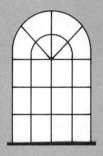

IN THIS CHAPTER, YOU WILL LEARN HOW TO PREVIEW the printed appearance of your document, how to make final formatting adjustments, how to set printer options, and how to generate the printed document copy. The chapter also includes an initial discussion on automatic hyphenation, since this procedure should be performed immediately before previewing a document.

PERFORMING AUTOMATIC HYPHENATION

In this section, you will learn how to have Word automatically hyphenate words within all or part of your document. To *hyphenate* a word means to insert a hyphen character into the word so that the letters before the hyphen, as well as the hyphen itself, can be moved up to the end of the previous line.

Paragraph justi-
fication and align-
ment are explained in
Chapter 15.

If a paragraph is left-aligned, hyphenating the appropriate words
can lessen the raggedness of the right edge of the paragraph. If the
paragraph is justified, hyphenating can reduce the amount of space
Word must insert between words to justify the lines.

Before learning how to perform automatic hyphenation, you
should understand the different types of hyphens that can be entered
into a Word document. Table 17.1 lists the different types of hyphen
characters, showing the appearance of each character and the keystroke used to enter it.

You learned how to
enter cm and en
dashes in Chapter 3.

Regular hyphens, *em* dashes, and *en* dashes always remain visible
on the screen and on the printed document. If you have inserted one
of these characters into a word, and if the word falls at an appropriate
position near the end of a line, Word will break the word at the location of the hyphen or dash.

Table 17.1: The Different Types of Hyphens

HYPHEN NAME:	APPEARANCE:	KEYSTROKE:
Regular	-	- (hyphen key)
Em dash	—	Alt-0150 (type number on numeric keypad with Num Lock on)
En dash	–	Alt-0151 (type number on numeric keypad with Num Lock on)
Nonbreaking	- *or* – (on screen)	Ctrl-Shift-hyphen
Optional	invisible *or* - *or* the logical not symbol (ASCII 170 or Windows ANSI 172) (on screen)	Ctrl-hyphen

Program bug: To enter a nonbreaking hyphen, you may have to press the *right* Ctrl key on a keyboard with two Ctrl keys.

If you do *not* want Word to break the word at the position of the hyphen, you can use a nonbreaking hyphen rather than a regular hyphen. If the Optional Hyphens option in the View/Preferences dialog box is enabled, a nonbreaking hyphen is displayed *on the screen* as a long dash (see Table 17.1); otherwise, it appears as a normal hyphen character. The Optional Hyphens option does not affect the way the hyphen is printed.

An optional hyphen inserted into a word exhibits the following properties:

- If the word falls *within* a line, the optional hyphen will not be printed.

- If the word falls at an appropriate position near the *end* of a line, Word will break the word at the position of the optional hyphen, and print the optional hyphen as a normal hyphen character.

- If you select the Optional Hyphens option within the View/ Preferences dialog box, the optional hyphen will always be displayed on the screen as the special character shown in Table 17.1.

- If you turn off the Optional Hyphens option, the optional hyphen will be displayed on the screen only when it occurs at the end of a line, within a broken word (in this case, it will appear as a normal hyphen character).

When you perform automatic hyphenation, Word inserts optional hyphens at the appropriate positions within words to help fill out the ends of the lines (or to reduce the amount of space that must be inserted between words within justified text).

To decide when it is appropriate to perform automatic hyphenation, consider the following guidelines:

If you edit or format text after hyphenating, you may lose some or all of the benefits of the hyphenation.

- You should hyphenate *after* entering all document text and *after* performing all basic formatting. Automatic hyphenation inserts optional hyphens *only* at those positions where line breaks can occur given the current arrangement of the text. If you change the content or format of the text, you should hyphenate again so that Word will insert optional hyphens in the *new* positions where line breaks can occur.

- You should hyphenate *before* previewing the printed appearance of your document (using the Page View or Print Preview mode, as described later), since hyphenation can change the positions of line and page breaks, and therefore alter the page layout that you are examining and adjusting.

- If you adjust the formatting while previewing your document, you may want to hyphenate the altered text *again,* for the reason explained under the first point.

Before performing automatic hyphenation, you should select the Display as Printed option within the View/Preferences dialog box. Selecting this option causes Word to display line breaks at the positions where they will occur on the printed copy of the document. Automatic hyphenation will then insert optional hyphens at the appropriate positions in the text. If the Display as Printed option is *not* selected, performing automatic hyphenation will improve the appearance of the text on the screen, but not the appearance of the text on the printed copy!

To automatically hyphenate a portion of your document, select the text you want to hyphenate. To hyphenate the entire document, either select the whole document or simply issue the hyphenation command without making a selection; if there is no selection, the hyphenation command automatically selects the entire document.

Next, choose the Utilities/Hyphenate menu command. Word will display the dialog box illustrated in Figure 17.1. Before beginning automatic hyphenation, you can select several options that affect the way Word performs the hyphenation.

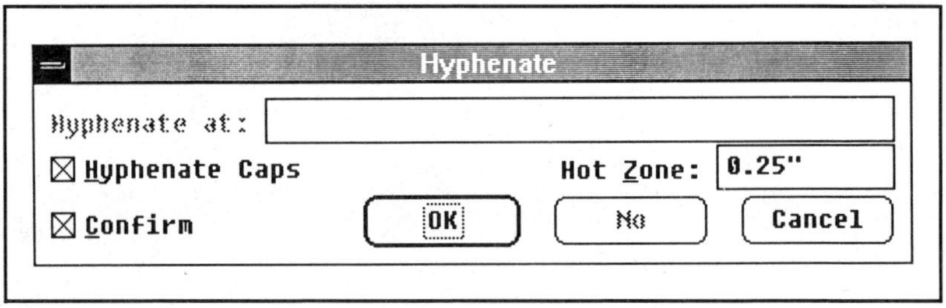

Figure 17.1: The Utilities/Hyphenate dialog box

First, if you select the Hyphenate Caps option, Word will attempt to hyphenate (if appropriate) words that consist entirely of capital letters—that is, words in all capital letters will be treated like any other words. If you turn this option off, Word will *not* attempt to hyphenate words all in capital letters.

Also, if you choose the Confirm option Word will pause before hyphenating each word and allow you to review the proposed hyphenation.

Finally, you can specify the hyphenation *hot zone* by entering a measurement into the Hot Zone box. The hot zone is the amount of empty space that Word must find at the end of a line before it attempts to hyphenate the first word on the next line. For example, if the hot zone is set to 0.5″, whenever there is at least 0.5″ of free space between the last character on the line and the right indent, Word will hyphenate (if possible) the first word on the following line. The default hot-zone value is 0.25″. In general, if you specify a smaller value, Word will attempt to hyphenate more words; a smaller value will thus result in a more even right margin (or in justified lines with less inserted space). If you specify a larger value, Word will attempt to hyphenate fewer words; a larger value will thus result in fewer hyphenations and fewer single syllables at the ends of lines.

When you have set the desired options and are ready to begin hyphenation, click the OK button. If you have *not* selected the Confirm option, Word will remove the dialog box and begin hyphenating. While Word is hyphenating, it displays the percentage of the selected text that it has completed. If you want to cancel the hyphenation process before it is finished, press Esc; Word will stop hyphenating, but will *not* remove any of the optional hyphens it has already inserted. (As you will see later, you can remove all hyphens already inserted by issuing the Undo command.)

If you *have* selected the Confirm option, Word will begin hyphenating and will leave the dialog box on the screen for you to review each proposed hyphenation. Whenever Word encounters a word that it wants to hyphenate, it displays the word within the **Hyphenate at** box.

If you want to remove the dialog box without performing hyphenation, click the Cancel button.

Hyphenate at: | per-cent█age

Each word appears divided into syllables, and the position of the proposed hyphen is marked by a flashing insertion point. You now have the following four choices:

- You can have Word insert an optional hyphen at the proposed location by clicking the Yes button.

- You can have Word insert an optional hyphen at another position within the word by moving the insertion point to the desired location and clicking the Yes button. To move the insertion point, press the ← or → key, or click the desired position. Notice that the word also contains a dotted vertical line, which indicates the position of the right indent; if the optional hyphen is inserted to the right of this line, Word will not be able to break the word at the hyphen. (In this case, the optional hyphen is nevertheless inserted at the position you designated; if the text in the paragraph is later rearranged, the word might be broken at this position.)

- You can omit hyphenating the current word, and move on to the next word, by clicking the No button.

- You can cancel the hyphenation process by clicking the Cancel button. Clicking this button prevents Word from inserting additional hyphens, but does not remove any hyphens that have already been inserted.

If you issue the Undo command immediately after performing an automatic hyphenation, Word will remove *all* hyphens that were inserted, whether or not the Confirm option was selected. To issue the Undo command, choose the Edit/Undo Hyphenate menu command or press Alt-Backspace.

PREVIEWING YOUR DOCUMENT

You can preview the printed appearance of your document using either the Page View or Print Preview document view. As you saw in Chapter 2, a document view is a particular way of looking at and working with a document. Table 17.2 summarizes the five basic document views provided by Word. By the end of this chapter, you will

Before clicking the Yes or No button to resume hyphenation, you can change any of the options contained in the Utilities/Hyphenate dialog box, which were described previously.

The Yes button replaces the OK button once the hyphenation process has started.

Table 17.2: The Five Document Views

DOCUMENT VIEW:	CHARACTERISTICS:
Galley View (Normal Editing View)	Default document view. Displays as printed: character and paragraph formatting features, line and page breaks, tab stop alignment, and pictures. Does *not* display as printed: headers, footers, footnote text, line numbering, multiple columns, and positioned objects. Provides all editing and formatting commands (intermediate speed).
Draft View	Displays all text using the system font, in a single character size. All character enhancements are displayed as underlined text. Displays pictures as empty frames. Provides all editing and formatting commands (fast).
Page View	Displays all features (except line numbering) exactly as they are printed. Text is displayed full size; thus, you can usually view only a portion of a page. Provides all editing and formatting commands (slow).
Print Preview	Displays one or two entire pages exactly as they will be printed. Text is reduced in size. Provides no editing or formatting commands, but allows you to move margins, headers, footers, page breaks, and positioned objects.
Outline View	Shows the organization of a document, and allows you to quickly rearrange the document content (see Chapter 24).

have learned about all of these views except outline view, which is described in Chapter 24.

Note that when you are in galley view (normal editing view), you can have Word display a more accurate representation of the printed appearance of the document by selecting the Display as Printed option within the View/Preferences dialog box. This option causes Word to display all character formatting features exactly as they will be printed. Also, Word will insert line breaks at the same positions where they will occur on the printed page.

PAGE VIEW

Print Preview is discussed in the next section.

To switch into Page View, choose the View/Page menu command. Page View provides a way of viewing and working with your document that is intermediate between galley view (normal editing view) and Print Preview. Page View shares the following features with galley view:

- You can typically see only a *portion* of the printed page at a given time; however, each character is fully legible.

- You can type text and perform normal editing and formatting tasks. Use the same techniques that have been described in this book for galley view.

Page View shares the following characteristics with Print Preview:

Page View does *not* display line numbering. Line numbering appears only in Print Preview and on the printed copy.

- You can see the boundaries of each page.

- Multiple snaking columns are displayed side-by-side, as they will be printed.

- Headers, footers, and footnotes are displayed on each page in their assigned positions.

Positioned paragraphs are described in Chapter 15.

- Positioned paragraphs appear in their assigned positions on the page.

You will probably want to enter the bulk of the document text while you are in galley or draft view, since scrolling and other commands operate more efficiently in these modes than in Page View. While you are creating the document, you might want to activate Page View occasionally to gain a more accurate picture of the printed appearance of the document, while still performing editing tasks. Immediately before printing the document, you can activate Print

Preview to see the overall layout of each page and make final formatting adjustments.

While you are in Page View, you can use the following two special techniques for navigating through the document:

- If the text is arranged in two or more columns, you can move the insertion point to the next column by pressing Alt-↑, or to the previous column by pressing Alt-↓.

- You can scroll immediately to the *previous* printed page of the document by clicking the page icon at the top of the vertical scroll bar.

- You can scroll to the *next* printed page by clicking the page icon at the bottom of the vertical scroll bar.

PRINT PREVIEW

To see the entire document page while you are in Print Preview, you should maximize the Word window, if it does not already fill the screen, by clicking the up-arrow icon in the upper right corner of the window.

To activate Print Preview, choose the File/Print Preview menu command. The Print Preview screen is illustrated in Figure 17.2. As you can see, Print Preview shows you a reduced view of one or two entire pages of your document. If Print Preview is currently displaying a single page, clicking the Two Pages button at the top of the window causes it to display two pages; if it is displaying two pages, clicking the One Page button causes it to display a single page.

Although each character is normally too small to read (unless you have assigned a large character size), Print Preview provides a good overall view of the layout of each page of the document. Using Print Preview to examine the page layout of a document immediately before printing can greatly reduce the amount of trial and error in generating the desired final result.

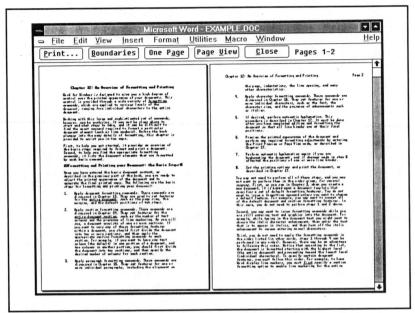

Figure 17.2: The Print Preview screen showing two document pages

While Print Preview is active, many menu and keyboard commands are unavailable.

While in Print Preview, you can scroll through the document using the vertical scroll bar, or by pressing the PgDn key to view the next page and the PgUp key to view the previous page. Word displays the current page number or numbers to the right of the row of buttons displayed at the top of the window.

In Print Preview, you can adjust the position on the page of any of the following objects:

- Page margins

- Headers and footers

- Page breaks

- Positioned objects (that is, paragraphs that have been assigned specific positions on the page through the Format/Position command, described in Chapter 15).

In Print Preview, you cannot move an object to a different page.

To move one or more of these objects, first click the Boundaries button. Word will draw a line indicating each margin, and will draw a box around each header, footer, page break, or positioned object. If you are currently viewing two pages, Word will display boundary lines within only one page. You can move the lines to the other page by clicking anywhere within this page. Clicking the Boundaries button again removes the lines and boxes.

Once boundary lines are displayed, you can adjust a document margin using the following steps:

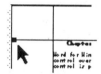 While you are moving an object in Print Preview, Word displays the current coordinates of the object on the page at the right end of the row of buttons at the top of the window.

1. Move the mouse pointer to the black square on the line that marks the margin you want to move.

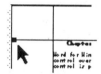

The mouse pointer will become a cross.

2. Drag the margin to the desired new position. That is, press the left mouse button, and while holding down the button, move the line to the new position and then release the button.

3. To have Word draw the margin in its new position, click the Print Preview window anywhere *outside* of the page.

Since the margin position is a document formatting feature, adjusting a margin on one page automatically changes it on all other pages of the document.

While boundary lines are displayed, you can also move headers, footers, page breaks, and positioned objects. To move one of these objects, use the following steps:

1. Place the mouse pointer within the box surrounding the object you want to move. The arrow pointer will turn into a cross.

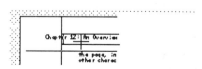

2. Drag the object to the desired new location on the page.

3. Click the Print Preview window anywhere outside of the page to have Word display the object in its new position.

Note that unless you have formatted a header or footer as a positioned object (through the Format/Position command), you can move the header or footer only in the vertical direction, and you cannot move it across the margin into the text area of the page. Since headers and footers are features assigned to a document section, moving a header or footer on one page automatically moves it on all pages within the same section.

While in Print Preview, you can print the document by clicking the Print button, by choosing the File/Print menu item, or by pressing **P**. Word does *not* immediately start printing the document; rather, it opens the File/Print dialog box, described in the next section. You can terminate Print Preview using one of the following methods:

- Click the Page View button to activate Page View.

- Click the Cancel or Close button, or press Esc, to activate whatever document view was active before you switched into Print Preview (the Cancel button becomes the Close button after you make a change to the document in Print Preview). You can also choose the File/Print Preview menu item, or the Close item on the document control menu, to restore the former document view.

- Choose the desired document view from the View menu by choosing the Outline, Draft, or Page item.

SETTING UP YOUR PRINTER

Before you can print using Word, or any other Windows application, you must install a printer within the Windows environment, and choose the desired printer options. Also, if you install more than one printer, you must select which printer is to receive output from Windows programs (known as the *default* printer). Normally, you

You can run the Windows Control Panel from within Word by choosing the Run command from the Word control menu (in the upper left corner of the Word window), selecting the Control Panel option, and clicking the OK button.

For information on using the Control Panel, see the manual supplied with your version of Windows.

Refer to the Word for Windows *Printer Guide* for information on specific printers.

perform these steps when you install Windows using the Setup program. However, you can later install one or more additional printers, change printer settings, or select the default printer, using the Windows Control Panel.

You can also select the default printer (if you have installed more than one printer), and adjust the printer options, through the Word File/Printer Setup menu command. You can issue this command at any time before printing the document. Note, however, that changing the default printer or altering the printer setup can change the appearance of your document. For example, it can alter the available fonts and character enhancements, and the position of line and page breaks. Ideally, therefore, you should install and set up the desired printer *before* entering and formatting document text. If you later change the printer setup, you should make sure that the page layout and other document features are correct before sending the document to the printer. To examine these features, you can use the Page View and Print Preview document modes, as described previously in this chapter.

When you choose the File/Printer Setup command, Word displays the dialog box illustrated in Figure 17.3. The Printer list box contains a list of printers that have been installed in the Windows environment. The description of each printer includes the name of the computer *port* that the printer connects to (such as LPT1 or LPT2, or None if it is not connected to a port). A port is a receptacle, typically on the back of the computer, into which you can plug a computer cable; a computer may have several ports so that you can attach several printers at the same time.

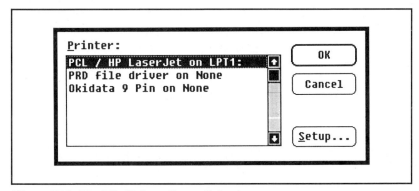

Figure 17.3: The File/Printer Setup dialog box

If the default printer is not attached to a port, you cannot switch into Print Preview document mode.

The name of the default printer is highlighted. If you want to change the default printer so that you can direct Word output to another printer, select the desired printer within this list by clicking it or moving the highlight with the ↑ or ↓ key. Note, however, that you *cannot* print to a printer that is not attached to a port (that is, if the printer description is followed by the expression **on None**); if you want to select such a printer, you must attach it to a port by running the Windows Control Panel (you cannot attach more than one printer to the same port at a given time).

To change one or more options for the default printer, click the Setup button. The appearance of the dialog box that Word displays depends upon the specific printer. For example, if the default printer is an HP LaserJet II, Word displays the dialog box shown in Figure 17.4.

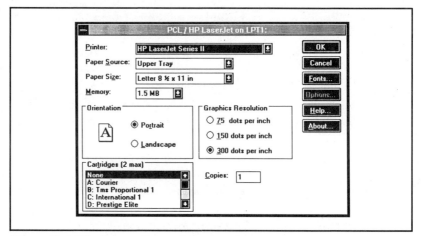

Figure 17.4: The Printer Setup dialog box for an HP LaserJet II printer

The following are several options commonly found in the Printer Setup dialog box:

- The size of the paper on which you are printing. This size should be the same as the page size entered into the Format/Document dialog box (if the sizes are different, Word issues a warning).

- The graphics *resolution,* which is the amount of detail that is printed, measured in *dots per (linear) inch.* This option will be available if your printer can print graphics at more than one resolution.

- The *orientation* of the paper. In *portrait* orientation, the document is printed from top to bottom on the page.

In *landscape* orientation, the document is printed sideways on the page; this orientation is convenient for printing envelopes on a laser printer.

The printer options you set through the File/Printer Setup command remain in effect until you explicitly change one or more of them through this same command, or through the Windows Control Panel. These options affect printing from Word as well as other Windows applications. In contrast, the printer options you set through the File/Print dialog box affect only the printing of a single Word document.

PRINTING YOUR DOCUMENT

See Chapter 18 for information on printing multiple customized copies of a document. See Chapter 26 for information on having Word print an entire group of documents.

When you are finally ready to print your document, choose the File/Print menu command. Word will display the dialog box illustrated in Figure 17.5.

First make sure that **Document** is selected within the Print box so that Word will print the document. You can have Word print other items, such as the document summary information or the document annotations, by selecting the appropriate item from the pull-down list attached to the Print box. Each of the other items you can print will be discussed in the chapter covering the feature.

Enter the number of copies of the document you want Word to print into the Copies box (the default is 1). The portion of the document that is to be printed is specified through the options in the Pages

Unlike the print options set through the File/Printer Setup command, the options set in the File/Print dialog box affect only the printing of the Word document in the active window. You must set the desired options each time you issue the File/Print command.

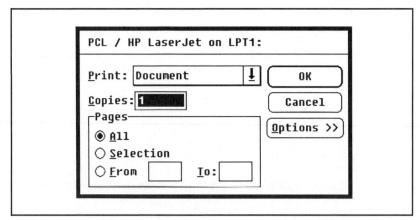

Figure 17.5: The File/Print dialog box

area of the dialog box:

All
Selection
From...To

If you choose the All option (the default), Word will print the entire document. If you choose the Selection option, Word will print only the current selection. If you choose the From option, Word will print a range of pages within your document. Enter the first page in the desired range into the From box and the last page into the To box.

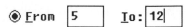

To select additional printing options, click the Options button. Word will enlarge the File/Print dialog box to reveal the remaining options. The expanded dialog box is illustrated in Figure 17.6. The effect of each of these additional options is described in Table 17.3.

When you have chosen all desired options and are ready to begin printing, click the OK button. Word will display a message at the bottom of the screen indicating that it is printing the document, and specifying the page it is currently printing. You can cancel the printing process by pressing Esc.

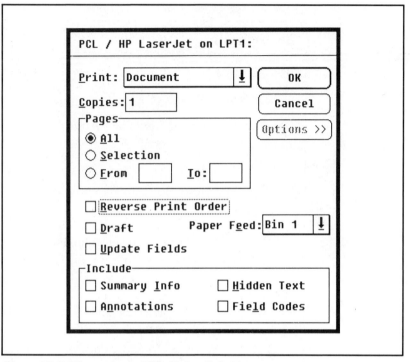

Figure 17.6: The expanded File/Print dialog box

SUMMARY

- You can improve the printed appearance of your document by having Word automatically hyphenate it.

- You should perform automatic hyphenation *after* entering and formatting the document text, but *before* previewing the final printed appearance of the document using Page View or Print Preview.

- To hyphenate the selected text (or the entire document if there is no selection), use the Utilities/Hyphenate menu command. If you want to confirm each hyphenation, select the Confirm option within the dialog box.

Outline view is described in Chapter 24.

- Word provides five different document views: galley view (normal editing view), draft view, Page View, Print Preview, and outline view. These views are summarized in Table 17.2.

Table 17.3: The Additional Print Options

PRINT OPTION:	EFFECT:
Reverse Print Order	Prints document pages from last to first. This option is helpful for printers that stack pages in reverse order (such as some early laser printer models).
Draft	Eliminates character formatting when printing, and prints pictures as empty boxes (all characters assigned enhancements, such as italics, are simply underlined). This option increases printing speed when formatting and graphics are not required.
Update Fields	Causes Word to update all fields before printing the document. Fields are instructions to the Word program embedded within a document.*
Paper Feed	From the pull-down list attached to this box, allows you to specify the source of the paper (for example, from a particular printer bin, manual feed, and so on). The available options depend upon the current default printer.
Include, Summary Info	Prints the document summary information (see Chapter 26) on a separate page following the document itself.
Include, Annotations	Prints any annotations (see Chapter 25) starting on a separate page following the document.
Include, Hidden Text	Prints any hidden text (see Chapter 16) in the document. Note that this can change the positions of line and page breaks.
Include, Field Codes	Prints the codes for any fields contained in the document (that is, the special { } characters and the text within them), rather than printing the results of the fields.*

* For information on fields, see the Word *User's Reference* or *Technical Reference,* under the topic "Fields."

- To activate Page View, choose the View/Page menu option. This view displays all features (except line numbering) exactly as they will be printed. Since text is displayed full size, you can usually view only a portion of the printed page at a time. However, you can issue all normal editing and formatting commands.

- To activate Print Preview, choose the File/Print Preview menu option. This document view displays one or two entire pages exactly as they will be printed. Text is reduced in size, and you cannot employ the usual editing or formatting commands.

- In Print Preview, you can directly move margins, header, footer, page break, or a positioned object by dragging the item to the desired location on the page.

- By choosing the File/Printer Setup menu command, you can select the printer that is to receive output, and also select options that affect the way printed output from Windows programs is handled.

- To print your document, choose the File/Print menu command. Word will display a dialog box so you can select options that determine the way the current document is printed. When you have selected the desired options, click the OK button to begin printing.

18

PRINTING FORM LETTERS

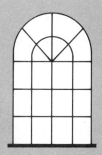

THE WORD *PRINT MERGE* FACILITY AUTOMATICALLY prints multiple copies of a document, customizing each copy according to your instructions. You can use this facility to create form letters, mailing labels, and other documents that require each copy to be different.

When you use the print merge command, Word combines a *main document*, which contains the text that is the same for every printed copy, with a *data document*, which contains the text that is unique for each copy. In this chapter, you will learn how to create the main document, how to create the data document, and how to print customized copies by combining these two documents with the print merge command. Finally, you will learn how to use some additional instructions in your print merge documents.

CREATING THE MAIN DOCUMENT

The main document contains the text and graphics that are to be the same on every printed copy of the document, plus instructions for inserting variable text from the data file. Figure 18.1 shows an example of a main print merge document.

Print merge instructions are inserted into the main document as Word fields. The main document must include a DATA field that tells the print merge facility the name of the data file containing the variable text. The DATA field should come before any of the other print merge fields described in this chapter. The following are the steps for inserting the DATA field:

> As you first saw in Chapter 4, a field is an instruction to the Word program that is embedded in the document text. Fields are used to control the print merge facility and for many other purposes. See the Word *User's Reference* or *Technical Reference,* under the topic "Fields."

1. Place the insertion point at the position in the document where you want to insert the field (before any other print merge fields).

2. Press the Ctrl-F9 keystroke to enter an empty field.

{|}

```
┌─────────────────────────────────────────────────────────────┐
│  ═                   Microsoft Word - EXAMPLE.DOC        ▼ ▲  │
│  ▭  File  Edit  View  Insert  Format  Utilities  Macro  Window      Help │
│                    {DATA sales}Carnivorous Plants by Mail          ↑ │
│                           178 Butterwort Lane                        │
│                          Mill Valley, CA 94941                       │
│                                                                      │
│           Dear {REF customer}:                                       │
│                                                                      │
│           Thank you for ordering a {REF item}. Your order was received on {REF date}, and will │
│           receive prompt attention. Please allow 8-10 weeks for delivery. │
│                                                                      │
│           Sincerely,                                                 │
│                                                                      │
│                                                                      │
│           Lily Sundew, President                                     │
│           ──                                                         │
│                                                                    ↓ │
│  Pg 1   Sec 1    1/1    │At      Ln      Col 23 │                    │
└─────────────────────────────────────────────────────────────┘
```

Figure 18.1: An example print merge main document

3. While the insertion point is between the bracket characters ({}), type the word **DATA** (you can use uppercase or lowercase letters), followed by the name of the data file containing the variable text (in the next section, you will see how to create this file). If you don't include an extension in the file name, Word assumes that the file has the .DOC extension. If the data file will not be in the current directory at the time you run the print merge command, you must specify the full path name:

{DATA C:\\DOCUMENTS\\SALES}

The example main document in Figure 18.1 begins with the field

{DATA sales}

> To enter a backslash character (\) into a field, you must type *two* backslashes (\\).

which causes the print merge command to obtain the variable text from the file SALES.DOC in the current disk directory.

You should also enter a REF field at each location in the main document where you want to insert an item from the data file. To insert a REF field, use the following steps:

1. Place the insertion point at the position in the main document where you want the variable data printed when you run the print merge command.

2. Press the Ctrl-F9 keystroke to enter an empty field.

> If you do not use REF, you run the risk of using a reserved field word as your field name—for example, {date} or {author}.

3. While the insertion point is between the bracket characters ({}), type the word **REF**, followed by the name of the item in the data file that you want to insert. In the next section, you will see how to assign names to items in the data file.

As an example, the following field in the main document shown in Figure 18.1 causes the print merge facility to print the appropriate customer name (obtained from the data file) on each printed copy:

{REF customer}

> Several additional fields that you can use with the print merge command are discussed near the end of the chapter, in the section "Using Other Print Merge Instructions."

Note that after you have previewed or printed the main document, a print merge field may become invisible on the screen, or it may be replaced with a specific value from the data file. To view the field instructions that you entered, enable the View/Field Codes menu item.

CREATING THE DATA DOCUMENT

The data document contains the actual text that is printed at the position of each REF field in the main document. Figure 18.2 illustrates an example of a data document that you could use in conjunction with the main document shown in Figure 18.1. Paragraph marks are enabled in this figure to show you the locations of the paragraphs.

Use the following steps to create a data document:

1. Open a new document by issuing the File/New command.

2. Into the first paragraph, type a name for each item you want to insert into the main document. This paragraph is known as the *header*. The names you enter into the header are the same names used in the REF fields within the main document to identify the text items that you want the print merge command to insert. Separate the names with commas or tab characters.

Notice that the header in the data document of Figure 18.2 contains three item names: **customer**, **item**, and **date**, separated with commas.

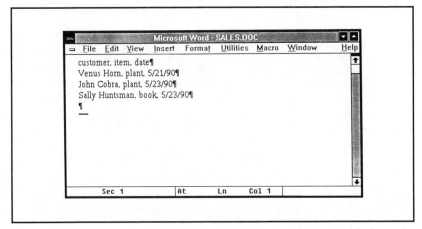

Figure 18.2: An example data document that you could merge with the main document of Figure 18.1

3. Into the next paragraph, type the actual text items that are to be inserted into the first copy of the print merge document. This paragraph is known as a data *record*. You must type an item for each name you entered into the header. The first item in the record will be identified (in a REF field in the main document) by the first name in the header, the second will be identified by the second name in the header, and so on.

If a text item contains one or more leading space characters, a comma, or a tab character—that is, a field separator—you must enclose the entire item in quote characters. The first item in the following record is an example:

"Horn, Venus", plant, 5/21/90

To enter a quote character (") or a backslash character (\) into a text item, you must type a backslash in front of the character. For example, the two items in the record

Jack \"Nick\" Nicholson, C:\\DOCUMENTS

would be printed on the print merge document as

Jack "Nick" Nicholson

and

C:\DOCUMENTS

You may not want to enter a text item for each name in the header. For example, if the header specifies two lines for the customer's address, but the address requires only a single line, you would omit the corresponding text item. To omit a text item, you must include an extra separator, as in the following example:

Sally Huntsman, 234 Lark Lane,, Ventura CA 90305

4. In the same manner, enter an additional record for each copy of the print merge document that you want to generate. Each record must be contained in its own paragraph, and you must not leave empty paragraphs between records.

5. Save the data document. The document must be saved on disk before you can use it to generate the printed copies of the print merge document.

Word tables are discussed in Chapter 8.

Alternatively, you can place both the header and all records in a single Word *table*. The header should be placed in the first row of the table, with one name in each cell. The records should be placed within subsequent table rows, with each data item in a separate cell. If you use a table, all characters entered into the cell (except a backslash) will be printed. Thus, you can include leading spaces, commas, and tabs without surrounding the entire item in quotes, and you can include a quote character without preceding it with a backslash. However, to print a backslash, you must enter a *double* backslash. Figure 18.3 illustrates the same data document shown in Figure 18.2, arranged within a Word table.

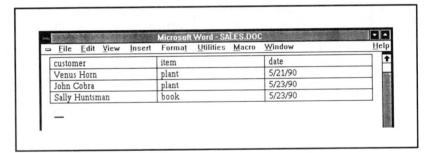

Figure 18.3: A data document using a Word table

MERGING THE MAIN DOCUMENT AND DATA DOCUMENT

When you are ready to produce the printed copies of the print merge document, open the main document and choose the File/Print Merge menu command. Word will display the dialog box shown in Figure 18.4.

To print a document copy for *every* record in the data document, select the All option. To print a document for only a *range* of records, select the From option, and enter the beginning and ending records in the desired

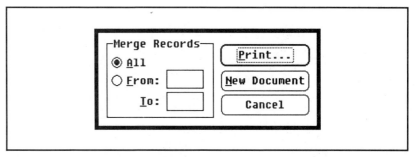

Figure 18.4: The File/Print Merge dialog box

range into the From and To boxes. For example, the following choices would cause Word to print 6 document copies, using data records 5 through 10:

◉ **F**rom: 5
   To: 10

The options in the File/Print dialog box are explained in Chapter 17, in the section "Printing Your Document."

To set options for printing the copies of the print merge document, click the Print button. Word will display the same dialog box used by the File/Print command; the following options, however, are unavailable:

- Print, for selecting the item to print. You can select only the document.

- Selection, for printing only the current selection. You must print either the entire document or a range of pages.

- Update fields, for updating all fields in the document.

When you are ready to begin producing the printed copies, click the OK button. Figure 18.5 illustrates the result of merging the main document of Figure 18.1 with the data document of Figure 18.2.

To send all copies of the merge document to a new Word document rather than to the printer, click the New Document button within the File/Print Merge dialog box. Word will insert all copies of the print merge document into the new file, separating each copy with a section break.

Carnivorous Plants by Mail
178 Butterwort Lane
Mill Valley, CA 94941

Dear Venus Horn:

Thank you for ordering a plant. Your order was received on 5/21/90, and will receive
prompt attention. Please allow 8-10 weeks for delivery.

Sincerely,

Lily Sundew, President

Carnivorous Plants by Mail
178 Butterwort Lane
Mill Valley, CA 94941

Dear John Cobra:

Thank you for ordering a plant. Your order was received on 5/23/90, and will receive
prompt attention. Please allow 8-10 weeks for delivery.

Sincerely,

Lily Sundew, President

Carnivorous Plants by Mail
178 Butterwort Lane
Mill Valley, CA 94941

Dear Sally Huntsman:

Thank you for ordering a book. Your order was received on 5/23/90, and will receive
prompt attention. Please allow 8-10 weeks for delivery.

Sincerely,

Lily Sundew, President

Figure 18.5: The printed copies resulting from merging the data document of Figure 18.1 with the data document of Figure 18.2

USING OTHER
PRINT MERGE INSTRUCTIONS

For complete infor-
mation on these
fields, as well as others
that might be useful for
print merge documents,
see the topic "Fields" in
the Word *User's Reference*
or the Word *Technical
Reference.*

In addition to the DATA and REF fields, several other Word fields
are useful for creating print merge documents. This section introduces the IF, NEXT, NEXTIF, and SKIPIF fields. To enter one of
these fields, press the Ctrl-F9 key to insert an empty field, and while
the insertion point is inside the bracket characters ({}), type the
instructions specified in the following sections.

THE IF FIELD

The IF field causes Word to print a text expression *only if a specified
condition is true.* This field has the following format:

{IF *Condition Text*}

If *Condition* is true, then Word will print *Text.* Specify *Condition* in the
following manner:

First_expression Comparison Second_expression

The expressions can be either text or numeric values. If an expression includes one or more spaces, tabs, or paragraph marks, it must
be surrounded with quote characters (" "). *Comparison* can be one of
the following:

COMPARISON	MEANING
=	Equals
>	Greater than
<	Less than
> =	Greater than or equal to
< =	Less than or equal to
< >	Not equal to

Figure 18.6 illustrates a main print merge document that uses IF
fields to avoid printing a blank line if the second line of the address

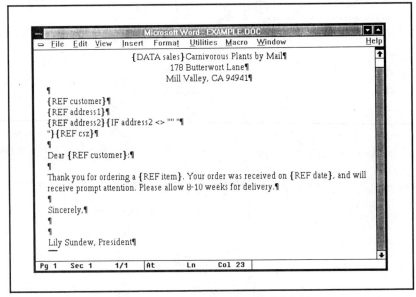

Figure 18.6: A main document demonstrating an IF field

(**address2**) is blank (in this figure, paragraph marks are visible). If the address2 item within the current record is *not* blank, Word will print the paragraph (notice the paragraph mark in quotes), creating a new line.

```
{REF address2}{IF address2 <> "" "¶
"}{REF csz}¶
```

If, however, address2 is blank, Word will not print a new paragraph, thus avoiding an extraneous blank line for customers that do not have a second address line.

Figure 18.7 shows a data document to be merged with the main document in Figure 18.6, and Figure 18.8 shows the final printed copies resulting from merging these two documents.

THE NEXT FIELD

The NEXT field has the form

```
{NEXT}
```

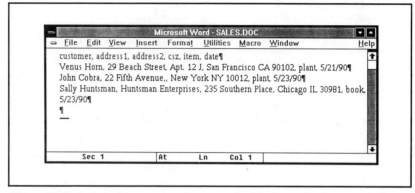

Figure 18.7: A data document to be merged with the main document of Figure 18.6

The NEXT field will have no effect unless one or more REF fields are inserted after the NEXT field in the main document.

When the print merge command encounters this field in the main document, it continues printing the current copy of the print merge document, but begins reading text items from the *next record* in the data document (rather than waiting until it has completed printing the current copy).

The NEXT field is useful if you want to include text from more than one data record within a single copy of the document. For example, if you are printing address labels, you would typically place each address in a separate record in the data document. The main document can print an entire page of addresses by placing a NEXT field after the fields for each address (if the NEXT fields were not included, the *same* address would be printed repeatedly).

THE NEXTIF FIELD

The NEXTIF field has the format

{NEXTIF *Condition*}

If *Condition* is true, this field has the same effect as the NEXT field; otherwise, it has no effect. *Condition* is specified in the same manner as the condition for the IF command, explained previously in the chapter.

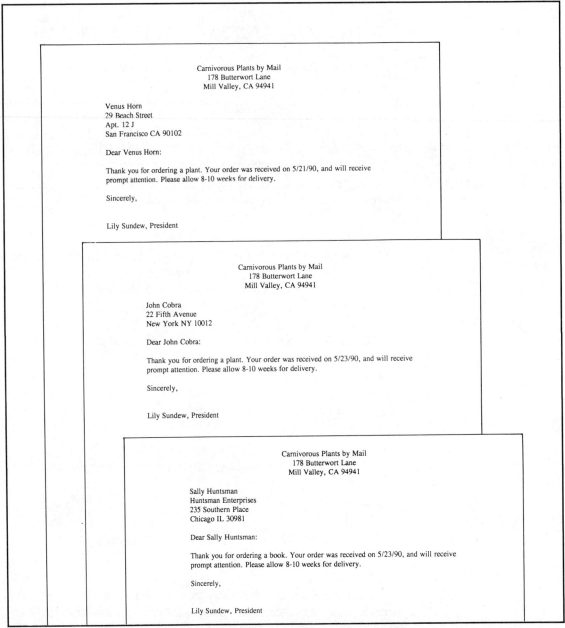

Figure 18.8: The printed copies resulting from merging the main document of Figure 18.6 with the data document of Figure 18.7

THE SKIPIF FIELD

The SKIPIF field has the form

{SKIPIF *Condition*}

Condition is specified like the condition for the IF command, explained previously in the chapter. If *Condition* is true, then Word begins using the next record in the data document; this effect is the same as that produced by the NEXT or NEXTIF command. However, unlike the NEXT or NEXTIF command, Word stops printing the current copy of the print merge document, and begins printing a new copy from the beginning of the main document. In other words, if *Condition* is true, the SKIPIF command has the same effect as reaching the end of the current copy of the main document.

As an example, consider the following field, inserted immediately after the DATA field at the beginning of a main document for producing invoices:

{SKIPIF numplants < 5}

In this field, **numplants** is the name of an item in the data records that contains the number of plants purchased. As a result of this field, the print merge command would not print an invoice for any customer who purchased fewer than five plants.

SUMMARY

- Using the print merge facility, you can print many copies of a document, incorporating custom text items into each copy.

- When using the print merge command, you must create a main document and a data document.

- The main document contains the text that is to be the same for all printed copies. It also contains instructions telling Word the name of the data document, and where to insert text from the data document.

- You must specify the name of the data document at the beginning of the main document with a DATA field.

- At each location in the main document where you want to print text from the data document, you must insert a REF field that specifies the name of the desired text item.

- The data document contains the text that is different for each printed copy.

- The first paragraph in the data document must list the names of the data items that are to be inserted into the main document when the print merge command is run. The names should be separated with commas or tabs. This paragraph is known as the *header*.

- Each subsequent paragraph in the data document contains the text items for a single copy of the print merge document. Each of these paragraphs is known as a *record*, and contains a text item for each name listed in the header. The text items should be separated with commas or tabs.

- When you have created both the main document and the data document, you can generate the printed copies by opening the main document and choosing the File/Print Merge menu command.

- By using the IF field, you can have Word print a text item only if a specified condition is true.

- By using the NEXT or NEXTIF command, you can have Word start printing text items from the next record in the data file.

- By using the SKIPIF command, you can prevent Word from making copies for selected records in the data document.

DOCUMENT TEMPLATES AND OTHER SPECIAL FEATURES

A *template* is the framework upon which a document is built. A document template is a great timesaver. Once you have set up a template for a particular type of document, documents you create based upon this template automatically acquire all features assigned to the template, such as boilerplate text, formatting, styles, and other important elements.

In Chapter 19, you will learn about templates themselves: how to use, modify, and create them. In the remaining chapters in this part of the book, you will learn about each of the basic features you can assign to a template: styles, glossary entries, macros, and custom keyboard and menu assignments.

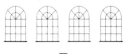

19

AN OVERVIEW OF DOCUMENT TEMPLATES

If you want to find out the name of the document template for the current document, choose the Edit/Summary Info menu command and then click the Statistics button.

A DOCUMENT TEMPLATE RESIDES IN A SPECIALLY formatted disk file, which is usually named with the .DOT file extension and is stored in the Word for Windows program directory on your hard disk (\WINWORD).

All new Word documents are based upon a specific document template. As you have seen, when you create a new document by issuing the File/New menu command, you can select the name of the document template.

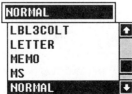

The template NORMAL, as it is supplied by Microsoft, does not contain any text. Thus, all new documents based upon it are initially empty.

The new document automatically acquires all of the features assigned to the document template. The Word for Windows package includes a variety of templates, including NORMAL, ARTICLE, ENVELOPE, LETTER, and many others. NORMAL is a general-purpose template, and the others are designed for specific types of documents.

In this chapter, you will learn the following facts about templates:

- The document features that can be assigned to templates
- The special properties of the NORMAL template
- The relationship between the document and the document template
- How to change the template assigned to a document
- How to create a new template or modify an existing one

FEATURES THAT CAN BE ASSIGNED TO TEMPLATES

The following features can be assigned to a document template, and are automatically acquired by all new documents based upon the template:

- Text and text formatting
- Styles
- Glossary entries
- Macros
- Menu and keyboard assignments

TEXT AND FORMATTING

A template can contain text (or pictures). When you create a new document based upon the template, Word automatically inserts all text from the template into the new document, together with any character or paragraph formatting that is assigned to the text. A template can also be assigned section or document formatting features, which are likewise automatically acquired by all new documents based upon the template.

For example, a template used for creating letters might contain the heading, salutation, and other elements common to all letters you write. Such common text is known as *boilerplate text*.

STYLES

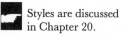
Styles are discussed in Chapter 20.

A *style* is a collection of character and paragraph formatting features that is identified by name and can be applied to paragraphs in a document. Style definitions can be assigned to a template; any new document based upon the template automatically acquires these definitions.

GLOSSARY ENTRIES

Glossaries are discussed in Chapter 21.

Each template has its own *glossary*, which can store one or more blocks of text or graphics (known as *glossary entries*). A glossary entry is identified by name, and can be inserted anywhere within a document. A document has access to all entries contained in the glossary belonging to the document template.

MACROS

Macros are discussed in Chapter 22.

A *macro* stores a series of keystrokes and mouse actions. You can have Word automatically execute these keystrokes and mouse actions by *running* the macro. Macros are identified by name, and are stored in a document template. While you are working on a document, you can run any of the macros assigned to the document template.

MENU AND KEYBOARD ASSIGNMENTS

Chapter 23 discusses how to create custom menu and keyboard assignments.

You can remove commands from or add commands to the default Word menus. You can also specify the keystrokes that execute specific commands or execute macros that you have created. Menu and keyboard assignments are stored in a document template and are automatically available while you are working on any document based upon the template.

NORMAL AND OTHER TEMPLATES

Later in the chapter, you will see how to change the document template after a document has already been created.

In this section, you will learn some of the special properties of the NORMAL template. When you create a new document by using the File/New command, Word initially suggests NORMAL as the document template. You can, of course, pick another template from the list.

Also, when you start Word without specifying a document name, it automatically creates a new document using NORMAL as the document template. Thus, NORMAL is the default document template.

When the document template is NORMAL, the document simply acquires all features that have been assigned to NORMAL (those features initially assigned by Microsoft, as well as any features you have explicitly assigned). However, if the document template is *not* NORMAL, the document acquires or can access all features assigned to the document template, *plus* all of the following features assigned to the NORMAL template:

- Glossary entries

- Macro definitions

- Keyboard assignments

- Menu assignments

For example, if you create a new document based upon the template LETTER, the document will acquire all text, styles, glossary entries, macro definitions, keyboard assignments, and menu assignments belonging to LETTER. It *also* acquires all glossary entries, macro definitions, and menu and keyboard assignments belonging to NORMAL.

Accordingly, the NORMAL template is known as the *global* template, and affects *all* documents, even those assigned different document templates. Note, however, that if there is a conflict between an element belonging to NORMAL and an element belonging to the document template, the element belonging to the document template *overrides* the conflicting feature belonging to NORMAL. For example, if the document template is LETTER, and if both LETTER and NORMAL have a glossary entry named **head** (and the entries have different text), inserting **head** will produce the text belonging to the *LETTER* glossary entry rather than that belonging to NORMAL.

Also, if you have assigned the same keystroke to both LETTER and NORMAL, and you have associated the keystroke with different commands, pressing the keystroke will issue the command assigned to *LETTER* rather than that assigned to NORMAL.

Note, finally, that when the document template is NORMAL, Word sometimes indicates that there is *no* document template. For example, the Statistics dialog box (displayed when you issue the Edit/ Summary Info menu command and click the Statistics button) displays the template name **None** when the document template is NORMAL.

THE RELATIONSHIP BETWEEN A DOCUMENT AND ITS TEMPLATE

As you have seen, when a *new* document is created, it acquires all features that belong to the template it is based upon. After a document has already been created, however, what is the relationship between the document and the document template? Does changing the template affect the document? Does changing the document affect the template?

In answering these questions, the features can be divided into two groups:

- Text, graphics, formatting, and styles
- Glossary entries, macros, and menu and keyboard assignments

TEXT, GRAPHICS, FORMATTING, AND STYLES

When a new document is created, it acquires all text, graphics, formatting, and styles belonging to the template upon which it is based. These elements are copied into the new document, where they are stored separately from the template. Thus, if you later change one of these elements within the template, the document is *not* automatically affected. Likewise, if you edit the text or graphics within the document, or change the formatting or styles, the document template is *not* automatically affected.

However, as you will see later in the chapter (in the section "Modifying a Template"), you can explicitly copy elements between a document and a template in the following two ways:

- You can transfer all of the document formatting features assigned to the current document to the document template by clicking the Set Default button within the Format/Document dialog box.

- You can transfer styles from a document to the document template, or transfer styles from a specified template to the current document. These operations are performed through the Format/Define Styles menu command.

GLOSSARY ENTRIES, MACROS, AND MENU AND KEYBOARD ASSIGNMENTS

Later in the chapter, in the section "Modifying a Template," you will learn how to make changes to a template.

When you create a new document, it acquires all glossary entries, macros, and menu and keyboard assignments belonging to the global template, NORMAL, *and* those belonging to the document template (assuming that the document template is not NORMAL). Unlike the features described in the previous section, however, glossary entries, macros, and menu and keyboard assignments are stored within the template (or templates) and *not* within the document itself. Therefore, if you later add, remove, or modify any of these features within a template, the changes affect all documents associated with the template. (Changing one of the features in NORMAL affects *all* documents.)

CHANGING THE TEMPLATE ASSIGNED TO A DOCUMENT

You can change the document template at any time after the document has already been created through the following steps:

1. Issue the Format/Document menu command.

2. Type the name of the desired template into the Template box. If the template is not in the \WINWORD directory, you must specify the full path name. Alternatively, if the template is in \WINWORD, you can choose it from the associated pull-down list.

Changing the document template *after* the document has already been created does *not* alter the document text, formatting, or style definitions. These elements are acquired from a template only when the document is first created, and they are stored separately within the document itself.

In contrast, when you assign a new template, the document immediately acquires the glossary entries, macros, and menu and keyboard assignments defined in the new template (since these elements are stored in the template and not in the document itself).

CREATING
OR MODIFYING A TEMPLATE

Microsoft supplies a large number of useful templates with the Word for Windows package; these are explained in the Word *Sampler* book. You can also create new templates or modify existing ones to suit your exact needs.

CREATING A NEW TEMPLATE

To create a new template, issue the File/New menu command and select the Template option within the dialog box.

Like a document, a new template is based upon an existing template, and automatically acquires all the features of this template. You must therefore choose the desired template from the Use Template box.

You can now assign all desired features to the template. As you have seen, you can assign the following features to a template:

- Text and text formatting
- Styles
- Glossary entries
- Macros
- Menu and keyboard assignments

Instructions for assigning these features are given in the remaining chapters of this part of the book (except for the first item). When you have added all desired features, save the template using the File/Save or File/Save As menu command. Enter a file name for the template into the Save File Name box.

Save File Name:

```
BOOK.DOT
```

The template name should have the .DOT file extension; if you do not include an extension in the name you type, Word will automatically supply the .DOT extension. If you do not specify a directory name, Word will place the template file in the \WINWORD directory on your hard disk. It is best to place the template in this directory, since Word automatically lists all templates found in this directory when you create a new document.

Alternatively, you can create a new template by opening an existing template, modifying it, and then saving it under a new name. Use the following steps:

1. Choose the File/Open menu command.

See Chapter 3 for complete instructions on using the File/ Open dialog box.

2. Type the full path name of the existing template into the Open File Name box. As an alternative method, you can type ***.DOT** into the Open File Name box, switch into the directory containing the desired template using the Directories list box, and then select the desired template from the Files list. Click the OK button to open the file.

3. Make the desired modifications to the template.

4. Save the modified version under a new name by choosing the File/Save As menu command, entering a name for the new template into the Save File Name box, and clicking the OK button.

Finally, you can create a new template by opening an existing *document*, making any desired modifications, and then saving the file in the template format under a new name. By using an existing document, you can take advantage of text you have already entered, and definitions you have already specified. Open and modify the document as explained previously. To save the modified version as a template, perform the following steps:

1. Issue the File/Save As menu command.

2. Type a name for the template into the Save File Name box, as explained previously in this section.

3. Before clicking the OK button to save the template, click the Options button and choose the Document Template item from the File Format list box (see Figure 19.1).

4. Click OK after entering document summary information.

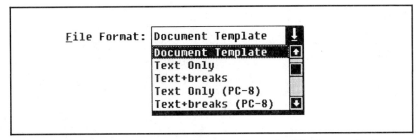

Figure 19.1: Choosing Document Template from the File Format list box

MODIFYING A TEMPLATE

To modify a template, you can either open and modify the template file itself, *or* you can make changes while working on a document based upon the template and then save these changes to the template.

Modifying a Template Directly

To modify a template directly, use the following steps:

1. Open the desired template using the File/Open menu command. See the instructions for opening a template given previously in the chapter (in the section "Creating a New Template").

2. Make the desired modifications using the techniques presented in this book.

3. Save the template by choosing the File/Save command.

Modifying a Template through a Document

You can also modify a template indirectly by making changes to a document based upon the template. The technique for modifying a template through a document depends upon the specific feature you want to change. For the purposes of this discussion, template features can be divided into the following three groups:

- Text and formatting

- Styles

- Glossary entries, macros, and menu and keyboard assignments

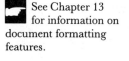 See Chapter 13 for information on document formatting features.

After changing one or more document formatting features through the Format/Document menu command, you can copy these changes to the document template by clicking the Set Default button within the Format/Document dialog box.

To make these changes permanent, you must save the .DOT file, which you are prompted to do when you close the associated .DOC file. Alternatively, you can use File/Save All.

To alter text, graphics, or any other forms of formatting belonging to a template, you must edit the template directly, as described previously in the chapter.

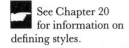 See Chapter 20 for information on defining styles.

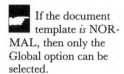 If the document template *is* NOR-MAL, then only the Global option can be selected.

Style definitions are stored within each document. If you add, delete, or modify a style definition, the change is saved together with the document itself, and does not automatically affect the document template.

As you will see in Chapter 20, however, you can transfer styles from a document to the document template, or transfer styles from a specified template to the current document. These operations are performed through the Format/Define Styles menu command.

As you will see in the following chapters, when you define a glossary entry, macro, or menu or keyboard assignment, you must specify the *context* of the definition. The dialog box for defining each of these features allows you to choose one of the following options:

For each feature, the Global option causes Word to save the definition in the NORMAL template, and the Template option causes it to save the option in the document template.

When you make a change that affects a template, Word does *not* automatically write the change to the template file. You must save any changes by issuing the File/Save All menu command. This command will save any change that affects a template, prompting you before saving each template file.

Also, if you quit the program without saving your changes, Word will allow you to save any altered template file in the same manner as the File/Save As command.

SUMMARY

- When you create a new Word document, it acquires all of the features belonging to the *template* upon which it is based.

- A template can be assigned the following features: text, formatting, styles, glossary entries, macros, menu assignments, and keyboard assignments.

- A new document based upon the NORMAL template acquires all features belonging to this template. A new document based upon any other template acquires all features of this template *plus* those belonging to NORMAL. NORMAL is therefore known as the *global* template.

- A new document acquires a separate *copy* of the text, graphics, formatting, and styles belonging to its template. If you later change any of these elements in a template, the documents based upon the template are not affected.

- A new document *gains access* to the glossary entries, macros, menu assignments, and keyboard assignments belonging to its template. These elements are stored only within the template. Therefore, changing any of them within the template affects all documents based upon the template.

- You can change the document template to another template through the Template box within the Format/Document dialog box.

- You can create a new template by choosing the File/New command and selecting the Template option. Alternatively, you can open an existing template or document, modify it, and save it as a template under a new name.

- You can modify a template by opening it through the File/Open menu command, making the desired changes, and then saving it using the File/Save menu command.

- Alternatively, you can modify a template by changing the features of a document based upon the template, and then saving these features to the template file.

20

DEFINING STYLES
TO SIMPLIFY FORMATTING

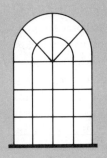

A STYLE IS A COLLECTION OF CHARACTER AND paragraph formatting features that is identified by name, and can be applied to one or more paragraphs in a document. For example, you might create a style named **quote** that contains the formatting features you normally apply to paragraphs of quoted text.

Using styles rather than applying individual formatting commands can save you time in two important ways. First, you can assign an entire set of formatting features to a style; once you have defined the style, you can apply all of these features to a paragraph through a *single* command. For example, the style **quote** could be assigned the following formatting features: $\frac{1}{2}''$ left indent, $\frac{1}{2}''$ right indent, and small capital characters. Once **quote** has been defined, you could apply all of these features to any paragraph by issuing a single command (which will be explained in this chapter).

See Chapter 6 for information on searching for styles and replacing styles within your document.

Second, if you *change* a style belonging to a document, the change is immediately applied to all text throughout the document that has been assigned the style. You do not need to go through the entire document and reformat each applicable paragraph. For example, if you decide that you want to indent quoted text by ³/₄″ rather than ½″, and you want the characters to be bold, you can simply make these changes to the style *quote*; Word will instantly apply the changes to all paragraphs that have been assigned the *quote* style.

In this chapter, you will first learn about the predefined styles available in a new document. You will then learn how to apply a style, how to define a new style, and how to delete or alter an existing style.

THE PREDEFINED STYLES

See Chapter 19 for an explanation of document templates.

When you open a new document, various predefined styles are normally available; the exact collection of predefined styles depends upon the document template you selected when you created the document. If the document is based upon the NORMAL template (and if you haven't altered this template), it will possess a set of predefined styles known as *automatic* styles.

The automatic styles are listed in Table 20.1. As you can see in this table, Word automatically assigns these styles to various elements within the document. For example, it assigns the style *Normal* to ordinary document text, the style *footer* to footers (see Chapter 10), and the style *toc 1* to top-level items in tables of contents (see Chapter 11). In the third column of Table 20.1, you will see the style descriptions exactly as they appear in the Format/Define Styles dialog box and the Format/Styles dialog box.

Later in the chapter (in the section "Using the Format/Define Styles Command"), you will learn more about how one style can be based upon another.

Notice in the descriptions of the styles that all of the automatic styles are *based upon* the style Normal. This means that these styles have all of the features of Normal *plus* the additional features specified. In addition, the description

    Normal +

denotes the Normal style.

Table 20.1: The Automatic Word Styles

STYLE:	USE:	DESCRIPTION:
annotation reference	Annotation reference marks (see Chapter 25)	Normal + Font: 8 Point
annotation text	Annotation text (see Chapter 25)	Normal +
footer	Footer text (see Chapter 10)	Normal + Tab stops: 3″ Centered; 6″ Right Flush
footnote reference	Footnote reference marks (see Chapter 10)	Normal + Font: 8 Point, Superscript 3 Point
footnote text	Footnote text (see Chapter 10)	Normal +
header	Header text (see Chapter 10)	Normal + Tab stops: 3″ Centered; 6″ Right Flush
heading 1	Top-level outline heading (see Chapter 24)	Normal + Font: Helv 12 Point, Bold Underline, Space Before 12pt, Next Style: Normal
heading 2	Level 2 outline headings	Normal + Font: Helv 12 Point, Bold, Space Before 6pt, Next Style: Normal
heading 3	Level 3 outline headings	Normal + Font: 12 Point, Bold, Indent: Left 0.25″, Next Style: Normal Indent
heading 4	Level 4 outline headings	Normal + Font: 12 Point, Underline, Indent: Left 0.25″, Next Style: Normal Indent
heading 5	Level 5 outline headings	Normal + Bold, Indent: Left 0.5″, Next Style: Normal Indent
heading 6	Level 6 outline headings	Normal + Underline, Indent: Left 0.5″, Next Style: Normal Indent

Table 20.1: The Automatic Word Styles (continued)

STYLE:	USE:	DESCRIPTION:
heading 7	Level 7 outline headings	Normal + Italic, Indent: Left 0.5″, Next Style: Normal Indent
heading 8	Level 8 outline headings	Normal + Italic, Indent: Left 0.5″, Next Style: Normal Indent
heading 9	Level 9 outline headings	Normal + Italic, Indent: Left 0.5″, Next Style: Normal Indent
index 1	Top-level index item (see Chapter 11)	Normal +
index 2	Level 2 index item	Normal + Indent: Left 0.25″
index 3	Level 3 index item	Normal + Indent: Left 0.5″
index 4	Level 4 index item	Normal + Indent: Left 0.75″
index 5	Level 5 index item	Normal + Indent: Left 1″
index 6	Level 6 index item	Normal + Indent: Left 1.25″
index 7	Level 7 index item	Normal + Indent: Left 1.5″
index heading	Headings for index sections	Normal +
line number	Line numbers (see Chapter 14)	Normal +
Normal	Ordinary document text	Font: Tms Rmn 10 Point, Flush Left
Normal Indent	Text following outline heading level 3 and higher	Normal + Indent: Left 0.5″
toc 1	Top-level table of contents item (see Chapter 11)	Normal + Indent: Right 0.5″, Tab stops: 5.75″...; 6″ Right Flush
toc 2	Level 2 table of contents item	Normal + Indent: Left 0.5″ Right 0.5″, Tab stops: 5.75″...; 6″ Right Flush

Table 20.1: The Automatic Word Styles (continued)

STYLE:	USE:	DESCRIPTION:
toc 3	Level 3 table of contents item	Normal + Indent: Left 1.0″ Right 0.5″, Tab stops: 5.75″...; 6″ Right Flush
toc 4	Level 4 table of contents item	Normal + Indent: Left 1.5″ Right 0.5″, Tab stops: 5.75″...; 6″ Right Flush
toc 5	Level 5 table of contents item	Normal + Indent: Left 2.0″ Right 0.5″, Tab stops: 5.75″...; 6″ Right Flush
toc 6	Level 6 table of contents item	Normal + Indent: Left 2.5″ Right 0.5″, Tab stops: 5.75″...; 6″ Right Flush
toc 7	Level 7 table of contents item	Normal + Indent: Left 3.0″ Right 0.5″, Tab stops: 5.75″...; 6″ Right Flush
toc 8	Level 8 table of contents item	Normal + Indent: Left 3.5″ Right 0.5″, Tab stops: 5.75″...; 6″ Right Flush

Here are some examples to clarify the style descriptions. The toc 2 style for tables of contents

> Normal + Indent: Left 0.5″ Right 0.5″, Tab stops: 5.75″...; 6″ Right Flush

See Chapter 15 for details on tab formatting features.

means that it is based upon Normal (10-point Tms Rmn, flush left), and it also has left and right indents at ½″ and custom tab stops. The first tab, 5.75″ from the left margin, uses the leader character . . . (period characters) instead of blank spaces. The second tab is 6″ from the left margin, with the flush right style.

Similarly, the heading 2 style for outlines

See Chapter 24 for more information on outline styles.

> Normal + Font: Helv 12 Point, Bold, Space Before 6pt, Next Style: Normal

means that it is based upon Normal with several additional features. The font is 12-point bold Helv instead of 10-point Tms Rmn, and each second-level heading is preceded by 6 points of vertical space (above the paragraph). In addition, the paragraph that follows the heading (next style) has the Normal style. Note that outline headings in levels 3 to 9 use Normal Indent as the next style—that is, Normal style with a 1/2″ left indent.

Later in the chapter, you will see how to modify an automatic style, thereby changing the formatting of all document text assigned the style.

APPLYING A STYLE

> You will learn how to define your own styles later in the chapter.

All paragraphs in a document have an associated style. Unless you apply an alternative style, Word assigns the style Normal to paragraphs of ordinary text or graphics. In this section, you will learn how to change the style of a paragraph by explicitly applying another style.

You can apply a predefined style, or one that you have defined while working on the document, using one of the following basic methods:

- The Format/Styles menu command
- The Word ruler
- The keyboard

Before learning about each of these methods, you should know about a Word feature that makes it easier to work with styles: the *style area*. If you enter a measurement other than 0 into the Style Area Width box in the View Preferences dialog box, Word will display a style area to the left of the text within the window. The style area has the width specified in the Style Area Width box, and contains the name of the paragraph style adjacent to each paragraph. Figure 20.1 illustrates a window with a style area that is 0.75″ wide.

Note also that you can print a description of each of the document styles by choosing the File/Print menu command and selecting the Styles item from the Print list box (Figure 20.2).

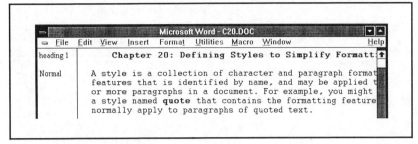

Figure 20.1: A window with a style name area

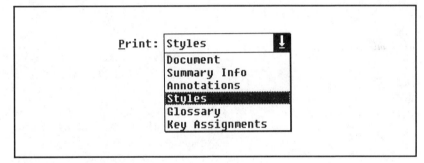

Figure 20.2: The Print list box

USING THE FORMAT/STYLES COMMAND

To use the Format/Styles command, first select the paragraph or paragraphs you want to assign a new style. If you want to assign a style to a single paragraph, you can simply place the insertion point within the paragraph. Next, choose the Format/Styles menu command. Word will display the dialog box illustrated in Figure 20.3. Alternatively, you can open the Format/Styles dialog box by pressing Ctrl-S twice, or by double-clicking within the style area (if it is displayed).

You can now type the name of the style you want to apply into the Style Name box. Alternatively, you can select a style name from the Style Name list. This list will display the names of all styles employed in the document, defined styles, plus the names of a few automatic styles that may not be in use (by default, heading 1, heading 2, heading 3). To have Word list *all* of the automatic styles given in Table 20.1, press Ctrl-A.

USING THE RULER

 If the ruler is not currently displayed, you can display it by choosing the View/Ruler menu command. Using the ruler is discussed in Chapter 15.

If the ruler is visible, you can apply a style to the current selection by typing the name of the desired style into the Style box and pressing ←. To place the insertion point within this box, either click inside the box with the mouse, or press Ctrl-S.

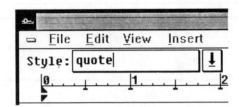

Alternatively, you can select a style from the Style pull-down list (see Figure 20.3). The style is applied as soon as you select it within the list; you do not need to press ←. The list contains the names of all automatic styles used within the document, all styles you have defined for the document, plus a few automatic styles that may not be in use (by default, heading 1, heading 2, heading 3). The Style list, unlike the list within the Format/Styles dialog box, does not display *all* automatic styles. Otherwise, specifying a style through the Style box within the ruler is the same as using the Format/Styles command, described in the previous section.

USING THE KEYBOARD

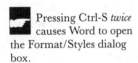 Pressing Ctrl-S *twice* causes Word to open the Format/Styles dialog box.

You can also apply a style to the current selection by pressing the Ctrl-S keystroke. Type the name of the desired style at the prompt that Word displays within the status bar.

Which style?

If the ruler is visible when you press Ctrl-S, Word will place the insertion point inside the Style box within the ruler rather than displaying a prompt within the status bar.

When specifying a style by typing Ctrl-S while the ruler is not displayed, you must type the correct style name; you do not have the

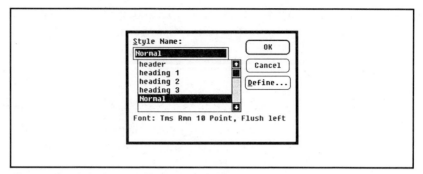

Figure 20.3: The Format/Styles dialog box

If you click the Define button within the Format/Styles dialog box, Word will open the dialog box normally activated through the Format/Define Styles menu command. This dialog box will allow you to modify a style definition, define a new style, and perform other operations on styles. It is explained later in the chapter (in the section "Using the Format/Define Styles Command").

When you are ready to apply the style to the selection, click the OK button.

Note that when using the Format/Styles command to apply a new style to a paragraph, you normally type into the Style Name box the name of an existing style *other* than the style already assigned to the selection. As you will see later in the chapter (in the section "Defining or Modifying Styles by Example"), by typing the name of the style already assigned to the selection, you can modify this style; also, by typing a name not already used for a style, you can create a *new* style based on the current selection.

When you apply a new style to a paragraph, the resulting character formatting is sometimes difficult to predict. If the entire paragraph, or a large portion of it, has been assigned a given character formatting feature, such as italic, applying the new style will *replace* this feature with the character formatting defined for the style. If, however, a character formatting feature has been applied to only a relatively small portion of the paragraph, assigning a style will leave this feature intact.

benefit of a list of valid style names. Otherwise, specifying a style through this keyboard command is the same as using the Format/ Styles command, described previously.

DEFINING STYLES

In this section, you will learn how to modify existing styles and define new styles. You will learn two basic methods for modifying or defining styles:

- You can define or modify a style through the Format/Define Styles dialog box, using commands to specify each formatting feature.
- You can define or modify a style by example; that is, you can base the features of the style upon the formatting features that have already been assigned to an existing paragraph.

USING THE FORMAT/DEFINE STYLES COMMAND

In this section, you will learn how to use the Format/Define Styles menu command to perform the following tasks:

- Define a new style
- Modify, rename, or delete an existing style
- Merge styles; that is, copy styles between the document and other documents or templates

When you choose the Format/Define Styles menu command, Word will display the dialog box illustrated in Figure 20.4.

Defining a New Style

To define a new style, first type the name you want to assign the style into the Define Style Name box within the Format/Define Styles dialog box.

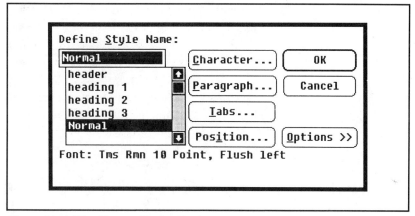

Figure 20.4: The Format/Define Styles dialog box

Define Style Name:

> quote|

The style name can contain up to 20 characters, and can include space characters. Be sure that you do not type the name of an existing style (either one you have defined, or one of the automatic styles listed in Table 20.1).

Initially, the new style is assigned all of the features of the paragraph that was selected when you chose the Format/Define Styles menu command. You can now freely add or remove individual formatting features. Notice that Word displays a description of the style below the list box.

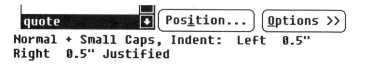

```
Normal + Small Caps, Indent:  Left   0.5"
Right   0.5" Justified
```

As you add or remove features, Word updates this description.

To assign a formatting feature to the new style, you can use a keyboard command or a dialog box, just as if you were formatting a paragraph within a document. To apply a paragraph formatting feature with the keyboard, you can issue any of the commands described in Chapter 15, in the section "Using the Keyboard" (except the Ctrl-S command). For example, if you press Ctrl-C, the style will be assigned the

Unfortunately, you can't use the Word ruler or ribbon to specify formatting features when defining a style with the Format/Define Styles command.

centered paragraph alignment style, and the word **Centered** will be added to the style description.

To apply a character formatting feature with the keyboard, you can issue any of the commands described in Chapter 16, in the section "Using the Keyboard."

To assign formatting features using a dialog box, click one of the following buttons to open a dialog box, and then select the desired features as if you were formatting a regular text selection.

- Click the Character button to open the Format/Character dialog box, which is described in Chapter 16.

- Click the Paragraph button to open the Format/Paragraph dialog box, described in Chapter 15.

- Click the Tabs button to open the Format/Tabs dialog box, described in Chapter 15.

- Click the Position button to open the Format/Position dialog box, described in Chapter 15.

If you click the Options button, you can choose one or more additional options.

The Format/Define Styles dialog box, with all options revealed, is illustrated in Figure 20.5.

First, you can specify another style as the basis for the style you are defining. A style is usually *based upon* another style. This means that the style has all of the features currently assigned to the base style, *plus* all features specifically assigned to the style. Many styles are based upon Normal. For example, consider the following style description:

Normal + Small Caps, Indent: Left 0.5″ Right 0.5″ Justified

This style is based upon Normal; it therefore has all of the features currently assigned to Normal. The style *also* has the Small Caps character formatting feature, both left and right half-inch margin indents,

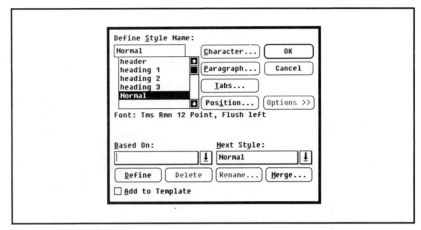

Figure 20.5: The Format/Define Styles dialog box with all options revealed

and justified paragraph alignment. Note that any feature explicitly assigned to the style overrides a conflicting feature assigned to the base style. For example, a paragraph assigned the style just described would be justified, even though the Normal style specifies flush left alignment.

If a style is modified, all styles based upon it will instantly reflect the change. For example, if all styles defined for a document are based upon Normal, and if you assign Normal the Courier font rather than the Tms Rmn font, all text in the document (including headers, footnotes, and other elements) will instantly be converted to the Courier font (except for any text assigned a style that specifies another font or text explicitly formatted with another font).

The Based On box contains the name of the current base style (if the style you are defining does not have a base style, this box is blank).

Based On:

If you want to change the base style, type the name of the desired style into the Based On box, or select a style from the pull-down list. If you do not want to base the style you are defining on another style, leave this box blank.

You can also specify a *next style*. The next style is the style that Word automatically assigns to the paragraph *following* a paragraph assigned the style you are defining. Usually, the next style is the same as the style you are defining, so that paragraphs you type one after the other will have the same style. It is sometimes useful, however, to have Word assign the next paragraph a different style.

Consider, for example, the *heading 1* automatic style, which is designed for creating document headings and is described in Table 20.1. This style is assigned Normal as the next style. Therefore, when you press ↵ after you have finished typing a heading assigned the heading 1 style, the next paragraph will be assigned the Normal style. This feature is convenient, since a title is typically followed by normal text, and not by another title.

When you are defining a new style, the Next Style box is initially empty. If you leave it empty, Word will make the next style the *same* as the style you are defining. If you want to specify a different next style, type the style name into the Next Style box, or select a style name from the pull-down list.

Document templates are discussed in Chapter 19.

If you select the Add to Template option, Word will copy the new style definition to the document template, so that the style will be available both within the current document *and* within any new documents based on the same template that are subsequently created.

Click the Define button to define the new style based upon the features you have specified. The dialog box will remain open so that you can continue to work with styles. Alternatively, you can click the OK button to define the style and close the dialog box.

Modifying, Deleting, or Renaming an Existing Style

You can modify an automatic style, but you cannot delete it or rename it.

You can modify, delete, or rename an existing style by entering its name into the Define Style Name box within the Format/Define Styles dialog box.

Define Style Name:

```
Normal
```

When you first choose the Format/Define Styles menu command, this box contains the name of the style assigned the current selection.

You can accept this name, type in the name of another existing style, or select a name from the pull-down list. To modify the style, you can now specify any formatting feature as described in the previous section. You can also change the base style and the next style, also according to the instructions in the previous section.

If you select the Add to Template option, the changes you make will be applied to the style within the current document *and* within the document template.

When you have completed specifying the features of the style you are modifying, click the Define button to redefine the style and leave the dialog box open. To redefine the style and close the dialog box, click the OK button.

To *delete* the style named in the Define Style Name box from the current document, click the Delete button. Clicking this button does *not* delete the style from the document template if it exists there; to delete it from the template, you must open the template file and delete it through the Format/Define Styles menu command.

Finally, you can rename the style by clicking the Rename button. Word will display a dialog box that allows you to specify the new name.

Merging Styles

As you saw in the previous section, you can copy a new or modified style definition to the document template by selecting the Add to Template option within the Format/Define Styles dialog box. In this section, you will learn how to copy *all* document styles to the document template or to the global template (NORMAL). You will also learn how to copy styles from a template or another document *to* the current document.

To copy styles, click the Merge button.

Word will display the dialog box shown in Figure 20.6.

You can now either copy all styles from the current document to a document template, or copy all styles from a template or other document to the current document.

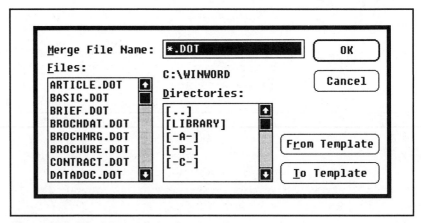

Figure 20.6: The Merge dialog box

When copying styles, a copied style with the same name as an existing style in the target document or template will *replace* the existing style.

To copy all styles from the current document to a template, click the To Template button within the Merge dialog box, observing the following guidelines:

- If the Merge File Name box does *not* contain a specific template file name when you click the To Template button (or if it contains the name of the document template), Word will automatically copy all styles defined in the document to the document template.

- You can have Word copy all styles from the current document to the global template (NORMAL), whether or not NORMAL is the document template. Choose the \WINWORD directory within the Directories list box, and select NORMAL. The list boxes can be used in the same manner as the list boxes in the File/Open command, described in Chapter 3.

- If the Merge File Name box contains the name of a template or document other than the document template or NORMAL, the To Template button is grayed, and cannot be clicked. Thus, the Merge dialog box allows you to transfer styles only to the document or global template.

To copy all styles from a template or other document to the current document, click the From Template or OK button, observing the following guidelines:

- To quickly copy all styles from the document template to the current document, simply click the From Template button. Make sure, however, that the Merge File Name box does not contain the name of a specific template or document; otherwise, styles will be copied from the specified file. (It can contain a *general* name, such as *.DOT.)

- To copy all styles from another document or template, first switch to the appropriate directory and select the name of the document or template using the Files and Directories list boxes (in the same manner described for the File/Open command in Chapter 3). Then click either the From Template or OK button.

DEFINING OR MODIFYING STYLES BY EXAMPLE

You can create a new style or alter an existing one based upon the character and paragraph formatting features of an existing paragraph. This method is useful for quickly creating a new style, or for altering an existing one, after you have already applied the desired formatting commands to a paragraph. Also, it enables you to see how the formatting commands look and to make sure they are correct before assigning them to a style. A final advantage of this method is that it allows you to apply formatting features using the Word ruler or ribbon (remember that you cannot use the ruler or ribbon when defining a style through the Format/Define Styles dialog box).

Once you have created a new style by example, you can later enhance the style, if desired, through the Format/Define Styles menu command.

The first step is to apply the desired character and paragraph formatting to a paragraph in your document. When choosing the paragraph you want to use as an example, keep in mind the following guidelines:

To apply the desired formatting features, use any of the menu or keyboard commands, or ruler or ribbon techniques, described in Chapters 15 and 16.

- If you are creating a new style, you can use *any* paragraph as an example. It makes sense, however, to choose one that is as close as possible to the desired format.

- If you want to modify an existing style, you must use a paragraph that is assigned this style.

Note that if a given character formatting feature varies within the paragraph, Word will use the feature applied to the majority of the characters. For example, if some characters are assigned the Helv font, but most are assigned the Courier font, Word will assign the Courier font to the style you define.

Next, make sure that the insertion point is within the example paragraph, or that you have selected part or all of this paragraph (if the selection encompasses more than one paragraph, Word will use the settings of the *first* paragraph within the selection to define the style).

You can now use either of the following methods:

- The ruler or keyboard
- The Format/Styles menu command

USING THE RULER OR KEYBOARD

If the ruler is *not* currently displayed, type the Ctrl-S keystroke. Word will display the following prompt within the status bar:

Which style?

If the ruler *is* displayed, either type Ctrl-S or click within the Style box at the left end of the ruler. Word will place the insertion point within the Style box.

Next, type the name you want to assign to the new style you are defining and press ←. Word will ask you if you want to define the new style based upon the selection. Click the Yes button to complete the definition.

If you are creating a new style, you should type a name that is not already used for a style defined within the document, or for one of the automatic styles listed in Table 20.1.

If you want to redefine the style applied to the selected paragraph, follow these steps:

1. If the ruler is *not* displayed, type the name of the style of the selected paragraph at the prompt within the status bar and

The name of the style will be displayed in the ruler unless the current selection encompasses two or more files formatted with different styles.

press ←. If the ruler *is* displayed, the name of this style should already be contained in the Style box within the ruler; you can simply press ←.

2. Word will ask you if you want to redefine the style based upon the selection. Click the Yes button. (If you click the No button, Word will *reapply* the style to the selected paragraph, eliminating any formatting features you have manually added.) Note that if you type or select the name of an existing style *other* than the one assigned to the selected paragraph, Word will apply the specified style to the paragraph, replacing both the original style and any formatting you have manually applied.

USING THE FORMAT/STYLES MENU COMMAND

The Format/Styles dialog box was described previously in the chapter, in the section "Applying a Style."

As an alternative method for defining or modifying a style by example, you can use the Format/Styles menu command. After choosing this command, enter the name you want to assign to the new style and click the OK button. Make sure that you enter a name not already used for a style. Word will ask you if you want to define the new style based on the selection. Click Yes to complete the definition.

To redefine the style assigned to the selected paragraph, use the following steps:

1. The name of the style assigned to the selected paragraph should already be displayed in the Style Name box of the Format/Styles dialog box. You can simply click the OK button.

2. Word will ask you if you want to redefine the style based upon the selection. Click the Yes button. See the additional comments given under step 2 in the previous section.

SUMMARY

- A style is a set of character and paragraph formatting features; it is identified by name and may be applied to one or more paragraphs in a document.

- Every paragraph within a document is assigned a style. Word provides a number of predefined, or *automatic*, styles that it assigns to various types of text within your document. For example, ordinary text is assigned the style Normal. The automatic styles are listed in Table 20.1.

- You can assign the desired style (an automatic style or one that you have defined) to one or more paragraphs in a document using the Format/Styles command, the Word ruler, or the keyboard.

- The Format/Styles menu command allows you to type the name of the desired style, or select it from a list. The style is applied to the selected paragraph or paragraphs.

- When the ruler is displayed, you can assign a style to the current selection by typing a style name into the Style box, or by selecting a style from the pull-down list. First place the insertion point within the Style box by clicking in the box, or by pressing Ctrl-S.

- If the ruler is not displayed, you can apply a style to the selection by pressing Ctrl-S and typing the style name at the status bar prompt.

- You can define a new style or modify an existing one by specifying each feature through the Format/Define Styles menu command, or by using an existing paragraph as a model for the new style.

- To define or modify a style using the Format/Define Styles menu command, enter the style name into the Define Style Name box, and then assign the desired character and paragraph formatting features. You can assign a feature by clicking the appropriate button to open a dialog box, or by typing a keyboard command as if you were formatting text.

- The Format/Define Styles dialog box also allows you to choose a style to serve as a basis for the style you are defining, and to specify a style that Word automatically assigns to the paragraph following a paragraph whose style you are defining.

- You can also delete or rename an existing style through the Format/Define Styles dialog box, and you can copy styles *to* a template or *from* a template or other document.

- You can define or modify a style by using an existing paragraph as an example. The new style acquires all character and paragraph formatting features of the example paragraph.

- To define a style by example, first select the paragraph that has the desired features, and then type the style name into the Styles box within the ruler, at the prompt after typing Ctrl-S, or within the Style Name box in the Format/Styles dialog box.

21

USING THE GLOSSARY TO SAVE TYPING

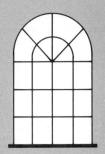

YOU CAN USE A WORD *GLOSSARY* TO STORE BLOCKS of text or graphics. Each block—termed a *glossary entry*—is identified by name, and it can be inserted into any document location. You can save time by storing frequently used blocks of text or graphics as glossary entries and inserting them whenever required, rather than retyping the text or importing the picture each time it is needed. Unlike the Windows Clipboard, which you usually use to store text or graphics temporarily, a glossary provides permanent storage and can hold many entries.

In this chapter, you will learn how to store a selection within a glossary and how to insert a glossary entry into your document. Finally, you will learn how to use a special glossary entry known as the Spike.

STORING A
SELECTION IN A GLOSSARY

To insert a block of text or graphics into a glossary, first select the desired block. Next, choose the Edit/Glossary menu command. Word will display the dialog box illustrated in Figure 21.1. Type a name for the new glossary entry into the Glossary Name box. A glossary name can be from 1 to 31 characters in length, and can include space characters.

If you type the name of an existing glossary entry, Word will *redefine* this entry using the current selection. When you start typing in the glossary name, Word will display the current selection at the bottom of the dialog box—that is, the text that will become the contents of the glossary entry. If there is insufficient room, Word will display only the first 38 characters of the selection, and terminate it with an ellipsis (...).

Before completing the definition, you should choose the *context* for the entry from the Context box. Remember from Chapter 19 that glossary entries are actually stored within a template, and not within the document itself. Each template has its own glossary. If you choose the Global option, the glossary entry will be stored within the global template (NORMAL); in this case, the Template option is displayed in gray letters and cannot be selected. Alternatively, if the document template is *not* the global template, you can choose the Template option to store the entry within the document template.

Click the Define button to store the selection in the glossary and remove the dialog box.

Before redefining an existing entry, Word will display a message box, allowing you to decide whether you want to redefine the entry.

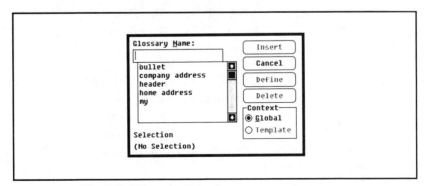

Figure 21.1: The Edit/Glossary dialog box

While the Edit/Glossary dialog box is open, you can delete a glossary entry by typing its name into the Glossary Name box, or by selecting its name from the list box, and then clicking the Delete button.

You can print the glossary entires available for the current document by choosing the File/Print command, and selecting the Glossary item from the Print list box (see Figure 21.2). Word will print the name of each glossary entry, together with its contents. It will print the entries within the document template, followed by the entries in the global template.

If the document template is the global template, Word will simply print the global template entries.

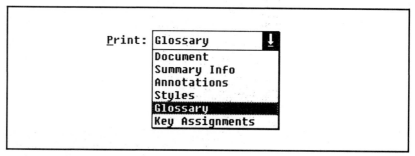

Figure 21.2: The File/Print list box

INSERTING A GLOSSARY ENTRY INTO A DOCUMENT

You can insert a glossary entry at the current position of the insertion point using either a dialog box or a keyboard command.

To insert a glossary entry using a dialog box, choose the Edit/Glossary menu command. Word will display the dialog box that was illustrated in Figure 21.1, earlier in the chapter. Now, either enter the name of the desired glossary entry into the Glossary Name box, or select a name within the list, as shown in Figure 21.3.

When the entry name has been typed into the Glossary Name box, or when the name has been selected in the list, Word displays the contents of the entry below the list. If there is not enough room to display

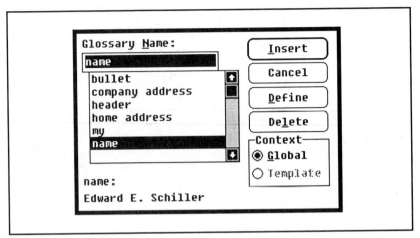

Figure 21.3: Selecting a glossary entry in the Edit/Glossary dialog box

the entire contents of the entry, Word displays the first 38 characters of the entry and terminates it with an ellipsis (...). Click the Insert button to insert the specified entry into your document.

To insert a glossary entry using the keyboard, type the name of the entry directly into your document at the position where you want the entry to be inserted. While the insertion point is to the immediate right of the glossary name, press the F3 key. Word will immediately replace the glossary name with the glossary contents. Alternatively, you can select the glossary name before pressing F3.

USING THE SPIKE

Normally, when you store a selection in an existing glossary entry, it replaces the former contents of the entry. Word, however, provides a special glossary entry named **Spike**, which allows you to store multiple blocks of text or graphics, and then insert all of the text as a single block at the desired location in a document.

To add a block of text or graphics to the Spike, select the block and press the Ctrl-F3 keystroke. The block is *removed from the document* (that is, it is *cut*) and is added to the Spike. It is stored in the Spike in addition to any blocks that were previously stored in this glossary entry.

To insert the current contents of the Spike into a document, place the insertion point at the desired position in the text and press the

Ctrl-Shift-F3 keystroke. All entries stored in the Spike will be inserted into your document as a single block *in the same order that they were added to the Spike*. Also, the Spike will be emptied; therefore, using the Ctrl-Shift-F3 keystroke you can insert the Spike contents only once.

You can, however, insert the Spike contents repeatedly by choosing the Edit/Glossary menu command and selecting the name **Spike**, or by typing the word **Spike** into your document and then pressing F3. (See the previous section for details.)

SUMMARY

- You can store blocks of text or graphics as glossary entries, which are identified by name and can be inserted into your document whenever required.

- To store a block in a glossary, select the block within your document and choose the Edit/Glossary menu command. Type a name for the glossary entry into the Glossary Name box.

- Glossary entries are stored within a template, not within the document. Select the Global option in the Context box to add the entry to the global template, or the Template option to add it to the document template. Click the Define button to complete the definition.

- While the Edit/Glossary dialog box is still open, you can delete the glossary entry displayed in the Glossary Name box by clicking the Delete button.

- You can insert a glossary entry at the position of the insertion point by choosing the Edit/Glossary menu command, selecting the name of the entry in the Glossary Name box, and clicking the Insert button.

- Alternatively, you can type the name of the glossary entry directly into your document and then press the F3 key while the insertion point is to the immediate right of the name.

- Word provides a special glossary entry known as the Spike. You can store multiple blocks of text or graphics in this entry, and then insert them as a single block at the desired location.

- To remove a block from your document and add it to the Spike, select the block and press Ctrl-F3. To insert the current contents of the Spike, place the insertion point at the desired position in your document and press Ctrl-Shift-F3.

22

WRITING MACROS TO SAVE WORK

YOU CAN RECORD A SERIES OF EDITING OR FORMATTING actions as a Word *macro*. You can then repeat these actions at any time by running the macro. Macros are like new Word commands that you create yourself. By issuing a single command (running the macro) you can have Word perform an entire series of actions. You can save time by creating macros to perform complex tasks or tasks that you perform frequently.

In this chapter, you will learn how to record a macro, how to edit a macro, and how to run a macro.

RECORDING A MACRO

The easiest way to create a simple macro is to record your actions as you perform them. To begin recording your actions, choose the

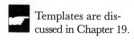 Windows 3.0 provides a Macro Recorder that allows you to record and run macros within one or more Windows applications. See your Windows *User's Guide* for information.

Templates are discussed in Chapter 19.

If the document template is the global template, the template option is displayed in gray letters and cannot be selected.

Macro/Record menu command. Word will display the dialog box shown in Figure 22.1.

First, type the name you want to assign the macro into the Record Macro Name box. Word proposes the name **Macro1** for the first macro you record, **Macro2** for the second, and so on. You can accept these names, or you can enter more descriptive names of your own. A macro name cannot contain space characters.

Next, you can specify the macro *context* by choosing one of the options within the Context box. Like glossary entries, macros are stored in a template, not in the document itself. If you choose the Global option, the macro you record will be stored within the global template (NORMAL). In this case, the macro will be available when you are working with any document.

Alternatively, if the document template is *not* the global template, you can choose the Template option to store the macro within the document template. In this case, the macro will be available only when you are working with a document created with the same template.

Before starting to record the macro, you can also enter a description into the Description box. Word will later display your description if you select the macro within one of the following dialog boxes: Macro/Run, Macro/Edit, Macro/Assign to Key, Macro/Assign to Menu (these dialog boxes are described later). The description can help you choose the appropriate macro when using any of these dialog boxes. Also, if you assign the macro to a menu (as described in Chapter 23), Word will display the description within the status bar when the menu item is highlighted. You can later edit the description you enter through the Macro/Edit command, described later in the chapter (in the section "Editing a Macro").

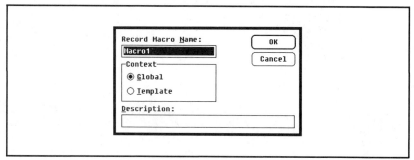

Figure 22.1: The Macro/Record dialog box

When you are ready to begin recording, click the OK button. Word will remove the dialog box, and will display the letters **REC** within the right side of the status bar to let you know that your actions are being recorded.

Now perform the series of actions you want to store in the macro. You can perform almost any editing action or Word command. Note, however, that you cannot use the mouse except to choose menu commands and to select options within dialog boxes. While the mouse pointer is in the text area, it is displayed as a transparent arrow rather than the usual I-beam, and you cannot use the mouse to perform such actions as moving the insertion point or selecting or copying text.

> Once you start recording a macro, the Record item on the Macro menu is replaced with the Stop Recorder item.

When you have completed performing the actions you want to record, choose the Macro/Stop Recorder menu command. Word will immediately stop recording the macro without displaying a dialog box. It will also remove the letters **REC** from the status bar. Later in the chapter, you will see how to run the macro.

If you have created or modified one or more macros, Word will prompt you to save your changes to the appropriate template when you quit the program (or if you issue the File/Save All menu command).

AUTOMATIC MACROS

If you assign a macro you create one of the following names, Word will run the macro *automatically* whenever the appropriate situation arises:

> Although Word runs automatic macros automatically, you can also run them manually using the Macro/Run command, described later in the chapter.

- AutoExec
- AutoExit
- AutoOpen
- AutoNew
- AutoClose

You can prevent Word from running the macro if you hold down the Shift key while performing an action that would normally activate the macro.

AutoExec

If you assign a macro the name **AutoExec**, the macro will run automatically when you start Word. For example, if you want to open a specific document each time you start Word, you could create a macro as follows:

1. Choose the Macro/Record menu command. Type **AutoExec** into the Record Macro Name box, select the Global context, and enter a description if desired.

2. Click the OK button to begin recording. Word will remove the dialog box.

3. Using the File/Open menu command, open the file you want to appear each time you start Word.

4. Choose the Macro/Stop Recorder menu command.

Note that you can *prevent* Word from running the **AutoExec** macro by including the **/m** switch in the command line when you start the program. For example, if you start Word using the Windows Program Manager File/Run command, type the following in the Command Line box to start Word without running the AutoExec macro:

```
winword   /m
```

AutoExit

If you assign a macro the name **AutoExit**, the macro will run automatically whenever you quit Word. You can record in this macro any final tasks you want to perform each time you quit Word.

AutoOpen

If you name your macro **AutoOpen**, it will run automatically whenever you open an *existing* document. It does not run when you open a new document.

If you choose the Template context option in the Macro/Record dialog box, the macro will run only when you open a document that has the *same* document template as the document in which you recorded the macro.

AutoNew

If you name your macro **AutoNew**, it will run whenever you open a *new* document. It does not run when you open an existing document.

If you choose the Template context option in the Macro/Record dialog box, the macro will run only when you create a new document that has the *same* document template as the document in which you recorded the macro.

AutoClose

A macro named **AutoClose** will run whenever you close a document. Quitting Word or quitting Windows before closing the document will also trigger this macro.

EDITING A MACRO

For a description of the macro programming language, see the Word *Technical Reference.*

Using the Macro/Edit menu command, you can delete a macro, rename a macro, or edit a macro description.

You can also use the OK button in the Macro/Edit dialog box to open a special window for editing the commands within the macro itself, or for creating a new macro from scratch. Editing or creating a macro within this window, however, requires knowledge of the macro programming language used by Word. This language allows you to include Word commands as well as control structures, and to create sophisticated macros; however, it is beyond the scope of this book.

When you choose the Macro/Edit menu command, Word displays the dialog box shown in Figure 22.2. The first step is to select the name of the desired macro from the Edit Macro Name box. Before selecting a name, however, you must make sure that the appropriate context is selected in the Context box. If the Global option is selected, Word will display all macros that were assigned the Global context when they were recorded; likewise, if the Template option is selected, Word will show only the macros that were assigned the Template context when they were recorded. If you select the Show All option, Word will list all Word commands in addition to macros that have been defined.

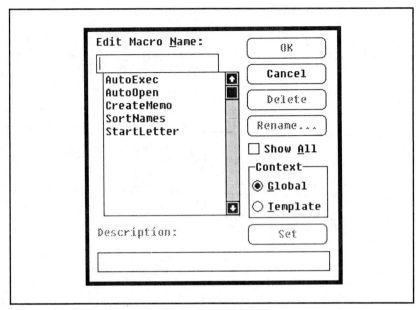

Figure 22.2: The Macro/Edit dialog box

To delete the macro, click the Delete button. To assign the macro a new name, click the Rename button, and type the new name at the prompt.

To edit the macro description, place the insertion point within the Description box by clicking in this box or by pressing Alt-I. You can modify the text using normal editing operations. When the description is the way you want it, click the Set button to record the changes.

To remove the Macro/Edit dialog box, click the Close button (the Cancel button becomes the Close button once you perform an operation within or from this box).

> Don't click the OK button to remove the dialog box, since this button opens the macro command editing window described previously, rather than returning you to the document window.

RUNNING A MACRO

When you want to run a macro, choose the Macro/Run menu command. Word will display the dialog box shown in Figure 22.3. Type the name of the macro you want to run into the Run Macro Name box, or select the name from the list. Word displays the description (if any) of the selected macro within the Description box.

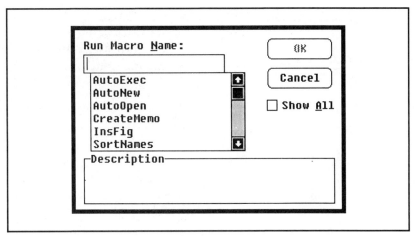

Figure 22.3: The Macro/Run dialog box

The list contains the names of all macros available to the current document (those stored in the document template as well as those stored in the global template).

If you select the Show All option, Word will display the names of all Word program commands in addition to the names of the available macros. Each program command is given a name and is assigned a description; it can be selected and run in the same manner as a macro.

Click the OK button when you are ready to run the macro. When you run a macro, Word performs all of the recorded actions; it does not, however, display any dialog boxes used while recording the macro, unless additional information is required through a dialog box.

You can start Word and have it automatically run a macro by including the /m flag on the command line. For example, if you have created a macro called **Initialize**, you could start Word and run this macro by typing the following command line at the Program Manager File/Run prompt:

    winword   /minitialize

As you will learn in the next chapter, you can assign a key combination to a macro, so that you can run the macro by simply pressing this keystroke. You can also include a macro on a Word menu so that you can run the macro by choosing the menu item.

As you saw previously, if you have defined a macro named AutoExec, including the /m flag prevents this macro from running automatically.

Do not press the spacebar between /m and the name of the macro to execute.

SUMMARY

- You can record a series of Word commands and store them as a macro. You can then run the macro at any time you want to perform these commands.

- To begin recording your actions in a macro, choose the Macro/Record menu command. To make the macro available to all documents, select the Global option; to make it available only to documents that have the same document template, select the Template option. If desired, you can enter a description into the Description box.

- Click OK to remove the dialog box and begin recording your actions.

- While your actions are being recorded in a macro, the letters **REC** are displayed in the status bar, and you cannot use the mouse except for choosing menu commands and selecting options within dialog boxes.

- To stop recording your actions, choose the Macro/Stop Recorder menu command.

- You can have Word automatically run a macro at a designated time by assigning it one of the following names: AutoExec, AutoExit, AutoOpen, AutoNew, or AutoClose.

- You can delete or rename a macro, or change the macro description, by choosing the Macro/Edit menu command and selecting the macro name from the list. Select the Global context option to see all globally defined macros, or the Template option to see the macros defined for the document template.

- To delete the selected macro, click the Delete button. To rename the macro, click the Rename button. To change the macro description, edit the text in the Description box and click the Set button. To remove the dialog box, click the Close button.

- If you click the OK button in the Edit/Macro dialog box, Word will open a window for editing the commands within

the macro. Editing the commands, however, requires knowledge of Word's macro programming language, described in
the *Technical Reference*.

- To run a macro, choose the Macro/Run menu command.
  Either type the macro name into the Run Macro Name box,
  or select the macro from the list.

- To select a standard Word command rather than a macro
  that you have defined, select the Show All option in the
  Macro/Run dialog box, and select the name of the desired
  command from the list.

- When you are ready to run the command, click the OK button.

- In the next chapter, you will learn how to assign keyboard
  combinations to a macro so that you can run it by simply
  pressing a keystroke. You will also learn how to add a macro
  name to a Word menu so that you can run it by choosing the
  menu item.

23

CUSTOMIZING MENUS, KEYBOARD COMMANDS, AND OTHER FEATURES

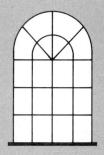

IN THIS CHAPTER, YOU WILL LEARN HOW TO customize your working environment in Word. You will learn how to add or remove commands or macros from Word menus, how to assign keystrokes to commands or macros, and how to customize other Word features.

Keep in mind that the techniques described throughout this book are based upon the original menu and command configuration supplied with Word. Therefore, it is best not to remove existing commands from Word menus, or to change the keystrokes that issue standard Word commands, until you have finished working with the book. In the meanwhile, you can use the techniques given in this chapter to add additional items to menus, or to assign keystrokes to macros you have defined as described in the previous chapter.

CUSTOMIZING MENUS

Menu customiza-
tions affect only *full*
menus. If short menus
are displayed, choose the
View/Full Menus menu
command.

Creating macros
is discussed in
Chapter 22.

Word allows you to extensively customize the menus that it displays. You can customize the menus for all documents, or you can customize the menus that are displayed only when working with a document based upon a specific template.

You can add or remove from any Word menu either a standard Word command or a macro that you have created. Initially, the menus contain only a subset of the full collection of standard Word commands. You can have Word display additional commands that you use frequently, or remove commands that you seldom use. Also, when you first create a macro, the only way to run the macro is to choose the Macro/Run command and specify the macro name in the dialog box. After adding a macro to a menu, however, you can run it by simply choosing the menu item.

To add or remove a macro or Word command from a menu, choose the Macro/Assign to Menu command. Word will display the dialog box shown in Figure 23.1.

To *add* a Word command or macro to a menu, first select the name of the command or macro from the Assign Macro Name list. When you select an item in the list, Word displays the associated description at the bottom of the dialog box to help you find the correct name.

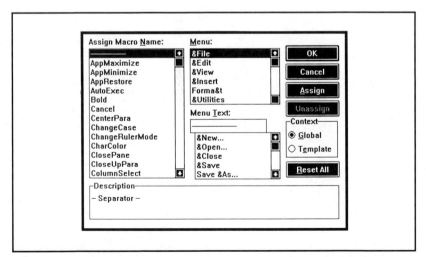

Figure 23.1: The Macro/Assign to Menu dialog box

Notice that the first item in the list is a horizontal line, described as **Separator**. This item is not an actual command or macro; rather, selecting it allows you to insert a horizontal line after the last menu item. Thus, you can separate existing menu items from items that you subsequently add to the menu.

Next, you should choose the Word menu on which you want to place the new command. Select the name of the desired menu from the Menu list.

The Menu Text box contains the actual text that will be displayed on the menu. When you select the name of a command or macro from the Assign Macro Name list, Word automatically enters this name into the Menu Text box. If you want to change the text for the menu item, you can edit the contents of this box.

In the Menu Text box, the ampersand character (&) is not actually printed as part of the menu text. Rather, it causes Word to underline the following character. For example, typing the text

Menu Text:

| &SortNames |

would result in the menu item

| SortNames |

with *S* underlined. You should underline exactly one character within the text for the menu item, by inserting an ampersand in front of this character. When the menu containing the item is open, you can choose the item by pressing the underlined character. If, however, two or more items on a given menu have the *same* underlined character, pressing the character will not choose the item; rather, it will move the highlight to the next item with the character. To choose the item, you must then press ◄┘. You should therefore assign each menu item a unique underlined character, to make the item easier to choose.

Templates are discussed in Chapter 19.

Next, you should select the appropriate option from the Context box. Choosing the Global option will add the item to the menu displayed when working with any document. If the document template is *not* the global template (NORMAL), you can choose the Template option; in this case, the item will appear on the menu only when you are working with a document based upon the same template as the current document.

Click the OK button to complete the menu assignment and remove the dialog box, or click the Assign button to complete the assignment and leave the dialog box open so that you can continue to customize menus.

The command or macro will generally be added to the *end* of the specified menu, with two exceptions: first, the command or macro will be placed immediately *before* the list of files at the end of the File or Window menu; second, if you add a standard menu item that was previously removed, it is placed back in its former location.

To *remove* a command or macro from a menu, perform the following steps in the Macro/Assign to Menu dialog box:

1. Choose the Global option to remove an item from *all* menus, or the Template option to remove it from menus for documents based upon the same template as the current document.

2. In the Menu list, select the Word menu containing the command or macro you want to remove. Word will now list all items on this menu in the list below the Menu Text box.

3. In the list below the Menu Text box, select the specific item you want to remove.

4. Click the Unassign button.

You can also change the text displayed for an existing menu item by first performing steps 1 through 3 given above; then, rather than clicking the Unassign button, edit the text within the Menu Text box. To accept the change to the menu text, click the Assign button (to leave the dialog box open) or the OK button (to close the dialog box).

After you have made one or more changes to Word menus, you can *restore* the original Word menus supplied with the program through the following two steps:

1. Choose the Global option to restore *all* menus, or the Template option to restore menus only for documents based upon the same template as the current document.

2. Click the Reset All button.

Note that when you are working with a document that is not based upon the global template, menu changes applied to the document template override changes applied to the global template, in the following ways:

- If you add a menu item to the global template, it will initially appear in all documents. If, however, you then explicitly remove it from a nonglobal document template (using the Unassign button), it will *no longer* appear in any document based upon this template.

- If you remove a menu item from the global template, it will initially be removed from all documents. If, however, you then explicitly add it back to a nonglobal document template (using the Assign button), it will reappear in documents based upon this template.

ASSIGNING KEYSTROKES

Word also allows you to customize the key combinations used to issue standard Word commands or macros that you have defined. You can perform the following basic operations:

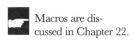
Macros are discussed in Chapter 22.

- Assign a keystroke to a specific command or macro. Once you have made this assignment, pressing the keystroke will execute the command or run the macro.

- Remove a keystroke assignment from a command or macro. Once you have removed the assignment, pressing the keystroke will no longer execute the command or macro.

- Restore the original keyboard assignments made by Microsoft. This will eliminate any keyboard changes you have made.

You can employ these operations, for example, to assign a convenient keystroke to a Word command that you use frequently. Also, you can assign a keystroke to a macro so that you can run the macro more quickly than choosing the Macro/Run menu command.

To perform one of these operations, choose the Macro/Assign to Key menu command. Word will display the dialog box illustrated in Figure 23.2.

The next step is to choose the context for the change you make to the current keyboard assignments. Choosing the Global option within the Context area will affect the keyboard configuration for *all* documents. Choosing the Template option will affect the keyboard configuration for only those documents based upon the template that you have changed.

ASSIGNING A KEYSTROKE TO A COMMAND OR MACRO

To assign a keystroke to a command or macro, use the following steps:

1. Select the name of the command or macro from the Assign Macro Name list. If you press a letter key, Word will quickly select the next name starting with this letter. Notice that as soon as you select a name, any keystrokes currently assigned to the command or macro are listed in the Current Keys box.

2. Press the exact keystroke you want to assign to the selected command.

You can enter one of the following key combinations:

- A function key (F2 to F12)
- A Ctrl-*key* combination, where *key* is a letter or function key
- A Ctrl-Shift-*key* combination, where *key* is a letter or function key

As soon as you press a valid key combination, Word displays a description of the keystroke in the Key box. If the keystroke you press is invalid, Word will ignore the keystroke and will *not* display its description in the Key box.

You can print a list of current keyboard assignments by choosing the File/Print menu item and selecting the Key Assignments item from the Print pull-down list. You will obtain a list of key assignments you've made, not including Word's default key assignments.

In Word's original configuration, all function keys and almost all Ctrl-*key* combinations are assigned to standard Word commands. However, most of the Ctrl-Shift-*key* combinations are initially unassigned.

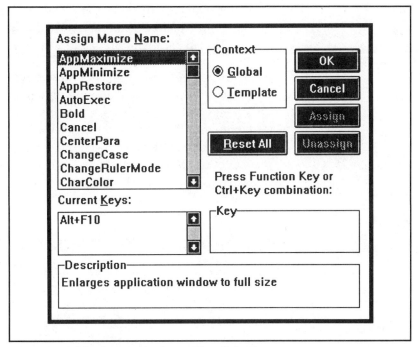

Figure 23.2: The Macro/Assign to Key dialog box

If the keystroke you press has already been assigned to another command, Word will indicate the name of this command within the Key box, following the description of the keystroke.

┌─Key─────────────
│ Ctrl+R
│ Bold
└─────────────────

If the keystroke has not already been assigned, Word will display the words **currently unassigned** following the description.

   3. Click the Assign button to assign the keystroke appearing in the Key box to the command or macro selected within the Assign Macro Name list. The keystroke will now appear in the Current Keys box. If the keystroke was already assigned to another command or macro, it is *reassigned* to the command or macro selected in the Assign Macro Name box.

*The Cancel button be-
comes the Close but-
ton after you have changed
a key assignment.*

4. When you have completed making key assignments, click the Close button to remove the dialog box. Alternatively, you can perform steps 3 and 4 by simply pressing the OK button.

Once you have completed these steps, pressing the assigned keystroke will immediately execute the designated command or macro. When you quit the program, or if you issue the File/Save All menu command, Word will prompt you to save any changes to the appropriate template file.

Note that you can assign several keystrokes to a command or macro, but you cannot assign the same keystroke to more than one command or macro.

REMOVING A KEYSTROKE ASSIGNMENT

To remove a keystroke assignment when the Macro/Assign to Key dialog box is open, do the following:

*Word has preas-
signed Alt-key
combinations to certain
commands. You cannot
remove Alt-key keystrokes
from commands, since
Word does not allow you
to enter these key combi-
nations into the Key box.*

1. Press the keystroke you want to remove. Word will display a description of the keystroke in the Key box, together with the name of the command or macro to which it is currently assigned.

Alternatively, you can first select in the Assign Macro Name box the command or macro to which the keystroke has been assigned; Word will display the keystrokes currently assigned to this command in the Current Keys box. If you select the desired keystroke within this box, Word will automatically copy the description to the Key box.

2. Click the Unassign button.

3. When you have finished altering key assignments, click the Close button to remove the dialog box.

*Be careful using the
Reset All button,
since it will remove all
keyboard assignments
you have made within
the specified context.*

RESTORING THE ORIGINAL KEYBOARD ASSIGNMENTS

To restore all keyboard assignments to the values originally set by Microsoft, click the Reset All button. Word will immediately restore all original keyboard assignments within the global template (if the Global context option is selected) or within the document template (if the Template context option is selected).

CUSTOMIZING OTHER WORD FEATURES

To complete the discussion on customizing Word, this section summarizes some other useful commands and options for customizing the Word environment. Many of these options are also described elsewhere in the book.

THE UTILITIES/CUSTOMIZE COMMAND

First, the Utilities/Customize command provides various options for customizing Word. This command displays the dialog box shown

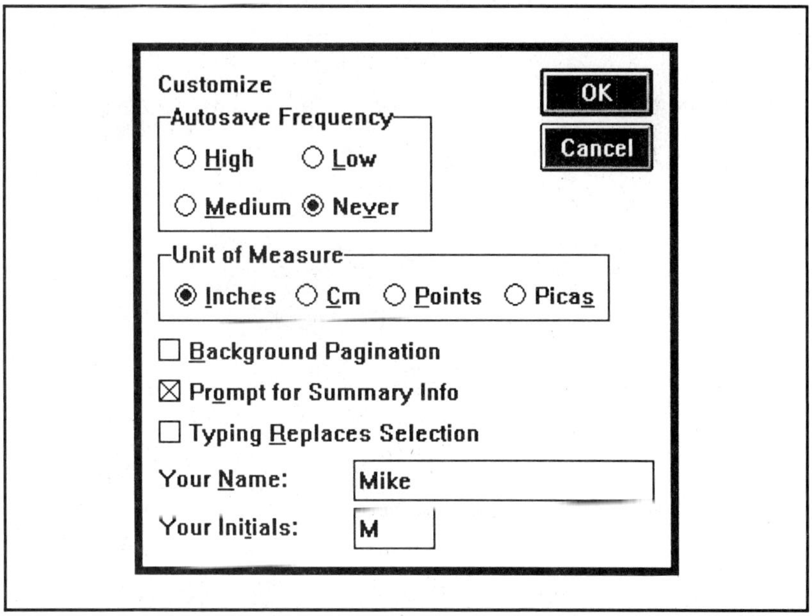

Figure 23.3: The Utilities/Customize dialog box

in Figure 23.3. The options in this dialog box are as follows:

OPTION	EFFECT
Autosave Frequency	Specifies whether Word will automatically prompt you to save your document, and how often it should do so (see Chapter 3).
Unit of Measure	Specifies the default unit of measurement displayed on the ruler and accepted by numeric fields in dialog boxes (see Appendix B).
Background Pagination	Causes Word to divide the document into pages as you work (see Chapter 4).
Typing Replaces Selection	Causes Word to automatically delete the selected text when you insert a character (the character replaces the selection; see Chapter 5).
Prompt for Summary Info	Causes Word to automatically display the Edit/Summary Info dialog box the first time you save a new document.
Your Name	The name you enter here is used as the default in the Author box within the Edit/Summary Info dialog box for all new documents. Also, it is used to identify the author when you lock a document for annotations (see Chapter 25).
Your Initials	The character or characters you enter here are included in annotation marks (see Chapter 25).

THE VIEW/PREFERENCES COMMAND

You can choose several options for customizing the Word screen display by issuing the View/Preferences menu command. The dialog box opened through this command is shown in Figure 23.4. The options in this dialog box are as follows:

OPTION	EFFECT
Tabs	Displays tabs as right arrows (see Chapter 3).

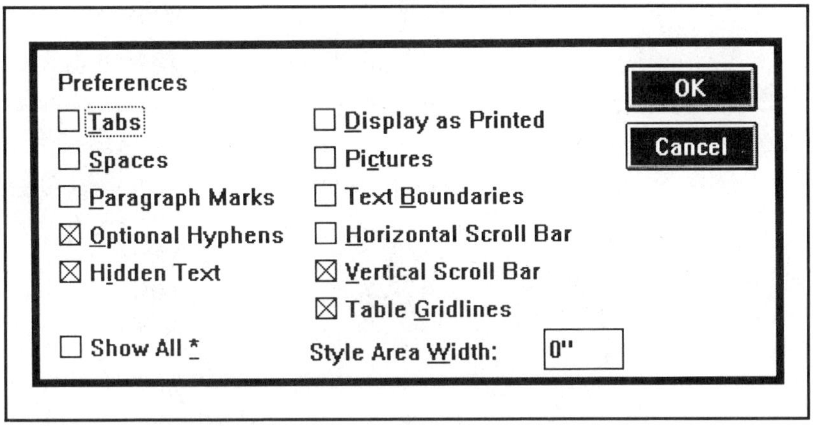

```
┌─────────────────────────────────────────────────────────┐
│  ┌───────────────────────────────────────────────────┐  │
│  │ Preferences                          ┌─────────┐   │  │
│  │ ☐ T̲abs            ☐ D̲isplay as Printed│   OK    │   │  │
│  │ ☐ S̲paces          ☐ Pic̲tures         └─────────┘   │  │
│  │ ☐ P̲aragraph Marks ☐ Text B̲oundaries  ┌─────────┐   │  │
│  │ ☒ O̲ptional Hyphens☐ H̲orizontal Scroll│ Cancel  │   │  │
│  │ ☒ Hi̲dden Text      Bar                └─────────┘   │  │
│  │                   ☒ V̲ertical Scroll Bar            │  │
│  │                   ☒ Table G̲ridlines                │  │
│  │ ☐ Show All *      Style Area W̲idth: ┌────┐         │  │
│  │                                     │0"  │         │  │
│  │                                     └────┘         │  │
│  └───────────────────────────────────────────────────┘  │
└─────────────────────────────────────────────────────────┘
```

Figure 23.4: The View/Preferences dialog box

OPTION	EFFECT
Spaces	Displays normal spaces as small centered dots, and nonbreaking spaces as degree symbols (see Chapter 3).
Paragraph Marks	Displays paragraph marks, newline characters (Chapter 3), and end-of-cell marks in tables (Chapter 8).
Optional Hyphens	Toggles the display of nonbreaking hyphens (as a special character) and optional hyphens (see Chapter 17).
Hidden Text	Displays characters formatted as hidden text with a dotted underline (see Chapter 16).
Show All *	Displays *all* special characters listed above. Equivalent to selecting all options in first column of the View/Preferences dialog box.
Display as Printed	Displays all character formatting, line breaks, and tab stop alignment exactly as printed (see Chapter 17).

OPTION	*EFFECT*
Pictures	Displays pictures. If option turned off, pictures are displayed as empty boxes (see Chapter 9).
Text Boundaries	Marks all margins, headers, footers, and positioned objects in page view (sec Chapter 17).
Horizontal Scroll Bar	Displays horizontal scroll bar.
Vertical Scroll Bar	Displays vertical scroll bar.
Table Gridlines	Displays a box around each cell in a table (the lines do not print; see Chapter 8).
Style Area Width	Entering a nonzero measurement displays a style area having the specified width (see Chapter 20).

SUMMARY

- You can customize the Word environment by adding or removing commands or macros from Word menus, by assigning keystrokes to various commands or macros, and by adjusting other program features.

- To add an item to a menu, choose the Macro/Assign to Menu command, select the name of the desired command or macro, and select the menu on which to put it. You can also edit the item text that will appear on the menu. Click the Assign or OK button to complete the assignment.

- To remove an item from a menu, choose the Macro/Assign to Menu command, select the menu containing the item, select the item itself, and click the Unassign button.

- To restore the original Word menu configuration, click the Reset All button within the Macro/Assign to Menu dialog box.

- To assign a keystroke to a command or macro, choose the Macro/Assign to Key menu command, select the name of the command or macro, type the desired keystroke, and click the Assign or OK button.

- To remove a keystroke assignment, choose the Macro/ Assign to Key menu command, type the keystroke you want to remove, and click the Unassign button.

- To restore all original keyboard assignments, click the Reset All button within the Macro/Assign to Key dialog box.

- Choosing the Utilities/Customize menu command lets you customize a variety of Word features.

- The View/Preferences menu command lets you choose options that affect the way Word displays your documents.

LARGE PROJECTS

Now that you have learned basic Word editing and formatting techniques, as well as how to use the time-saving features that can be incorporated into document templates, this part of the book presents techniques that will assist you with larger-scale projects.

In Chapter 24, you will learn how to use Word's outline view to make large documents more manageable. In Chapter 25, you will learn how to add annotations and mark revisions—two features that help you keep track of changes to a document, and make it easier for several people to work on the same document. Finally, in Chapter 26, you will learn how to work with large manuscripts and manage collections of documents.

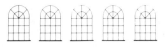

24

OUTLINING
YOUR DOCUMENTS

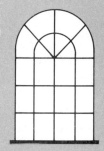

Table 17.2 in Chapter 17 summarizes the five basic document views.

THE OUTLINE DOCUMENT VIEW CAN HELP YOU create and organize a document. Outline view provides you with an overview of the structure of the document. You can vary the amount of document detail that is shown, and you can quickly rearrange large blocks of text within the document. You can also use outline view to quickly find particular topics within a large document.

When you use outline view, the outline is not separate from the document. Rather, outline view is merely a unique way of looking at and working with the document. Any changes made in outline view are reflected in all other document views, since they are changes made to the document itself.

In this chapter, you will learn how to examine and organize your document in outline view, how to have Word automatically number your outline headings, and how to create a table of contents directly from outline headings.

WORKING WITH OUTLINE VIEW

To switch into outline view, choose the View/Outline menu command. To turn off outline view, choose this command again. Figure 24.1 illustrates a short document in outline view. Notice that Word displays a *icon bar* at the top of the window; the use of each of the icons in this bar is discussed later in the section.

A document in outline view has two types of paragraphs: *outline headings* and *body text*.

You can change the formatting features of a particular heading level by redefining the corresponding predefined style (heading 1, heading 2, and so on), as described in Table 20.1 of Chapter 20. You cannot, however, change the amount a heading is indented in outline view, since this is defined independently of the style.

An outline heading is a paragraph that has been assigned a special predefined style. The specific style determines the heading level. A top-level heading is assigned the heading 1 style, a second level heading is assigned the heading 2 style, and so on. The lowest possible heading level is heading 9. In outline view, a top-level heading is aligned with the left margin; levels 2 through 9, however, are successively indented, so that each heading level is placed farther to the right than the preceding heading level. In other document views, the indent of a heading depends upon its paragraph formatting.

A paragraph of body text within an outline is one that has *not* been assigned an outline heading style (that is, a paragraph assigned a style other than heading 1, heading 2, and so on).

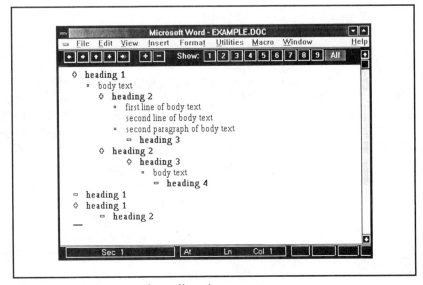

Figure 24.1: A document in outline view

The term *subtext* refers to all subordinate headings (headings at lower levels), plus all body text, that immediately follow an outline heading. For example, in Figure 24.1, the subtext belonging to the first top-level heading consists of five subordinate headings and four paragraphs of body text—that is, everything up to the next heading at the same level. The second top-level heading has no subtext.

Notice also in Figure 24.1 that Word marks all headings that have subtext with a large plus icon, all headings without subtext with a large minus icon, and all paragraphs of body text with a small square icon. These icons will be referred to as *paragraph icons*. Later in the chapter, you will see several ways that you can manipulate a paragraph by using the mouse in conjunction with the paragraph icons.

You can create a new document in outline view, or you can work with an existing document in this view. If you open a new document and then immediately switch into outline view, the document will consist of a single top-level heading containing the insertion point. Each time you press ←, Word will insert another top-level heading beneath the one containing the insertion point, and it will move the insertion point to the beginning of this heading (in the same manner that Word inserts new paragraphs when you type text into a document in other views). In this chapter, you will see how to convert a heading to another level, and how to covert a heading to body text.

If you have already created a document in another view, and then switch into outline view, the document will initially consist of only body text (unless you have previously applied a heading style to one or more paragraphs). In this chapter, you will learn how to convert body text to a heading.

In this section, you will learn the following techniques:

- How to select text in outline view.

- How to promote or demote outline text; that is, how to change the level of a heading or convert between a heading and body text.

- How to collapse or expand an outline heading; that is, how to hide or reveal various amounts of subtext belonging to a heading.

- How to quickly move a heading—together with varying amounts of its subtext—within the document.

- How to use outline view to rapidly find a topic within a document.

You will learn both mouse and keyboard methods for each of these operations. Note that the keyboard methods can also be used when you are not in outline view.

SELECTING IN OUTLINE VIEW

The first step in performing many of the operations discussed in this chapter is to select the appropriate text within the outline. In general, you can use any of the basic selection methods discussed in Chapter 5. The following, however, are some unique features of selecting when in outline view:

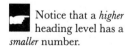
Notice that when the mouse pointer is on top of the paragraph icon, it becomes a four-pointed arrow.

- You can select a heading together with all of its subtext (whether expanded or collapsed) by clicking the paragraph icon or by double-clicking in the selection bar next to the paragraph.

- You can select one or more characters within a paragraph using a standard selection method (for example, by pressing an arrow key while holding down Shift). However, as soon as you extend the selection past a paragraph boundary, both adjoining paragraphs are selected.

PROMOTING AND DEMOTING OUTLINE TEXT

Using promoting and demoting techniques, you can change the level of a heading, convert body text to a heading, or convert a heading to body text.

Notice that a *higher* heading level has a *smaller* number.

The first step is to select the block of text in the outline that you want to promote or demote. You can select one or more headings or paragraphs of body text, using the methods described in Chapter 5 and in the previous section. To promote or demote a single heading or paragraph of body text, you can simply place the insertion point anywhere within the paragraph.

When you promote a heading (level 2 through level 9), it is assigned the next higher level. It is also moved to the left, together with any body text that immediately follows it (whether or not the body text is included in the selection). For example, a level 3 heading (assigned the style heading 3) becomes a level 2 heading (assigned the style heading 2).

Demoting a heading (level 1 through level 8) has the opposite effect. Namely, the heading is assigned the next lower level and is indented farther to the right, together with any body text that immediately follows it.

If you promote a paragraph of body text, it is converted to a heading having the same level as the heading immediately above it. If you demote a paragraph of body text, it is converted to a heading that is one level lower than the heading immediately above it.

Note, however, that to convert body text to a heading, the selection *cannot* contain a heading; if the selection contains a heading, body text can be moved, but it remains body text.

Once you have selected the desired block, you can use any of the following methods to promote or demote the selection:

- Use the icons on the outline icon bar. To promote the selection, click the left arrow on the icon bar.

  To demote the selection, click the right arrow (→) on the icon bar.

- Press the Alt-Shift-← keystroke to promote the selection, or press the Alt-Shift-→ keystroke to demote it.

- To promote a heading together with all of its subtext, drag the paragraph icon (the hollow plus sign preceding the heading level) to the left.

- To demote a heading and its subtext, drag the paragraph icon to the right. Notice that as soon as you click on a paragraph icon, Word automatically selects the heading together with all of its subtext. You therefore cannot use this method to promote or demote more than one heading at a time, or a heading without all of its subtext.

Assigning styles is discussed in Chapter 20.

According to the Word *User's Manual*, the Alt-Shift-5 keystroke (5 on the numeric keypad) is supposed to convert a heading to body text. On some computers, however, this keystroke does not work. Also, the *User's Manual* states that you can convert a heading to body text by "dragging it to the right"; this method, however, merely demotes the heading and does *not* convert it to body text.

Rather than selecting a single heading, you can simply place the insertion point within it.

- To promote or demote a heading or body text, you can simply assign it the desired style. For example, to demote a top-level heading one level, you can assign it the heading 2 style.

As you have seen, you can convert body text to a heading by simply promoting or demoting it. To convert a selected heading to a body text, you can use one of the following methods:

- Click the double-right-arrow icon within the outline icon bar.

- Assign the heading the Normal style, or some style other than heading 1 through heading 9.

COLLAPSING AND EXPANDING HEADINGS

To *collapse* a heading means to hide some or all of the subtext belonging to the heading. To *expand* a heading means to make visible subtext that was previously hidden. You can collapse and expand individual headings, or headings throughout the entire document.

Collapsing and Expanding Individual Headings

To collapse one or more headings, perform the following steps:

1. Select the desired heading or headings.
2. Click the – icon on the icon bar.

or press the minus key (–) on the numeric keypad, or press the Alt-Shift-minus keystroke (using either minus key).

Word will collapse the heading by one level; that is, it will hide the lowest-level subordinate heading that is currently visible. Note that

Notice that Word partially underlines a heading that is partly or fully collapsed, to let you know that the heading has hidden subtext.

body text is considered to be at a lower level than a level 9 heading. For instance, if the heading is fully expanded and includes body text, the first time you perform this step, all body text under the heading or under any of its subordinate headings is hidden.

3. Repeat step 2 for each additional level you want to collapse. If you continue to collapse levels, eventually only the heading itself will be visible.

Alternatively, you can double-click the paragraph icon next to the heading. If the heading is fully expanded, Word will completely collapse it (that is, it will hide all its subtext). If, however, it is partially or fully collapsed, Word will fully expand it.

To expand one or more headings, perform the following steps:

1. Select the desired heading or headings.

2. Click the + icon on the icon bar, press the plus key (+) on the numeric keypad, or press the Alt-Shift-plus keystroke (using either plus key).

Rather than selecting a single heading, you can simply place the insertion point within it.

Word will expand the heading by one level; that is, it will reveal the highest level of subtext that was previously hidden. For example, if a level 2 heading is completely collapsed, performing this step will display all level 3 subordinate headings that belong to it.

3. Repeat step 2 for each additional level you want to expand. If you continue to expand levels, eventually all subtext will be visible.

Alternatively, if the heading is fully or partially collapsed, you can fully expand it by double-clicking the paragraph icon belonging to the heading.

Collapsing and Expanding the Entire Outline

By clicking the appropriate numbered icon within the icon bar, you can collapse or expand headings throughout the entire outline.

If you click the icon numbered 1, Word will display only top-level headings; all headings with levels 2 through 9, as well as all body text, will be hidden. If you click the icon numbered 2, Word will display all headings with levels 1 or 2, and everything will be hidden; if you click the icon numbered 3, Word will display all headings with levels 1, 2, or 3; and so on. Clicking the icon numbered 9 will reveal all headings, but no body text. Finally, clicking the All icon will cause Word to display all headings and all body text (that is, the entire outline will become visible).

Rather than clicking a numbered icon, you can press the Alt-Shift-*number* keystroke, where *number* is a number between 1 and 9 indicating the heading levels you want visible. You must press a number key on the top row of the keyboard, rather than a number key on the numeric keypad. For example, pressing the Alt-Shift-3 keystroke is the same as clicking the icon numbered 3. Also, pressing Alt-Shift-A is the same as clicking the All icon.

Finally, if you press the Alt-Shift-F keystroke, Word will display *only the first line* of each paragraph of body text throughout the outline. Word indicates the presence of the hidden lines of body text by terminating each first line with an ellipsis (. . .). Pressing Alt-Shift-F again causes Word to display all lines of body text.

According to the Word *User's Guide,* pressing the Alt-Shift-* key combination (* on the numeric keypad) is the same as pressing the Alt-Shift-A keystroke or clicking the All icon. On some computers, however, this keystroke does not work.

Unless body text is already visible, you will not immediately see the effect of pressing Alt-Shift-F.

MOVING A HEADING AND ITS SUBTEXT

In outline view, you can easily move any of the following objects:

- A heading
- A heading together with some or all of its subtext
- Several headings, together with their subtext
- One or more paragraphs of body text

By moving headings together with their subtext, you can quickly rearrange a document.

The first step is to select the outline text you want to move. To move a single heading or paragraph of body text, you can simply place the insertion point anywhere within the paragraph. If you select a heading without its subtext, Word will move the heading, but will leave the subtext in its current position. If, however, a heading is collapsed, Word will move both the heading and its subtext, even if only the heading is selected.

You can now use one of the following methods:

- Click the ↑ on the icon bar to move the selection up in the outline.

- Click the ↓ on the icon bar to move the selection down in the outline.

- Press the Alt-Shift-↑ keystroke to move the selection up, or the Alt-Shift-↓ keystroke to move it down.

- Drag a paragraph icon either up or down. Using this method, you can move only a single paragraph of body text, or a heading together with all of its subtext.

USING OUTLINE VIEW TO FIND TOPICS

You can use outline view to help you find a topic within your document. This is done as follows:

1. While working with a document using another document view, you can switch into outline view by choosing the View/Outline menu command.

2. Collapse the outline so that only the desired level of headings is shown (see the section "Collapsing and Expanding the Entire Outline").

3. Scroll through the document to find the desired topic. You can scroll quickly, since only the headings are displayed.

4. When you find the desired location in the document, place the insertion point at this position.

5. Switch out of outline view. Word will display the beginning of the document.

6. Press Shift-F5 to scroll instantly to the position of the insertion point.

Alternatively, you can locate a desired position in your document by activating outline view in a separate window pane. Use the following steps:

See Chapter 26 for more information on working with split windows.

1. While working on a document in normal editing view, divide the window into two panes by dragging the split bar down to the approximate center of the screen.

2. Activate outline view in the pane containing the insertion point by choosing the View/Outline menu command. Notice that the *other* pane remains in normal editing view.

3. Collapse the outline to the desired level of headings.

4. Scroll through the outline to find the desired topic. Notice that the other pane (in normal editing view) *automatically scrolls to the same position in the document viewed through the pane in outline view.*

5. Once you have found the desired topic, you can now remove the outline pane by dragging the split bar all the way to the top of the window (if the outline pane is on top), or to the bottom of the window (if the outline pane is on the bottom).

NUMBERING OUTLINE HEADINGS

You can have Word number the headings within your outline, using the following steps:

Word will number only paragraphs that are currently displayed.

1. Collapse or expand the headings within your document to reveal the portions of the outline that you want to number.

2. Select the paragraphs within the document you want to number. If there is no selection, all visible paragraphs throughout the document will be numbered.

3. Choose the Utilities/Renumber menu command. Word will display the dialog box shown in Figure 24.2.

4. Select one of the three options in the Renumber Paragraphs area of the Utilities/Renumber dialog box.

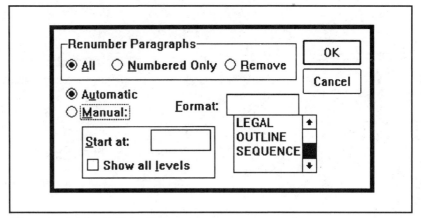

Figure 24.2: The Utilities/Renumber menu command

The Renumber Paragraph options have the following effects:

- **All**: Numbers all visible paragraphs that are currently selected (or all visible paragraphs in the entire document if there is no selection).

- **Numbered Only**: Numbers only the paragraphs that already have a number in front of them.

- **Remove**: Removes numbers that are in front of all visible selected paragraphs.

If you select automatic numbering, explained next, the actual values of the numbered paragraphs are ignored, and renumbering begins at 1. If you select manual numbering, Word uses the existing number of the first paragraph at a given outline level as the starting number.

5. Select either the Automatic or Manual option.

The **Automatic** option generates paragraph numbers that are automatically updated (kept in proper order) whenever you delete one or more paragraphs or rearrange paragraphs. (If, however, you insert a new paragraph, it is not automatically numbered; you have to issue the Utilities/Renumber command again.) Automatic numbering always begins with 1 or A; you cannot control the starting number.

Also, you can have only one sequence of numbers in a document (for example, you could not number top-level headings 1, 2, 3, and so on, in more than one location in the document).

The **Manual** option inserts paragraph numbers that are not updated automatically. If you delete, insert, or rearrange one or more paragraphs, you must update manual numbering by issuing the Utilities/ Renumber command again. With manual numbering, however, you can choose the starting number, and you can have more than one numbering sequence in the same document.

6. Choose a numbering format from the Format list.

If you have selected automatic numbering, you can choose the LEGAL, OUTLINE, or SEQUENCE numbering format. These formats are illustrated in Figure 24.3.

> If there are no existing numbers, choosing the LEARN format results in SEQUENCE numbering.

If you have selected manual numbering, you can choose any of these formats *or* the LEARN format. The LEARN format uses the format of existing numbers within the document. For each outline level, it uses the format of the first number at that level.

7. If you have selected manual numbering, you can now choose the starting number by entering it into the **Start at** box.

8. If you have selected manual numbering and the OUTLINE or SEQUENCE format, you can select the **Show all levels**

```
◊  1.  LEGAL numbering
    ◊  1.1.      LEGAL numbering
        ▫  1.1.1.     LEGAL numbering
◊  I.  OUTLINE numbering
    ◊  A. OUTLINE numbering
        ▫  1.  OUTLINE numbering
◊  1.  SEQUENCE numbering
    ◊  1.  SEQUENCE numbering
        ▫  1.  SEQUENCE numbering
```

Figure 24.3: Numbering formats for outlines

option to cause Word to include *all* levels in each paragraph number.

For example, these are several OUTLINE headings *without* the Show all levels option:

✧ I. **OUTLINE numbering**
   ✧ A. **OUTLINE numbering**
      ▫ 1. **OUTLINE numbering**

These are the same headings *with* the Show all levels option:

✧ I. **OUTLINE numbering**
   ✧ I.A.   **OUTLINE numbering**
      ▫ I.A.1.   **OUTLINE numbering**

CREATING A TABLE OF CONTENTS FROM OUTLINE HEADINGS

See Chapter 11 for additional information on creating tables of contents.

In Chapter 11, you learned how to create a table of contents from entries manually inserted into the document. If you have included outline headings in your document, you can also create a table of contents directly from these headings, without the need to manually insert table of contents entries. Once you have finished adding outline headings to your document, use the following steps to create a table of contents from these headings:

1. Place the insertion point at the position in your document where you want the table of contents.

2. Choose the Insert/Table of Contents menu command. Word will display the dialog box shown in Figure 24.4.

3. Select the Use Heading Paragraphs option within the Insert/ Table of Contents dialog box.

4. Select the All or From option.

Select All if you want Word to include all outline headings in the table of contents. Select the From option if you want Word to use only

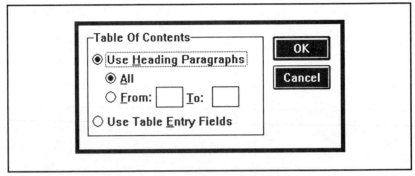

Figure 24.4: The Insert/Table of Contents dialog box

the outline headings within a range of levels, and enter the starting and ending levels into the From and To boxes. To use a single level, you can type the same number into both boxes.

You can use the From option to create several tables within a single document. For example, if you use outline levels 1 through 5 for topic headings, and outline level 6 for figure captions, you could create a general table of contents by specifying outline levels 1 through 5, and *also* create a table of figures by specifying level 6 headings.

5. Click the OK button. Word will insert the table of contents at the position of the insertion point.

SUMMARY

- In outline view, you can visualize and reorganize the overall structure of your document.

- To switch into outline view, choose the View/Outline menu command. To switch out of outline view, choose this command again.

- In outline view, a document consists of headings (paragraphs assigned the special predefined styles heading 1 through heading 9), and body text (paragraphs having any other style).

- A heading is assigned one of nine different levels. A level 1 heading is a top-level heading and is not indented in outline view. A level 2 heading is considered the next lower level, and is indented. Each subsequent level is indented farther to the right.

- The term *subtext* refers to all subordinate headings, as well as all body text, that immediately follow an outline heading.

- In outline view, you can quickly select a heading, together with all its subtext, by clicking the paragraph icon to the left of the heading.

- You can *promote* a heading to a higher level (or convert body text to a heading) by selecting it and then clicking the ← icon on the outline icon bar, by pressing the Alt-Shift-← key, or by dragging the paragraph icon to the left. You can *demote* the selected heading to a lower level by clicking the → icon, by pressing the Alt-Shift-→ key, or by dragging the paragraph icon to the right.

- You can convert a heading to body text by selecting it and then clicking the double-right-arrow icon on the icon bar, or by applying a style other than a heading style.

- You can *collapse* a heading (hide subtext) by selecting it and either clicking the − icon on the icon bar or pressing the − key on the numeric keypad. You can *expand* a heading (display subtext) by selecting it and clicking either the + icon on the icon bar or pressing the + key on the numeric keypad.

- You can collapse or expand headings throughout the entire outline to the desired level by clicking one of the numeric icons on the outline icon bar. Clicking the All icon will display all headings and subtext throughout the outline.

- You can move a heading (with or without its subtext), or a paragraph of body text, by selecting it and then clicking the ↑ or ↓ on the outline icon bar, or pressing the Alt-Shift-↑ or Alt-Shift-↓ keystroke.

- When working on a document in another document view, you can temporarily switch into outline view, or activate outline view in a separate window pane, to make it easy to find a topic.

- You can have Word automatically number the headings in your outline by issuing the Utilities/Renumber menu command, and specifying the desired options in the dialog box.

- To create a table of contents from outline headings, use the Insert/Table of Contents command.

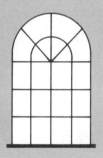

25

ADDING ANNOTATIONS AND MARKING REVISIONS

THIS CHAPTER PRESENTS TWO WORD FEATURES
that help you to work with other authors and editors, and to develop
the final version of your document: annotations and revision marking. Annotations allow you or another writer to add comments to a
document. Revision marks help you keep track of the changes you
make to a document.

ADDING ANNOTATIONS ─────────

Using annotations, you can add comments to a document without
inserting them directly into the document text. Each annotation is
labeled with the initials of the person who wrote it. Thus, if several
people are working on the same document, annotations allow them

to exchange comments and ideas on the manuscript without altering the manuscript itself.

Like a footnote, an annotation consists of two elements: the annotation mark and the annotation text. The annotation mark contains the initials of the creator of the annotation plus a number identifying that annotation. It is inserted into the document text, but it is formatted as hidden text so that it will normally not appear on the printed copy of the document. The annotation mark should be placed within the portion of the document that is discussed in the annotation text.

The annotation text is displayed in a separate window pane; it is *not* part of the document itself. The annotation text begins with the same annotation mark inserted into the document, so that you can find the text that goes with a particular mark.

Figure 25.1 illustrates a document containing annotations, and an open annotation pane.

The following are the steps for adding an annotation to a document:

1. Choose the Insert/Annotation menu command.

Word will open an annotation window pane (as shown in Figure 25.1), it will automatically insert the annotation mark into the document (as hidden text) *and* into the annotation pane, and it will place the insertion point after this mark in the annotation pane.

The initials incorporated into the annotation mark are the author's initials that you entered the first time you ran Word. You can *change*

While the annotation pane is open, Word automatically turns on the Hidden Text option within the View/ Preferences dialog box, so that you can see the annotation marks within the document. If the annotation pane is not open, you can turn on this option so that annotation marks remain visible.

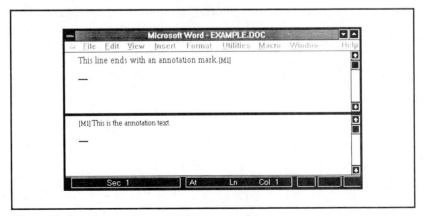

Figure 25.1: A document containing annotations

The Utilities/ Customize dialog box is discussed near the end of Chapter 23.

the author's initials at any time by entering the desired character or characters into the Your Initials box within the Utilities/Customize dialog box.

If another person works on your document, using a different copy of Word on a different machine, the annotations entered by this person will normally contain *different* initials. You can thus identify the writer of an annotation.

Notice that the annotation mark also contains a number. The first annotation entered by a person is numbered 1, the second annotation entered by the same person is numbered 2, and so on. If annotations are subsequently inserted or deleted, Word maintains the correct numbering.

2. You can now type the text for the annotation directly into the annotation pane. To move the insertion point back and forth between the annotation pane and the document pane, press the F6 key or click in the desired pane.

3. Once you have completed entering the annotation text, you can either leave the annotation pane open, or you can close it. To close the annotation pane, drag the split bar all the way to the top or the bottom of the window, *or* turn off the View/ Annotations menu option.

4. You can later edit the annotation. First open the annotation pane, if necessary, by turning on the View/Annotations menu option, or by pressing the Ctrl key while dragging the split bar down the window. You can then use standard techniques to edit the annotation text.

When you insert an annotation, the View/Annotations menu option is automatically turned on. You can manually turn it off to remove the annotation pane. If the annotation pane is not visible, you can manually turn it on to display it.

You can copy annotation text into the document itself using any of the techniques for copying text explained in Chapter 5.

You can *delete* an annotation by selecting the annotation mark in the document, and pressing the Del key. Word will remove both the annotation mark and the associated annotation text.

You can also move an annotation mark *together with its associated annotation text* by simply moving the annotation mark. To move the annotation mark, you can cut and paste it as described in Chapter 5.

CHANGING ANNOTATION FORMATTING

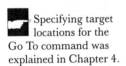
You can change the formatting features of annotation marks or text by redefining the corresponding automatic style, as explained in Chapter 20.

Annotation marks are assigned the automatic style annotation reference, and paragraphs of annotation text are assigned the automatic style annotation text. The features of these styles are listed in Table 20.1 in Chapter 20.

FINDING ANNOTATION MARKS AND READING ANNOTATIONS

You can use the Word Go To command to move the insertion point to a specific annotation mark in your document by means of the following steps:

1. Choose the Edit/Go To menu command, or press the F5 key.

2. At the prompt, type **a** to go to the *next* annotation mark, or **a** and a number to go to a specific annotation mark.

Specifying target locations for the Go To command was explained in Chapter 4.

Here are several examples using Go To:

INSTRUCTION	MOVES INSERTION POINT TO:
a4	The fourth annotation within the document
a + 3	The third annotation mark after the insertion point
a – 2	The second annotation before the insertion point
a	The *next* annotation in the document

Once you have located the desired annotation mark in the document, you can read or edit the corresponding annotation text in the annotation pane.

Notice that the annotation pane is linked with the document pane. When you scroll through the document, Word automatically scrolls the text in the annotation pane, if necessary, to display the text corresponding to the annotation mark near the insertion point in the document pane. Likewise, if you scroll through the annotation pane,

Word automatically scrolls the document pane, if necessary, to display the annotation mark corresponding to the annotation text near the insertion point in the annotation pane.

PRINTING ANNOTATIONS

Normally, annotations do not appear on the printed copy of the document. By selecting appropriate print options, however, you can either print the document together with all annotations, or print *only* the annotations attached to a document.

You can print both the document and the annotations as follows:

1. Choose the File/Print menu command.

2. Click the Options button within the File/Print dialog box.

3. Select the Annotations option within the Include area of the dialog box.

4. Click the OK button to begin printing.

Word will print all hidden text, including annotation marks, and will print all annotation text *after* the document text. The text for each annotation will include the page number of the annotation mark, the creator's initials, and the annotation number.

To print only the annotations, perform the following steps:

1. Choose the File/Print menu command.

2. Select the Annotations item from the Print pull-down list within the File/Print dialog box.

3. Click the OK button to begin printing.

The text for each annotation will include the page number of the annotation mark, plus the initials of the writer of the annotation and the annotation number.

LOCKING A DOCUMENT

If you *lock* a document when you save it, only you or another user of your copy of Word will be able to modify the document. People

Menu commands and options that change the document content are displayed in gray and cannot be selected.

using other copies of Word on other machines will be able to add annotations, but will not be able to modify the document.

Use the following steps to lock a document:

1. Choose the File/Save As menu command, or press the F12 or Alt-F2 keystroke.

2. Click the Options button within the dialog box to reveal additional options.

3. Select the Lock for Annotations option.

4. Click the OK button. Word will save the document under its original name, as a locked document.

You can later unlock the document by saving it with the File/Save As command and turning *off* the Lock for Annotations option before saving the file. Only the author of the document can lock or unlock a document (if the current user is not the author, this option is grayed).

How does Word know who the author of the document is? When you first ran the Word program, you entered an author's name. The first time you save a new document, Word stores the author's name within the document, to identify the author of the document.

You can change the author's name by entering another name into the Your Name box within the Utilities/Customize dialog box (see Chapter 23).

If a document is locked and the author's name stored within the document does not match the author's name stored by the current copy of the Word program, Word will not permit changes to the document. You can defeat this mechanism, however, by changing the name entered into the Your Name field of the Utilities/Customize dialog box to match the name of the author of the document.

MARKING REVISIONS

You can have Word mark all additions or deletions of text within a document, either as you make the changes or by comparing the current document with a previous version.

Word marks each change in the document as follows:

If you print the document, all revision markings will appear on the printed copy (unless you have disabled their display).

- It places a vertical line in the margin adjacent to the change. This line is known as a *revision bar.* If desired, you can prevent Word from printing revision bars.

- If you delete text, Word leaves the text in the document, but formats it as strikethrough characters.

| ~~This line has been deleted. It is formatted as strikethrough text.~~

- If you add new text, Word marks it in the manner you specify (for example, by formatting it as underlined characters). If desired, you can prevent Word from marking new text.

Figure 25.2 illustrates a paragraph containing revision marks.

> This paragraph contains revision markings. ~~This sentence has been deleted.~~ <u>This sentence has been added.</u>

Figure 25.2: Text with revision marks

As you will see later in the chapter, you can *remove* revision marking, either accepting or undoing all marked revisions.

MARKING CHANGES AS YOU MAKE THEM

To begin marking revisions in your document as you make them, use the following procedure:

1. Choose the Utilities/Revision Marks menu command. Word will open the dialog box shown in Figure 25.3.

2. Select the Mark Revisions option.

3. Choose the type of revision bars you want Word to display by selecting an option from the Revision Bars area.

The Revision Bars options have the following effects:

OPTION	EFFECT
None	Revision bars are eliminated.
Left	Revision bars are printed in the left margins.

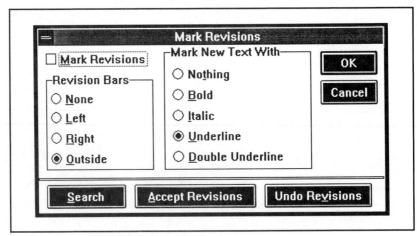

Figure 25.3: The Utilities/Revision Marks dialog box

OPTION	EFFECT
Right	Revision bars are printed in the right margin.
Outside	Revision bars are printed in the left margin on even-numbered (left-hand) pages and in the right margin on odd numbered (right-hand) pages. If the document is printed on both sides of the page, the revision marks will always be on the outside.

Note that even if you choose the Right or Outside option, the revision marks will be displayed within the *left* margin in normal editing view (galley view). They will appear in the designated margin in Page View and Print Preview, and on the printed copy.

4. Choose an option specifying the way you want Word to mark new text from the Mark New Text With area.

The Mark New Text With options have the following effects:

OPTION	EFFECT
Nothing	New text is not marked; however, if you have enabled revision bars, Word will display and print a revision bar adjacent to the new text.

OPTION	*EFFECT*
Bold	New text is formatted as bold characters.
Italic	New text is formatted as italic characters.
Underline	New text is formatted as underlined characters.
Double Underline	New text is formatted as double-underlined characters.

5. Click the OK button. Word will begin marking all insertions or deletions within the current document.

Note that you can later open the Utilities/Mark Revision dialog box and change either the Revision Bars option or the Mark New Text With option. The change you make will affect not only subsequent markings, but also all markings already in the current document.

Although you can choose the type of revision bars and the marking style for new text, deleted text is always marked with strikethrough characters.

Later in the chapter, you will see how to remove the existing markings, either permanently implementing the changes or undoing them.

You can stop revision marking by selecting the Utilities/Revision Marks command again, turning off the Mark Revisions option, and clicking the OK button. Word will no longer mark revisions; however, any markings made previously will remain intact.

COMPARING WITH A PREVIOUS VERSION OF THE DOCUMENT

Rather than having Word mark all changes to the current document as you make them, you can have Word mark all changes in the current document *compared to a previous version of the document*. Use the following steps:

1. Choose the Utilities/Compare Versions menu command. Word will display the dialog box illustrated in Figure 25.4.

2. Type the name of the former version of the document into the Compare File Name box. Alternatively, you can select the name by means of the Files and Directories lists; use the

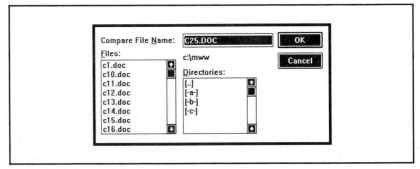

Figure 25.4: The Utilities/Compare Versions dialog box

techniques explained for the Open command in Chapter 3, in the section "Opening a Document within Word."

3. Click the OK button.

Word will mark all characters *added* to the previous version by formatting them as underlined text. If, however, you previously issued the Utilities/Revision Marks command and specified a different marking style, it will use the indicated style. Also, Word marks each paragraph containing added text with a revision mark (unless you previously issued the Utilities/Revision Marks command and disabled revision marks).

Unfortunately, however, Word does not indicate text that was *deleted* in the current version but present in the document on disk. Also, Word is overzealous in marking added text. For example, if you inserted text at the beginning of a paragraph, it marks the *entire* paragraph as new text.

SEARCHING FOR REVISIONS

You can find revision marks in your document as follows:

1. Issue the Utilities/Revision Marks menu command.

2. Click the Search button within the Utilities/Revision Marks dialog box.

Word will highlight the first revision mark it finds past the position of the insertion point, and will leave the dialog box open. If you have selected text, Word searches from the beginning of the selection, but does not confine its search to the selection. When Word reaches the end of the document, it asks you if you want to continue searching from the beginning; click the Yes button to continue the search.

3. To search for the next revision mark, click the Search button again.

When you search for revisions using the Utilities/Revision Marks dialog box, Word highlights either new *or* deleted text. Alternatively, you can search specifically for new text or for deleted text using the following method:

See Chapter 6 for information on other options available when using the Edit/ Search menu command.

1. Choose the Edit/Search menu command. Word will display a dialog box.

2. Delete any text within the Search For box.

3. While the insertion point is in the Search For box, type Ctrl-N to find new text, or Ctrl-Z to find deleted text.

4. Click the OK button.

ACCEPTING OR UNDOING REVISIONS

To accept all revisions within the current selection (or within the entire document if there is no selection), click the Accept Revisions button within the Utilities/Revision Marks dialog box. Word will remove all revision marking and will permanently incorporate all changes into the document. Specifically, clicking the Accept Revisions button has the following effects:

- Text formatted as strikethrough characters is deleted.

- Text that is marked as new (formatted as you specified) is permanently inserted into the document, with the marking removed.

- Revision bars are removed from the margins.

To reverse all revisions within the current selection (or within the entire document if there is no selection), click the Undo Revisions button. This will remove any revisions made since you enabled revision marking, or any revisions marked in the current document after issuing the Utilities/Compare Versions command. It also removes all revision marking. Specifically, clicking the Undo Revisions button has the following effects:

- Text formatted in strikethrough characters is left in the document, but the strikethrough formatting is removed.

- Text that is marked as new (formatted as you specified) is deleted.

- Revision bars are removed from the margins.

SUMMARY

- An annotation is a comment attached to a specific location in a document.

- An annotation consists of an annotation mark, which is inserted into the document text as hidden text, and annotation text, which is displayed in a separate window pane.

- An annotation mark contains the initials of the person who enters it, as well as a number identifying the specific annotation entered by that person.

- To enter an annotation at the current position of the insertion point, choose the Insert/Annotation menu command and type the text for the annotation into the separate window pane that Word opens.

- You can find annotations in your document by choosing the Edit/Go To menu command, or by pressing F5, and typing **a** followed by the number of the annotation you want to find (type **a** alone to find the *next* annotation).

- You can lock a document so that anyone can enter annotations, but only the author can make changes to the document. Save the file using the File/Save As command, selecting the Lock for Annotations option.

- You can have Word mark all additions or deletions of text within the current document by choosing the Utilities/Revision Marks menu command, selecting the Mark Revisions option, and clicking the OK button. You can also specify the location of the revision bar that Word places in the margin adjacent to each revision, and the character formatting that Word uses to mark new text. Word always marks deleted text using strikethrough characters.

- Alternatively, you can have Word mark all changes to the current document compared to a previous version of the document, by means of the Utilities/Compare Versions menu command.

- You can search for marked revisions in the document by clicking the Search button in the Utilities/Revision Marks dialog box.

- You can remove revision marks and permanently incorporate the changes into the document by clicking the Accept Revisions button in the Utilities/Revision Marks dialog box.

- You can remove revision marks and eliminate the revisions by clicking the Undo Revisions button in the Utilities/Revision Marks dialog box.

26

Managing Collections of Documents

AFTER WORKING WITH WORD FOR A WHILE, YOU MAY acquire a large collection of documents. In this chapter, you will learn how to use Word's document retrieval facility to help you find documents and perform operations on groups of documents. You will then learn how to manage Word windows so that you can work with several open documents at the same time.

RETRIEVING DOCUMENTS

Using the File/Find command, you can obtain a list of Word documents or files in other formats that match a specified set of search criteria. For example, you can obtain a list of all documents written by a particular author; or a list of all documents created within a certain range of dates. Once you have obtained the list, you can use the File/

Find dialog box to perform any of the following operations:

- Sort the list of documents
- Open documents on the list
- Print documents on the list
- Delete documents on the list
- Read or edit summary information for documents on the list

OBTAINING A LIST OF DOCUMENTS

For more information on DOS directories, see Appendix A.

To obtain a list of documents matching a set of search criteria, choose the File/Find menu command. The first time you issue this command, Word will automatically begin constructing a list of all documents on the current disk drive (that is, all files with the .DOC extension, in all directories). This process can be quite lengthy; if you want to stop it, click the Cancel button or press Esc. When Word finishes compiling the list of files (or if you abort the search), it displays the File/Find dialog box, which is illustrated in Figure 26.1. This dialog box contains the names of all documents obtained in the search (if you stopped the search, the list will contain only the files found before the search was aborted).

To obtain a list of documents matching a narrower set of criteria, click the Search button. Word will now open the dialog box shown in Figure 26.2.

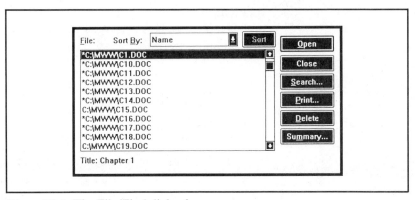

Figure 26.1: The File/Find dialog box

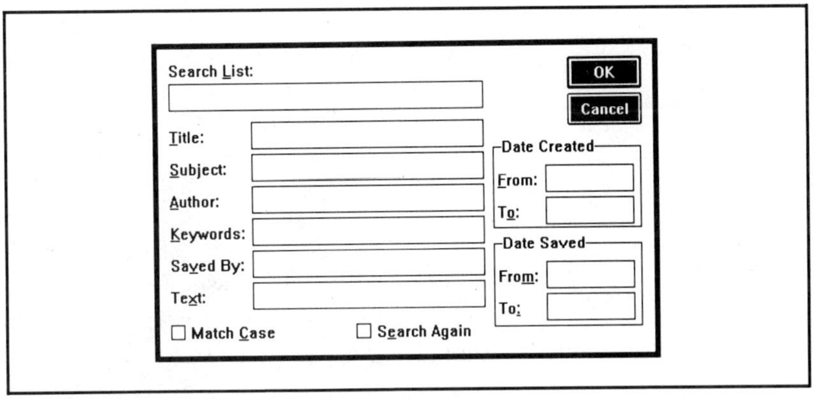

Figure 26.2: The Search dialog box

You should first specify the location and possibly the general name of the documents you want to search by entering one or more path names into the Search List box. Each path name should include the full name of a directory. For example, the following path name would cause Word to search *all* documents (that is, files with the .DOC extension) in the \DOCUMENT\LETTERS directory on the current disk drive:

\DOCUMENT\LETTERS

A path name can also include a general file name, specified using the standard DOS wildcard characters (* and ?; see Appendix A). For example, the following path name would cause Word to search all documents beginning with CHAP, in the \BOOK directory on drive C:

C:\BOOK\CHAP*.DOC

The following path name would cause Word to search all files with the .TXT extension in the BIRD directory on the current drive:

\BIRD*.TXT

You can include more than one path name, separating each name with a comma or semicolon. For example, the following path name would cause Word to search all documents in the \CARP directory *and* all documents with the .TXT extension in the \GUPPY directory, on the current disk drive:

`\CARP;\GUPPY\*.TXT`

If you leave the Search List box empty, Word will search for all documents in all directories on the current disk drive.

You can specify additional search criteria by entering the appropriate text into one or more of the other text boxes within the Search dialog box. The other criteria you can specify are summarized in Table 26.1. Notice that many of these criteria are based upon items contained in the document summary information. For example, if you type **Ivan** into the Author box in the Search dialog box, Word will list only files that contain the name Ivan in the Author field of the document summary information.

If you do not specify any of the criteria listed in Table 26.1, Word will list all files that conform to the path names listed in the Search List box. If you specify one or more of the criteria in Table 26.1, Word will *combine* the criteria. For example, if you enter the following path name into the Search List box

`\LETTERS`

and the following name into the Author box

T. Jones

Word will list the names of all documents that are in the LETTERS directory on the current disk drive *and* are written by T. Jones. If, in addition to specifying an Author criteria, you also entered the following word into the Keywords box

nasturtium

Word will list the names of all documents that are in the LETTERS directory on the current disk drive, are written by T. Jones, *and* contain the keyword **nasturtium** in the Keywords box of the document summary information.

In the section "Reading and Editing Document Summary Information," you will learn how to read and edit the summary information belonging to any document.

Table 26.1: Criteria for Finding Documents

OPTIONAL SEARCH CRITERIA:	EFFECT IF YOU ENTER TEXT INTO SEARCH CRITERIA BOX.
Title	Lists documents that have this text within the Title box of the document summary information.
Subject	Lists documents that have this text within the Subject box of the document summary information.
Author	Lists documents that have this text within the Author box of the document summary information.
Keywords	Lists documents that have this text within the Keywords box of the document summary information.
Saved By	Lists documents that have this text within the name of author who last saved the document (the name is displayed in the Last saved by field of the Statistics dialog box).
Text	Lists documents that contain this text (document must not have been saved with the Fast Save option).
Date Created	Lists documents created within the range of dates specified in From and To boxes.
Date Saved	Lists documents last saved within the range of dates specified in From and To boxes.

Note that the text you enter into a criteria box need only match a *portion* of the text in the corresponding box of the document summary information. For example, entering **T** into the Author box of the Search dialog box would match documents with any of the following names in the Author box of the document summary information: T. Jones, John Tussey, or Tomaso Albinoni.

In the File list, Word displays an asterisk (*) in front of the name of each document saved with the Fast Save option.

Note also that entering characters into the Text box causes Word to search for text within the document itself, rather than within the document summary information. Searching for text, however, is unreliable if you have saved one or more of the searched documents using the Fast Save option. If you want to search for specific text within documents, you should save the documents without the Fast Save option, using the following steps:

1. Choose the File/Save As menu command. Word will display a dialog box.

2. Click the Options button within this dialog box, and turn off the Fast Save option.

3. Click OK to save the document.

Unfortunately, you must repeat this entire procedure each time you want to save the document, since Word automatically turns the Fast Save option back on after you have turned it off.

When you type text into a text box (other than the Search List box) within the Search dialog box, you can also enter one or more of the special characters described in Table 26.2. For example, if you entered the following expression into the Text box, Word would search for documents containing the word **Partridge** *and* the word **Sophia** (the two words do *not* need to be together in the document):

Partridge & Sophia

If you select the Match Case option within the Search dialog box, Word will search for the exact combination of uppercase and lowercase letters entered into the Text box. If the Match Case option is not selected, Word will ignore the case of all letters when searching for text within documents. The Match Case option does not affect criteria other than that specified in the Text box.

Normally, Word searches *all* files specified by the path names in the Search List box. If, however, you select the Search Again option, Word will search only the files already listed in the File/Find dialog box. This option is useful for narrowing a list of files. For example, you might conduct a search and obtain a long list of files. You could

Table 26.2: Special Characters You Can Enter into the Text for Document Search Criteria

CHARACTER:	EFFECT:
?	Matches any single character (for example, **a?e** would match **abe**, **ace**, **age**, and so on).
*	Matches any group of one or more characters (for example, **a*** would match **at**, **ace**, **apple**, and so on).
^	Treats the following special character as a normal character (for example, **^?** would match a question mark).
,	Means "or" (for example, entering **bat, cat** into the Keywords box would cause Word to search for documents that have either **bat** *or* **cat**, or both, within the Keywords box of the document summary information).
&	Means "and" (for example, entering **bat & cat** into the Keywords box would cause Word to search for documents that have *both* **bat** *and* **cat** within the Keywords box of the document summary information).
~	Means "not" (for example, entering **~bat** into the Keywords box would cause Word to search for documents that do *not* have the word **bat** within the Keywords box of the document summary information).

then click the Search button again and add one or more search criteria to eliminate unwanted files from the list. Rather than having Word again search *all* files specified in the Search List box, you can have it search only the files already in the list by turning on the Search Again option.

When you have specified all desired criteria and options within the Search dialog box, click the OK button. Word will compile a list of all documents that meet your specifications. It will remove the Search dialog box, and display the list of documents within the File/Find dialog box. You can now select one or more of these files and perform any of the operations described in the following sections.

To close the File/Find dialog box, click the Cancel or Close button. The next time you open the dialog box by choosing the File/Find command, Word will display the same set of documents. If changes have occurred within the search directories, Word will perform the search again and display an updated version of the list. It will use the same criteria previously entered into the Search dialog box. You can work with this list, or you can obtain a new list of files by clicking the Search button and revising the search criteria.

The Cancel button becomes the Close button after you perform an operation with the dialog box.

SORTING THE LIST

Once Word has built a list of documents, you can sort this list using the desired sorting order. To sort the list, perform the following two steps:

1. Select the desired sorting order from the Sort By pull-down list in the File/Find dialog box (see Figure 26.3).

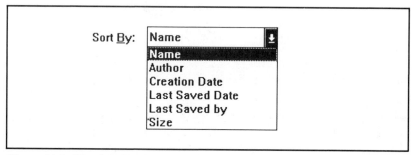

Figure 26.3: The Sort By list

The sorting options are explained in Table 26.3. Note that merely selecting a new sorting option does *not* cause Word to sort the list.

2. Click the Sort button.

If more than one file is selected, it displays the information for the *first* selected file in the list.

Word displays information on the selected file at the bottom of the dialog box. The information that Word displays depends upon the sort order you selected in the Sort By box. For example, if you

Table 26.3: File Sorting Orders

SORT OPTION:	EFFECT:
Name	Sorts files alphabetically by file name.
Author	Sorts files alphabetically by Author name field of document summary information.
Creation Date	Sorts files chronologically by date of creation.
Last Saved Date	Sorts files chronologically by date of most recent save.
Last Saved By	Sorts files alphabetically by name of the user who most recently saved each file.
Size	Sorts files from smallest to largest.

sort files by creation date, Word will display the creation date of the selected file.

OPENING DOCUMENTS

You cannot open more than nine documents at the same time (this is the maximum number of open windows).

To open one or more documents listed in the File/Find dialog box, first select the name or names from the list. To select more than one name, hold down the Shift key while clicking each desired name in the list. Next, click the Open button. Word will remove the File/Find dialog box and will open the selected documents, each one in a separate window.

See the section "Opening Several Document Windows," later in the chapter, for information on managing windows.

You can also open a single file in the File list by double-clicking the file name.

PRINTING DOCUMENTS

You can print one or more files in the File list by selecting the file or files, and then clicking the Print button. Before printing the files, Word will display the File/Print dialog box, which was explained in Chapter 17. The options you enter into this dialog box, such as a printing a range of pages, will affect all of the documents printed (Word displays the dialog box only once, before printing the first document).

DELETING DOCUMENTS

You can delete one or more files in the File list by selecting the file or files, and then clicking the Delete button. Word will display a message box, asking you to confirm the deletion of the files. After performing the deletion, Word leaves the File/Find dialog box open.

READING AND EDITING DOCUMENT SUMMARY INFORMATION

As you saw in Chapter 1, when you first save a new document, Word automatically prompts you for document summary information (unless you have turned off the Prompt for Summary Info option within the Utilities/Customize dialog box). Word stores the document summary information in the disk file, together with the document text.

You can add or revise the document summary information for a document within the File list of the File/Find dialog box, by selecting the name of the file and clicking the Summary button. Word will display the Summary Information dialog box, which is illustrated in Figure 26.4. This is the same dialog box that is automatically displayed when you first save a new document and you are prompted for summary information. Opening the Document Summary Information dialog box for a document does not cause Word to open the document itself.

You can also add or revise the document summary information for the current document by choosing the Edit/ Summary Info menu command.

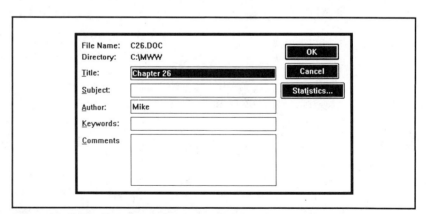

Figure 26.4: The Document Summary Information dialog box

Table 26.4 summarizes each of the items you can enter into the Document Summary Information dialog box. You can enter up to 255 characters for each item.

If you click the Statistics button within the Document Summary Information dialog box, Word will display the Statistics dialog box, which shows a variety of information on the current document. The Statistics dialog box is illustrated in Figure 26.5. Note that the three items at the bottom of the dialog box, following the label **As of last update**, may not contain the current correct values. They are updated, however, when you print the entire document or click the Update button within the Statistics dialog box.

You can print the document summary information, either by itself or together with the document. To print the document summary information alone, select the Summary Info item from the Print list

Table 26.4: Items You Can Enter into the Document Summary Information Dialog Box

ITEM:	PURPOSE:
Title	A title for the document. You can enter a more descriptive name than that provided by the file name (which can be only eight characters long).
Subject	A description of the content of the document.
Author	The name of the writer of the document. Word initially inserts the name from the Your Name box in the Utilities/Customize dialog box. If desired, you can enter another name.
Keywords	One or more words, each of which describes an important topic or term covered in the document. The words should be separated by a space. Supplying keywords makes it easy to find the desired document through the File/Find command (you can enter a keyword into the Keywords box within the Search dialog box).
Comments	Free-form notes on the document for future reference.

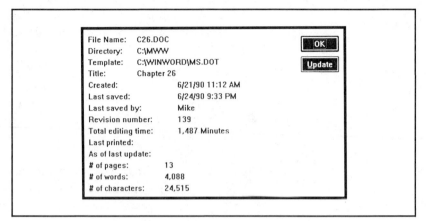

File Name:	C26.DOC	
Directory:	C:\MWW	
Template:	C:\WINWORD\MS.DOT	
Title:	Chapter 26	
Created:	6/21/90 11:12 AM	
Last saved:	6/24/90 9:33 PM	
Last saved by:	Mike	
Revision number:	139	
Total editing time:	1,487 Minutes	
Last printed:		
As of last update:		
# of pages:	13	
# of words:	4,088	
# of characters:	24,515	

Figure 26.5: The Statistics dialog box

box within the File/Print dialog box. To print the document summary information together with the document, choose the Document item from the Print list box, and turn on the Summary Info option within the Include area of the File/Print dialog box (to reveal this option, you must click the Options button).

As you have seen, supplying document summary information for a document is optional. However, providing this information can make it easier to find a specific document, using the File/Find command as described previously in the chapter.

WORKING WITH WINDOWS IN WORD

In this section, you will learn how to work with the various windows belonging to the Word program. Specifically, you will learn the following techniques:

- How to work with the Word window

- How to work with a document window

- How to open and manage several documents at the same time

- How to work with a single document in several windows

- How to split a window

If you need more information on any of these methods, read the user's guide accompanying your copy of Windows, or the booklet *Basic Skills for Windows Applications,* supplied with Word for Windows.

Before reading this section, you should be familiar with the following basic Microsoft Windows techniques for manipulating a window:

- Maximizing, minimizing, and restoring a window
- Moving a window on the screen
- Adjusting the size of a window

WORKING WITH THE WORD WINDOW

The term *Word window* refers to the main window displayed by the Word program. The following features belong to the Word window:

- A title bar at the top of the window, with the label **Microsoft Word**. If the active document window (discussed shortly) is maximized (that is, expanded to fill the entire area within the Word window), this title bar also contains the name of the active document.

- The Word control icon

which opens into the Word control menu (see Figure 26.6).

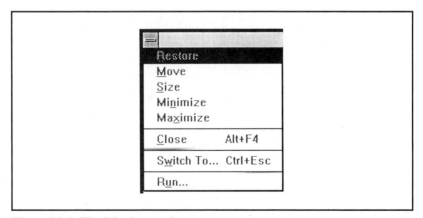

Figure 26.6: The Word control menu

- Minimize and maximize (or restore) icons

- The menu bar. If the active document window is maximized, the document control menu icon for this window is placed at the left end of the menu bar.

- The status bar (provided that the View/Status Bar menu option is turned on).

The Word window may contain one or more document windows. It is the *parent* of these windows, which means that the document windows are always contained within the boundaries of the Word window.

When you first run the Word program, the Word window is maximized so that it fills the entire screen. You can restore it to a window that fills only a portion of the Windows screen by clicking the restore icon.

You can now move the Word window anywhere on the screen, and you can adjust its size. If you click the minimize icon (the downward-pointing triangle) on the Word window, it is reduced to the program icon:

WORKING WITH A DOCUMENT WINDOW

Each open document is displayed within a *document window*. A document window is a *child* of the Word window, meaning that it is always contained within the boundaries of the Word window. A document window contains the following elements:

- A title bar at the top of the window containing the name of the document. If the document window is maximized, it shares a title bar with the main Word window; the shared title bar contains both the label **Microsoft Word** and the name of the document.

 If the document window is maximized, the document control icon will be displayed at the left end of the menu bar belonging to the Word window; otherwise, it is displayed at the left end of the title bar belonging to the document window.

- The document control icon

which opens into the document control menu (Figure 26.7).

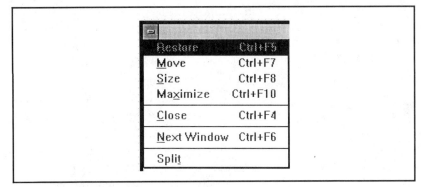

Figure 26.7: The document control menu

- A maximize icon (an upward-pointing triangle), unless the window is already maximized.

- A vertical scroll bar, provided that the Vertical Scroll Bar option within the View/Preferences dialog box is turned on.

- A horizontal scroll bar, provided that the Horizontal Scroll Bar option within the View/Preferences dialog box is turned on.

When you first run Word and open a document, the document window is maximized, meaning that it fills the entire available space within the Word window. To reduce the document window so that it fills only a portion of the Word window, choose the Restore item on the document control menu.

When the document window is no longer maximized, you can move it or change its size, using standard techniques. However, the document window always remains within the boundaries of the Word window.

OPENING SEVERAL DOCUMENT WINDOWS

If a document is displayed in more than one window, the title bar of each document window is numbered to identify the particular window.

When you open a document within Word, the document you are working on (if any) is not closed. Rather, Word opens an *additional* document window. Also, if you choose the Window/New Window menu command, Word will open another window containing the *same* document you are currently working on. Therefore, at a given time, Word can contain up to nine open document windows.

The document window you are working within is known as the *active document window*. Its title bar is highlighted, it contains the insertion point (or selection), and menu commands act upon it. You can switch among open document windows (that is, activate the next open document window) by pressing the Ctrl-F6 keystroke, or by choosing the name of the desired document from the Window menu. You can also switch between windows by clicking the mouse in the window you wish to make active (if it is visible on the screen).

When several documents are open at the same time, you can easily exchange text among them using the Windows Clipboard, as described in Chapter 5.

You can arrange the document windows within the Word window so that you can view more than one of them at a time. Use the standard techniques for moving and changing the size of windows to arrange them in a convenient pattern. If the active window is currently maximized, you will first have to reduce its size by choosing the Restore command from the document control menu.

Alternatively, you can choose the Window/Arrange All menu command. Word will automatically arrange the open document windows so that they may all be viewed at the same time.

To close the active window, double-click the document control icon, choose the Close item from the document control menu, or press the Ctrl-F4 keystroke. If the current document is contained in more than one window, this command will close the current window, but *not* the document itself (that is, all other windows containing the document remain open). Alternatively, if you choose the File/Close menu command, Word will close the current document itself by closing *all* windows containing the document.

SPLITTING A WINDOW

If you want to see two views of the same document, it may be easier to split the active document window, rather than opening a new window. When a window is split into two panes, you can scroll independently in each pane, and you can edit the document in either pane. To move the insertion point from one pane to another, press the F6 key or simply click in the other pane.

To split a window using the mouse, drag the split bar (the black bar at the top of the vertical scroll bar) down the window to the point where you want to split the window. You can adjust the size of the panes at any time by dragging the split bar to a new position. To remove the split, drag the split bar all the way to the top or the bottom of the window.

To split a window using the keyboard, use the following steps:

See Chapter 24 for a discussion on activating outline view in one pane and normal editing view in the other pane.

1. Choose the Split command from the document control menu. Word will display a horizontal dotted line in the middle of the document window.

2. Use the ↑ or ↓ key to move the dotted line to the desired position of the split.

3. Press ←⏎.

You can adjust the position of the split using this same method. To remove the split, follow the same procedure, but move the dotted line all the way to the top or bottom of the window before pressing ←⏎.

SUMMARY

- You can use the File/Find command to obtain a list of documents meeting a specified set of search criteria. You can then open, print, delete, or edit the summary information for one or more documents in the list.

- To obtain a list of documents, first choose the File/Find menu command, and click the Search button to reach the Search dialog box. Specify the documents you want Word to search by entering one or more file path names into the Search List box in the Search dialog box. You can specify the file search criteria by entering the appropriate text into one or more of the remaining text boxes within the Search dialog box. These text boxes are described in Table 26.1. Click the OK button in the Search dialog box to have Word remove the dialog box and display the list of files meeting your criteria.

- You can sort the list of files in the File/Find dialog box by choosing a sort order from the Sort By pull-down list, and clicking the Sort button.

- You can open, print, or delete one or more files by selecting the files from the File list and clicking the appropriate button in the File/Find dialog box.

- To edit the document summary information for the selected file, click the Summary button, and enter the desired values into the Document Summary Information dialog box that Word displays.

- While the Document Summary Information dialog box is open, you can obtain information on the document by clicking the Statistics button.

- The main Word program can contain one or more document windows.

- You can move the Word window on the Windows screen and control its size using standard Windows techniques.

- You can open up to nine document windows. Each document window can contain a different document, or you can open more than one window displaying the same document. Document windows are always contained within the Word window.

- To switch among open windows, press the Ctrl-F6 keystroke or choose the name of a document from the Windows menu (or click with the mouse). The window containing the document you are currently working on is known as the *active window*.

- You can view several windows at the same time by using standard Windows techniques to arrange the windows on the screen in a convenient pattern. Alternatively, you can have Word arrange all open windows, so that you can view them simultaneously, by choosing the Window/Arrange All menu command.

- You can see two views of the same document by splitting the active window, rather than opening a separate window. To split the window, drag the split bar down the window to the desired position of the split. To remove the split, drag the split bar all the way to the top or bottom of the window.

A

UNDERSTANDING THE DOS FILE SYSTEM

MICROSOFT WINDOWS—AND WORD FOR WINDOWS—run under the DOS operating system, and they use the DOS file system. When you read or write Word documents or other files, therefore, it is important to understand how DOS organizes files. In this appendix, you will learn about DOS file directories and how to specify the full path name of a file. You will then learn about the current disk and directory, and how to specify the partial path name of a file. Finally, you will discover how to specify a group of files by using *wildcard* characters within the file name.

HOW FILES ARE ORGANIZED

The DOS file system is *hierarchical,* or tree-like. First of all, your computer probably has one or more disk drives. For example, it may have two floppy-disk drives, known as drive A and drive B, and a hard disk drive, known as drive C.

Each disk drive contains a primary storage area, known as its *root directory*. The root directory can contain one or more files (such as Word documents or application programs); it can also contain other directories. Like the root directory, each of these other directories can store files as well as additional directories. Figure A.1 illustrates a simple collection of files and directories on drive C and shows the tree-like structure that results from the ability to store directories within other directories.

For instructions on creating or removing directories, see a DOS handbook, or the user's manual that came with your version of Windows.

The root directory is always present on a disk drive. When you install a program such as Word for Windows, it creates one or more additional directories. You can also create or remove directories yourself using DOS, or the Windows File Manager (or the Windows MS-DOS Executive for versions of Windows prior to 3.0).

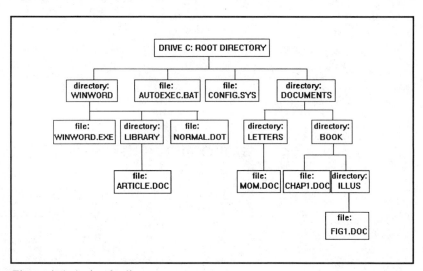

Figure A.1: A simple directory structure

SPECIFYING FULL PATH NAMES

The full path name for a file specifies both the name of the file and the exact location of the file within the computer's directory structure. A full path name begins with the drive specification, then indicates each of the directories containing the file, and finally supplies the file name.

The details of typing a full path name are best explained by giving some examples. As the first example, the full path name for the file AUTOEXEC.BAT in Figure A.1 would be the following:

C:\AUTOEXEC.BAT

The **C:** indicates that the file is on drive C; the \ character represents the root directory; and **AUTOEXEC.BAT** is the name of the file. This path name thus indicates that the file AUTOEXEC.BAT is in the root directory on drive C.

As another example, the full path name for the file ARTICLE-.DOC in Figure A.1 would be

C:\WINWORD\LIBRARY\ARTICLE.DOC

As in the previous path name, the *first* \ indicates the root directory. The subsequent \ characters, however, are simply separators between directory or file names. This path name indicates that the file ARTICLE.DOC is in the LIBRARY directory, which is in the WINWORD directory, which is in the root directory of drive C.

SPECIFYING PARTIAL PATH NAMES

When Word prompts you for a file name (for example, in the File/Open dialog box), you can always specify the full path name of the desired file. If, however, you understand the concept of the *current drive* and *current directory,* you can save time when typing a file name.

At any given time, Word designates one of the disk drives in your system as the *current drive.* If a file is on the current drive, you *do not have to specify the drive in the path name.* For example, if drive C is the current drive, you can fully identify the file WINWORD.EXE of Figure A.1 through the following name:

\WINWORD\WINWORD.EXE

You can change the current drive by double-clicking the name of the desired drive within any Word dialog box that provides a list of drive names (such as the File/Open dialog box, explained in Chapter 3).

Since this path name does not contain a drive specification, Word assumes the current drive (C).

You can change the current directory by double-clicking the name of the desired directory within any dialog box that lists directory names (such as the File/Open dialog box, described in Chapter 3).

Similarly, on each drive, Word designates one directory as the *current directory*. You can omit the path of the current directory from any file name. The following examples are taken from the file structure illustrated in Figure A.1. If the current directory on drive C is the root directory, you could specify the file CONFIG.SYS with the name

C:CONFIG.SYS

and the file NORMAL.DOT with the name

C:WINWORD\NORMAL.DOT

Since these path names do not start from the root (there is no leading \), Word assumes that the specified path begins from the current directory. Note also that if drive C is the current drive, you could also omit the drive specification; thus, you could identify these files with

CONFIG.SYS

and

WINWORD\NORMAL.DOT

As another example, if the current directory is DOCUMENTS, you could specify the file CHAP01.DOC with the name

C:BOOK\CHAP1.DOC

Note that there is *no* leading \ after the drive designation (otherwise, this would be a full, but invalid, path name; Word would look for the BOOK directory within the root directory).

USING WILDCARDS IN FILE NAMES

You can specify an entire *set* of files by including one of the *wildcard* characters, ? or *, within a file name. The ? character stands for *any single character*. For example, the name

CHAP??.DOC

indicates any file name beginning with the characters CHAP, followed by any two characters, followed by the .DOC extension (such as CHAP01.DOC or CHAP05.DOC).

The * character stands for any number of characters (0 or more). For example, the name

    C*.DOC

indicates any file name beginning with C and having the .DOC extension (such as CHAP03.DOC, CATS.DOC, or C.DOC).

You can use a wildcard character when entering the name of a file into a Word dialog box, to obtain a list of all files matching the name. For example, if you entered the name

    *.TXT

into the Open File Name box within the File/Open dialog box, Word would list all files in the current directory having the .TXT extension.

B

ENTERING MEASUREMENTS IN WORD

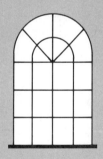

Chapter 23 discusses the Utilities/Customize command.

MANY OF THE WORD DIALOG BOXES REQUIRE YOU to enter measurements. If you specify the measurement in the *default unit,* you can simply type the number, and you do not have to indicate the units. For example, if the default unit of measurements is inches, you can simply type the number **8.5** into the Page Width box in the Format/Document dialog box; Word will interpret this value as inches and will automatically add the abbreviation for inches (") after you click the OK button (as you will see the next time you open the dialog box).

You can set the default unit used for *most* measurement boxes through the Utilities/Customize menu command. For certain text boxes, however, Word always uses a specific default unit, regardless of the default you specify with the Utilities/Customize command. For example, the default unit for specifying paragraph spacing (in the Format/Paragraph dialog box) is always lines (li).

It is easy to determine the default unit used for a given text box, since the current measurement is displayed in the default unit.

You can enter a value into a text box in a unit other than the default unit for that text box; however, *you must specify the desired unit using the correct abbreviation for this unit.* For example, if the current default unit for a text box is inches, you could enter a value in centimeters by including **cm** after the number, as in the following example:

2.54 cm

The next time you open the dialog box, you will discover that Word has converted all measurements to the default unit.

Table B.1 provides the abbreviation for each of the units used by Word. For each unit, it also gives the equivalent number of each of the other units, to help you convert from one unit to another. For example, the table indicates that 1 inch is equal to 2.54 centimeters, 6 lines, 6 picas, or 72 points.

Table B.1: Abbreviations and Conversion Factors for Measurements Used in Word

Unit	Abbreviation	Centimeters	Inches	Lines	Picas	Points
Centimeters	cm	1	.39	2.38	2.38	28.35
Inches	" *or* in	2.54	1	6	6	72
Lines	li	.42	$1/6$	1	1	12
Picas	pi	.42	$1/6$	1	1	12
Points	pt	.035	$1/72$	$1/12$	$1/12$	1

INDEX

A

annotations, 57, 489
  adding, 489–491
  deleting, 491
  formatting, 492
  moving, 491
  printing, 493
  searching for, 492–493
ANSI (American National
  Standards Institute) character
  set, 45–46
arrow keys, 21
AutoClose macro, 449
AutoExec macro, 448, 451
AutoExit macro, 448
automatic styles, 416–420
automatic word wrap, 8, 41
AutoNew macro, 449
AutoOpen macro, 448
Autosave option, 58–59

B

Backspace key, 9, 22, 48
backup procedure, 57
blank frame, 192–193
block operations, 03
  copying, 93–100
  deleting, 91–93
  footnotes, 225–226
  indexes, 241–242, 247
  moving, 93–100

  with pictures, 201
  in tables, 153–157, 159–161
  text selection, 84–85. *See also*
    text selection
boldface, 355
bookmarks, 69, 72–74, 84, 172,
  243–244
borders
  around cells, 165–168
  around paragraphs, 317–318
  around pictures, 200–201

C

calculating, 168–173
Caps Lock key, 39–40
cells, 144, 147
  borders around, 165–168
  deleting, 152–157
  inserting, 152–157
  merging, 157–158
  width of, 335–336
character formatting, 268,
  347–350
  bold, 355
  color, 353–354
  condensing, 357
  expanding, 357
  font selection, 350–352
  italics, 355
  with keyboard, 360–361
  with ribbon, 357–360
  selecting for, 348

size, 352–353
subscript, 356
superscript, 356
underlining, 355
viewing, 348–349
Clipboard, 97, 117, 159
    pictures and, 186–191
color, 353–354
column breaks, 43, 301
columns, 144, 293
    boundaries for, 333
    formatting, 297–302
    inserting, 152–157
    newspaper, 298–300
    spacing of, 163
    width of, 146, 162–163
comments, 57, 489. *See also*
    annotations
condensed spacing, 357
control menu, 14
Copy command, 94–95
copying, 93–100
    blocks, 93–100
    footnotes, 225–226
    index entries, 241–242
    indexes, 247
    pictures, 201
    in tables, 159–161
Create Backup option, 57
cropping, 195–200
current directories, 37, 55,
    525–526
current drive, 525
cursor control, 7, 21. *See also* Go To
    command; scrolling
    Go Back key, 76
    with keyboard, 64–65
    with mouse, 65–68

pictures and, 188
for ruler, 332
scrolling, 65–68
Search command, 76–77
status bar and, 78–80
in tables, 147–148
Customize command, 463–464
Cut command, 94–95, 160

D

data document, 385, 388–390
DATA field, 386–387
DDE (dynamic data exchange),
    100, 190
decimal alignment, 322
default printer, 26
Del key, 22, 48, 91
deleting
    annotations, 491
    blocks, 91–93
    cells, 152–157
    characters, 9, 22, 48
    columns, 92–93
    files, 512
    footnotes, 225–226
    index entries, 241–242
    indexes, 247
    pictures, 201
    tab stops, 323–324
    in tables, 159–161
dialog box, 11
directories
    current, 37, 55, 525–526
    .DOC file extension, 38, 55
    parent, 38
    root, 524
documents, 3

document formatting, 273–274
  default settings for, 283
  footnotes, 227–231, 281
  margins, 333. *See also* margins
  orphan control, 282
  page size, 274–275
  section overriding, 283–284
  tab stops, 281
  templates, 33–34, 282, 399,
    401. *See also* templates
  widow control, 281–282
document preview, 24–26
document summary information,
  12–13, 34, 53, 512–514
document template, 33
document view, 24
document window, 6
DOS directory structure, 523–524
.DOT file extension, 33, 401, 408
draft view, 77, 371
dynamic data exchange (DDE),
  100, 190

E

editing
  document summary
    information, 512–514
  footnotes, 224–225
em dash, 366
en dash, 366
end notes, 231
end-of-cell mark, 148
end-of-file mark, 7
Esc key, 25–26
exiting, 13–15, 27
expanded spacing, 357
expression field, 171

F

Fast Save option, 56–57
fields, 114, 171, 240–241
file extensions, 11, 36
  .DOC, 38, 55
  .DOT, 33, 401, 408
file names, 11
files
  opening, 511
  printing, 511
  searching for, 503–510
  sorting, 510–511
fonts, 350–352
footers, 207–208. *See also* headers
footnotes, 221
  copying, 225–226
  deleting, 225–226
  editing, 224–225
  inserting, 222–224
  moving, 225–226, 304
  numbering scheme for, 231
  positioning, 227–231, 281, 304
  separator characters, 226–227
  specifying reference mark,
    222–223
form letters, 385
  data document creation,
    388–390
DATA field and, 386–387
document merging, 390–392
IF field and, 393–394
main document creation,
  386–388
NEXT field and, 394–395
NEXTIF field and, 395
REF field and, 387–389
SKIPIF field and, 397

formatting, 263–269. *See also*
    printing
  annotations, 492
  characters. *See* character
      formatting
  columns, 297–302
  documents. *See* document
      formatting
  indexes, 247–253
  paragraphs. *See* paragraph
      formatting
  sections. *See* section formatting

G

galley view, 24–25, 77, 371
glossaries, 97, 403, 437
  importing entries to document,
      439–440
  spike and, 440–441
  storing text in, 438–439
Go Back key, 76
Go To command, 69–70, 72, 109,
      114, 224, 290–291, 492
  targeting annotations, 72
  targeting bookmarks, 72–74
  targeting footnotes, 72
  targeting lines, 71–72
  targeting pages, 70–71
  targeting sections, 71
graphic filter, 191
graphics, 185–186. *See also* pictures
gutter margins, 276, 280

H

hard page breaks, 42
headers, 207–208. *See also* footnotes

for data documents, 388–389
  different first page, 217
  different odd/even pages,
      217–218
  distance from page edge, 220
  entering, 209–213
  formatting, 214–215
  linking to document sections,
      213–214
  page numbering, 208–209,
      218–219
  positioning, 215–216
help features, 13
hidden text, 241, 356
horizontal scroll bar, 67
hyphenating, 41, 365–370
hyphenation hot zone, 369

I

icons, 4
icon bar, 472
icon bar mode, 212
IF field, 393–394
indents, 311–314, 326–327,
      332–333. *See also* margins for
      columns, 313–314
indexes, 237
  block operations in, 241–242,
      247
  bookmarks in, 243–244
  compiling, 246
  cross-references in, 245
  formatting, 247–253
  inserting entries in document,
      238–246
  page number ranges in, 243
  subheadings in, 242

switch options for, 249–253
switch options for entries,
    244–246
updating, 247
inserting
    cells, 152–157
    columns, 152–157
    footnotes, 222–224
insertion point. *See* cursor control
insert mode, 8, 48
installing, 4–5
italics, 355

J

justifing, 315

K

keyboard, customizing, 459–463
KEYCAPS.DOC file, 47
keystroke definitions, 459–463

L

landscape orientation, 378
leaders, 322
left justification, 315
lines, 316
    breaks, 42
    numbering, 302–304, 319–320,
        372
    spacing, 316
Lock for Annotations option, 57
locking documents, 493–494

M

macros, 403, 445
    AutoClose, 449
    AutoExec, 448, 451
    AutoExit, 448
    automatic, 447–449
    AutoNew, 449
    AutoOpen, 448
    editing, 449–450
    keystroke assignment to,
        459–463
    as a menu selection, 456–459
    recording, 445–447
    running, 450–451
main document, 385–388
margin view, 334
margins, 275–280, 333. *See also*
    indents
    gutter, 276, 280
    mirror, 278–280
    using ruler to set, 333–335
measurement units, 529–530
menus
    adding selections, 456–458
    customizing, 456–459
    removing selections, 458
merging cells, 157–158
mirror margins, 278–280
moving, 93–100
    annotations, 491
    footnotes, 225–226, 304
    index entries, 241–242
    indexes, 247
    pictures, 201
    in tables, 159–161

N

newline, 41
newspaper columns, 298–300
NEXT field, 394–395
NEXTIF field, 395
next style, 428
nonbreaking hyphens, 41, 367
NORMAL.DOT file, 34
NORMAL template, 404–406,
    411, 416, 438, 446, 458

O

opening, 32–33, 511
    existing documents, 35–39
    within Word, 33–39
opening screens, 6–7
optional hyphens, 41, 367
orientation
    landscape, 378
    portrait, 378
orphan control, 282
outline view, 77, 371. *See also*
    outlining
outlining, 253, 471–474
    changing heading levels,
      474–476
    collapsing headings, 476–478
    expanding headings, 476–478
    headings for, 472–474
    moving headings and subtext,
      478–479
    numbering formats for,
      480–483
    selecting text in, 474
    subtext in, 473
    tables of contents and, 483–484
    topic location using, 479–480

P

pages
    breaks, 42–43, 318–319
    numbering, 208–209, 218–219
    size, 274–275
    view, 371–373
panes, 210–211
paragraph breaks, 41
paragraph formatting, 267–268,
    307, 309–311
    alignment, 314–315, 327
    borders, 317–318
    default values for, 308
    indents, 311–314, 326–327,
      332–333
    with keyboard commands,
      336–338
    line numbering, 319–320
    page breaks, 318–319
    paragraph selection, 307–309
    positioning, 338–343
    spacing, 316, 327–329
    style, 317, 329
    tab stops. *See* tab stops
paragraph icon, 473
paragraph marks, 308
parent directories, 38
Paste command, 94–95
PATH command, 5, 32
path names, 20, 35
    full, 524–525
    partial, 525–526
picture formatting, 193–194
    borders, 200–201
    cropping, 195–200
    picture selection, 194–195
    scaling, 195–200
pictures, 85, 185–186

captioning, 203–204
copying, 201
cursor control and, 188
deleting, 201
formatting. *See* picture formatting
importing from Clipboard, 186–191
importing from disk file, 191–192
inserting a blank frame, 192–193
linking with source, 189–191
maximum size of, 188
moving, 201
positioning, 201–204
scrolling and, 188–189
updating, 190–191
point size, 352–353
portrait orientation, 378
positioned object, 202, 339
Preferences command, 464–466
previewing, 370–372. *See also* hyphenation; printing
page view, 371–373
print preview, 371, 373–376
printer, default, 26
printing, 26–27, 379–381. *See also* formatting; previewing
annotations, 57, 489
default printer selection, 377
graphics resolution selection, 378
installing, 376–379
paper orientation, 378
paper size selection, 378
port selection, 377
print merge facility. *See* form letters

Print Preview, 24–26, 371, 373–376
Program Manager, 6, 32, 35

R

REF field, 387–389
repagination, 43
Repeat command, 51–52
Replace command, 105, 115
replacing, 115. *See also* searching
case sensitivity, 118
Clipboard and, 117
formatting features, 120–122
multiple features, 121–122
styles, 120–122
text, 115–119
revision bar, 494
revision marks, 77, 114–115, 494–497
accepting, 499–500
document comparison with, 497–498
searching for, 498–499
undoing, 499–500
ribbon, 203, 269, 357–360
right justification, 315
root directories, 524
rows, 144
aligning, 165
height of, 164–165
indenting, 163–164
inserting, 152–157
ruler, 269, 275, 324–325
cursor control for, 332
paragraph formatting with keyboard, 331–333

paragraph formatting with
mouse, 325–331
ruler mode, 331–332
ruler view icon, 325
run-time version of Windows, 4–5,
20, 32

S

Save All command, 58
Save As command, 53–57
Save command, 53
saving, 9–13, 24, 52–53
Autosave option, 58–59
Fast Save option, 56–57
scaling, 195–200
screen customizing, 464–466
scroll bar, 66–67
scrolling, 65–68, 77–78. *See also*
cursor control
pictures and, 188–189
Search command, 76–77, 105
searching. *See also* Go To
command; replacing
for annotations, 492–493
case sensitivity and, 109
for character formatting
commands, 110–112
directory, 503–510
for documents, 115, 503–510
for fields, 114
for multiple features, 113–114
for paragraph formatting
commands, 112–113
for revision markings, 114–115
for special characters, 107
string, 106–109
for style commands, 113

wildcard characters and, 108,
509
section breaks, 43, 288
section formatting, 267, 287,
291–292
columns, 293, 297–302
document division for, 287–291
line numbering, 302–304
specifying section start, 292–294
vertical alignment, 294–297
security, 493–494
selection bar, 89
sizing handles, 195, 198
SKIPIF field, 397
snaking columns, 298–300
soft page breaks, 43
sort key, 175–177
sort order, 179–180
sorting, 173
case sensitivity and, 177
document lists, 510–511
by field, 178–179
order, 179–180
sort key selection, 175–177
sort record selection, 174–175
spacing
columns, 163
condensed, 357
expanded, 357
line, 316
spell checker, 125–127
spell checking. *See also* thesaurus
alternative spellings, 134
change word, 133
document, 129–135
ignore word, 132–133
single word, 127–128
supplemental dictionaries and,
128, 130–131, 134–135

Spell key, 135–136
spike, 440–441
startup procedure, 5–6, 32
status bar, 78–80
style area, 420
styles, 415–416
    applying with keyboard,
        423–424, 432–433
    applying with ruler, 423,
        432–433
    automatic, 416–420
    copying, 429–431
    defining a new style, 424–428
    defining by example, 431–432
    deleting, 428–429
    merging, 429–431
    modifying, 428–429
    modifying by example, 431–432
    names of, 425
    next, 428
    predefined, 416–420
    renaming, 428–429
Styles command, 421–422, 433
subscript, 356
summary information, 12–13,
    34, 53
superscript, 356
synonyms, 136–139

T

Tab key, 41
tab stops, 320–321
    decimal alignment of, 322
    default, 320
    defining custom, 321–323
    deleting, 323–324

    editing custom, 323–324
    leader for, 322
    setting with ruler and keyboard,
        333
    setting with ruler and mouse,
        329–331
tables, 143
    block operations in, 153–157,
        159–161
    calculation within, 168–173
    cell borders in, 165–168
    cell deletion, 152–157
    cell insertion, 152–157
    cell merging, 157–158
    column spacing, 163
    column width, 146, 162–163
    converting text to, 149–151
    converting to text, 151
    creating, 143–146
    cursor control in, 147–148
    dividing, 158–159
    entering text in, 147
    form letters and, 390
    grid lines in, 146
    paragraphs within, 148–149
    row alignment in, 165
    row height in, 164–165
    row indent in, 163–164
    sorting within. *See* sorting
    using ruler to set cell width in,
        335–336
tables of contents, 253
    compiling, 257
    creating from outline headings,
        483–484
    inserting entries in document,
        253–255
    positioning, 256

switch options for, 257–258
switch options for entries,
    255–256
updating, 256
tagged image file format (TIFF)
    file, 191
templates, 33–34, 282, 399, 401
    for boilerplate text, 403
    creating, 407–409
    document, 33
    glossary entries and, 403, 406
    keystroke definitions and, 403,
        406
    macros and, 403, 406
    modifying, 406–407, 409–411
    NORMAL, 404–406, 411, 416,
        438, 446, 458
    relationship to parent
        document, 405–406
    style definitions and, 403
text entry, 8–9, 39–41
    ANSI characters, 45–46
    error correction, 47–52
    hard page breaks, 42
    line breaks, 42
    newline, 41
    paragraph breaks, 41
    Repeat command, 51–52
    Undo command, 50–51
text selection, 84–85
    with keyboard, 85–88
    with mouse, 90
    selection bar, 89

    undoing, 90
thesaurus, 136–139. *See also* spell
    checking
TIFF (tagged image file format),
    191
title bar, 7
typeover mode, 8, 48

U

underlining, 355
Undo command, 50–51, 91, 120,
    175
units of measurement, 529–530

V

vertical scroll bar, 66

W

widow control, 281–282
wildcard characters, 38, 108, 509,
    526–527
windows, 514–515
    document, 516–517
    multiple, 518
    splitting, 518–519
    Word, 515–516
Windows installation, 4–5
Word installation, 4–5
word wrap, 8, 41

Selections from The SYBEX Library

WORD PROCESSING

The ABC's of Microsoft Word (Third Edition)
Alan R. Neibauer
461pp. Ref. 604-9

This is for the novice WORD user who wants to begin producing documents in the shortest time possible. Each chapter has short, easy-to-follow lessons for both keyboard and mouse, including all the basic editing, formatting and printing functions. Version 5.0.

The ABC's of WordPerfect
Alan R. Neibauer
239pp. Ref. 425-9

This basic introduction to WordPefect consists of short, step-by-step lessons—for new users who want to get going fast. Topics range from simple editing and formatting, to merging, sorting, macros, and more. Includes version 4.2

The ABC's of WordPerfect 5
Alan R. Neibauer
283pp. Ref. 504-2

This introduction explains the basics of desktop publishing with WordPerfect 5: editing, layout, formatting, printing, sorting, merging, and more. Readers are shown how to use WordPerfect 5's new features to produce great-looking reports.

The ABC's of WordPerfect 5.1
Alan R. Neibauer
352pp. Ref. 672-3

Neibauer's delightful writing style makes this clear tutorial an especially effective learning tool. Learn all about 5.1's new drop-down menus and mouse capabilities that reduce the tedious memorization of function keys.

Advanced Techniques in Microsoft Word (Second Edition)
Alan R. Neibauer
462pp. Ref. 615-4

This highly acclaimed guide to WORD is an excellent tutorial for intermediate to advanced users. Topics include word processing fundamentals, desktop publishing with graphics, data management, and working in a multiuser environment. For Versions 4 and 5.

Advanced Techniques in MultiMate
Chris Gilbert
275pp. Ref. 412-7

A textbook on efficient use of MultiMate for business applications, in a series of self-contained lessons on such topics as multiple columns, high-speed merging, mailing-list printing and Key Procedures.

Advanced Techniques in WordPerfect 5
Kay Yarborough Nelson
586pp. Ref. 511-5

Now updated for Version 5, this invaluable guide to the advanced features of Word-Perfect provides step-by-step instructions and practical examples covering those specialized techniques which have most perplexed users—indexing, outlining, foreign-language typing, mathematical functions, and more.

The Complete Guide to MultiMate
Carol Holcomb Dreger
200pp. Ref. 229-9

This step-by-step tutorial is also an excellent reference guide to MultiMate features and uses. Topics include search/replace, library and merge functions, repagination, document defaults and more.

Encyclopedia WordPerfect 5.1
Greg Harvey
Kay Yarborough Nelson
1100pp. Ref. 676-6
This comprehensive, up-to-date Word-Perfect reference is a must for beginning and experienced users alike. With complete, easy-to-find information on every WordPerfect feature and command -- and it's organized by practical functions, with business users in mind.

Introduction to WordStar
Arthur Naiman
208pp. Ref. 134-9
This all time bestseller is an engaging first-time introduction to word processing as well as a complete guide to using WordStar—from basic editing to blocks, global searches, formatting, dot commands, SpellStar and MailMerge. Through Version 3.3.

Mastering DisplayWrite 4
Michael E. McCarthy
447pp. Ref. 510-7
Total training, reference and support for users at all levels—in plain, non-technical language. Novices will be up and running in an hour's time; everyone will gain complete word-processing and document-management skills.

Mastering Microsoft Word on the IBM PC (Fourth Edition)
Matthew Holtz
680pp. Ref. 597-2
This comprehensive, step-by-step guide details all the new desktop publishing developments in this versatile word processor, including details on editing, formatting, printing, and laser printing. Holtz uses sample business documents to demonstrate the use of different fonts, graphics, and complex documents. Includes Fast Track speed notes. For Versions 4 and 5.

Mastering MultiMate Advantage II
Charles Ackerman
407pp. Ref. 482-8

This comprehensive tutorial covers all the capabilities of MultiMate, and highlights the differences between MultiMate Advantage II and previous versions—in pathway support, sorting, math, DOS access, using dBASE III, and more. With many practical examples, and a chapter on the On-File database.

Mastering WordPerfect
Susan Baake Kelly
435pp. Ref. 332-5
Step-by-step training from startup to mastery, featuring practical uses (form letters, newsletters and more), plus advanced topics such as document security and macro creation, sorting and columnar math. Through Version 4.2.

Mastering WordPerfect 5
Susan Baake Kelly
709pp. Ref. 500-X
The revised and expanded version of this definitive guide is now on WordPerfect 5 and covers wordprocessing and basic desktop publishing. As more than 200,000 readers of the original edition can attest, no tutorial approaches it for clarity and depth of treatment. Sorting, line drawing, and laser printing included.

Mastering WordPerfect 5.1
Alan Simpson
1050pp. Ref. 670-7
The ultimate guide for the WordPerfect user. Alan Simpson, the "master communicator," puts you in charge of the latest features of 5.1: new dropdown menus and mouse capabilities, along with the desktop publishing, macro programming, and file conversion functions that have made WordPerfect the most popular word processing program on the market.

Mastering WordStar Release 5.5
Greg Harvey
David J. Clark
450pp. Ref. 491-7
This book is the ultimate reference book for the newest version of WordStar. Readers may use Mastering to look up any word processing function, including the new Version 5 and 5.5 features and enhancements, and

find detailed instructions for fundamental to advanced operations.

Microsoft Word Instant Reference for the IBM PC
Matthew Holtz

266pp. Ref. 692-8

Turn here for fast, easy access to concise information on every command and feature of Microsoft Word version 5.0 -- for editing, formatting, merging, style sheets, macros, and more. With exact keystroke sequences, discussion of command options, and commonly-performed tasks.

Practical WordStar Uses
Julie Anne Arca

303pp. Ref. 107-1

A hands-on guide to WordStar and MailMerge applications, with solutions to comon problems and "recipes" for day-to-day tasks. Formatting, merge-printing and much more; plus a quick-reference command chart and notes on CP/M and PC-DOS. For Version 3.3.

Understanding Professional Write
Gerry Litton

400pp. Ref. 656-1

A complete guide to Professional Write that takes you from creating your first simple document, into a detailed description of all major aspects of the software. Special features place an emphasis on the use of different typestyles to create attractive documents as well as potential problems and suggestions on how to get around them.

Understanding WordStar 2000
David Kolodney
Thomas Blackadar

275pp. Ref. 554-9

This engaging, fast-paced series of tutorials covers everything from moving the cursor to print enhancements, format files, key glossaries, windows and MailMerge. With practical examples, and notes for former WordStar users.

Visual Guide to WordPerfect
Jeff Woodward

457pp. Ref. 591-3

This is a visual hands-on guide which is ideal for brand new users as the book shows each activity keystroke-by-keystroke. Clear illustrations of computer screen menus are included at every stage. Covers basic editing, formatting lines, paragraphs, and pages, using the block feature, footnotes, search and replace, and more. Through Version 5.

WordPerfect 5 Desktop Companion
SYBEX Ready Reference Series
Greg Harvey
Kay Yarborough Nelson

1006pp. Ref. 522-0

Desktop publishing features have been added to this compact encyclopedia. This title offers more detailed, cross-referenced entries on every software features including page formatting and layout, laser printing and word processing macros. New users of WordPerfect, and those new to Version 5 and desktop publishing will find this easy to use for on-the-job help.

WordPerfect Instant Reference
SYBEX Prompter Series
Greg Harvey
Kay Yarborough Nelson

254pp. Ref. 476-3, 4 ¾" × 8"

When you don't have time to go digging through the manuals, this fingertip guide offers clear, concise answers: command summaries, correct usage, and exact keystroke sequences for on-the-job tasks. Convenient organization reflects the structure of WordPerfect. Through Version 4.2.

WordPerfect 5 Instant Reference
SYBEX Prompter Series
Greg Harvey
Kay Yarborough Nelson

316pp. Ref. 535-0, 4 ¾" × 8"

This pocket-sized reference has all the program commands for the powerful WordPerfect 5 organized alphabetically for quick access. Each command entry has the exact key sequence, any reveal codes, a list of available options, and option-by-option discussions.

WordPerfect 5.1 Instant Reference

Greg Harvey
Kay Yarborough Nelson

252pp. Ref. 674-X

Instant access to all features and commands of WordPerfect 5.0 and 5.1, highlighting the newest software features. Complete, alphabetical entries provide exact key sequences, codes and options, and step-by-step instructions for many important tasks.

WordPerfect 5 Macro Handbook

Kay Yarborough Nelson

488pp. Ref. 483-6

Readers can create macros custom-tailored to their own needs with this excellent tutorial and reference. Nelson's expertise guides the WordPerfect 5 user through nested and chained macros, macro libraries, specialized macros, and much more.

WordPerfect 5.1 Tips and Tricks (Fourth Edition)

Alan R. Neibauer

675pp. Ref. 681-2

This new edition is a real timesaver. For on-the-job guidance and creative new uses, this title covers all versions of WordPerfect up to and including 5.1—streamlining documents, automating with macros, new print enhancements, and more.

WordStar Instant Reference SYBEX Prompter Series

David J. Clark

314pp. Ref. 543-3, 4 ¾" × 8"

This quick reference provides reminders on the use of the editing, formatting, mailmerge, and document processing commands available through WordStar 4 and 5. Operations are organized alphabetically for easy access. The text includes a survey of the menu system and instructions for installing and customizing WordStar.

DESKTOP PUBLISHING

The ABC's of the New Print Shop

Vivian Dubrovin

340pp. Ref. 640-4

This beginner's guide stresses fun, practicality and original ideas. Hands-on tutorials show how to create greeting cards, invitations, signs, flyers, letterheads, banners, and calendars.

The ABC's of Ventura

Robert Cowart
Steve Cummings

390pp. Ref. 537-9

Created especially for new desktop publishers, this is an easy introduction to a complex program. Cowart provides details on using the mouse, the Ventura side bar, and page layout, with careful explanations of publishing terminology. The new Ventura menus are all carefully explained. For Version 2.

Mastering COREL DRAW!

Steve Rimmer

403pp. Ref. 685-5

This four-color tutorial and user's guide covers drawing and tracing, text and special effects, file interchange, and adding new fonts. With in-depth treatment of design principles. For version 1.1.

Mastering PageMaker on the IBM PC (Second Edition)

Antonia Stacy Jolles

384pp. Ref. 521-2

A guide to every aspect of desktop publishing with PageMaker: the vocabulary and basics of page design, layout, graphics and typography, plus instructions for creating finished typeset publications of all kinds.

Mastering Ventura (Second Edition)

Matthew Holtz

613pp. Ref. 581-6
A complete, step-by-step guide to IBM PC desktop publishing with Xerox Ventura Publisher. Practical examples show how to use style sheets, format pages, cut and paste, enhance layouts, import material from other programs, and more. For Version 2.

Understanding PFS: First Publisher
Gerry Litton
310pp. Ref. 616-2
This complete guide takes users from the basics all the way through the most complex features available. Discusses working with text and graphics, columns, clip art, and add-on software enhancements. Many page layout suggestions are introduced. Includes Fast Track speed notes.

Understanding PostScript Programming (Second Edition)
David A. Holzgang
472pp. Ref. 566-2
In-depth treatment of PostScript for programmers and advanced users working on custom desktop publishing tasks. Hands-on development of programs for font creation, integrating graphics, printer implementations and more.

Ventura Instant Reference SYBEX Prompter Series
Matthew Holtz
320pp. Ref. 544-1, 4 ¾" × 8"
This compact volume offers easy access to the complex details of Ventura modes and options, commands, side-bars, file management, output device configuration, and control. Written for versions through Ventura 2, it also includes standard procedures for project and job control.

Ventura Power Tools
Rick Altman
318pp. Ref. 592-1
Renowned Ventura expert, Rick Altman, presents strategies and techniques for the most efficient use of Ventura Publisher 2.

This includes a power disk with DOS utilities which is specially designed for optimizing Ventura use. Learn how to soup up Ventura, edit CHP files, avoid design tragedies, handle very large documents, and improve form.

Your HP LaserJet Handbook
Alan R. Neibauer
564pp. Ref. 618-9
Get the most from your printer with this step-by-step instruction book for using LaserJet text and graphics features such as cartridge and soft fonts, type selection, memory and processor enhancements, PCL programming, and PostScript solutions. This hands-on guide provides specific instructions for working with a variety of software.

OPERATING SYSTEMS

The ABC's of DOS 4
Alan R. Miller
275pp. Ref. 583-2
This step-by-step introduction to using DOS 4 is written especially for beginners. Filled with simple examples, *The ABC's of DOS 4* covers the basics of hardware, software, disks, the system editor EDLIN, DOS commands, and more.

ABC's of MS-DOS (Second Edition)
Alan R. Miller
233pp. Ref. 493-3
This handy guide to MS-DOS is all many PC users need to manage their computer files, organize floppy and hard disks, use EDLIN, and keep their computers organized. Additional information is given about utilities like Sidekick, and there is a DOS command and program summary. The second edition is fully updated for Version 3.3.

DOS Assembly Language Programming
Alan R. Miller

365pp. 487-9

This book covers PC-DOS through 3.3, and gives clear explanations of how to assemble, link, and debug 8086, 8088, 80286, and 80386 programs. The example assembly language routines are valuable for students and programmers alike.

DOS Instant Reference
SYBEX Prompter Series
Greg Harvey
Kay Yarborough Nelson

220pp. Ref. 477-1, 4 ¾" × 8"

A complete fingertip reference for fast, easy on-line help:command summaries, syntax, usage and error messages. Organized by function—system commands, file commands, disk management, directories, batch files, I/O, networking, programming, and more. Through Version 3.3.

DOS User's Desktop Companion
SYBEX Ready Reference Series
Judd Robbins

969pp. Ref. 505-0

This comprehensive reference covers DOS commands, batch files, memory enhancements, printing, communications and more information on optimizing each user's DOS environment. Written with step-by-step instructions and plenty of examples, this volume covers all versions through 3.3.

Encyclopedia DOS
Judd Robbins

1030pp. Ref. 699-5

A comprehensive reference and user's guide to all versions of DOS through 4.0. Offers complete information on every DOS command, with all possible switches and parameters -- plus examples of effective usage. An invaluable tool.

Essential OS/2
(Second Edition)
Judd Robbins

445pp. Ref. 609-X

Written by an OS/2 expert, this is the guide to the powerful new resources of the OS/2 operating system standard edition 1.1 with presentation manager. Robbins introduces the standard edition, and details multitasking under OS/2, and the range of commands for installing, starting up, configuring, and running applications. For Version 1.1 Standard Edition.

Essential PC-DOS
(Second Edition)
Myril Clement Shaw
Susan Soltis Shaw

332pp. Ref. 413-5

An authoritative guide to PC-DOS, including version 3.2. Designed to make experts out of beginners, it explores everything from disk management to batch file programming. Includes an 85-page command summary. Through Version 3.2.

Graphics Programming
Under Windows
Brian Myers
Chris Doner

646pp. Ref. 448-8

Straightforward discussion, abundant examples, and a concise reference guide to graphics commands make this book a must for Windows programmers. Topics range from how Windows works to programming for business, animation, CAD, and desktop publishing. For Version 2.

Hard Disk Instant Reference
SYBEX Prompter Series
Judd Robbins

256pp. Ref. 587-5, 4 ¾" × 8"

Compact yet comprehensive, this pocket-sized reference presents the essential information on DOS commands used in managing directories and files, and in optimizing disk configuration. Includes a survey of third-party utility capabilities. Through DOS 4.0.

The IBM PC-DOS Handbook
(Third Edition)
Richard Allen King

359pp. Ref. 512-3

A guide to the inner workings of PC-DOS 3.2, for intermediate to advanced users and programmers of the IBM PC series. Topics include disk, screen and port control, batch files, networks, compatibility, and more. Through Version 3.3.

Inside DOS: A Programmer's Guide
Michael J. Young
490pp. Ref. 710-X
A collection of practical techniques (with source code listings) designed to help you take advantage of the rich resources intrinsic to MS-DOS machines. Designed for the experienced programmer with a basic understanding of C and 8086 assembly language, and DOS fundamentals.

Mastering DOS (Second Edition)
Judd Robbins
722pp. Ref. 555-7
"The most useful DOS book." This seven-part, in-depth tutorial addresses the needs of users at all levels. Topics range from running applications, to managing files and directories, configuring the system, batch file programming, and techniques for system developers. Through Version 4.

MS-DOS Advanced Programming
Michael J. Young
490pp. Ref. 578-6
Practical techniques for maximizing performance in MS-DOS software by making best use of system resources. Topics include functions, interrupts, devices, multitasking, memory residency and more, with examples in C and assembler. Through Version 3.3.

MS-DOS Handbook (Third Edition)
Richard Allen King
362pp. Ref. 492-5
This classic has been fully expanded and revised to include the latest features of MS-DOS Version 3.3. Two reference books in one, this title has separate sections for programmer and user. Multi-DOS partitons, 3 ½-inch disk format, batch file

call and return feature, and comprehensive coverage of MS-DOS commands are included. Through Version 3.3.

MS-DOS Power User's Guide, Volume I (Second Edition)
Jonathan Kamin
482pp. Ref. 473-9
A fully revised, expanded edition of our best-selling guide to high-performance DOS techniques and utilities—with details on Version 3.3. Configuration, I/O, directory structures, hard disks, RAM disks, batch file programming, the ANSI.SYS device driver, more. Through Version 3.3.

Programmers Guide to the OS/2 Presentation Manager
Michael J. Young
683pp. Ref. 569-7
This is the definitive tutorial guide to writing programs for the OS/2 Presentation Manager. Young starts with basic architecture, and explores every important feature including scroll bars, keyboard and mouse interface, menus and accelerators, dialogue boxes, clipboards, multitasking, and much more.

Programmer's Guide to Windows (Second Edition)
David Durant
Geta Carlson
Paul Yao
704pp. Ref. 496-8
The first edition of this programmer's guide was hailed as a classic. This new edition covers Windows 2 and Windows/386 in depth. Special emphasis is given to over fifty new routines to the Windows interface, and to preparation for OS/2 Presentation Manager compatibility.

Understanding DOS 3.3
Judd Robbins
678pp. Ref. 648-0
This best selling, in-depth tutorial addresses the needs of users at all levels with many examples and hands-on exercises. Robbins discusses the fundamentals of DOS, then covers manipulating

files and directories, using the DOS editor, printing, communicating, and finishes with a full section on batch files.

Understanding Hard Disk Management on the PC
Jonathan Kamin
500pp. Ref. 561-1
This title is a key productivity tool for all hard disk users who want efficient, error-free file management and organization. Includes details on the best ways to conserve hard disk space when using several memory-guzzling programs. Through DOS 4.

Up & Running with Your Hard Disk
Klaus M Rubsam
140pp. Ref. 666-9
A far-sighted, compact introduction to hard disk installation and basic DOS use. Perfect for PC users who want the practical essentials in the shortest possible time. In 20 basic steps, learn to choose your hard disk, work with accessories, back up data, use DOS utilities to save time, and more.

Up & Running with Windows 286/386
Gabriele Wentges
132pp. Ref. 691-X
This handy 20-step overview gives PC users all the essentials of using Windows - - whether for evaluating the software, or getting a fast start. Each self-contained lesson takes just 15 minutes to one hour to complete.

COMMUNICATIONS

Mastering Crosstalk XVI (Second Edition)
Peter W. Gofton
225pp. Ref. 642-1
Introducing the communications program Crosstalk XVI for the IBM PC. As well as providing extensive examples of command and script files for programming Crosstalk, this book includes a detailed description of how to use the program's more advanced features, such as windows, talking to mini or mainframe, customizing the keyboard and answering calls and background mode.

Mastering PROCOMM PLUS
Bob Campbell
400pp. Ref. 657-X
Learn all about communications and information retrieval as you master and use PROCOMM PLUS. Topics include choosing and using a modem; automatic dialing; using on-line services (featuring CompuServe) and more. Through Version 1.1b; also covers PROCOMM, the "shareware" version.

Mastering Serial Communications
Peter W. Gofton
289pp. Ref. 180-2
The software side of communications, with details on the IBM PC's serial programming, the XMODEM and Kermit protocols, non-ASCII data transfer, interrupt-level programming and more. Sample programs in C, assembly language and BASIC.

SYBEX®

TO JOIN THE SYBEX MAILING LIST OR ORDER BOOKS
PLEASE COMPLETE THIS FORM

NAME _____ COMPANY _____

STREET _____ CITY _____

STATE _____ ZIP _____

☐ PLEASE MAIL ME MORE INFORMATION ABOUT **SYBEX** TITLES

ORDER FORM (There is no obligation to order)

PLEASE SEND ME THE FOLLOWING:

TITLE	QTY	PRICE
_____	____	____
_____	____	____
_____	____	____
_____	____	____

TOTAL BOOK ORDER   ____ $____

CUSTOMER SIGNATURE _____

SHIPPING AND HANDLING PLEASE ADD $2.00 PER BOOK VIA UPS   ____

FOR OVERSEAS SURFACE ADD $5.25 PER BOOK PLUS $4.40 REGISTRATION FEE   ____

FOR OVERSEAS AIRMAIL ADD $18.25 PER BOOK PLUS $4.40 REGISTRATION FEE   ____

CALIFORNIA RESIDENTS PLEASE ADD APPLICABLE SALES TAX   ____

TOTAL AMOUNT PAYABLE   ____

☐ CHECK ENCLOSED   ☐ VISA
☐ MASTERCARD   ☐ AMERICAN EXPRESS

ACCOUNT NUMBER _____

EXPIR. DATE _____ DAYTIME PHONE _____

CHECK AREA OF COMPUTER INTEREST:

☐ BUSINESS SOFTWARE

☐ TECHNICAL PROGRAMMING

☐ OTHER: _____

THE FACTOR THAT WAS MOST IMPORTANT IN YOUR SELECTION:

☐ THE SYBEX NAME

☐ QUALITY

☐ PRICE

☐ EXTRA FEATURES

☐ COMPREHENSIVENESS

☐ CLEAR WRITING

☐ OTHER _____

OTHER COMPUTER TITLES YOU WOULD LIKE TO SEE IN PRINT:

_____

_____

OCCUPATION

☐ PROGRAMMER   ☐ TEACHER

☐ SENIOR EXECUTIVE   ☐ HOMEMAKER

☐ COMPUTER CONSULTANT   ☐ RETIRED

☐ SUPERVISOR   ☐ STUDENT

☐ MIDDLE MANAGEMENT   ☐ OTHER:

☐ ENGINEER/TECHNICAL   _____

☐ CLERICAL/SERVICE

☐ BUSINESS OWNER/SELF EMPLOYED

CHECK YOUR LEVEL OF COMPUTER USE

☐ NEW TO COMPUTERS

☐ INFREQUENT COMPUTER USER

☐ FREQUENT USER OF ONE SOFTWARE

PACKAGE:

NAME _____

☐ FREQUENT USER OF MANY SOFTWARE

PACKAGES

☐ PROFESSIONAL PROGRAMMER

OTHER COMMENTS:

_____
_____
_____
_____
_____
_____
_____

PLEASE FOLD, SEAL, AND MAIL TO SYBEX

SYBEX, INC.
2021 CHALLENGER DR. #100
ALAMEDA, CALIFORNIA USA
94501

SEAL

SYBEX Computer Books are different.

Here is why . . .

At SYBEX, each book is designed with you in mind. Every manuscript is carefully selected and supervised by our editors, who are themselves computer experts. We publish the best authors, whose technical expertise is matched by an ability to write clearly and to communicate effectively. Programs are thoroughly tested for accuracy by our technical staff. Our computerized production department goes to great lengths to make sure that each book is well-designed.

In the pursuit of timeliness, SYBEX has achieved many publishing firsts. SYBEX was among the first to integrate personal computers used by authors and staff into the publishing process. SYBEX was the first to publish books on the CP/M operating system, microprocessor interfacing techniques, word processing, and many more topics.

Expertise in computers and dedication to the highest quality product have made SYBEX a world leader in computer book publishing. Translated into fourteen languages, SYBEX books have helped millions of people around the world to get the most from their computers. We hope we have helped you, too.

For a complete catalog of our publications:

SYBEX, Inc. 2021 Challenger Drive, #100, Alameda, CA 94501
Tel: (415) 523-8233/(800) 227-2346   Telex: 336311
Fax: (415) 523-2373

Command	Key Combination	Menu Item
Macro, Edit	Alt-M, *then* E	Macro/Edit
Maximize Document Window	Alt-hyphen, *then* X Ctrl-F10	Document Control/Maximize
Maximize Word Window	Alt-spacebar, *then* X	Word Control/Maximize
Menus, Short/Full	Alt-V, *then* M	View/Short Menus, View/Full Menus
Menus, Customizing	Alt-M, *then* M	Macro/Assign to Menu
Minimize Word Window	Alt-spacebar, *then* N	Word Control/Minimize
Move Document Window	Alt-hyphen, *then* M Ctrl-F7	Document Control/Move
Move Word Window	Alt-spacebar, *then* M	Word Control/Move
New Document	Alt-F, *then* N	File/New
Next Document Window	Alt-hyphen, *then* N Ctrl-F6	Document Control/Next Window
Number Paragraphs	Alt-U, *then* R	Utilities/Renumber
Open Document	Alt-F, *then* O Ctrl-F12	File/Open
Options, Display	Alt-V, *then* E	View/Preferences
Outline Document View	Alt-V, *then* O	View/Outline
Page Numbers, Print at Top or Bottom of Page	Alt-I, *then* U	Insert/Page Numbers
Page View Document View	Alt-V, *then* P	View/Page
Paragraph, Format	Alt-T, *then* P	Format/Paragraph
Paste Contents of Clipboard	Alt-E, *then* P Shift-Ins	Edit/Paste
Paste Link	Alt-E, *then* L	Edit/Paste Link
Picture, Insert	Alt-I, *then* P	Insert/Picture
Picture, Format	Alt-T, *then* R	Format/Picture
Position Paragraph	Alt-T, *then* O	Format/Position
Print Document	Alt-F, *then* P Ctrl-Shift-F12	File/Print
Print Merge	Alt-F, *then* M	File/Print Merge
Print Preview Document View	Alt-F, *then* V	File/Print Preview
Printer Setup	Alt-F, *then* R	File/Printer Setup
Repaginate	Alt-U, *then* P	Utilities/Repaginate Now
Repeat Last Command	Alt-E, *then* R F4	Edit/Repeat
Replace	Alt-E, *then* E	Edit/Replace
Restore Document Window	Alt-hyphen, *then* R Ctrl-F5	Document Control/Restore